D0065565

HOW THE WEB WAS WON

HOW
THE
WEB
WAS
WON

**MICROSOFT FROM
WINDOWS TO THE WEB**

*The Inside Story of How Bill Gates and His Band of
Internet Idealists Transformed a Software Empire*

PAUL ANDREWS

broadway books ∘ new york

Library of Congress Cataloging-in-Publication Data
Andrews, Paul, 1949–
   How the web was won : Microsoft from windows to the web : the inside story of how Bill Gates and his band of internet idealists transformed a software empire / by Paul Andrews.
     p.   cm.
   ISBN 0-7679-0048-0
   1. Gates, Bill, 1955– . 2. Microsoft Corporation—History. 3. Businessmen—United States—Biography. 4. Computer software industry—United States—History.   I. Title.
HD9696.63.U64M532   1999
338.7′610053′0973—dc21   99-14176
                                                                          CIP

FIRST EDITION

Designed by Pei Loi Koay

99 00 01 02 03 10 9 8 7 6 5 4 3 2 1

We're talking about life and death in every piece of e-mail.

—BILL GATES

We believed in open standards and the power of Windows and what they could do together to transform the way people used information. We had to fight and fight hard. The online contingent had Bill's ear better than we did. But we believed in ourselves and we hung in there and we pushed hard and kept pushing. And in the end, all the work was worth it. We knew the Internet belonged in Windows. And we were right.

—BRAD SILVERBERG

For Cecile and Maggie,

who bring passion and spirit

to everything we do

T

his book tells the story of Microsoft's rise on the Internet through the lives of the people most directly involved. Behind any sweeping historical transformation are the names and faces of those who make things happen. The visionaries. The leaders. The doers. With all the attention that has been focused on the Internet boom, the world still does not know who the Microsoft players are, what motivates them, where their contributions fit, and how they were able to lead their company to success.

Microsoft's emergence on the Internet makes an especially compelling tale because at first the company was deemed to have arrived at the party so late. Throughout the early 1990s, Internet denizens wrote Microsoft off, saying the software giant was too clueless, insular, and proprietary to "get the Net." Microsoft itself did little to counter the public perception until late 1995, when Bill Gates delivered a sweeping Internet strategy pronouncement to analysts and media on December 7, the anniversary of the Japanese Pearl Harbor attack that ignited U.S. participation in World War II.

Within two years Microsoft had transformed its Internet presence so powerfully that the U.S. Department of Justice was compelled to take Microsoft to court on antitrust charges. The action prompted further investigation and a broad Sherman Act lawsuit against the company filed on May 18, 1998.

The lawsuit was confirmation of Microsoft's immense and unstoppable impact on the Internet. Yet it did little to explain the mechanics of Microsoft's turnaround. For all the charges, countercharges, depositions, direct testimony, memos, and e-mail, no clear picture emerged of how

Microsoft accomplished what can arguably be called the business coup of the century.

That story is best told through the hopes and dreams of a core band of idealists at Microsoft who fought public disdain, corporate inertia, and even one another as they drove their company to "embrace and extend" the Internet. Their unsinkable persistence in the face of skepticism, intransigence, and misunderstanding is a classic story of rebellion against the forces of status quo and conventionality. The fact that they succeeded in getting heard and pushing through their agenda says as much about the company they work for as it does about their own refusal to be denied.

I first studied Microsoft culture ten years ago, while researching an article titled "The Velvet Sweatshop" for the *Seattle Times'* Sunday Pacific magazine. Then, with Stephen Manes, I coauthored a 1993 biography chronicling the rise of Bill Gates and his "smart guys"—*Gates: How Microsoft's Mogul Reinvented an Industry and Made Himself the Richest Man in America*. Throughout the past decade much of my writing for the *Seattle Times* has focused on the unique alchemy of Microsoft's achievement. However one feels about Microsoft, it is a continually fascinating artifact of this century and, one can assume, the next.

How the Web Was Won is an independent work of narrative nonfiction that tells Microsoft's Internet story through the eyes, ears, and voices of the players themselves. People may wonder about "the other side of the story." The question misses the point of the book, which is to explore the inner workings and consciousness of a company grappling with a new marketplace and defending itself against the threat of extinction in a highly competitive, ceaselessly evolving industry. My hope is that readers, in gaining an understanding of what makes Microsoft tick, will be better able to judge for themselves the validity of accusations facing the company. By exploring the personal side of Microsoft's emergence on the Internet, I hope to impart some grain of insight into the nature of technology and the human spirit as we approach the millennium.

BILL GATES: The Microsoft cofounder's 1990 vision of "Information At Your Fingertips" was a philosophical seedbed for his company's Internet awareness.

STEVE BALLMER: No. 2 in command, Ballmer initiated talk of merging Windows with the Internet with a strategic e-mail to Microsoft executives.

BRAD SILVERBERG: Mr. Windows of the 1990s, Silverberg pushed early for integration of Web browsing with Microsoft's operating system.

JOHN LUDWIG: A behind-the-scenes doer who brought networking and Internet savvy to the Windows effort.

J ALLARD: Microsoft's first Internet idealist, Allard drove much of the "plumbing" for merging Windows with the Internet and then led Microsoft's Web server efforts.

STEVEN SINOFSKY: As Gates's technical assistant, Sinofsky alerted the Microsoft chairman to the Internet's potential, particularly in publishing, then helped merge Microsoft Office with the Web.

BEN SLIVKA: The man who built Microsoft's browser, Internet Explorer, and commanded the company's later Java development.

PETER PATHE: Microsoft's first Internet product, Word Assistant, was Pathe's inspiration.

PAUL MARITZ: Microsoft's field marshal for operating systems in the 1990s emerged as the key strategist for browser and Java technologies.

THOMAS REARDON: Responsible for the technological breakthrough that enabled Windows to match Novell's NetWare as a network operating system, Reardon drove early browser deals and Internet strategy.

BERNARD ABOBA: Author of *The Online User's Encyclopedia*, Aboba drove Internet support in Microsoft Network, or MSN.

BOB MUGLIA: During the critical 1996 to 1997 time frame, the responsibility for Microsoft's tenuous relationship with Sun and Java fell on Muglia's shoulders.

JIM ALLCHIN: Fought early for Internet compatibility in Microsoft networking products, then led the Windows NT effort responsible for making NT a powerhouse in corporate and Internet networking.

BRAD CHASE: The "Other Brad," Chase teamed with Silverberg on Windows and Internet marketing efforts.

RUSS SIEGELMAN: The creator of Microsoft Network, Siegelman had to serve the company's online and Internet strategies in a juggling act that repeatedly stumbled.

DAN ROSEN: The congenial former AT&T executive tried to get Microsoft and Netscape to partner but wound up in the middle of one of the Internet's—and software's—biggest battles ever.

CONTENTS

1990

11/12/90
Bill Gates unveils "Information At Your Fingertips," a vision of interconnected computing that later serves as a philosophical basis for Microsoft Internet strategy.

1992

1/20/92
Winsock 1.0, enabling Windows applications to run on a standard TCP/IP implementation, is announced.

5/16/91
Gates issues "Think Week" memo outlining Microsoft networking challenges.

1993

3/8/93
Keith Moore writes Microsoft's ftp server in a five-day frenzy.

11/20/93
White House issues press release extolling the release of Mosaic, the "digital cannon felt around the world," on Windows, Macintosh and UNIX platforms.

5/2/91
Microsoft.com is registered on the Internet.

1991

9/10/91
On his second day at Microsoft, J Allard is asked by Steve Ballmer to "make the pain go away" with TCP/IP, the standard Internet protocol.

10/92
J Allard registers Microsoft's ftp address.

11/18/93
Microsoft ftp server with DOS 6.2 as bait for Internet compatibility tests attracts 10,000 users in a 40-hour period.

12/7/93
Microsoft second-in-command Steve Ballmer sends "What think?" e-mail to colleagues asking about Internet integration into Windows.

9/12/94
At the NetWorld + Interop show in Atlanta, Mosaic Communications announces its new browser, called NetScape, and server, NetSite.

10/6/94
Slivka e-mail details features for Microsoft "Explorer" browser. The same day Gates issues a "Think Week" memo outlining Microsoft challenges in Internet publishing.

10/13/94
Mosaic Communications issues its NetScape browser, version 0.9.

11/14/94
Mosaic Communications is renamed again, this time to Netscape Communications.

12/12/94
Microsoft licenses Mosaic browser from Spyglass.

9/21/94
Windows NT 3.5, code-named Daytona, released.

10/11/94
IBM rolls out OS/2 Warp (version 3.0), the first PC operating system with its own browser, WebExplorer.

11/9/94
America Online announces it has purchased BookLink browser, sending shockwaves through Microsoft.

11/14/94
Microsoft Network is announced at Fall Comdex in Las Vegas. Also shown is first Microsoft Internet application, Word Assistant.

1/13/95
Microsoft announces deal with UUNet to provide Internet access for Microsoft Network.

1995

11/20/96
Netscape's Jim Barksdale shows off "Constellation," a counter to Microsoft's Active Desktop, at Fall Comdex in Las Vegas.

3/25/96
Steven Levy article in *Newsweek*, citing "Blood in the Browser War," puts new phrase into the Internet lexicon.

8/12/96
Microsoft releases Internet Explorer 3.0, its breakthrough version.

1997

9/30/97
Microsoft rolls out Internet Explorer 4.0, merging Windows with the Web.

10/20/97
Microsoft is charged by the Department of Justice with violating its 1994 consent decree.

7/31/96
Windows NT 4.0, code-named Cairo, released to manufacturing with Internet Information Server and Windows 95 interface.

8/19/96
Netscape releases Navigator 3.0. The ensuing product comparisons and strategic jockeying popularize the browser wars in mainstream consciousness.

12/11/96
In an attempt to align industry against Microsoft, Sun announces "100 Percent Pure Java" initiative.

10/7/97
Sun sues Microsoft in federal district court for violation of Java contract.

11/21/97
Work on Internet Information Server 4.0 is completed.

MICROSOFT'S INTERNET EVOLUTION

1994

1/25/94
Allard distributes his wide-ranging memo, "Windows: The Next Killer Application on the Internet," containing the kernels of Microsoft's ensuing Internet strategy.

4/5/94
Microsoft executives discuss integrating Windows with the Internet at a brainstorming session at the stately Shumway Mansion in the Seattle suburb of Kirkland.

4/12/94
Having decided their new company should write a Web browser, Jim Clark and Marc Andreessen visit Champaign, Illinois, to recruit Mosaic team programmers from National Center for Supercomputing Applications.

5/9/94
Clark changes the name of Electric Media to Mosaic Communications Corp., suggesting its new focus.

6/12/94
J Allard begins assembling team for Internet Information Server, Microsoft's Web server.

2/7/94
Noticing the rise of Internet use on campus while trapped at his alma mater in a snowstorm, Steven Sinofsky sends an e-mail to colleagues headed "Cornell is WIRED!"

4/7/94
Articles of incorporation are approved for Electric Media, Inc., the company that eventually becomes Netscape Communications.

4/16/94
Gates issues sweeping follow-up memo to Shumway retreat, outlining a variety of strategic paths for integrating the Internet into Windows.

5/23/94
Strolling the floor of Spring Comdex in Atlanta, Brad Silverberg and Steven Sinofsky take a look at a new browser, BookLink Internetworks, featuring strong Windows technology. Negotiations later begin for Microsoft to license or purchase BookLink.

8/22/94
Ben Slivka sends e-mail stating he has started interface design on a Microsoft "WWW (World Wide Web) Explorer" browser.

12/7/95
On the 54th anniversary of the Pearl Harbor Day bombing, and second anniversary of Ballmer's "What think?" e-mail, Gates announces to media and analysts, "The sleeping giant has awakened." Microsoft announces licensing of Java and expansion of its Spyglass license to provide Internet Explorer for Windows 3.X, Macintosh and UNIX.

3/5/96
Netscape holds DevCon, its developers conference, unveiling its strategy to make its browser and servers a platform capable of supplanting Windows on the Internet.

5/23/95
Sun Microsystems announces Java, with Netscape the first licensee.

6/2/95
Paul Maritz hosts offsite Internet strategy session addressing browser and Java initiatives.

8/9/95
Netscape IPO, creating a $2.2 billion company in a day, sets new standard for Internet valuations.

5/26/95
Bill Gates issues pivotal "Think Week" memo, "The Internet Tidal Wave."

6/21/95
In a session the Justice Department later cites as anticompetitive, Microsoft and Netscape meet in Mountain View, California, to discuss potential partnership.

8/24/95
Windows 95 is released, featuring built-in Internet plumbing and, on new computers, the Internet Explorer 1.0 browser. IE is available as well in separate Windows 95 add-on retail package, Microsoft Plus! Pack.

2/20/96
Gates announces creation of the Internet Platform and Tools Division, to be headed by Silverberg.

1996

3/12/96
Microsoft holds its Professional Developers Conference, announcing ActiveX as a counter to Java and a deal to put AOL in a folder on the Windows 95 desktop.

1998

1/22/98
Netscape announces that it will make its own browser free and post source code on the Internet.

6/25/98
Windows 98 is released, incorporating Web functionality.

9/4/98
Microsoft tops General Electric as world's highest-valued company in market capitalization.

11/24/98
America Online acquires Netscape for $4.2 billion.

3/1/99
MIcrosoft is ranked America's third most-admired company by *Fortune* magazine.

5/18/98
Justice Department and attorneys general for 20 states file a sweeping Sherman Act antitrust suit against Microsoft.

7/21/98
Steve Ballmer is named president of Microsoft.

9/28/98
Microsoft passes Netscape in browser share, according to market analysis firm International Data Corporation.

2/5/99
Following appearances by key executives Paul Maritz and Jim Allchin at the antitrust trial in Washington, D.C., Microsoft is widely considered to have lost the case.

1999

Part 1

INSIGHT

WHAT THINK?

t 4:51 P.M. on Tuesday, December 7, 1993—the fifty-second anniversary of the bombing of Pearl Harbor—Steve Ballmer, Microsoft's head of worldwide sales, sat down in front of his computer and began animatedly typing out an e-mail to his colleague Mike Maples, overseer of Microsoft applications development. It was an act destined to transform their company and alter the course of the Information Age. The day before, Ballmer had returned from a visit to his alma mater, Harvard, stunned and confused. Here he was, the Microsoft guy, the No. 2 in command of the world's biggest personal computer company, and all anyone could talk to him about was something Microsoft had nothing to do with: the Internet. It was like some kind of new designer drug. When the subject of the Net came up, students' faces lit up, their eyes blazed, their voices rose, their skin flushed, and their speech accelerated. Ballmer recalled witnessing a similar fascination nearly two decades earlier, while a callow undergraduate on the Cambridge, Massachusetts, campus. It happened when his friend and classmate, a skinny, mop-haired, poker-playing math geek named Bill Gates, started riffing on computers. Computers were going to change the world, Gates would tell him. Everyone was going to be connected. Everyone would be able to send messages and files and data and God knew what else to one another over a vast global electronic matrix—what Gates's friend Paul Allen called the Wired World. Ballmer did not know much about computers. He was into sports and math and literature and campus stuff like the Fox Club. But it struck him how the subject of computers enraptured his friend. Now he was seeing the same expression on the Harvard kids' faces, hearing the same urgency in their voices, when they talked about the Internet. Something was happening here, something big. Where did Microsoft fit in? Ballmer wondered. How could Windows tap into this strange new world? It was time to start asking questions.

Somehow, Ballmer sensed, Chicago had to take advantage of the Internet. Chicago was the code name for the next version of Windows, the upgrade that promised to revolutionize the way people used personal computers. Chicago would be easier to use, more intuitive, more user friendly. Yet it would also be more powerful, enabling users to operate several programs and perform several functions at the same time. An idea suddenly seized Ballmer. He began furiously typing out his e-mail to Maples. If Microsoft could say that Chicago is the greatest front end to the Internet, Ballmer mused, it would really help popularize the upgrade "not only amongst students but all the other random people I talk to who have Internet addresses." Could Chicago make it easy to connect to the Net? Ballmer asked. "Could we let you be a node on the Internet directly (is that dumb)?" Not dumb, actually, just the opposite. But not, in 1993, a question easily answered. There was more: Could the Chicago team do an Internet e-mail connection to the Net? In other words, could you just click on an icon in Windows and *blam!* be connected to e-mail on the Net? Could there be Internet chat in Chicago? Chat was all the Harvard kids could talk about. Chat was like talking on the phone, only typing. You hooked up with a person or persons over the Net and typed messages back and forth in real time, each able to see the other's postings. Several people could be involved, all banging away on their keyboards. What if you just had a button in Windows that you clicked to join a chat room? Ballmer thought. Wouldn't that be cool?

Ballmer was getting into it now. The juices were really flowing. Type, type, type, clackety-clack, his keyboard almost splitting under the jackhammer pounding of his thick fingers. How about linked and embedded objects—a technology that would enable things like a spreadsheet graphic from Excel to be circulated over the Net in a document or e-mail message?

Could there be newsgroup discussions? The Net was full of newsgroups gossiping about everyone from Princess Di to Mr. Spock, interpreting everything from Nirvana's lyrics to Seinfeld's jokes, lampooning everyone from Rush Limbaugh to Barney the Dinosaur. Someone would set up a topic for discussion, others would contribute, and pretty soon you had this electronic equivalent of a town hall discussion going. Was there any way, Ballmer wondered, for Microsoft to make newsgroups easier to access and more fun to participate in via Windows?

When Ballmer got excited, his thoughts began cascading on one another in a rush of inspiration, his adrenaline began coursing like a basketball player about to shoot the winning hoop, and his fingers started moving faster than the keyboard could keep up. Could Microsoft package "some of the greta internbet shareware stuff"? he asked Maples. Shareware—free software—was all over the Internet. A lot of it was worth the asking price, but there was valuable stuff as well. Maybe Windows could make it easier to get at the good stuff. Ballmer concluded with a flourish:

> I do not really understand what I am saying or asking for but I sense an opportunity
> could/should someone look into this I was at harbard talking to studnets Mon
> theya ll have a view of what would be cool Iw ant to sell mail and chicago somehow
> this way what think
>
> --

What think indeed. The trademark stream-of-consciousness prose style once led Maples to comment that e-mail from Ballmer sometimes looked like nothing more than a randomly typed collection of letters on the screen. But not to worry. Ballmer's point was coming across loud and clear. Ballmer's head-scratching demeanor was, to paraphrase the Yeats quotation about education, meant to light a fire, not fill a bucket. Ballmer always understood more than he was willing to let on. There was a cunningness to his perplexity on any topic. Bottom line: Ballmer did not really need to understand a technology to know it was important. And the Internet, he knew, was important.

As was routine at Microsoft, Ballmer copied his e-mail to Bill Gates and Paul Maritz. Copying was a chain-of-command protocol that Microsoft early on had perfected as its use of e-mail accelerated. You sent e-mail to the person or persons with direct responsibility for the topic at hand. You copied people who had interest in the topic or tangential responsibility for one of the areas discussed. Gates had an interest in just about everything going on at Microsoft. It was routine to copy him—to keep him in the loop, even if he had no direct involvement. Maritz oversaw Microsoft's operating-system division, of which Windows was the anchor.

One piece of e-mail could take on a life of its own at Microsoft. The following morning, December 8, 1993, at 9:12 A.M., Maritz forwarded the Ballmer epistle to Darryl Rubin, a longtime networking guru at Microsoft, and to e-mail executives Laura Jennings and Tom Evslin. Maritz also copied the two top Windows executives, Brad Silverberg and Brad Chase, otherwise known as the Two Brads. With his forward, Maritz appended a comment that was as laconic and pointed as Ballmer's had been expansive. It was classic Maritz. Compact. Efficient. Lucid. Right to the point.

"What are the plans?" he asked.

Within forty minutes of Maritz's mail, Rubin responded with a long note describing different means of corporate and individual access to the Internet. Certainly Ballmer's e-mail initiatives were doable, Rubin replied. For Windows users on a corporate network, access could be provided through an Internet mail gateway, a kind of electronic turnstile that let e-mail from one network pass into another network. Concerning Internet discussion groups, Rubin suggested they could be represented as public folders in Microsoft's Exchange mail system. For Windows users not on corporate networks—folks logging in from home—things were a little more tricky. Only a couple of companies had announced Windows software for accessing the Internet, Rubin noted. It might be possible to do a deal with an Internet service provider to get Chicago users easy access to the Net, Rubin suggested.

Rubin also copied his response to the Two Brads.

By 1:16 P.M. Silverberg weighed in with a note to John Ludwig, the Chicago networking manager, as well as Brad Chase, Chicago's marketing manager, and David Cole, Chicago's programming lead. These were Silverberg's guys, the systems aces who had taken DOS and Windows to new heights over the previous three and a half years, since Windows 3.0 had created a firestorm of demand for IBM-and-compatible PCs beginning the spring of 1990. Never in the short but explosive history of personal computing had two industry-leading programs undergone such rapid and successful upgrades. DOS 5. Windows 3.1. Windows for Workgroups 3.1. DOS 6. Windows for Workgroups 3.11. With the possible exception of Windows for Workgroups 3.1, each had surprised analysts and Wall Street with immediate popularity and booming sales. Even Silverberg and his gang had been amazed. It wasn't like each upgrade was perfect out of the box, after all. Systems upgrades never were. But for all the various bugs and glitches and complaints, computer users loved Windows. And Chicago, Silverberg and his team had early on decided, was going to be the biggest Windows of all.

Silverberg had long experience with the Internet, having first used its Arpanet incarnation as a computer science researcher at SRI, formerly known as the Stanford Research Institute, in Menlo Park in the late 1970s. The morning he responded to Maritz's forward of Ballmer's e-mail, Silverberg had read an article on a "treasure map" to the Internet written by John Markoff in the *New York Times*. A particular quote in the article had caught Silverberg's eye. The piece was about Mosaic, a new software program that helped computer users view electronic documents on the Internet via something called the World Wide Web. The quote that alerted Silverberg to Mosaic's potential was from Brian Reid, technical director for the Network Systems Laboratory at Digital Equipment Corporation in Palo Alto, California. "Mosaic has given me a sense of limitless opportunity," Reid had told Markoff. Silverberg had followed Reid's work since the late 1970s and respected his opinion.

"I see a big opportunity here," Silverberg wrote in his e-mail to his Chicago cohorts. "Chicago as the gateway to the information highway." Less than half an hour later, David Cole responded. "Having a great front end to the Internet would be cool," Cole wrote. "It would help sell Chicago." The Internet was gaining visibility. "We should leverage," Cole added. The Net was even popping up on TV shows about technology. For all the talk about the information highway, Cole noted, the Net was, really, the only information highway.

When Bill Gates saw Ballmer's e-mail, he thought about a recent demonstration of the Internet by his technical assistant, Steven Sinofsky, during Gates's semiannual Think Week. Twice a year the Microsoft and industry icon liked to take time out to catch up on reading, industry trends, and company strategy. Sinofsky, a twenty-seven-year-old programming whiz out of Cornell University who had joined Microsoft just four years earlier, sensed that the Internet's popularity was about to explode. Some of the Internet's components, things like telnet and gopher and file transfer protocol, enabled the user to find and exchange information in uniquely vast, globally connected ways. Although still crude, they represented to Sinofsky the building blocks of the grand vision of "Information At Your Fingertips" first extolled by Gates three years earlier as the computer industry's challenge for the '90s. Gates, who had used the Internet in the mid-1970s as an undergraduate at Harvard University, was a tough sell. The Net was still too hard to learn for the average computer user, he felt, and besides, where was the business model? How did a software company make money in a venue where everything was free? With time, Sinofsky believed, all questions would be answered. His initial goal of planting a seed had been accomplished.

J Allard, just two years out of college and in charge of Internet protocol development at Microsoft, did not know about Ballmer's ruminations or Gates's Think Week demonstration. While eddies of Internet awareness swirled around the upper echelons, Allard agitated among the rank and file. In November he had begun work on a long, quixotic ramble of an essay about the opportunities the Internet presented for Microsoft's Windows operating system. The memo was part anthem, part carpe diem. Allard sang the praises of the Internet and believed it to be on the verge of exploding. If Microsoft did not seize the day, it risked being swept aside by the biggest communications phenomenon of the century. In terms of Microsoft's history, Allard's alert was comparable to the December day in 1974 when Paul Allen ran across Harvard Square to his friend Bill Gates's room after seeing the Altair 8800 on the cover of *Popular Electronics* on a newsstand. "This is it! Somebody's finally put the computer together!" Allen exclaimed, excitedly. "We should do BASIC!" Allard was sending e-mail, stopping coworkers in hallways, circulating his treatise for reaction to anyone he thought interested enough to give it a read. "In the early days when you saw J coming down the hall kind of bouncing off the walls, you knew he had something new to say about the Internet," recalled Henry Sanders, a top network programmer at Microsoft. If Ballmer was the messenger anointed for Microsoft and the Internet, Allard was the messenger virus.

Lighting a fire: The Ballmer e-mail, Sinofsky demonstration, and Allard memo were in their own ways helping to ignite a collective unconscious at Microsoft. Through e-mail, memos, and hallway talk over the course of fall 1993, the Microsoft journey to Chicago had gained a major roadside attraction. Inside the upper reaches of Microsoft management, Ballmer had gotten the ball rolling toward integrating key Internet capabilities into Windows. Like e-mail. Chat. Newsgroups. Publishing. If the process went well, Chicago would literally become the window of Windows to the Internet. There were still lots of issues on the table. Much work needed to be done.

The technology would require years of programmer hours. Eventually there would be competitor allegations and government investigations to endure.

For now everything looked wide open. The massive Microsoft machinery had engaged. Microsoft's long march to merge Windows with the Web had begun.

Chapter 1

NIGHTMARE

You would never have known it from his wealth, fame, and reputation, but Bill Gates was a worried, worried man.

On April 30, 1991, the software king isolated himself for a week at the family compound he had built along the southeastern shore of Hood Canal in Washington State's Puget Sound. The canal, a long, narrow stretch of inlet that ran the length of the sound, was one of Gates's favorite spots on earth. Growing up in Seattle, Gates had spent some of his happiest times visiting Hood Canal, going water-skiing, attending summer camp, staying with his grandmother Adelle Maxwell, whom he and the rest of the family called Gam, at her summer cabin there. After she passed away, Gates had built as a monument to his grandmother Gateaway, a four-house compound on three and a half acres, for family and executive retreats. An hour and a half's drive from Seattle, Gateaway was well known to Microsofties as the site for Microgames, an annual summertime adventure competition where teams of players matched wits and motor skills in a sort of extreme games for the brainy set. The compound also hosted periodic strategic planning sessions for Microsoft's inner circle, guys like Steve Ballmer, Paul

Maritz, Jeff Raikes, Brad Silverberg, Jim Allchin. And Gates liked to bring in friends like megainvestor Warren Buffett and *Washington Post* publisher Katharine Graham for occasional get-togethers.

That week, Gates was alone.

There was something calming yet energizing about the canal. The damp air seemed to enclose you in a cocoon of concentration and focus. Your mind cleared out. Issues and challenges became more defined. Ideas flowed more easily. It was amazing how when you eluded the noise and demands of the everyday world, you could grab hold of the things that really mattered. Drilling down, augering in — call it what you wanted, the misty isolation of Hood Canal really allowed you to bring things into focus.

Gates had been poring over a stack of technology-oriented reading material — memos, white papers, journals, magazines, and books — early that afternoon. The software king loved to read. The bookshelves in the living room of his compound quarters held some of his recent perusings. There was *Running Critical* by Patrick Tyler, examining the Cold War power struggle between Admiral Hyman Rickover and General Dynamics. There was Robert Lacey's look at Ford and *God Knows*, the bleak Joseph Heller novel. *The Great Getty*, by Bob Lenzner, on the oil baron turned art patron; *Honorable Justice* by Sheldon Novick, on Oliver Wendell Holmes; *The Second Creation*, a look at twentieth-century physics; *The Bishop's Boys*, Tom Crouch's study of the Wright brothers, and *Liar's Poker*, Michael Lewis's look at Wall Street. Gates gravitated toward historical biographies. Part of his fascination derived from his own sense of history and his role in one of the great revolutions of the twentieth century: the Information Age. By any measure, Gates and Microsoft were successes — amazingly, astonishingly so. Founded in 1975 by Gates and his Seattle private-school chum Paul Allen, Microsoft had grown sixteen years later into an international software empire generating $1.8 billion in revenues and 25 percent after-tax profits. Microsoft's third version of Windows, issued a year earlier on May 22, 1990, had sold 9 million copies and was well on its way to supplanting MS-DOS as the bestselling software program ever written. Within five months Gates, thirty-five years old and worth $4.8 billion, would ride the success of Microsoft and Windows to the No. 2 position on the Forbes 400 list of the richest Americans, a distinction Gates considered more a distraction than an honor.

To the world at large, Microsoft was a mighty kingdom, yes. But to Gates, that just made it a bigger target. The way he saw things, Microsoft was under assault from every front. And if the company relaxed its defense for a moment, if it made the wrong strategic decision or pursued the wrong technology, the whole thing could go up in smoke tomorrow. It was one reason he liked to tell executives at Microsoft, "For every piece of good news you send me, tell me a piece of bad news." Gates mentally ticked off the challenges Microsoft faced. First there was IBM, upset about the success of Windows versus OS/2—the big, next-generation PC operating system that Big Blue wanted to use to supplant Microsoft's DOS and Windows. The delicate partnership that had defined personal computing through the 1980s had in the fall of 1990 finally dissipated in a miasma of distrust and reprobation. "IBM always had these projects to wipe us out, so every company retreat we're saying, 'It looks like IBM is going to try and replace us,'" Gates would recall. "What can we do to prevent that? What's our strategy once that happens?"

The two companies were still working together under a three-year agreement to share some technologies, but IBM's strategy was for OS/2 to supersede Windows by the time the agreement expired in 1993.

Besides Big Blue, there was Big Brother to worry about. The Federal Trade Commission was investigating possible antitrust violations related to the way Microsoft licensed DOS to computer manufacturers. Then there was the Apple lawsuit, filed three years earlier and still hanging fire. Perhaps worst of all, Microsoft was having to bear the ignominy of being crushed by Novell, the Provo, Utah, PC networking software company. For eight years Microsoft had been trying to come up with a good networking strategy. And each year it seemed to fall deeper and deeper off the chart. Starting in 1989 Microsoft had made overtures of a merger with Novell. But talks were desultory, and Gates held little hope the two companies would get together. Networking was an embarrassment, one that Gates repeatedly used as a reminder when someone started talking about how big and powerful and dominant Microsoft was becoming.

Gates thought about a memo he had been reading by John Walker, the founder of Autodesk. Warning his wildly successful computer-aided design company of complacency, Walker depicted a nightmare scenario where Microsoft decided to compete in the market Autodesk had built an empire upon. Gates considered Walker's notion irrelevant; getting Microsoft into CAD might spread the company too thin. On the other hand, Gates considered the notion of nightmare scenarios all too relevant. Unless he and his company could make the leap to the next paradigm, Gates mused, Microsoft would be tomorrow's WordStar. When the IBM PC had come out, WordStar was the No. 1 word processor, with something like 90 percent market share. Everyone knew what control-KD did. You could ask out loud, "How do you boldface?" And someone across the room would call out the command. WordStar had been the standard, the market leader, the dominant force in word processing.

And where was WordStar today?

If Microsoft continued to execute well on its core strategy, the company would do well, Gates knew. He could see DOS and Windows and Microsoft's desktop applications—Word, Excel, PowerPoint, and on down the line—continuing to thrive in their traditional market, the desktop computer. It was a good business, one that had brought Microsoft much of its success. The operating system standards Microsoft had created—first DOS, on the IBM PC and "clone" computers, and then Windows—empowered computer users to create and customize information in new and exciting ways. PCs had exploded in power, functionality, and popularity throughout the 1980s, putting the Gates-Allen vision of a computer on every desk and in every home ever more closely within reach. By 1990 computers were selling at the clip of more than 20 million a year. But peering down the road ahead, Gates saw a looming dead end. Ultimately the model of standalone computers on desks and in homes had a fundamental limitation that would prevent it from continuing to transform society. To be truly useful, to become as popular and effective as television and radio and the telephone, computers had to be linked together somehow. Like people, computers could get a lot done on their own. But like people, they became a real social force and powerful change agent when they networked together.

And networking, Gates knew, was Microsoft's bête noir.

By early afternoon Gates decided to take a stroll along the beach. It was overcast and still chilly, but windless, and Gates decided against his overcoat, figuring that his cotton sweater and khaki slacks would be enough protection against the elements. Besides, he liked the briskness of the salt Sound air. It kept you alert. It helped you think. Thinking, just thinking, had been one of his favorite pursuits since childhood. His parents liked to tell the story about how Gates as a youngster never seemed ready to go when the family went on an outing. When Mom or Dad asked him what he was doing, Gates would say he was thinking, that's right, thinking—before adding petulantly, "Don't *you* ever think?" In high school he learned to play bridge from Gam. Her strategy was summed up in two words that came to characterize Gates's approach to life: "Think smart! Think smart!"

Gates walked with a slight hunch, head forward, hands in his pockets. At five-foot-eleven and 145 pounds, slender and small-boned, Gates was not an imposing figure, particularly compared with his six-foot-six, 220-pound father, usually referred to as William Henry Gates Jr., even though he was originally the III. Dad Gates, apprehensive about ridicule, had dropped the numerical designation when he'd entered the army to serve in the Second World War. Family friends called them Big Bill and Little Bill, while the family distinguished between them by calling the younger Bill Trey because he periodically went by the III. Gates preferred his average dimensions as being more practical in a world of constant air travel and of needing to move around quickly without attracting attention. Although not yet a household name, Gates was recognized by enough people to appreciate the benefits of anonymity.

The tide was low, the beach littered with barnacled rocks, driftwood, and kelp. It was not often Gates got time like this to himself. Although he no longer put in the ninety-hour weeks of Microsoft's founding years, Gates still worked a good sixty to seventy hours a week. He tried to take at least one day off on the weekend to play a round of golf with his family, maybe, or spend with Melinda. But it was not easy to get away from the business, partly because he loved the business. As Ballmer liked to say, "Let's be clear! I love this company!" About that there could be no doubt. Gates had accumulated enough wealth to retire comfortably 1,000 times over, but he could not imagine a better way to spend his day than working for Microsoft.

Microsoft's networking flubs were not for lack of trying. In 1983 Gates made the rounds with several leading Microsoft customers, heralding a networking breakthrough for personal computers. On November 1, 1984, the company released Microsoft Networks, or MS-Net, an attempt to link IBM-and-compatible computers together (as with MS-DOS and the IBM-branded version PC-DOS, Microsoft supplied MS-Net to IBM in the form of a product called PC-Net).

MS-Net's origins actually harkened back to Gates's undergrad days at Harvard University, where he and his Seattle computing sidekick, Paul Allen, would talk about one day setting up an online service. Low transmission speeds were always a problem, however, and the two kept waiting, waiting for the right opportunity. Every year industry leaders and trade publications would herald the arrival of the "Year of Networking," the year online services would hook together corporate America and finally take off.

And every year it wouldn't happen. What did happen? Fax machines! They exploded! Instead of file sharing and universal e-mail and online documents, everyone was still working with paper. Converting paper to electronic form, sending it over a phone line, then reconverting it back to paper. It was low resolution. It was noneditable. It was yet another phone number to deal with. It required a whole new standalone device. There was nothing about faxing that, compared with sending documents over networks in electronic form, made logical sense. Gates and Allen and the Microsoft inner circle tore out their hair trying to fathom fax's popularity. And what it came down to, they decided, was this:

The directory. With a network, you never really knew how to link up with an individual. There was no phone book, no resource list. Nobody really had the names-based directory figured out. You needed machines running all the time, in touch with everyone on the system, up twenty-four hours a day. With faxes you knew you could reach the intended individual. If a fax line was busy you would call an intermediary, which would forward things along. That should not have been a reason for faxes to beat electronic communications, though. PC networks simply were not a useful mechanism, not yet anyway, for person-to-person communications.

The directory. The universal online contact mechanism. You hook up your PC, you fill out your ID, your e-mail address, whom you work for, and on down the line. You could even add hobbies, values, special interests. And the system all over the world would know who you were, how to locate you. For the directory to be useful, it had to be universally accessible. Directories within an organization were fairly easy. You either knew the person's logon and typed it in and the computer recognized it. Or you could look it up somewhere in the system. Directories among organizations or spanning society at large were considerably more problematic. You might know a Steve Smith by where he worked or lived or the fact he played fantasy baseball or collected stamps. You might know all that, but the computer did not. Computers had to have a way of sharing directories to make e-mail and file sharing and the network really work.

MS-Net did passably well in the low end of the networking business. If you just wanted to hook computers together to exchange files and mail, MS-Net worked fine. But MS-Net relied on NetBEUI, which was pronounced net-booey and was an enhanced version of IBM's protocol, Net-BIOS. NetBEUI had some nice features but lacked a critical one: routability. Networks needed routability in order to pass information among themselves. In October 1988 Microsoft released its big networking product of the future, called LAN (for local area network) Manager, aimed at providing network services for OS/2. Despite Microsoft's best and brightest efforts to market the product, proclaiming each ensuing January that this was to be the "Year of the LAN," LAN Manager was a struggle. Part of it was OS/2's sluggishness. But LAN Man also was built on top of NetBEUI and as such did not have the features for big-time networking. LAN Man also was not a product Microsoft sold: Instead it was available only from partners who modified it to their needs. Microsoft was a hostage to their implementation, keeping the company from establishing an identity of its own and controlling its destiny.

While MS-Net and LAN Man were wallowing around in IBM's corporate market space, Novell kept building and building and building the PC networking business. Novell's NetWare became the acknowledged standard, in large part because it was impressively fast, several times faster than LAN Man, and because its protocols enabled routability, which made file and print sharing much more efficient over NetWare networks. The fact was, Gates admitted to himself ruefully, when you thought of networking computers together, you thought of Novell. Or maybe UNIX, the academic standard. You did not think of Microsoft.

And in a way it was Microsoft's own fault. In 1983 a quixotically brilliant cherub-faced software genie named Bill Joy had approached Microsoft with a deal it should have found irresistible. Joy, a curly-haired redhead with a near-perpetual impish smile that confirmed his surname, already was a legend for his work on Berkeley UNIX, a favored flavor of the operating system developed by AT&T Labs in 1969. At the time of Joy's contact with Microsoft, UNIX was an emerging preference for high-end computers tied to academic, government, and institutional networks as well as the Internet. What Joy pitched Microsoft on was this: His employer Sun Microsystems, Microsoft, and a third company, Plexus, would codevelop a protocol enabling DOS computers to run on UNIX networks. The protocol would be an adaptation of Joy's NFS, or Network File System, for UNIX—the system that enabled data and services to be ferried around electronically via networks. For Microsoft it was a huge chance to establish itself in the networking field and to help shape a standard. Microsoft, which had its own UNIX system for PCs called XENIX, said no. Gates does not remember the proposal, and Joy is not sure whom he talked to at Microsoft. "We were still a small company," Gates said. "We're not a company where you have a vp of tracking this and a vp of tracking that." Joy was surprised at the dismissal but not shocked. Microsoft did not understand networking, he concluded, did not want to deal with networking. It was stuck steadfastly in the paradigm of the standalone desktop computer. Nobody then, even those on the Internet, knew how powerful the network would become.

And so Novell's success versus Microsoft had been enabled, Joy took great pains to point out ever since. In the mind-set of the early 1980s, corporations and organizations looking to build networks would have looked first for the company they were buying the computers from to supply the service. That was the way things were done. If you bought an IBM computer or a DEC computer, you asked those companies for network services. If you bought a PC, you would ask the PC maker, expecting that it would have worked up a networking strategy or made a deal with someone like Microsoft, since Microsoft supplied the operating system for the computer. But the PC maker did not have a network system to offer. Nor did Microsoft. Into the void stepped Novell.

Going with UNIX would not have been as easy a choice for Microsoft as Joy liked to portray. By adopting a DOS-UNIX strategy, Microsoft might have jeopardized its relationship with IBM. And back then, in 1983, IBM was the 800-pound gorilla. Whatever the if-buts, by the time Gates took his waterfront stroll in April 1991, Novell had a stronghold grip on PC networking, with 70 to 80 percent of the market. Microsoft had what most analysts considered to be 1 to 2 percent, although the figure was more like 7 to 15 percent if you included sales to computer makers, called OEMs, or original equipment manufacturers.

To Gates, MS-Net was not so much a failure as NetWare was a success. Novell engineer Drew Major figured out a way to "hook," or take advantage of, a call in DOS called Int (for Interrupt) 21. Major's breakthrough took some doing. Starting in 1980, Major had helped put together the first client-server network for personal computers, based on the DOS precursor, CP/M. Novell had an unlimited site license for CP/M and Major built networking into the operating system, which at the time ran dozens of PCs in different flavors, all incompatible with one another. Novell's breakthrough was to take one computer and put file-managing capability on it. The server acted as data traffic cop for other computers hooked to it. Novell called the server a "data management computer." Then one day Major was reading an article about Xerox, whose Palo Alto Research Center had without Novell's knowledge actually invented the concept earlier and called it a "file server." Major decided he liked Xerox's terminology better.

When the IBM PC began catching on in 1982, Major decided to do the file-server technology for DOS. He looked into licensing it, discovered it cost $60,000 to purchase source code, and figured that was too high. It would be easier simply to clone DOS. From Major's point of view, DOS was simply a clone of CP/M, which he already knew inside out. Still, cloning an operating system is no walk in the park. Then an inspiration hit him: "One day I was talking to my wife about it, and it dawned on me. Hey, I don't have to clone DOS. All I have to do is get in front of it. That would be easier, get in front of Int21, build what we called a shell that gets in front of Int21."

In so doing, Novell would fool the computer into thinking it was talking to DOS, when in reality it was dealing with Novell's networking operating system. It was a great hack. What inspired Major? "Just laziness. Not wanting to write all of DOS over again." The trick made Novell NetWare measurably faster than MS-Net and jump-started Novell into a huge new PC paradigm.

Gates's hat was off to Major. "Our guys thought, nah, you probably can't do it that way," Gates admitted. "But the stuff Drew Major did in the early days of Novell was very, very clever."

As he walked along Hood Canal, Gates thought about the missed opportunities. He had a philosophy about screwing up. All was forgiven as long as you learned something from your mistake and avoided repeating it. Microsoft product releases often worked out that way. Version 1.0 was usually a mess, version 2.0 was functional but inelegant, and Version 3.0 generally got things right. The way Gates saw it, MS-Net and OS/2 LAN Man had been versions 1.0 and 2.0 of Microsoft's networking initiative. The next time his people had to get it right. For computers to get on every desk and in every home, they had to be able to communicate. They had to be something more than standalone, self-contained boxes of data. They had to be connected together somehow in a simple, automatic way that did not require knowing arcane things like addresses and protocols. There had to be a new way of looking at the computer and the services it provided. A way of looking at the computer as something you could get information from and communicate with anywhere, any time, for any reason. A way of putting information at your fingertips.

The phrase had first entered the public consciousness the previous fall, at the Comdex trade show in Las Vegas on November 12, 1990, where Gates had rolled out his theme for the '90s. In a speech at a packed Las Vegas Hilton auditorium, Gates had transformed himself from the mop-topped nerd with a nose for a dollar to the mop-topped captain of a dynamic, exploding industry. The timing was propitious. Someone needed to step up. One by one the pioneers and pathfinders of personal computing had, after attaining unimaginable wealth, slipped out of the mainstream. Apple cofounder Steve Jobs had retreated with his brilliant but way-too-early NeXT machine. His cohort Steve Wozniak was studying and teaching and out of the industry. Gates's sidekick Paul Allen, the shyest of the industry's magnates, had a lot of irons in the fire but nothing as high impact as what he had done at Microsoft. Lotus's Mitch Kapor, the 1-2-3 spreadsheet wizard, had fallen off the radar screen in pursuit of important but abstract information-rights causes. Among the early trailblazers, the college dropouts and just-do-it entrepreneurs who had built a $100 billion industry from scratch in the basements and garages of Silicon Valley and Massachusetts, only Gates was left to carry the lantern for the computing masses into the 1990s.

The setting was right. At Comdex, Gates was a hero. The Monday morning he rolled out Information At Your Fingertips, the auditorium was shoulder-to-shoulder standing-room only. They came to hear Gates not because of his wealth or influence but because he was one of them—a guy as likely as the next geek to show up at one of the dozens of parties, to turn out at a user-group get-together, or to stroll the showroom floors. Gates could talk tech with the best of them, arguing over whether there should be a left-hand-only mouse (Gates is ambidextrous) or debating the merits of alt-key combinations versus point-and-click interfaces. For all his business acumen and managerial expertise, Gates was at core a technical guy, not a suit or a marketing weenie.

There was another reason the Comdex legions worshipped Gates. The industry, and the company he helped create, was making them rich too. It was he who, as a brash twenty-year-old, had first insisted in an outraged open letter to hobbyists that software, traditionally included free with purchases of computer hardware or created by and swapped among tech heads, was something meriting a price tag. "Hardware must be paid for, but software is something to share," the postadolescent capitalist had pointed out. "Who cares if the people who worked on it get paid?" Gates cared enough to break with accepted practice, to insist that his BASIC, written with Paul Allen and a Harvard math whiz, Monte Davidoff, was worth paying for. So an information revolution was sprung. By the early 1980s software programs like WordStar and VisiCalc and Lotus 1-2-3 and dBASE were making their progenitors rich and famous. Thousands of college graduates began getting into the act, writing games, utilities, add-ons, and enhancements that in turn generated more revenue and a faster positive-feedback cycle. MS-DOS was the bedrock of tens of thousands of imaginative, ingenious programs that put computers into the hands of businesses and consumers and money into the pockets of programmers. In DOS's footsteps had come Windows, and the cycle had started back up all over again. The typical computer hobbyist, the average software programmer, had not forgotten Gates's contribution. He was on another level, yes, but he still could talk the talk and walk the walk.

Let the guy have his money, they thought. He's helping me get mine.

The rhythm of the waves lapping on the shore had put Gates into a meditative state. He thought about that Comdex talk and smiled. He had been a little nervous, not a usual state for him. By then he had given thousands of industry speeches. But this was only his second keynote at Comdex. And the first had almost gone up in smoke when he had shown up with his slide projector but no remote control. This was in 1983, before software slides replaced film transparencies in the typical corporate presentation. With no way to advance the slides from the stage, Gates had recruited his dad to run the projector, and everything had worked out.

There was no slide projector this time around. IAYF was to slide projectors as the Jetsons were to the Flintstones. Gates's special-productions chief Jonathan Lazarus, working with Seattle-based producers Mark Dickison and David Merwyn, had seen to that. The theme was the popular *Twin Peaks* TV series by perversely trendy film director David Lynch. To get Gates psyched, Lazarus had gotten him all twelve videos of the series, which Gates, who prided himself on not owning a TV set, had never seen. Gates, however, did have a tunerless monitor hooked to a VCR. Gates quickly found himself addicted to the soap opera, ostensibly based on a town just a short drive from Microsoft headquarters. He liked the dark undertones of Lynch's style and, truth be told, he liked even more the dark-haired beauty of Sherilynn Fenn.

Cool! he told Lazarus. Let's go for it.

The Twin Peaks of IAYF—a fictitious universe called Twin Hills—was a world where people were linked electronically, instantly, all the time. Hand-held computers took their data out of the air. Giant databases containing all the knowledge of humankind on computer networks linked schools and academe. Communications and information blended together over wires, airwaves, and silicon to provide everything you needed to know, when you needed to know it, in a painless, stream-of-consciousness delivery. This rules, Gates told Lazarus. This is our holy grail for the '90s. The "Fingertips" motif centered on a coffee company loosely modeled after the emerging Starbucks megachain in Gates's hometown of Seattle. A distraught secretary talked about how hard it was to use her PC, fretting that "all the important information is locked away on minicomputers somewhere on the eighth floor, and I can't get access till later this afternoon when the IS people get in!" A truck driver said he wished he could pull inventory and sales data up in the field. A group of school kids called the PC irrelevant to their education. Gates promised to work on it.

You didn't need a keyboard in the world of IAYF: The truck driver used a pen-based hand-held pad to pull data from the office out of the airwaves. Your identity and information was protected by digital certification: The driver signed his name for password permission to his corporate database. There was 3-D: To show a couple what their remodeled house might look like, a "virtual reality" computer simulation. News on your desktop: At one point Gates simulated accessing a live news report of a Twin Hills fire via his computer. It seemed pretty futuristic, pretty far out there, but Gates wanted to make an impact. Dream a little, he thought. After all, things he had never even dreamed of happening on the PC had come true.

The audience at IAYF was appreciative but skeptical. Yeah, it could work. But it's going to take a long time. What Gates was saying made sense. Companies had to start thinking about what information they wanted to make available electronically to their employees and share electronically with customers, partners, and clients. The network was the key. The network joined people and data and information together like glue. The computer ought to not just process information but actually think for you. It ought to figure out by observing how you worked what you wanted, and remember it on an ongoing basis. Sure it was going to take a lot more hardware cycles and better software algorithms to do this. It was ambitious, in some ways it was crazy. But yeah, it could work someday. Later on Gates and Intel's Andy Grove and some other high-profile folks met in a suite at the Las Vegas Convention Center. They talked about how to download e-mail to computers' hard disks. This would let people read their e-mail without having to be connected to the network. It was a pretty radical concept at the time, when e-mail systems forced you to read and respond to mail while you were logged on. But e-mail was a cornerstone of IAYF, and that meant constant availability.

IAYF was the vision. Gates was happy with the vision. But as he strolled the beach along Hood Canal, he thought once again about the implementation—about the network. Microsoft was in a good position to supply a lot of parts. It had the Windows operating system to run the computers and applications like Word and Excel and PowerPoint, which, with a technology called object linking and embedding (OLE), could share information and graphics in a single document. It had an e-mail system, Microsoft Mail. It had a database strategy with SQL Server to provide a way of organizing, indexing, and managing networked data. But what about the glue? Somehow all the different software elements had to be linked together to share their data and services. Where was the glue that would attach the pieces of networked computers together going to come from?

Gates thought he had the answer: Build networking into the operating system. Put it into Windows. Build network file sharing, printing, e-mail, database connectivity, and other services right into Windows, where it belonged. Build user directories and make them universally accessible and available over the network. Make the glue part of Windows, and users would not have to worry about arcane configurations and protocols and system requests. Make the glue interoperable, routable, so anyone using a Windows computer would be able to connect to any other computer, on the next desk, in the next room or halfway around the world. Gates was not sure how all this would work. But somehow, someone had to come up with the glue for Windows.

The conceptual roots of IAYF extended years into the past. In July 1945 Vannevar Bush, a leading atomic scientist who was director of the Office of Scientific Research and Development under Franklin D. Roosevelt, published in the *Atlantic Monthly* an essay called "As We May Think" that envisioned a machine capable of storing and annotating text. Although World War II was not officially over, Bush recognized that scientists needed a new calling away from defense concerns. Mechanical devices seemed a logical pursuit. The typewriter, movie camera, automobile, and telephone worked remarkably reliably, Bush noted: "The world has arrived at an age of cheap complex devices of great reliability," he wrote three decades before the birth of the personal computer.

Bush explored several potential technologies, including speech recognition: "Will the author of the future cease writing by hand or typewriter and talk directly to the record? He does so indirectly, by talking to a stenographer or a wax cylinder; but the elements are all present if he wishes to have his talk directly produce a typed record." Bell Labs had a device called a Vocoder under development, Bush noted: "Speak to it, and the corresponding keys move."

Then there was his theoretical pet, the "memex," a "mechanized private file and library." Memex acted as a kind of electronic desk containing "slanting translucent screens" and linking key words to ideas and concepts in a seamless, easily accessed fashion. Indexing would be almost intuitive: "If the user wishes to consult a certain book, he taps its code on the keyboard, and the title page of the book promptly appears before him." The concept, which Bush dubbed "associative indexing," could create "a provision whereby any item may be caused at will to select immediately and automatically another." Numerous items could be linked together in "trails," Bush wrote. Trails persisted forever as the informational base expanded.

Bush's essay had numerous antecedents of its own, but for decades afterward it would be cited as the seminal work on database linking and as the theoretical blueprint for the World Wide Web. It took a Harvard graduate student in 1960 to give "associative indexing" a name that stuck, however. As a term project, Theodor "Ted" Nelson, the son of actress Celeste Holm, began working on a complex writing system for storing and comparing multiple versions of written text. Its first implementation was crude, consisting of 3-by-5 cards Nelson carried around, scribbling notes, quotations, and other arcana as the spirit moved, and then clipping them together for future reference. They could be sorted by date, content, and a numerical system Nelson devised. Nelson, who believes that as a child he may have been read the Vannevar Bush essay by his grandfather, presented a paper in 1965 to the Association for Computing Machinery convention extending Bush's concept. In the paper he discussed "zippered lists," where sections, pages, paragraphs, and concepts could be linked together among multiple documents. The paper was soon forgotten, but out of it came a term that stuck through the years: hypertext. Nelson defined it as "non-sequential writing, text that branches and allows choices to the reader, best read in an interactive screen." Needed: "A new layer able to create compatibilities between existing systems [and] . . . recombine what should never have been separate: word processing, outline processing, teleconferencing, electronic mail, electronic publishing, archiving." The closest antecedent: "the phone system, in its simplicity, universality, clarity, and fundamental character."

The notion of hypertext sprang Nelson, a lanky cynic with chiseled, wolfish features, on a lifelong odyssey to invent a global document-indexing system called Xanadu. The term stemmed somewhat opaquely from Samuel Taylor Coleridge's symbolic poem, "Kubla Khan," which lacks any reference, even granting poetic license, to associative thinking but did have relevance to favorite Nelson themes of dreams and inspiration. Alas, for Nelson hypertext was more Waterloo than Xanadu: Plagued by an habitual incapacity to finish projects, which he blamed on a "hummingbird mind,"

Nelson spent decades in feckless pursuit of a superstructure for implementing his grand design. In "Literary Machines" he proved uncannily prophetic: By the year 2020, "there will be hundreds of thousands of file servers . . . and there will be hundreds of millions of simultaneous users, able to read from billions of stored documents, with trillions of links among them. All of this is manifest destiny. There is no point in arguing it; either you see it or you don't." The Xanadu Project might not be it, Nelson admitted, "but some system of this type will, and can bring a new Golden Age to the human mind."

Ironically, perhaps even intentionally, Nelson became the embodiment of Bush's information automaton: Everywhere he went Nelson carried a camcorder, recording events and experiences for some personal hyperlinked legacy that future historians might find valuable. One can picture a future investigator in his lab, Bush had written, hands free and mobile afoot: "As he moves about and observes, he photographs and comments." In the evening he ponders his notes and "again talks his comments into the record." The machine transcribes everything; his life and archive are one and the same. Even though the Internet eventually usurped anything Nelson could accomplish individually, he continued to make plans for leveraging the Net's connectivity commercially through a digital copyrighting scheme that would collect a small payment—penny, nickel, dollar, whatever—each time a hyperlinked document was accessed, providing for the original author to be paid in digital cash on a per-access basis. Once the World Wide Web took off, micropayment, as the concept came to be known, was a stepping-off point for any discussion of electronic commerce.

The highest-profile precursor to IAYF, however, had been a tantalizing, slickly produced 1987 video, "The Knowledge Navigator," presented by John Sculley, chairman of Apple Computer. You talked to your computer, which was not a box on a desk but a video monitor filled with the facial image of a smiling, computerized helpbot. Home and office were the same. You walked into a room, and the Navigator gave you a news summary, told you your schedule, reminded you of things to do, and put you in touch with people you were trying to reach. You punched no keys, wrote nothing down. You merely spoke what you wanted to the Navigator—say "Please put me in touch with my daughter. Contact Jack and cancel golf Saturday. What's the latest on the global warming conference in Brazil?" Navigator was way cool. It got heavy air time at conferences, trade shows, Apple Computer events, and other industry get-togethers, giving the former Pepsi executive much-needed credibility among the tech set. But it was fanciful stuff. As it turned out, Navigator's problem was not the computer but the bandwidth: You needed lots of spectrum and lots of pipe to deliver the kind of information Sculley foresaw. Nevertheless, it showed compelling possibilities if communications were instantaneous and globally entwined. "Eventually, you will find yourself able to hook into a telephone 'highway' (an intelligent network) to get streams of information—voice, text, and images—over the same wire simultaneously," Sculley predicted. "By the early part of the next century . . . users won't even have to give a moment's thought to where the information resides—the tool will navigate its own way through these highways."

Thinking machines, hypertext, information highways. Vision, vision, vision. There was plenty of it floating around if you looked. It meant nothing without substance. Gates thought again about the glue. Overhead, a seagull's cry broke him from his reverie. Seagulls liked to pick up a shellfish, fly up high, and drop it on the rocky shore. The shell would break, giving the gull access to its next meal. Gates wondered how he could get Microsoft to break the shell surrounding networking. One thing was obvious: Microsoft would have to have help. A key element of Novell's success was in building a training organization that certified engineers on how to link, maintain, and troubleshoot NetWare networks. By 1990 Novell had 3,000 certified engineers, available to fix a network problem at the drop of a hat. That created a positive feedback cycle, one of Gates's favorite concepts, for attracting buyers and sellers to its product. Knowing Novell would support its product brought more buyers to the networking market. The more buyers there were, the more sellers. Microsoft support, by contrast, was an embarrassment. Callers had to wait too long to get help. Millions of customers were being left with bad impressions of Microsoft because of poor support. The company had set up support as a profit center, a separate product channel, which hid its costs from the product groups. Gates had a goal to cut by half the number of support calls. It was not going to be easy. Microsoft was going to need to partner with companies that knew what they were doing in the support arena. It was a business that his company had to learn to do.

A new world order was emerging at Microsoft, centered on IAYF. The company was attracting some of the best minds in the business, guys like Paul Maritz from Intel, Jim Allchin from Banyan, Brad Silverberg from Borland, Dave Cutler from DEC, Bob Muglia from Condor, John Ludwig from Booz-Allen. They had their work cut out for them, but when you brought a bunch of smart people together, great things happened. It was one of Gates's and Microsoft's core philosophies and had brought the company a long way.

It may have been an odd occasion for a multibillionaire software mogul to be worrying about his business strategy on a calm spring day. But long before Intel's Andy Grove popularized the phrase "Only the paranoid survive," Gates lived it. The man Sun's Scott McNealy called the most insecure CEO in America could never lower his guard. Gates liked to tell people the biggest secret of his success was running scared. He had to be constantly thinking of the next opportunity, the next paradigm shift, the next killer app. If he didn't, some kid just out of college would. Gates knew this perfectly well. It was the way he and Paul Allen had reinvented the world while IBM was scratching its head over what to do about this thing called the personal computer. Right now, in fact, while Gates took a leisurely, self-absorbed stroll, some college grad somewhere could be coming up with some brilliant new idea for a protocol or product capable of toppling everything Gates had built over the years. If he was lucky, the kid would work for Microsoft.

When the world's most powerful computer executive returned to Gateaway, he went straight to his desk and sat down in front of his computer. On the screen he began typing out the introduction to a memo he would subsequently distribute, on May 16, 1991, to his executive staff. "Every year," he wrote, "I set aside at least one Think Week to get away and update myself on the latest technical developments . . . " Microsoft had a lot of challenges on its plate. It was time to remind his inner circle of the need for speed.

Chapter 2

THE KID

J Allard did not know who the big bald guy was or what he did. But he looked and sounded important.

"How are you? Welcome aboard!" the big guy said, showing no interest in sitting down. He stood there in the doorway, an agitated impatience about him, his donkey's bray of a voice bleating out.

"Hey, I hear you know something about this TCP/IP thing," he said. "Bane of my existence!" He clapped both meaty hands dramatically to his oversize, Charlie Brown–round head. "You know, every time I get off an airplane in Washington, D.C., the government's beating me up about it! They need interoperability and it has to be routable and blah-de-blah-de-blah." The guy was really getting into it, moving his shoulders around like a boxer bobbing and weaving. "And I don't understand any of that crap." Allard felt the guy pause and look him over, as if sizing up the kid's chances of being able to pull it off. "Just make it go away, will you? Just make it go away!"

Then he was gone.

Allard sat in his office, stunned. Fresh out of college, just twenty-two years old, he had picked the biggest software company in the world to come

to work for, had come 3,000 miles from Boston to the moist climes of Redmond, Washington, for a job that required his skills and needed his vision.
He had his own office—well, half an office—and all the computer gear he
could ask for. They'd given him everything he could want. He thought he
had it made.

Where had he gone wrong?

It was September 10, 1991—Day 2 in his new job at Microsoft. And
some guy who acted like he ran the place had come into Allard's office and
in so many words revealed he was next to clueless about what it was Allard
did. Interoperability? It was the whole key to Microsoft's future! Routable?
You couldn't have a real network without it! Allard was beginning to feel
like a stranger in a strange land. Maybe this was not going to work after all.

At the age of twelve—or maybe he was thirteen—Allard had gone to a
computer trade show, something like PC Expo, in Boston's Hynes Convention Center. There he had encountered Microsoft for the first time.
This was 1983, before Windows, before the Apple Macintosh, long before
the World Wide Web. Allard remembers getting excited over Microsoft's
80-column cards for the Apple II. The Apple was a big game machine, and
Allard was a big gamer. The future of gaming, this prepubescent hacker was
convinced, was 3-D. Allard had even written a 3-D gaming graphics library
for the Apple II. He had thought about maybe selling the package right
there at the show, to some outfit like Broderbund, or Sierra, or even Microsoft. And the guys at the Microsoft booth, one of them may even have
been Bill Gates, Allard doesn't remember, were telling him, you don't understand. Microsoft is all about personal productivity applications. Microsoft is going to do WordStar and Lotus 1-2-3 and dBASE, only a whole
lot better. Microsoft is going to revolutionize desktop computing.

The hell with that! the kid muttered to himself. These guys just don't
get it!

As they were leaving the booth, he told his grandfather: "Someday I'm
going to work for Microsoft."

Sure the Microsoft guys were on the wrong track. But Allard had made
contact. It was their energy, their intelligence, their engagement. He knew
he had been talking to smart people. And Allard, even at a tender age, had
the evangelistic streak in him. The craving to win over the unenlightened.
Allard would rather convert heathens than preach to the choir. It was more
of a challenge that way, and Allard loved challenges. He didn't mind being
a maverick, as long as there was hope he could get the others to come
around. With smart people, there was always hope.

When he turned fourteen, Allard got his work permit and found a job in a computer store called Ray Supply in upstate New York. He was selling hardware, selling software, stuff for Apple and Commodore and the IBM PC. His schoolmates thought it was pretty rad. Shoppers couldn't believe this Little Lord Fauntleroy spouting processor speeds, motherboard specs, interface requirements. The kid was having the time of his life. Still, Allard never thought much about a career in computers. They were a hobby, something he did for fun. Nothing serious like what you would have to do for an actual livelihood.

Allard enrolled in Rensselaer Polytechnic Institute in Troy, New York, then moved to Boston University and began looking around for a calling. It was not easy. He took some classes in engineering, some in architecture. Interesting stuff, how a bridge stands up. Allard found himself fascinated to know how bridges worked, how buildings were constructed. But he found himself working it all out on computers. What made the process interesting was reconstructing it on a computer. He would never actually want to build a bridge. But figuring out how to build a bridge on a computer was fun.

Maybe there was something to a career in computers. Throughout his childhood Allard had been told by his father, You work way too hard not to love what you're doing. You put too much time into it, spend too much energy at it. Make sure when you pick a career you love what you're doing. Allard decided to follow his dad's advice. He turned to computer science courses and started working with UNIX, a computer operating system developed by Bell Labs. Academic institutions had standardized on UNIX for a litany of reasons. Its source code was readily available, meaning that any programmer could customize and enhance it. The principle was somewhat akin to a car buff, having obtained the shop manual, then being able to alter the makeup of his favorite rig. UNIX also connected easily to dumb terminals, the generic green screens found widely on campuses and in institutions. UNIX was scalable, meaning it was equally useful for a few or many thousands of users. It was network smart. Most important, it was free.

Allard immediately fell in love with the whole concept of networking. It was a way of bringing lots of people together. You could link networks with other networks, on and on, till the whole world was online. Think of the implications for changing society! Shrinking the globe! At Boston U Allard helped set up all kinds of shared applications, where students could collaborate on projects together, share calendars, play games in real time. He took responsibility for a number of the computer science department's distributed systems, like department accounting, course signups, online grade reports, network printing, and terminal reservations. He also worked on research in network security to earn credits. In November 1988 he and the rest of the country watched in spellbound horror as the deadly WORM virus, unleashed by a former Cornell University hacker, threatened to bring the Internet to a standstill. For all its harm, the WORM was, Allard liked to point out, the first real distributed application. Although in a negative way, it showed how an application could spread throughout the network all on its own, simply by being readily accessible. In altruistic hands, Allard reasoned, a program like the WORM could take advantage of the power of the Internet for the good of mankind. In its own way the WORM was an inspiration.

Allard saw e-mail as a huge, important application that would drive the Internet forward. But it wasn't what really interested him. The Net's true power lay in real-time collaboration and one-to-many communications, such as newsgroups. Things like Usenet news, roundtable mailing lists, and Internet chat were what excited him. You brought huge numbers of people together and anything could happen. Allard got into managing campus networks at the university, learning security issues, writing network code, tutoring others. Just about all his class projects centered on internetworking some way or other.

And what made it all possible, Allard discovered along the way, was TCP/IP.

TCP/IP stood for transmission control protocol/Internet protocol. A simplistic way of looking at what protocols do is to imagine two strangers in Europe trying to communicate. They try to find out what language they know in common: Sprechen Deutsche? Hablo Español? Parles Français? Speak English? Eventually (it is hoped) they hit on words they both understand and start exchanging conversation. The transmission control protocol, invented in 1973 by Internet pioneers Vinton Cerf and Robert Kahn, enabled data and files from one computer to be sent to another in electronic chunks called packets. Internet protocol decided how the data got routed over the network so it reached its right destination intact. It was a little like salmon returning to spawn from the ocean to the inland waterway, river, stream, creekbed. Somehow they knew which tributary to enter. You don't have to understand how TCP/IP works, thankfully, to recognize its importance. Without it, your computer cannot communicate with the Internet.

Allard became a TCP/IP weenie. TCP/IP was the key to making the Internet work. It was the glue.

When it came time to graduate in 1991, Allard knew he was destined for some job in networking. Most big companies had networks; it was just a matter of finding one with the right style. Working with heavy-duty workstations running UNIX on campus had shown Allard the power of linking PCs—in fact, his roommate and Allard had a PC running a bulletin-board system that they later connected to the Internet directly. But Allard had fallen victim to the classic big-box arrogance toward PCs. They were toys, playthings, glorified calculators, typewriters with screens. As for Microsoft, well, forget them. IBM knew networking, Novell knew networking, Sun knew networking. Microsoft was not even on the radar screen.

Allard saw a notice for a job fair at nearby MIT, where he had taken some classes and gotten to know a few people. He and his fiancée, Rebecca Norlander, decided it was time for a job. They printed up their résumés the night before, on watermarked paper in professional-looking PostScript typeface at the computer science lab they managed. They dressed up in suits, got leather portfolios, and went off to seek their fortunes. The job fair was a mob scene, thousands of kids running around, albeit none attired as formally as Allard and Rebecca. At the Kodak booth a woman asked to see his résumé. "Oh, what did you get your MA in?" she asked.

"MA?" Allard asked.

The woman pointed to a line on the résumé that said Boston, MA.

"That stands for Massachusetts," Allard said. "I don't have an MA."

Sorry, he was told, we're not interested in undergraduates. Allard, disgusted, took back the résumé. The watermarked paper had cost him 25 cents a sheet, after all.

He was about to ditch the fair when he stumbled by the Microsoft booth. There wasn't much point, he figured, but Rebecca was making the rounds and Allard had some time to kill and a stack of worthless résumés. What was it like to work at Microsoft? he asked the boothkeeper, Trish Millines, a manager in systems software at Microsoft. I hear all sorts of perspectives, he said.

"It's the greatest thing in the world," Millines said. They started talking, and pretty soon nearly an hour had passed. Millines thought Allard was pretty brash but also pretty smart. The thing she liked about him was, he had no issue with talking with a black woman about coming to Microsoft.

Usually at these things people were like, well, who's she? It was subtle, but she noticed it. Allard just dove right in. She found herself thinking, he's Microsoft material, even though she was having to do some selling on her company. Allard knew the salaries weren't all that great, so Millines had to explain the whole idea of stock options and working on cool products and getting to be at a place where everyone, not just one or two random folks, was as smart as he was. And you could write your own ticket. "It's just like running your own business," she said. "Once you get hold of a product or technology, you own it. It's basically yours." Millines, who had gotten her computer science degree in 1979 from Monmouth College in New Jersey and then worked at a couple of military contracting companies and PC companies before joining Microsoft as an independent contract worker in 1988, knew this would hook Allard. He seemed like the kind of kid who liked to call his own shots.

Allard figured it was just idle chatter, although later he would think back and realize that Millines really had been interviewing him. Allard went and brought back Rebecca to talk to Millines as well. Two weeks later Microsoft flew them both to corporate headquarters near Seattle, where they underwent a day of intensive interviewing. Allard was struck by a question from one of his interviewers, Brian Valentine, a networking manager at Microsoft. If you died tomorrow, Valentine asked him, what would you want your tombstone to read? Allard was quick with his reply: "Go big, or go home." Both he and Rebecca landed jobs. Within a couple of weeks Norlander joined Microsoft; Allard stayed in Boston through the summer to finish his degree. Eight days before his arrival at Microsoft, the two were wed.

Allard thought he was destined to work for Nathan Myhrvold, the former Princeton- and Cambridge-trained quantum physicist who at the time was in Microsoft's operating systems group. Myhrvold would be not a bad place to start. When you mentioned Myhrvold's name around Microsoft, it was like the E.F. Hutton commercial. People stopped and listened. Myhrvold had Bill Gates's ear. It was like being one step removed from the Man. Allard's responsibilities were to be in business application strategy and development, which sounded maybe interesting or maybe awful. But a headcount issue cropped up, Allard's position disappeared, and he found himself making the interview rounds again, trying to land somewhere appropriate. Everyone who interviewed him had the same bottom-line question: What would you *really* like to do? And Allard would say, I have to be honest with you, I'm not sure Microsoft is where I'm meant to be. He would say, I like Microsoft's high impact, that's great. But what I really want is a networking job, so it's really kind of weird I'm even out here talking to you. Allard thought of himself as the Internet punk out of college. If Microsoft could use him, fine. If he could get the Internet and Windows to work together, that would be phenomenal. Then his mom could get on the Net.

That was the ultimate goal, in Allard's mind: To get his mom onto the Net. Maybe even his dad! The only way he could see it happening was with Windows.

Finally something turned up in networking. Microsoft had a program called LAN Manager it was working on for OS/2. The LAN stood for local area network, a computer term for an in-house network linking several computers together. If you wanted to do networking at Microsoft, you had to do LAN Man. At the time, in 1991, Microsoft's relationship with IBM had pretty much collapsed. But the LAN Man development stumbled on, aimed at taking care of the big-business things Windows could not do. Microsoft loved to cover its bases. If OS/2 were to catch on among large enterprises, big accounting and brokerage and banking firms, say, or oil, transportation, and utility companies, Microsoft wanted to be there. Yes, LAN Man was a joke. But a lot of Microsoft products had started out as jokes. Windows itself had been a joke for seven years before finally catching on in 1990. Now it was taking over the world.

A recruiter called Allard up and told him the team had an opening. Microsoft needed someone to do something called "TC pip." At first Allard didn't make the connection. He thought, TC pip, what is it? Some kind of Microsoft proprietary LAN Man thing? But the guy said, No, it's TC-slash-pip. And Allard said, You mean, TCP-slash-IP? And the recruiter said, Oh, yeah, that's it. Hmmmm, Allard thought. The Internet really is a foreign language to Microsoft.

"You want to talk to those guys?" the recruiter asked.

"Sure," Allard said brightly. "Can't hurt."

So he talked to the LAN Man folks, got the job, got an office, got his equipment set up. And then on the second day, the big guy had come into his office, waving his arms, honking at him about making the pain go away.

On September 10, 1991, the Internet was still a limited-availability system, reserved for the military, for scientists, academicians, and government agencies. Created in the early 1970s as a Department of Defense project to enable strategic forces to keep communicating in event of a nuclear attack, the Internet was federally funded and controlled. Joe and Jill Citizen could not get an Internet account.

The World Wide Web barely existed. In late 1989 Tim Berners-Lee, a thirty-three-year-old British communications expert working at the CERN particle physics laboratory in Geneva, Switzerland, began drawing up specifications for network protocols that would enable documents to be linked, searched, and copied throughout the world via the Internet. The 1976 Oxford University graduate was enthralled with the notion of organizing information in the randomly associative way the brain works and had even developed a program he called Enquire that hyperlinked documents so you could hop from a topic in one to the same or related topic in another. Enquire, an early implementation of Ted Nelson's hypertext concept, was the seedbed from which Berners-Lee's CERN project grew. Berners-Lee and a Belgian colleague, Robert Cailliau, had an idea that seemed to them quite modest at the time. They wanted to link documents on the Internet somehow—by key words, by subject matter, by topic, whatever—so users could easily find and share information and assist others in finding and sharing information. What Berners-Lee and Cailliau came up with comprised three significant, breakthrough technologies. One was the hypertext markup language, referred to by its initials html. Another was hypertext transport protocol, or http. Related to http was the universal resource locator, or URL.

Html enabled programmers to format documents so they could be read and linked via the Internet. Using certain commands placed in brackets, html put headers, paragraphs, indentations, and other formatting features into documents. Most important, html enabled links. A certain command in html would, when invoked by the user (by hitting the ENTER key or clicking with a mouse), automatically bounce the user to another, related document on the Internet. Chances were that document also would have links bouncing to other documents. When a new document was placed on the Internet, not only would its author be able to link to other documents, but other Internet users would be able to link to the new document as well. Http was a way of enabling Internet users to access html documents directly by way of their location on the Net. The location was designated by the URL, which consisted of the document's host Internet server—the computer containing the document. When an Internet user or programmer registered his or her computer on the Net, it was given an address with a suffix indicating the nature of its origin. A company had the suffix "com," for example. A government agency was "gov," a nonprofit agency was "org," and a military agency "mil." So Widgets International might call its server widgets.com. And when Widgets would post a document, say its Gear Repair Manual, on its server using html, other Internet users would be able to access it by typing: www.widgets.com/gear.html.

The Berners-Lee/Cailliau system was a grand you-scratch-my-back-I'll-scratch-yours vision for building a global library of interconnected publications. A Dewey Decimal system on steroids for the Internet. A giant matrix of electronic documents. One of the marvelous inspirations of the system's inventors was the name Berners-Lee came up with to describe their creation: the World Wide Web.

As J Allard was arriving at Microsoft, the Web was on the verge of being released to the Internet community at large. It was largely text. Many of the world's personal computers could not even display graphical images, and Berners-Lee wanted his system to be as universal and openly accessible as possible.

What became known, accurately or not, as the first graphical browser was still nearly two years away from creation. The two University of Illinois undergraduates who would invent it, Marc Andreessen and Eric Bina, were working on computer graphics for scientific and data visualization at the university-affiliated National Center for Supercomputing Applications in Champaign. It would be another year and a half before their ingenious creation, Mosaic, began appearing on UNIX computers connected to the Web and another year to two after that before Mosaic became widely used enough to incite a revolution in the way people used computers.

And in 1991, Allard had discovered, Microsoft was the cave dweller of the Internet. TCP/IP was nothing but hieroglyphics. The Internet had nothing to do with the company's business plan, software strategy, or corporate vision. It was a checkbox item on a niche product that might or might not amount to anything for Microsoft. Allard bit his lip and shook his head. It was a long way to Tipperary.

Allard sat in his office as Mr. Loud disappeared down the hall. The young recruit's dream of marrying Windows with the Internet so his mom could log on seemed like a sick joke. He had crossed the continent to come to the world's biggest personal-computer software company, only to discover it had almost zero interest in the thing he was all about.

Allard turned to his office mate, Laurie Litwack. "Who was that?" he asked, his voice a blend of marvel and consternation.

Litwack looked at him as though she hadn't heard right. Everybody knew who the big bald guy was. He was Bill Gates's ex-Harvard buddy, hired to run operations at Microsoft in 1980, later the head Windows guy, the sales chief who ran the IBM relationship, Gates's occasional singing partner, loyal lieutenant, and best friend. The guy who in 1989 had shown his faith in the company by buying an unthinkable 945,000 shares of Microsoft stock after it took a rare tumble. The guy who had done the Crazy Eddie take-off, checkered sportcoat and all, hawking Windows when it was lame and unwanted, who revved the troops at the annual company meeting, who two years earlier swam the length of Lake Bill, a pond at Microsoft, in red underwear to fulfill a United Way bet with fellow executive Mike Maples. And on and on and on.

Litwack looked at the callow young recruit in front of her and said, "That was Steve Ballmer."

Steve Ballmer did not know what TCP/IP was.

But he knew it was good.

Ballmer strode down the corridor back toward his office. When he walked he was like a panther, eyes watchful, head moving, broad, round shoulders forward. Powerful yet fluid, and always with a sense of impending destination.

The world was changing. Employee No. 28 at Microsoft, who had started June 11, 1980, Ballmer could remember the days when he knew everyone on a first-name basis. If someone had been with the company for a few years, chances were Ballmer had hired, or at least signed off on, the person himself. The old-timers at Microsoft told riotous stories about being picked up by this raucous, excitable guy at Sea-Tac International Airport, driven to company headquarters in a Ford with old milk cartons and fragrant running shoes in back, and then being interviewed by the guy himself or having lunch or dinner with him during Microsoft's multiple-interview process. You never forgot a Ballmer interview. He had a philosophy about interviewing. You asked questions where the answer was not so much the point as was the process of trying to come up with the answer. You wanted to see what the candidate would do with the question. Like how many manholes there were in the city of New York. Some of them looked at you like you were crazy. Some tried to bluff it. The keepers thought about it a bit and started working through the process of how they would figure out the answer. What were manholes for, so how many were there per street, how many streets were there in the city. It was one way you managed to hire smart people.

With the possible exception of its cofounder and chairman, no one cared more for Microsoft than Steve Ballmer. Only two people besides Gates had been at the company longer: quiet, affable Bob O'Rear, one of the "Albuquerque 11" who had made the trip from New Mexico to the Seattle area in 1979 and was key to early DOS work for the IBM PC, and Gordon Letwin, a blunt-spoken systems programmer with a Merlinesque beard and reclusive aura. Both were within a couple of years of leaving Microsoft, however. Ballmer, at thirty-five, could not envision the day when he would hang it up.

Ballmer wondered about something. If he were coming in to Microsoft now and there was a Ballmer type interviewing him and asking him about TCP/IP, what would he say? These kids today knew so much coming in, they could make you feel dumb.

TCP/IP: The nation's big software accounts were screaming for it. The guys from the Department of Defense, the FBI, NSA, you name it. The Fortune 500. Big companies, medium-size companies. If Microsoft was going to be a player in the networked world, it had to offer TCP/IP connectivity. It had to enable people to get onto the Internet. If LAN Manager was going to run on big networks, it had to have TCP/IP. If Windows was going to become a big-enterprise standard on millions of desktops, it was going to need TCP/IP. Because those computers had to be hooked together somehow. They couldn't just sit by themselves, full of data other people needed to access. They had to communicate, and TCP/IP was one way the Big Boys wanted their computers to talk. Ballmer was not sure how much trouble TCP/IP would be, but he knew it would be worth whatever it took to get it. It did not take much to get Steve Ballmer's attention. After the second and third mention of something, he was on the case. These were big contracts, $10 million here, $25 million there. Even so, they were chicken feed compared to the business Microsoft could capture by becoming the networking standard for big shops around the globe—multinational corporations, government agencies, educational institutions. You were talking huge numbers, well into the billions of dollars. TCP/IP: Gotta get it, gotta have it!

And Microsoft's ability to deliver rested in the hands of a twenty-two-year-old kid fresh out of Boston University with a pony tail down the middle of his back. Ballmer shook his head in amusement. Man, the world was really changing.

Ballmer was the type of guy who kept pushing, pushing, pushing, till he got what he was after. With him life was one big grab for the brass ring. You were either on the bus or you were off the bus. You were either golden or screwed. But you gave it everything you had, so there were no regrets. Ballmer's hardcore persistence brought to mind the obsessiveness of Popeye the detective in the classic cop thriller, *The French Connection.* Popeye on a stakeout in the freezing cold, dining on limp pizza and putrid coffee while Frog 1 and Frog 2 sample prime rib and escargots in the pampered warmth of a five-star restaurant. Popeye commandeering a car and racing the elevated train through the streets of New York. Popeye taking the Lincoln into the shop, knowing it's dirty, and having it torn apart. And when at the end they can't find anything and the shop guy says, Give me a break, I've torn out everything except the rocker panels, Popeye jumping up, eyes blazing, snarling, "Come on, Irv, what the hell is *that?*"

Ballmer hoped he had not scared the kid. Focused and intense in any setting, Ballmer knew he could be intimidating. At six-foot-one, 225 pounds, stark bald, and Teamster-burly, he looked like a cross between Yoda and Oddjob the manservant. Around Microsoft, a company generally populated by skinny slide-rule types with little physical prowess, Ballmer was an imposing presence. Bill's best friend, the putative No. 2 guy, head of systems software. That meant DOS and Windows, the two pieces of software that accounted for 36 percent of Microsoft's revenues, were under his command. Ballmer carried a big stick. But he did not walk softly. He did nothing softly. Ballmer's voice, amplified by the lungs of a mule, projected loudly and emphatically whether in a face-to-face conversation or before thousands of Microsofties at a company meeting. It was his trademark, his defining characteristic. People told stories about it, joked about it, tried to imitate it. Everyone knew about Ballmer's vocal prowess. Like jets and chainsaws, you usually heard him before you saw him. And when you did see him, you knew it was high-impact time. Ballmer had the kind of photovoltaic persona that made the room go bright the minute he walked in.

But the kid, who had vaguely almond eyes, a high forehead with hair combed straight back, and compact build, lending a hint of the samurai to him, looked ready. As if he could hold his own.

Ballmer knew more about TCP/IP than he liked to let on. If you asked him, he would tell you he was not the most technical guy around. But that was in comparison to guys like Gates, Maritz, Allchin, Cutler. The high-wire acts. Guys who did or had done code. He did not talk about it much, but Ballmer had done some programming at Detroit's Country Day School. Nothing since then, but the fact was, he was technical enough to figure out how much he needed to know about TCP/IP and why Microsoft needed it. If he had no clue as to how it actually worked, that was okay. His job was not to write the code, it was to get other people fired up about writing the code. If Ballmer tried to come on like he knew something he did not, if he tried to throw some moves on the guys who worked for him, he knew he would get crucified in an instant. He had much better success backing off the technical stuff, making sure his charges understood that they knew a lot more than the boss. It gave them a sense of pride, a feeling of ownership. Ballmer knew that giving ownership was one of the great secrets of Microsoft. Over the years, Ballmer had worn a lot of hats at the company. But what stuck in the minds of Microsoft denizens most about Ballmer was his inspirational fire. Passion! That's what working at Microsoft was all about. You had to have fire in the belly! That's what you looked for when you went recruiting for Microsoft material. No fire, no hire!

The kid had fire. Ballmer could tell. There was something like a coiled spring to the way the kid sat at his chair, listening intently, eyes riveted on you. He was fearless. He talked fast, self-assuredly. He could take the ball and run with it.

Chapter 3

PASSION!

Steve Ballmer strode back to his office in Building 4, saying hello on the way to his longtime secretary, Debbie Hill, who had been with him practically since the start. He sat down and started rocking back in his chair, then picked up a Nerf ball and began shooting baskets at a mini-hoop set up on the opposite wall. Ballmer was famous for picking up sports paraphernalia and swinging or shooting or bouncing or just passing them from hand to hand during a meeting. He had huge, fleshy hands that swallowed toy balls like gumdrops. Ballmer had a history with bouncy balls. In the mid-1980s a stealth prankster at Microsoft, a Yale University recruit named Ray Drewry, began playing a distracting series of practical jokes using those incredibly bouncy superballs that were the fad of the day. The pranks got more and more elaborate until Ballmer issued an ultimatum banning the things. Shortly thereafter he returned, on his birthday, from a weeklong business trip to find his office filled with superballs. Or at least it looked that way. Drewry had erected a false wall out of corrugated cardboard in Ballmer's office, then filled the space between the wall and his windowed hallway relight to make it look like his entire office was filled with the things. When Ballmer opened the door, there was no way to prevent the balls from erupting into the hallway and bouncing madly all over the place. Ballmer saw his dilemma and roared. It was half in surprise, half in mock anger, and the other 50 percent in sheer delight at the ingenuity of the setup. Those present at the time later would end the story by saying Ballmer's outburst was the loudest of all the Ballmer loudnesses.

Ballmer loved sports, especially basketball. His office wall displayed a letter from Isiah Thomas, the Detroit superstar whom Ballmer had met during a Seattle SuperSonics game. Ballmer had the glow of a little kid when he talked about meeting Zeke. Through a friend he had scored two seats for the Detroit game right down on the court, next to the bench. Jovial Frank Gaudette, the Microsoft chief financial officer who had gone to grade school with one of the Pistons' assistant coaches, had told Ballmer to stick around, there were a couple guys he wanted Ballmer to meet. Before the game Ballmer met the assistant coach and head coach Chuck Daly. Then out of the blue Isiah had come up to him and said, "I hear you're from Farmington Hills," the Detroit suburb where Ballmer grew up. Ballmer was blown away.

Ballmer still managed to get out on the court for pickup games, and he kept in shape by jogging religiously, eight to ten miles every morning, rising from bed around 5:30 A.M. The classic Type A morning person overachiever. During his Harvard days, Ballmer had been something of a big man on campus. Publisher of the *Harvard Advocate*, the literary magazine. Ad manager for the *Crimson*, the school newspaper. Instructor of a precalculus class for undergraduates. Upon arriving on campus the fall of 1973, Ballmer had memorized the faces and names of each of his classmates from the freshman record. It made him a popular guy pretty quick. Built like a football center, Ballmer never actually played. But he stayed close to the sports scene, serving as general manager for the football team and statistician for basketball games.

The son of a Swiss father, who had served as a translator for the Nuremberg trials, and Detroit-born mother, Ballmer the high school math-science-physics whiz had applied to and been accepted at MIT, Cal Tech, and Harvard. He chose Harvard, first out of wanting a more balanced, less tech-slanted education and second because he knew his dad wanted him to go there. Ballmer's father was then an executive for Ford, where numerous senior executives were Harvard alums. And the Harvard recruiter for eastern Michigan taught at Ballmer's school. It was a case of Harvard, end of story. Visiting Harvard as a recruit in early 1973, Ballmer stayed with a cross-town Detroit freshman, Scott McNealy, in an ironic foreshadowing of what would become, with McNealy's rise to head Sun Microsystems, one of the computing industry's enduring rivalries.

Ballmer met Gates his sophomore year, when both roomed in Currier House, a dorm where the math-science types hung out. Both entered the prestigious national Putnam math competition, in which Currier House alone placed 9 finalists, as many as some schools, out of 1,800 entrants. Little-known fact: Ballmer actually scored higher than Gates on the test. Ballmer had heard about Gates, this crazy guy who slept without sheets on his bed and left for Christmas vacation with his room open, money on the desk, the windows wide open, when it was raining out. Their first night out together they went to one of those quirky art-house twin bills, *Singin' in the Rain* and *A Clockwork Orange*, the latter a futuristic psychodrama that turns the former's jaunty title song into a macabre anthem of hatred and rape. Ballmer and Gates hit it off. Ballmer found Gates a lot of fun—smart, talky, and sarcastic, and just enough off-center to keep you interested. After they drove back to campus in a car Gates was borrowing from Microsoft cofounder-to-be Paul Allen, they did a little singing of their own. Ballmer projected so well he almost came to blows with a dorm mate who proved unappreciative of the late-hour rendition.

The two made an unlikely pair. Slight and awkward, Gates was the reclusive poker-playing math geek who stayed up all night. Ballmer, big-hearted, boisterous, and outgoing, hated gambling and was an early riser. They took a graduate-level economics class, EC 2010, together, skipped all but a handful of the classes, then goaded each other on while cramming for the final in a male-bonding ritual of "We're golden" and "We're screwed." And Ballmer got Gates "punched," or initiated into, the campus's exclusive Fox Club. The initiation was a memorable occasion. Ballmer and two friends took a well-lubed Gates around the MIT campus blindfolded and in black tie. In the cafeteria Gates was required to give a lecture on programming and computer science. At the freshman union he had to sing from the balcony. Then the quartet went bar-hopping, where Gates was subjected to further impromptu humiliations. After a trip to Harvard Square, it was back to the club for the legendary crawl through a maze. There was no maze really, just the open floor, but in a blindfold, Gates could not tell the difference.

Gates dropped out his junior year to form Microsoft and sell the adaptation of the BASIC programming language that he, Paul Allen, and a Harvard math undergrad named Monte Davidoff had written. But Ballmer finished school. He was accepted at Stanford Business School but decided to defer postgraduate education and went to work for Procter & Gamble in Cincinnati. There he worked on marketing Duncan Hines mixes for a year and a half. At the bachelor-party pub crawl of a P&G pal, Ballmer showed off his impressive smarts, blowing away the competition in a trivia contest. He could remember things like what Beaver Cleaver said in episode 43, Steve Hamm later reported in *PC Week*. Eventually they got kicked out of the bar for being too noisy. Yes, there was a pattern here.

In 1979 Ballmer decided to seek his fortune in the balmier venue of Hollywood. Perhaps it was the Gilda Radner effect—Ballmer's and Radner's grandfathers were brothers, making his mother, Beatrice Dworkin, a first cousin of Radner's mother. Ballmer and Gilda had met, but well before her stardom on *Saturday Night Live*. In spring of 1977 Gates was in New York City working on a BASIC deal and hooked up with Ballmer at a Fox Club dinner. The two went out partying afterward and wound up at Studio 54, where they spotted Radner. It was the heyday of *SNL* and Radner was a celeb. Gates had to egg his friend on—"Come on, come on, she's your cousin!" Ballmer finally went over and introduced himself. Radner was skeptical till Ballmer dropped her grandfather's name. Then she warmed up and introduced him to her friend, John Belushi. It was a brief encounter—Belushi, well into the drug habit that killed him, made a joke about looking for white powder.

Beyond star fever, Ballmer's own natural flair for the theatric may have given him notions of getting into the movie business. Whatever, he went out to Hollywood and met with Jeff Sagansky, a fellow Harvard alum who later wound up president of CBS. Sagansky suggested Ballmer read scripts and do one-page synopses to get a feel for what worked. Ballmer gave it a whirl, but a few months of reading B-grade screenplays and parking cars at celebrity auctions persuaded him of a higher calling. It was off to Stanford, where he spent the 1979–1980 academic year working on his MBA. Looking for financial support to cover his college costs, Ballmer entered two competitions for separate $10,000 awards, put up by rival consulting firms, to go to the best first-year student. Ballmer won both. By spring he was lining up a summer job and was in the process of putting together a whirlwind five-day tour of companies interested in interviewing him, to be capped by a visit to see his parents in Detroit.

Then his college buddy Bill Gates came calling.

The previous summer, in July of 1979, Ballmer had visited Gates in

Seattle. It was only seven months after Gates's and Allen's fledgling company had moved from Albuquerque to Bellevue, Washington, a new-money Seattle bedroom community. Microsoft was located in an Old National Bank building in the heart of Bellevue. Ballmer hung out with Gates for a couple of weeks, but there was no talk of his hooking up with Microsoft. Ballmer had noticed one thing, though: His friend seemed tired. Gates was doing the rainmaker thing for the company, traveling around and generating business while also trying to run the place. He looked more frazzled than Ballmer had ever seen him, even during the crazed week they had crammed for the economics final together.

By the spring of 1980, Gates was seeing the handwriting on the wall, in a cursive that looked like Ballmer's. Microsoft was growing beyond his capacity to manage, and Gates needed someone with organizational skills to come in and run the business. Gates had watched his friend do "super well" at Procter & Gamble and Stanford Business School. Gates called him up and introduced the topic obliquely, complaining that he needed help bad, and did Ballmer know anyone available who was as smart as he was, and wasn't it too bad Ballmer didn't have a twin brother. Ballmer got to thinking about it and called Gates back at Microsoft but got Paul Allen instead. "Are you coming to work for us?" Allen asked. Then Ballmer called Gates's home and got Kay Nishi, Gates's buddy and Japanese liaison, who said, "So—you are coming to Microsoft, right?" Finally Ballmer got hold of Gates, who invited him to swing by Seattle at the end of his job tour. After a hectic frequent-flyer week—Monday in Chicago, Tuesday in New York, Wednesday and Thursday in Boston, Friday in Detroit, Ballmer was in Seattle. He and Bill had dinner with Gates's parents, Bill Jr. the prominent local attorney and Mary the civic activist involved in the national United Way and a recent appointee to the University of Washington board of regents. And the issue of what Steve wanted to do with his life kept coming up. Finally Gates asked him to come work at Microsoft. Ballmer gave him a tentative yes and drove Gates to the airport, where he flew off to the British Virgin Islands for his first vacation. Subsequently, riotous salary negotiations were carried out by ship-to-shore phone aboard a rented sailboat, the *DooWah*. Bill offered $45,000 but Ballmer held out for $50,000, which Gates acceded to amid inebriated heckling from his sailing companions. The salary was good for then, but Ballmer's coup was in scoring a performance-based qualification for stock options worth, eventually, 8.9 percent of the company and billionaire status.

Upon his arrival it was obvious to Ballmer what Microsoft needed. First, it had to become a real business. Microsoft was being run as a partnership between Gates and Allen. Ballmer figured to get the company on track it needed to incorporate. On January 29, 1981, he wrote a memo to Gates recommending incorporation and outside financing. Nobody was going to invest in a partnership, after all. Microsoft was doing well enough not to need outside financing, but Ballmer knew it would give the company legitimacy in the financial community and on Wall Street. It was never too early to be thinking about a public offering, especially with those stock options in the till. Apple had just the previous month completed its IPO, making bazillionaires out of the two Steves, Jobs and Wozniak. The Microsoft Steve had duly noted it. By July 1 Microsoft had made it official. In September Technology Venture Investors, in a deal marshaled by venture capitalist David Marquardt, bought 5 percent of the company for $1 million.

Ballmer also took custodianship of Microsoft's financial situation. Gates was trying to do everything managerial, even accounting, at the company. Ballmer's solution: Take over the books, look at the books, get the books under control. Then start bringing in more bodies. Allen, who wanted more folks for R&D to seed what eventually became Microsoft's lucrative applications business, backed up Ballmer's plan. Gates was not so sure. When Ballmer went on a hiring spree that brought in the first crop of what would become legendary names at Microsoft—Charles Simonyi, Mark Zbikowski, Doug Klunder, Jeff Harbers—Gates called him in for an upbraiding. What's this all about? he demanded. I brought you in to make sure that we are a responsible company and not hire a bunch of people and you're going to bankrupt us and you're going to bankrupt us and how could you do that?! Ballmer knew what the numbers said, though, and Microsoft could well afford the help. Besides . . . Ballmer was doing the stock options thing with the new hires too. It was payday on the come: If the company did well, they would do well. They had to be smart guys, though, good people. If they were lucky enough to get hired, and smart enough to hold on to the standard stock options package Ballmer granted, they were millionaires twice over within a decade.

Ballmer played a strategic role in other arenas as well, helping to negotiate the purchase of the original 86-DOS from Seattle Computer Products in 1981 and work on the DOS contract for the IBM PC, released in August. In late 1981 he became vice president of corporate statistics, a title that meant he basically took care of finance, hiring, legal, tech writing, and assorted other pursuits not directly related to programming and marketing. He held that role till August 1983, when Jon Shirley came from Tandy to be president of Microsoft. At that point Ballmer became vice president of marketing, a long way of saying he was Mr. IBM. The delicate relationship with Big Blue, under strain from a growing IBM "clone" market, needed Ballmer's deft business touch to keep on the straight and narrow. From 1980 to 1984 was what Ballmer liked to think of as his build-the-company phase. Build the company, get your arms around Big Blue. His Mr. IBM phase.

Getting even his big biceps around IBM was a heroic task for Ballmer. Almost from the time the ink dried on the August 1980 DOS contract, Microsoft had to walk and talk a delicate line with Big Blue. Microsoft had no choice. The three romanesque initials ruled the computing universe, making and breaking companies on a whim. From the time the first clone PCs began appearing after the 1982 success of the Compaq "sewing machine," a big and bulky but marvelously functional portable PC, IBM kept trying to make the PC a stepchild of its mainframe and miniframe business. PCs were toys. PCs were barely intelligent terminals, to be hooked into or used in conjunction with IBM "big iron." Yet Microsoft also depended on a clone market. Each machine meant another sale of MS-DOS. At $5 or so a pop, it represented just 1/500th to 1/1000th of the cost of the machine. But if enough machines were sold, it could turn into real money. And it was $5 more than Microsoft got from IBM for each IBM PC using DOS. The original DOS contract had, for $80,000, given IBM largely unlimited use of the operating system on its PCs. So Microsoft wanted things both ways: to keep IBM happy while still doing all it could to nurture a clone market. The demands of Microsoft's balancing act proved Wallenda-like. One example: When Microsoft announced Windows 1.0 at a November 10, 1983, fete, a lot of big names showed up to pledge support: Digital, Compaq, Hewlett-Packard, Radio Shack, Zenith, Convergent, Data General, on down the line. Huge in its absence was IBM. Big Blue not only was backing a competitor to Windows, the soon-to-be-forgotten VisiOn, it had ideas of its own for doing windowing systems on the PC.

Could this marriage be saved? In 1985 IBM made plans to replace DOS with a next-generation OS, eventually to be called, with typical Big Blue marketing flair, OS/2. Microsoft and IBM signed a renewal of vows called the Joint Operating Agreement to develop OS/2 and began the uneasy waltz: IBM wanting to supplant DOS and the clone market, Microsoft wanting to hold on to both—and Big Blue too. The couple seemed happy, or at least compatibly settled, when OS/2 1.0 shipped in December 1987. It went nowhere, however. Not only did OS/2 lack any useful mainstream applications, it required too much memory, which then cost as much as $200 a megabyte. And the user interface, typed commands on a blank screen, was retro to a fault at a time when the Macintosh was blazing a graphical user interface trail.

What to do? The obvious solution seemed to be: Run Windows on OS/2. Version 2.0 of Windows was not as nice as the Mac, but it was enough of an improvement over 1.0 to spark interest among leading-edge users and hobbyist types as well as a lawsuit (on St. Patrick's Day, 1988) for copyright violations by Apple Computer. But IBM balked: Adopting Windows might make it too beholden to the gang from Redmond. Instead, a plan was hatched to build a Windows-like interface for OS/2 and a PC to run it.

On the Microsoft side, Bill Gates asked the guy he knew who could crack the whip—and could tolerate Big Blue's ponderous bureaucracy— enough to get the job done: Steve Ballmer. Ballmer had proven his muster in similar straits a couple of years earlier. Back in 1984 he had come into the Windows project and found it behind schedule and in disarray. Ballmer's response was to start clarifying objectives, pinpointing schedules. He brought in key people like Neil Konzen and Chris Peters, real code wizards, and gradually things began taking shape. He got in the shorts of the manager of the project, who decided there was far too little room in his underwear for Ballmer, even metaphorically, and quit. Then Ballmer turned on the afterburners: Windows! Windows! Windows! Nothing would stand in his way! He was like a Mad Dog! By Fall Comdex 1985, Windows 1.0 was out the door. Cartoony, klunky, and unable to run on most existing PCs, Windows had a long way to go. But at least it was there.

Now all Ballmer had to do was sell the thing, and that involved doing the DOS jump-start all over again. Get Windows on IBM machines early and big-time, and use Windows' success on the IBM PC to kickstart adoption by the market at large. In early 1986 Ballmer made sixteen straight weekly trips to IBM's Boca Raton, Florida, laboratory. Sixteen weeks in a row, get on a plane to Boca, ten-hour meeting, get on a plane back to Seattle, a twenty-eight-hour turnaround. Finally he thought he had a deal. Nope: IBM wanted compatibility between Windows and TopView, an IBM point-and-click interface that never went anywhere. So Ballmer went out and found and bought a company, Dynamical Systems Research, in Berkeley. DSR had done a TopView clone. Ballmer figured they were the right guys to make Windows and TopView happy together. It turned out not to matter. On the same April day in 1987, IBM announced it was developing its own Windows-like interface, to be named Presentation Manager. And it was putting together its own PC to run OS/2, to be copacetically named the PS/2. And it was more or less telling Microsoft to back off, that it didn't need help from the Redmond gang anymore. That Windows had lost and Big Blue would go with its own solution, SAA, for Systems Application Architecture, a stab at a unified graphical interface system for microcomputers to mainframes that never went anywhere. It was yet another "replace Microsoft" scenario of the kind that kept Bill Gates up late at night. At Microsoft, nearly everyone was ready to throw in the towel—except Steve Ballmer. When Mr. OS/2 insisted his team could still work with IBM—to the point of putting Windows on OS/2—the programmers came up with an acronym to characterize the effort: BOGU. Bend Over, Grease Up. Gordon Letwin, a top Microsoft systems programmer, compared the project to a Mexican school bus destined to drive off a cliff. Ballmer and Gates both refused to believe Windows could survive without IBM. They still wanted it both ways: Microsoft wins, IBM wins too. Faced with rejection by a Big Blue strategic ploy, Gates would say, test our flexibility. Privately he characterized the OS/2 project as building the world's heaviest airplane.

Ballmer held no such equivocations. Mr. IBM was whole hog on OS/2, cajoling skeptics with the zeal of a Baptist preacher out to save a churchful of sinners. Faced with an October 1988 deadline to get PM out the door, Ballmer went on a death march. Nothing stood in his way! He raided the Windows team, the DOS team, any other team for the best talent he could find. He plundered any project. He was a Mad Dog! At analyst briefings, industry seminars, and company meetings, Ballmer would take the stage and wave his arms and pound his fist on the lectern with resounding praise for OS/2! OS/2! OS/2! At the 1989 company meeting, Ballmer was in the face of the Windows team. There was a new word processor for OS/2 that ran circles around anything on Windows. "DeScribe has multithreading this and unlimited undo that, and guess what! It only runs on OS/2! O-n-l-y on OS/2!" he shouted to the gathered throng.

By 1989 the marketplace was utterly confused. Should developers build the next versions of their word processor or spreadsheet or database or whatever for OS/2 and Presentation Manager? Or for Windows? The answer was open to unresolvable debate. By Fall Comdex 1989 messages on Windows and OS/2 had become so mixed that IBM and Microsoft felt compelled to issue a joint press release. Windows developers should aim for computers with up to 2 megabytes of memory—a lot more back then than it sounds like today. OS/2 programmers should aim for machines with more than 2 megs of memory, the high-end, expensive units. IBM was trying to figure out how to box Windows, limit Windows, contain Windows. Microsoft wanted to keep Windows alive in case OS/2 flopped. It was a dangerous liaison. Rumors floated around that IBM was coming out with a "lite" version of Presentation Manager. A Windows-killer, perhaps? And Microsoft was working on versions of its leading Excel and Word applications for Windows that would need more than 2 megabytes to run. Could this marriage be saved? To seasoned observers it looked like the two companies were paying lip service, staying together for the benefit of the kids. Once the kids grew up—who knew when that would be?—the two would be split city. It wasn't a death march they were on, it was a death watch.

The world changed on May 22, 1990. Windows 3.0 was released to acclaim from dozens of software and hardware vendors showing their wares at a New York City rollout. IBM PC czar Jim Cannavino originally had planned to be onstage with Gates and Allen to hail the rollout. At the last minute he pulled out when the companies could not agree to a joint development effort for Windows and OS/2. A bad sign, but Ballmer refused to be terminal. Test his flexibility! The plan was to split up OS/2 development so both companies could feel like they were contributing but without getting in each other's way. IBM would be responsible for OS/2 1.2 and 2.0, the next versions, and farther down the road Microsoft would roll out OS/2 3.0, which it already had in development. Back then OS/2 3.0 went by the name of NT, for New Technology. It was a separate project, being run under code god David Cutler, whom Gates had brought over from Digital Equipment Corp. the last day of October 1988. On August 20, 1990, in a strategic planning session at the restored Shumway Mansion in the Seattle suburb of Kirkland, Gates and Co. decided to bet the future of Microsoft on Windows. The key persuaders were Paul Maritz and Brad Silverberg, who proposed a plan to take Windows from the 16-bit platform of MS-DOS to the faster, more powerful and flexible 32-bit platform dominated by UNIX. For high-end computers with lots of memory and power, the aim was NT. For consumer computers with less capability, 32-bit computing would be a slower ramp. It would not show up till Chicago, or Windows 95. Within days of the Shumway summit several dozen OS/2 programmers at Microsoft were told to drop what they were doing, fold up their tents, and transfer to other projects. For many of them it was done without warning, abruptly and rudely, leaving them feeling uprooted and bitter. But it had to be: IBM was taking over the near-term OS/2 development. NT, not even really a functional system yet, was not due to appear for at least two years. In the interim, Microsoft was going to have to live or die by Windows.

It turned out to be the former. Windows 3.0 became a raging success among individual end users and the consuming public. By October 1990 Microsoft had shipped more than 1 million units and Gates felt comfortable enough with its momentum to declare that Windows had won the battle for the graphical user interface—the thing composed of menus and icons that users saw when they logged on to their computers. At least, over OS/2 and its Windows equivalent, Presentation Manager. The Macintosh was still hanging in there. It was important to get Presentation Manager out of the way. Without it, IBM would have to adopt Windows. And if IBM used Windows, evangelized Windows, spread Windows, then Microsoft could continue to ride the Big Blue coattails. If you asked in Redmond, just about everyone was saying good riddance to OS/2. Everyone, that is, except Steve Ballmer.

Can't live with it, can't shoot it. For all the headaches OS/2 caused over the years, it gave Microsoft a lasting positive legacy. It helped keep Microsoft in the networking business. Without the IBM tie, Microsoft had almost no presence at all in networking. With OS/2 it was on the radar screen. In September 1990, *InfoWorld* blared the headline: Divorce! IBM and Microsoft were splitsville over OS/2. Ballmer begged, wheedled, cajoled everyone he talked to: Please, don't use the word divorce. More like a temporary separation with visitation rights. It did little good. Especially since the world was embracing Windows 3.0 and all but ignoring OS/2 and Presentation Manager.

On January 29, 1991, Ballmer stood up before a press-and-analysts briefing in Redmond and told how IBM and Microsoft were going to continue to work together. For consumer, low-end, and mid-range PCs, DOS and Windows would be the place for programmers to concentrate their efforts. For high-end computers, OS/2 1.X and 2.X with Presentation Manager and SAA would be the focus. Eventually NT would come along and subsume everything under one big roof, but not till the mid-1990s. To test the strategy, Microsoft had run it by software vendors at a recent conference. Ninety-five percent assented. This was Microsoft's crusade, its holy war, its jihad, Ballmer said. One more time: Low and mid-range, DOS and Windows. High-end, OS/2. Down the road, NT. Am I being perfectly clear? Yes, said Alex. Brown analyst Ruthann Quindlen, clear as mud. How could any software vendor plan a business around such a hydra-headed strategic initiative? "I suggest if you poll people here, you'll find 95 percent opposition," she said. Others in attendance applauded in agreement. Ballmer stood at the lectern, leaned his hulking torso over the top, and took a deep breath. "All right," he said, "one more time."

What Ballmer believed even if the audience did not was that Microsoft had to have OS/2 if it wanted to take Windows to the next level. Here was the situation: Although Windows had sold 2.75 million units in seven months, an average of 11,000 a day, it still lacked credibility with corporate America. It lacked C2 security, mission-critical dependability, fault tolerance, portability, and distributed platform capabilities, blah-de-blah-de-blah. Forget the lingo: Translated, it meant that Windows was not ready for corporate, government, and academic prime time. But OS/2 was. OS/2 had sold just a tenth the number of units and had only a tenth as many applications (100 compared to 1,000) as Windows 3.0. Yet until Windows gained "robustness," as Ballmer liked to put it, it would have to ride OS/2's coattails. That was the real jihad: hanging on for dear life to the IBM mother ship while hoping to advance your own technology far enough to break away some day.

Ballmer thought back over Microsoft's networking software strategy. As successful as the company had been in transitioning from one software category to the next, going from languages like BASIC and FORTRAN and COBOL to operating systems like DOS and Windows and OS/2 and productivity applications like Word and Excel and PowerPoint . . . as successful as the company had been in expanding and adjusting and taking advantage, it had utterly failed in the world of networking. It was time to get it right.

Lots needed to be done. On the low end there was a little $20 million Tucson, Arizona, company called Artisoft whose LAN-tastic networking program was selling like hotcakes. The Windows 3.X guys were working on an answer to that market. Henry Sanders, a 1988 Intel import and network programming ace, and John Ludwig, from the network program management side, were on the case with a forthcoming edition called Windows for Workgroups 3.1. Novell was going great guns in the client-server space with NetWare. So was UNIX. The NT guys would have to rise to that occasion. And IBM continued to crank along in the large enterprise environment. OS/2 LAN Manager was Microsoft's responsibility there.

They all had to do networking, and doing a complete job on networking meant they would have to have TCP/IP. All Windows and NT and LAN Man needed was those five little initials and Mr. B would be happy. And this whole deal was riding on the shoulders of a twenty-two-year-old pup from Boston University.

It was a good thing the kid knew what he was doing.

Chapter 4

GO BIG

When he arrived at Microsoft on September 9, 1991, J Allard went by his birth name, James Allard. Following the e-mail convention of the company—first name, and then as many initials of the last name as it took to distinguish from others—Allard took the logon of jamesal@microsoft.com. All went well till people started getting him confused with Jim Allchin, whose e-mail logon was jimall@microsoft.com. Next to Brad Silverberg, who preceded him at Microsoft by five months, Allchin was one of Gates's toughest recruits ever. Allchin had been with network services pioneer Banyan Vines virtually from the start, having joined the company fresh from receiving his doctorate at Georgia Tech in 1983. Beginning in 1989 Gates spent more than a year recruiting Allchin, who at first wondered why all the interest. Microsoft was not exactly known for its network prowess. Eventually Gates "made this incredibly good argument that if you want to impact people, if the number of people you touch with software is your No. 1 goal, there's no better place than Microsoft." That was the pitch that stuck. Banyan tried to block Allchin's departure, however—to the extent that Mike Murray, head of Microsoft's Network

Business Unit, sent him a pair of boxing gloves. Allchin, in charge of the super-secret and megapowerful Cairo project, got some interesting mail at Microsoft. Cairo was the code name for a next-generation version of Windows intended to bring powerful new features to the operating system's interface, not the least of which was network awareness. When Allchin had arrived at Microsoft, his initial two proposals were as combative as Murray's gift: "Within a month I did a presentation enumerating the hard questions the company had to answer," he says. "I remember going to the board room and walking through them, and it was very clear to me that LAN Man was a dead-end product. And that OS/2 was a disaster from a technical perspective. We were throwing good money after bad by investing in the system the way we were doing it."

Second, Allchin was aghast when the Microsoft information systems group proposed wiring the Redmond campus with a non-TCP/IP standard protocol. "I said, You're crazy. It's TCP. It's obvious it's TCP. Boy, I'm telling you I remember having discussions where they were presenting to Bill, and I'm sitting there objecting, objecting, and objecting, saying, It's got to be TCP."

While Allard and Allchin obviously were soul mates on network protocols, they were in far different strata in Microsoft's reporting structure and product strategy. Eventually the two would team up together and do great things. For now, forwarding Allchin's mail was a pain. Allard changed his logon to jallard@microsoft.com. At Microsoft you became known as readily by your logon as by your given name; Gates was billg, Ballmer was steveb, Maritz was paulma, and Muglia was bobmu, and so on. Jallard became "J" Allard and he stuck with the abbreviation, which he used without a period primarily because, in the ephemeral text-only environment of e-mail, you avoid typing as many characters as you can.

A few weeks after arriving at Microsoft, Allard ran into Trish Millines, the manager he had talked to at the MIT job fair. She greeted him warmly, then said she had a question she had to ask. What was a tall white kid doing at a minority job fair? she wondered. In a suit, no less.

Minority job fair? Allard asked, with a sideways glance that indicated he had no idea what Millines was talking about.

Yeah, said Millines. That was a minority job fair.

Oh, Allard said. There was a little pause, and then they both burst out laughing. Allard and his wife-to-be had crashed the job fair, not being enrolled students at MIT. In the caper, the fine print about intended invitees had eluded them.

Finding himself in a company where the Internet was treated like a foreign country, Allard went about his business like a secret agent. Early in life he had decided that it was better to apologize than to ask permission. His mission, now that he had decided to accept it, was to get the Internet into Microsoft as much as possible without the company really knowing what was happening. Justifying his actions ahead of time, Allard figured, would be like trying to describe the elephant to the blind man. He could accomplish far more by forging ahead and dealing with the whys later.

The first thing Allard did after his meeting with Steve Ballmer was to order business cards. There was just one problem. He had no title. No one really knew what he did, or at least was going to be doing. Rather than ask, Allard decided he would simply make up a title—one that would get people to ask questions about what he did, giving him the opening to evangelize the Internet. His first batch of 500 Microsoft cards read: James Allard, program manager, TCP/IP technologies. With a few exceptions, people had two reactions: "Oh." (Not knowing what else to say.) And, "Say what?" Both were perfect entrée.

Fortunately, one Internet housekeeping task had already been done by the time of Allard's arrival. On May 2, 1991, microsoft.com had been registered as an Internet domain name by a Microsoft operations analyst named David Pond. The move was largely to set up an e-mail gateway; Microsoft's UUCP connection was far slower, sometimes taking a day or more to deliver a message, than a Net gateway. Pond, a Net neophyte, cobbled together a system built on Microsoft's aging XENIX setup that queued up outgoing mail and dumped it onto the Net every fifteen minutes. It quickly overloaded and had to be monitored to distinguish between legitimate mail uses and pastimes like Dungeons and Dragons.

By normal Internet standards the registration was late in the game for a powerhouse like Microsoft. Apple had registered apple.com on February 19, 1987. Sun had been registered March 19, 1986, and 3COM on December 1, 1986. But at least Microsoft had been registered. Having the domain meant Allard could get on the Net through Microsoft and start building the company's presence with the Internet community. Allard had no staff, no budget, no imprimatur. But he was blessed with a winning, persuasive personality and figured if he talked to enough people and got them excited, the details would take care of themselves.

At the time he had been trying to decide whether to go to work for Microsoft, Allard had a job offer from the Cambridge, Massachusetts–based Free Software Foundation, headed by a pioneering and cyber-rights activist named Richard Stallman. Stallman's philosophy was that software should be freely available for all users to tinker with, improve upon, and distribute. His was a throwback to the formative days of software development, when what you paid for was the computer—the software came free. Gates's empire, and the huge industry surrounding it, had been built on the premise that software was far more valuable than hardware, in the way that movies, say, are more valuable than camera equipment. Allard was amused at his bipolar vocational choice, kind of like having to choose between Walden Pond and Las Vegas. His reason for going with Microsoft was telling, however. For all his altruism and purist motives, Stallman put a ceiling on things, Allard thought. Richard had a set audience, a defined agenda, a proscribed series of goals. It was all kind of religious. Whereas Allard figured Gates to be a no-limits kind of guy. Bill's notion was just to go big, and if you could come up with a better way to go bigger, do it.

The only thing was, in this case, Allard was having to start very, very small.

The first step was to get himself an Internet connection. This was a tricky procedure at Microsoft in 1991. The company had a sophisticated global WAN—wide area network—that it used to communicate with regional offices around the world. It ran off dedicated telephone lines and was not hooked to the Internet. In fact, the only Net connections were to a few information systems engineers and some folks doing advanced research. Security issues made getting a Net connection a nontrivial procedure. Microsoft had to be certain no outside hacker could gain entry to its network via the Internet. It was not till early 1992 that Allard persuaded Microsoft's network gods that he could handle his own Net connection. When he finally hooked up, he was the eleventh Microsoft employee on the Internet. The computer was a Sun SPARCstation, a high-end workstation that ran SunOS, Sun's version of the UNIX operating system.

The front item on Allard's plate was TCP/IP. Allard was in charge of putting the Internet protocol into Microsoft's LAN Manager—its network system for OS/2. At the time there were lots of TCP/IP stacks, or layers of code that translated data to and from the Internet. Microsoft had licensed Hewlett-Packard's stack, which in turn had been based on a 3COM stack. The H-P stack fit the bill partly because it was well-implemented, partly because H-P was a big player in the UNIX arena, but also because Microsoft's and H-P's relationship went back quite a few years, to the early 1980s. H-P had been an early supporter of Windows, lending its weight and reputation on stage at the first Windows announcement in 1983, and had supported early MS-Net development as well. H-P also knew Windows backward and forward. Its New Wave system, an implementation of Windows for businesses and corporations, was artfully enough done that Apple based its infamous look-and-feel suit against Windows actually on New Wave (as well as Microsoft Windows)—a historical point quickly forgotten. The H-P part of the suit never went anywhere, and neither did New Wave. But H-P remained a strong and loyal partner of Microsoft.

Adapting H-P's TCP/IP stack to LAN Man proved little challenge to Allard. For one thing, he was fast. Growing up, Allard's favorite cartoon had been *Underdog*, whose motto was "speed of lightning, roar of thunder!" Allard talked fast, walked fast, thought fast, and worked fast. He even drove fast. Allard's idea of kicking back involved racing 52 horsepower, 125cc shifter carts, supercharged go-carts capable of going from zero to sixty to zero in about three seconds and reaching 130 miles an hour. "You get about half an inch off the ground at full throttle" was the way Allard characterized it. "You wear a helmet, you wear a neck brace, you wear a suit that slides real well when you flip." Allard brought the same manic passion to his work at Microsoft.

Within three months LAN Man 2.1 with Allard's TCP/IP was ready to roll. Its announcement in December 1991 hardly sent lightning bolts through the personal computing sky. With Microsoft's shift toward networking in Windows rather than OS/2, LAN Manager was no longer the focus of old. Work was well under way for Windows for Workgroups, the first Windows networking product, which would be released ten months later in October 1992. However, it would be nearly two years—the fall of 1993—before Windows for Workgroups would have TCP/IP. Allard was well ahead of the game. Despite LAN Man's falling star, Allard's work on TCP/IP gave him a breakthrough inspiration.

Talking to people at Microsoft about the company's success, Allard came to understand that a key factor was ownership of the API, or applications programming interface. APIs were absolutely crucial because they enabled programmers to write applications for a platform—in Microsoft's case, DOS and, more significantly, Windows. Microsoft worked closely with programmers for all kinds of companies, from small utility makers to the big players like Lotus, WordPerfect, and Borland, to make sure they were happy with Microsoft's APIs. It was a win-win relationship: Without the software vendors writing to Microsoft's APIs, Windows could not succeed and make money. Without good APIs for a platform like Windows, software vendors would be unable to write applications and make money. Microsoft watchers of all stripes over the years liked to point to the company's careful currying of developers as an often-overlooked taproot of its success. Developers tended to be smart, impatient, perfectionist, and less than delicate about expressing their opinions. If you could manage their personality factor, though, and meet their demands, they could do wonders for your platform.

If Windows were to become the platform for the Internet, Allard realized, developers would want a robust API set. Allard's work with UNIX had taught him the value of an open environment, where code was freely shared and APIs were open and published. One reason UNIX worked so well with the Internet, Allard knew, was sockets. Allard had written thousands of lines of code around the sockets API, called Berkeley sockets after the work at the University of California in the late 1970s. In the way a lamp uses a socket to plug into the vast electricity network, a UNIX application used a socket to plug into the Internet. You did not have to know how electricity worked, or who provided the current, to get the light to turn on. Sockets shielded the user from having to think about the connection. Give Windows "sockets," Allard reasoned, and it would open up the Internet to hordes of Windows programs, and vice versa. It would be a classic expression of Gates's beloved positive feedback cycle of software development: The more programs get written for it, the more popular a platform becomes. The more popular the platform becomes, the more programs get written for it.

As excited as Allard was when the inspiration hit, he knew he had some heavy persuading to do in-house. The Internet was little used and even less understood within Microsoft. Any plan to open Windows up to Internet development was bound to be met with suspicion and skepticism. What about hackers? Who would use the APIs? Where's the business model? How do we make money? Microsoft customers and Windows users, after all, were not pounding down the doors of Redmond clamoring for Internet access. Most daunting, the Microsoft mind-set was heavily proprietary. The company liked to stamp things with the Microsoft logo and keep lots of control over how they were used. The wild wooliness of the Internet, frankly, scared Microsoft. Being the open-minded kind of UNIX guy, Allard saw himself as a real rebel. He didn't act like Microsofties, didn't talk like them, he thought "open" when they thought "proprietary." Networking was all about interoperability and routability and sharing. Microsoft's instinct, as Ballmer had so uniquely expressed it, was just to make it go away, please.

But Allard was nothing if not persistent. He started talking up the notion of Windows sockets, encountered mostly rebuffs or blank stares, but then got the breakthrough he needed. Flipping through a company directory one day, Allard ran across a reference to Microsoft's developer-relations group, or DRG. It sounded like someone there would have a clue about his base strategy at least. Allard hooked up with one of the group's executives, Alistair Banks, and bam! Banks got it. I can help make the industry connection with the Windows platform happen, Banks told Allard. I'm your guy.

Banks also had the greed for speed. Within a couple of weeks he had set up a meeting with thirty-one companies, a lot of them unknowns to the general public but big players in the TCP/IP space. They comprised a mix of vendors who did the network components that provided compatibility with the local network and the Internet, and applications vendors who wrote programs that enabled information sharing over the Net. Each vendor sold its own TCP/IP stack, usually with a bunch of additional software as well, for $400 to $500. While TCP/IP provided a respectable revenue stream for vendors, having multiple stacks was a nightmare for users. The stacks were not compatible, meaning that an application written for Net-Manage's TCP/IP would not run on FTP Software's stack. Thus most application vendors were forced to go the painful route of writing an adaptation layer, or doing a different version of their application for each TCP/IP stack. To Allard the whole thing smacked of using a word processor back in the early 1980s. To get your document to print you had to make sure the printer you bought was compatible with the word processor you were using, and if you liked word processor X and printer Y, and they were incompatible, you were hosed. In all there were nearly a dozen TCP/IP stacks, all with slightly different APIs, and none was particularly well integrated with Windows. It didn't really matter whose worked the best with Windows; what mattered was getting them all to talk to applications the same way.

There was another factor in favor of a single API. TCP/IP stacks were boring. They were a means to a far more interesting end—applications, where the fun was. Asking around, Allard discovered that what vendors really wanted to do was to focus on their cool applications. They wanted to do file transfer clients, X Windows (a flavor of UNIX) software, e-mail packages—ways to locate and grab and display information from around the Net. Allard's message to them: Okay, we'll free you up to do that. We'll take care of the stupid plumbing stuff for you. We'll enable you to reassign your best programmers to the cool stuff, so they don't have to mess with TCP/IP infrastructural garbage. And it will be a value proposition: Ultimately a great application will earn you far more than hacking on TCP/IP anyway.

Look at Windows: By taking care of the boring stuff like printer drivers and video drivers and mouse drivers and keyboard drivers and making it part of the operating system, Microsoft enabled applications vendors like Word-Perfect and PageMaker and Lotus to focus on making their products better. The way Allard put it was this: Someday, he did not know when, the combination of TCP/IP and Windows sockets built into the operating system was going to enable some little company to do something great that would just blow everybody's socks off. It was a conscious pun. Windows sockets was usually shortened to Winsock.

The first Winsock API meeting was at InterOp, the leading industry conference on interoperability and the Internet, in San Jose in October 1991. Over the course of the next three months the participating companies hammered out a Winsock 1.0 specification. A "spec," as it was abbreviated to, laid out the general features of the program so everyone could agree on what it was meant to accomplish. Banks and Allard were joined on the Microsoft contingent by David Treadwell, a 1988 Princeton electrical engineering graduate who before he wound up at Microsoft had figured on a hardware career. Interviewing with Dave Cutler's small, fledgling NT team persuaded Treadwell otherwise, and he signed up as employee No. 13. Another degree holder from the Microsoft School of Fast Talking, Treadwell was on his way to being Microsoft's ace of Winsock.

The Winsock process was not always smooth. It was like trying to get the world's superpowers to agree on a nuclear test ban treaty. In principle, all the participating companies more or less agreed that a single API was a good thing, even though it was going to cost them big to give up their proprietary stacks. TCP/IP was a $150 million business; a single Winsock API built into Windows would zap much of that revenue stream. Vendors assumed that with a common API, they would be able to focus on, enhance, and sell the applications. Windows would give them a much bigger TCP/IP pie. They would make more money, even if their slice of the pie was smaller. But arriving at an exact specification meant that participating programmers would have to agree on the One True Way of doing things. When it came to settling on common ground, programmers were like economists. You could lay them all end to end and never reach a conclusion.

The companies haggled over whose features were going to be adopted and which would be abandoned. NetManage argued that its implementation should be adopted whole cloth. That seemed to defeat the spirit of the consortium, even if NetManage's implementation was the most compatible with Windows. The same held true for FTP Software, the TCP/IP market leader. Despite its dominant position giving it de facto veto power, FTP helped drive the Winsock effort. "If their goal had been to maintain the proprietary advantages, then they might have tried to derail the Winsock effort as the No. 1 TCP vendor," Treadwell pointed out. "Fortunately, their goal was to extend the Internet."

By January 20, 1992, the Winsock 1.0 specification had gotten enough support for Microsoft to announce it was backing the spec and would make it available free to software developers over online bulletin boards by March. Although Martin Hall, the moderator of the Winsock consortium, pointed out its significance in the announcement—"Now developers can write to one standard sockets interface and run without modification against a wide variety of TCP/IP networks"—the world at large was unaware of the occasion. It was a banner day in J Allard's book, however. A huge initial hurdle had been leapt in the steeplechase toward merging Windows with the Internet.

Winsock 1.0 was not ready for prime time. Within a few months Treadwell had put together 1.1, a more compatible, better debugged version. To get everybody on the same page with the specification, the companies held real-time testing sessions called bake-offs. All the vendors would get together under one roof and hammer on the specification, ironing out incompatibilities, agreeing on the most efficient approach. The first bake-off was at FTP Software near Boston in the winter of 1992. The second was also in Boston, but at the offices there of Sun Microsystems, the Silicon Valley high-end UNIX workstation vendor. That session turned into a marathon peace talks summit. For days participants argued over an obscure but vital technical issue. Eventually everyone sort of wore one another out and the debate fizzled. The 1.1 spec remained unchanged. When the consortium moved to decide a Winsock 2.0 standard—an effort Treadwell referred to as an attempt to solve world hunger—it overshadowed even the 1.1 flap. Microsoft had put in some of its own improvements, designed to help PowerPoint users under Windows NT 3.5. The modifications crashed FTP Software's TCP/IP stack, however. Because the changes had not been sanctioned by the Winsock committee, Hall accused Microsoft of a power grab—trying to set the standard before everyone had a shot at oversight and approval. Treadwell worked with the Winsock committee to iron things out but acknowledged "it was a bit of a fight there for a while."

The Winsock effort marked the first of what would turn out to be many standardization initiatives for the Internet that Microsoft helped lead. For all the controversy over Microsoft's competitiveness in the software industry in general, its reputation on the standards front has been stalwart. The Winsock initiative, culminating with built-in TCP/IP support in Windows 95, usurped millions of dollars' worth of business from independent TCP/IP vendors such as FTP Software and NetManage. But it created an industry worth billions more. "As far as I'm concerned, Winsock is the unsung hero of the Internet" is the way Bob Quinn, a programmer with FTP Software and an early Winsock developer, put it. Quinn places Winsock on par with Berners-Lee's http in spawning the Internet boom.

Heartened by the initial Winsock momentum, Allard made his mission getting Microsoft onto the radar screen for the entire Internet community. In November 1991 he represented Microsoft at a meeting of the Internet Engineering Task Force in San Jose, California. The IETF, as it was blessedly shortened to, had first met in January 1986 with an underwhelming roster of fifteen attendees. It dealt with gritty issues involving infrastructure and protocols and standards, and it was composed of some of the biggest names in Net computing. Being around legends of the culture was heady stuff for a brash upstart, but Allard's age and fresh-scrubbed look were not what people wondered about when he showed up in San Jose. Why was Microsoft there? they wanted to know. "Are you on vacation, boy?" they asked Allard. For all its success in the personal computer arena, Microsoft was deemed benighted and out of touch in the world of the Internet. It was not a player; it had no real presence on the Net. What was this guy Allard up to, anyway?

Allard reacted without defensiveness. He was perfectly aware that many on the IETF viewed Microsoft as a proprietary enterprise bent on owning the known universe. After all, he himself had held that view only months earlier. The key was simply to get involved, let them know you're sincere, be open about your goals, and let the process take you where it could best benefit all parties. It was an attitude Allard took with him to a number of Internet organizations. From the fall of 1991 over the next three years, Allard was certain to be involved in anything having to do with TCP/IP and Microsoft. In 1992 Microsoft became a founding member of the Internet Society, an international group of professionals dedicated to spreading the Internet through standards that enabled connecting a wide variety of systems. Allard later was asked to serve on the IETF's Internet Architecture Board, which helped determine the future of Internet protocols. In 1993 Allard joined the seventeen-member IPng Directorate within the IETF to advise on the future of TCP/IP and design its successor. This was a key effort to wrestle with limitations in the TCP/IP design such as the issue of Internet addresses, which were projected to be in short supply due to increased demand on the Net.

Allard's big move at Microsoft came in 1992, when he shifted to the company's NT development effort. His mission was to help engineer a core TCP/IP technology for all Windows development. Three products were on the boards: Windows for Workgroups 3.1, useful for tying together small numbers of Windows computers to share files and data; Windows 95, at the time code-named Chicago and in its infancy; and NT, the high-end Windows system that ultimately was meant to enable large corporations, institutions, and government agencies to run all-Windows networks across thousands and thousands of computers. The coding mantle for getting TCP/IP and Winsock into the Windows suite would fall to the engineering wizardry of a handful of program aces: Henry Sanders, a TCP/IP specialist who had been hired from Intel to work on LAN Man for OS/2; David Treadwell, the god of Winsock; David Thompson, a systems specialist in charge of networking for NT; Pete Ostenson, in charge of TCP/IP testing for NT; Mike Massa, Sanders's TCP/IP sidekick; and Keith Moore, an NT systems ace. If they succeeded, anyone using any version of Windows would be able to log on to the Internet automatically. In 1992 that kind of ease of connection was unheard of. Allard was a happy camper. His goal was increasingly within shouting distance.

Joining the NT effort was yet another bold step for Allard, still a relatively wet-eared ingenue within Microsoft. But coming into NT cold would be an adventure for anyone. NT was headed by David Cutler, who had been brought by Gates to Microsoft in October 1988 to begin building the Microsoft operating system of the future. A no-nonsense perfectionist with little patience for pretense or dissemblance, Cutler had a reputation for tyranny and gruffness. He was the kind of guy you knew was just waiting to pounce on a misstatement or screw-up. Fearless as ever, Allard preferred to give just about anyone the benefit of the doubt.

The two were destined to meet on ostensibly neutral ground—a golf course. Thompson, figuring on a trial by fire to check Allard out, set up an early round at a local municipal links. Allard, antsy as ever, arrived early—well before the first tee-off at 5:30 A.M. As a result he was first in line for tee assignments. Cutler rolled in somewhat later, spotted his new protégé, and said, "You're Allard, right? You're that program manager who works in my organization, right?" Cutler had a reputation for hating program managers, considering them akin to tits on a bull. Allard gulped, nodded, and said, brightly, "Yup!" "So what spot are we on the tee?" Cutler asked. "Well, we're first, Dave," Allard responded. Cutler looked him up and down and broke into a beaming grin. "I like you already!" he said with a chuckle.

Allard's efforts to spread the Winsock DNA once again paid off quickly. By September 1992, just weeks before the release of Windows for Workgroups, LAN Man 2.2 was ready, with TCP/IP and Winsock. As a viable product, LAN Man still wasn't going anywhere, but its core technology now gave Microsoft a product and strategy to build from. A founding principle at Microsoft, built on the Gates-Allen experience with their first BASIC, held that remarkable things could happen once you got a product out the door, even if it was not quite ready for prime time, even if it played in a market of dubious scope. With LAN Man 2.2, built-in Internet access for Windows was on its way. Allard's heroics were not in time to get TCP/IP and Winsock into Windows for Workgroups 3.1, which shipped on October 27, 1992, but Workgroups was designed to tie into LAN Man networks; TCP/IP connectivity was there for those doing a Microsoft solution. That was the good news. The bad news was that LAN Man still held less than 10 percent of the networking market.

Allard's next step, in October, was to register ftp.microsoft.com on the Net. Ftp stood for file transfer protocol and was at the time the chief way users obtained files over the Internet. In terms of doing what it did well, ftp was more than adequate. But it was hardly user friendly. It required learning some pretty arcane text-based commands, and it required familiarity with at least a smattering of UNIX. Applications writers in fact were at work trying to come up with easy-to-use ftp variations for Windows. Allard's move was significant in making Microsoft a destination site on the Net. A player. A sharer of technology in the spirit of the Net.

Microsoft was opening its doors to the Internet community. Not that the company overall had that much more of a clue about the Net. Allard and the TCP/IP gang were still a lonesome band of desperadoes in many respects. In early 1993 Allard started an in-house discussion group on the Internet, which he dubbed "inetdisc" in the shorthand of the medium. Out of a company with 14,400 employees, 5 people joined: Sanders, Thompson, Treadwell, Moore, and Massa. Allard and the NT Gang of Five. Oh, well. You had to start somewhere.

Microsoft's ftp status not only gave the company credence on the Net, it boosted the fortunes of Windows NT. On May 24, 1993, Microsoft introduced NT 3.1 at the Windows World trade show, held in conjunction with Spring Comdex, in Atlanta. Everyone at Microsoft from Bill Gates on down deemed NT the company's most significant product release ever. In the months building toward NT's release, analysts were predicting unit sales in seven figures for NT the first year out of the gate. A bullish Piper Jaffray report dated September 18, 1992, summed up expectations: "Surprisingly, our research shows that many UNIX users are seriously evaluating Windows NT. We have heard that Microsoft shipment estimates are in the 2-to-3 million unit range for calendar 1993 and may approach 10 million units for calendar 1994." Microsoft's estimates were in part based on rapid response to software developer kits for NT—the programming tools that software developers use to build applications for an operating system. Within six months of their release, Microsoft sold 50,000 kits. Developer interest was usually a bellwether, "like housing starts and the economy," said Dwayne Walker, NT product manager at the time. "When you see that happening, it usually means people are betting pretty heavy."

But the new operating system crawled out of the gate, not even released to manufacturing till the end of July, two months after its celebrated rollout, and not in customers' hands till the middle of August. Even then, it was hardly welcomed with open arms. The vast majority of PCs in use—386 machines with 2 to 4 megabytes of memory—could not begin to handle NT. There were virtually no applications for it. Not even Microsoft's flagship Excel or Word products were ready when NT shipped. It was big and slow. Jim Allchin looked around and saw people writing the thing off: "There'd been these predictions of how many units were going to be sold. So when we created a management team that was really going to have a marketing plan, and we did a hard look at what we had to do, it was a pretty depressing play list. . . . Competitiors were very afraid, so they were going to hammer us. We'd built things up in the press, so they were going to hammer us. No one in Office was using it. Networking wasn't being supported in Windows 95. The teams internal to the company weren't going to give us any support."

Moreover, NT was doing little to shake Novell's grip on PC networking. Ironically, the Windows 3.X boom was bolstering Novell's fortunes just as Novell, by providing Windows networking, was bolstering Windows. So where did NT fit into the mix? How would NT ever make headway against the Novell empire?

The way Allard saw it, NetWare was great at running printing and file-sharing services. But it did little for making applications run on a network. To be really useful, Allard knew from his UNIX background, a network had to be able to run applications. Database programs, accounting programs, transaction programs, publishing programs. Human resources management. Purchasing and orders. Annual budgets. Advertising brochures. The kind of things big collections of people running corporations and institutions did together.

Allard wanted those applications to run over the Internet, and he wanted them to be *Windows* applications. To make that happen, Microsoft had to build Internet compatibility into Windows in an organized, consistent way. All three versions of Windows—3.1, the standard desktop flavor; Windows for Workgroups 3.1, the "lite" networking version; and NT, the powerful high-end version—had to be compatible over the Internet with one another. That meant making NT server as compatible as possible with all the various TCP/IP implementations. The only way to do that was to test them, scores of them, hundreds of them. Microsoft's little Winsock cabal—Allard, Treadwell, Sanders, Massa, Moore—started collecting TCP/IP stacks everywhere it could, whether for MS-DOS, miniframes, mainframes, whatever. Soon they had garnered several dozen and had a massive testing problem on their hands. They were having to expand the lab, hire more testers . . . it was costing a fortune simply to do this brute-force testing. Then the *aha!* hit Allard. Instead of going out and getting all the implementations of TCP/IP and bringing them back in for testing, why not do a stealth test? Simply set up a Windows NT Internet ftp server, invite Netheads to come by for a look, and see if their TCP/IP version actually worked with the Microsoft server. Keith Moore drew the ftp server assignment. Over a five-day grind starting March 8, 1993, while his wife, Sonia, an editor in the NT documentation group, visited home in Texas, Moore hammered together the server riding a buzz of adrenaline and diet Pepsi. Moore would work till 4:00 or 5:00 A.M., go home, sleep for a couple of hours, shower and change clothes, and be back by 7:00 or 8:00 in the morning. It helped that he and Sonia lived across the street from the Microsoft campus. The server was not the most efficient thing in the world, Moore said. It sucked up a lot of resources and burned a ton of threads. But the main thing was to get it out the door, and he did. Allard considered it an act of heroism.

After the ftp site was set up later in the year, Allard figured he needed some bait to get users to visit. Something that would lure Internet surfers to use the Microsoft server. He approached Brad Chase, Microsoft's MS-DOS marketing chief, and asked if the TCP/IP crew could post the new DOS 6.2 upgrade, released November 1, 1993, on the server. The upgrade enhanced DOS DoubleSpace, a utility for compressing data on hard disks. Compression utilities were big back then—hard disks were, like RAM, expensive. At the same time, operating systems and applications were getting bigger, and users had more data archived over several years of computer use. Rather than buy costly new disks, most users preferred to compress data on the hard drives they had. DOS 6.2 also had ScanDisk, an improved utility for finding and fixing broken files. Allard figured there would be a high demand for it. Chase had to think about it a bit because, officially, the company used CompuServe for its online support. Eventually he said, Sure, give it a ride. Allard's crew put DOS 6.2 on the ftp server and Bingo! Word traveled fast around the Net. Soon hundreds of accesses were coming in, confirming Allard's suspicions about the demand potential of the Internet. On November 18, 1993, Allard messaged the NT networking group that ftp.microsoft.com had lured 10,000 users in the previous forty hours: "Pretty serious capacity and a tremendous service to Microsoft customers in the Internet community," he noted. Allard continued to monitor use of the server and found it was transferring an average of 75,000 file downloads to around 25,000 users a week. By January 24, 1994, he had clocked some riveting statistics. Internet downloads of DOS 6.2 were more than double CompuServe's count: 45,921 to 22,924. (Another 4,400 had downloaded 6.2 from the ZiffNet forum on CompuServe.)

As it turned out, Microsoft's TCP/IP implementation was pretty good. Many of the downloads went without a hitch. The ones that did not tended to crash the server. So the server would go down every couple of hours, and the Microsoft crew would "sniff" the connection (trace the problem), identify the bug, if possible, and do the fix. That made the connection all the more robust for the next round of downloads. It was perhaps the most efficient beta test Microsoft had ever conducted, particularly since the testers had no inkling of their unwitting contribution. In the usual scenario, bugs reported by outsiders would have had to be reported to the NT team, which then would have to replicate them in order to figure out their cause. The server not only hastened the process, it made it far more efficient. A lot of problems in NT were uncovered along the way. And, incredible as it seems today, the ftp site was just one pretty ordinary computer, a Northgate 486-33 PC, sitting in the hall outside Mike Massa's office.

The download scheme had yet another accidental benefit. Allard was astounded by the feedback cycle that his group's simple little ftp server had produced. Maybe there was something significant there for Microsoft's interaction with its customers. Word was getting out on the Net—Did you hear that Microsoft has an ftp server up and running? Allard added a tease to his e-mail signature. At the bottom of every mail he sent was the line:

"On the Internet, nobody knows you're running Windows NT." Everyone on the Net got the reference. It was a play on a June 1993 *New Yorker* cartoon, showing a dog in front of a computer terminal. The caption read: "On the Internet, nobody knows you're a dog." The cartoon had spawned a whole subculture of sendups, like: "On the Internet, nobody knows you love hockey" and "On the Internet, nobody knows you're a nobody," sort of like the "Honk if you love . . ." bumper sticker craze. Allard had a copy of it posted on his office wall. A friend, Steve Brown, who was doing contract programming for Microsoft, came up with the inspiration of putting together a sticker with Allard's e-mail tagline slogan. Brown had 1,000 printed up. The two men started distributing them at demos, conferences, and presentations. One night on a whim they slapped a sticker on Gates's maroon Lexus. Within seconds Microsoft security was paying them a little visit. Eventually the stickers became a cult item around Microsoft. After a few months, only a handful remained.

As it turned out, there was an obscure way to determine whether a site was running Windows NT after all. One day Allard called up his e-mail to find a posting that challenged his "nobody knows" assertion. "Nonsense!" the mail read. It turned out the author had done a search with a tool called "Dump." The resulting readout confirmed that the computer running Microsoft's ftp server was an Intel 486 box using Windows NT 3.5. Allard had been "outed." So much for the "skunkworks" approach. But hey, it had worked for most.

The ftp campaign was working. Word was getting out: Microsoft was starting to "get" the Net. The network dweebs and infonauts haunting the Internet, the leading-edge types who evangelized the Net with friends, coworkers, and corporate higher-ups were discovering to their shock and amazement that the gang from Redmond was for real. This guy Allard seemed to know what he was doing. Allard, in the open-door ethic of the Internet, published his ID and phone number at the bottom of his e-mail. Popularity had its downside, however. At one point Allard, laid up with a knee injury from snowboarding, did not post on the Internet for a few days. The next thing he knew, he got a call from a complete stranger in Wisconsin, wanting to know why he had not been doing e-mail. "I'm heavily medicated on the couch watching *Gilligan's Island* reruns, and here this guy calls out of the blue wanting to make sure I was all right and hadn't died or anything," Allard recalled. He immediately called the phone company and got a new number.

Allard was thinking about how the Net opened up all these opportunities for interacting with Microsoft customers, thinking about the incredible impact a simple thing like an Internet server could have. If there was a way Microsoft could provide content people wanted, like DOS 6.2, while also providing the means for connecting to and obtaining the content, like an ftp server, the process could open up the Internet to millions of Microsoft customers around the world and make the PC the standard way people used the Internet. From that base Microsoft could build all kinds of new and revolutionary Net features into its products. As modest as the experiment with DOS 6.2 and the ftp server was, it held huge implications for the future of the Internet. By May 1994 the 1 millionth hit—access—of the ftp server had occurred. Allard and Brown decided they had to track down the user to commemorate the occasion. It took three days of e-mail searching to find him: Lieutenant Commander Michael W. Lott, an information systems officer at the Naval Medical Center in Oakland. At the unveiling of Microsoft's SQL Server '95, the database server for NT, in San Francisco that summer, Jim Allchin presented the grinning officer a plaque containing an NT CD-ROM signed by Allard, Allchin, Cutler, and Gates. The success of the ftp server eventually laid the philosophical foundation for Allard's next breakthrough project, Internet Information Server, Microsoft's Web server.

Part 2

MOBILIZATION

Chapter 5

PROVOCATEUR

J Allard became obsessed with talking up Microsoft's Internet opportunities to anyone who would listen. He was like a bottle rocket pres-
surizing toward take-off. Inside the ideas were growing, multiplying, expanding almost daily, but Allard had few outlets other than friends and
colleagues to run stuff by. He was just this program manager/Internet guy,
he had little clout, little audience with higher-ups. But he buttonholed
folks at any opportunity. One day in the summer of 1993, Allard approached Allchin, not long after the latter had assumed control of the NT
project. Allchin wanted NT to be faster, smaller, and more responsive to
customer needs. Allard was bouncing along in that spring-loaded, energized way he had of walking. Jim, Allard said, the Internet is the key to all
this! We can set up a feedback cycle with our customer base, we can test
software, we can interact with the Net community and let them help us improve the product and expand our presence. We've gotta take advantage!
I'll give you a memo, he said, I'm writing all this down, there's a ton of stuff
going on.

Go for it, Allchin said, thinking: We got a live one here.

Allard's notion was that Windows ought to provide the "killer app" for the Internet. Whenever a new way of thinking arose in the computer community, everyone looked for a killer application to drive adoption. It was really just another way of characterizing a technology's true impact on society. Electricity's killer app was the light bulb. Television's killer app was the *Ed Sullivan Show*. The personal computer's original killer app was the spreadsheet—first VisiCalc on the Apple II and then Lotus 1-2-3 on DOS, followed by Microsoft's Excel on the Macintosh. Originally, when he had first started working on the idea of Winsock and TCP/IP for the Internet, Allard thought the killer app was going to be real-time videoconferencing with a program like Excel. You would make multiple connections with other users on the Net, your computers would have microphones and cameras so you could hear and see one another, and you would open a document together and manipulate it on your screens in real time as you worked through the data. You might own one column or row, and a colleague in Boston would own another column, and one in London a third column, and so on. It was a compelling notion. Big companies like AT&T had invested millions in videoconferencing, but they were using closed connections that took special equipment and dedicated phone lines. Intel was working on a similar system, which it eventually called ProShare, for PCs. The way Allard figured it, the Internet would supply the infrastructure—or infostructure, as he dubbed it. All you needed to do was make Excel "Internet aware" and you were on your way.

The ftp experiment had Allard revising his thinking. Yes, there were opportunities for videoconferencing. But other, just as compelling, applications were becoming apparent. Using the Internet as a communications and file-transfer medium, Microsoft could drastically reduce costs of providing support to its customers. The ftp server had just gotten the DOS upgrade into tens of thousands of customers' hands. Consider the cost of goods associated with supplying the upgrade through Egghead Software stores, or even via the post office on a floppy diskette. Allard estimated the ftp server's savings at a quarter of a million dollars over its first two months of operation.

Allard also saw the Internet as a powerful R&D and marketing tool for Microsoft. In just a few hours of Net surfing, a single individual with a computer and printer could accomplish what it would take a traditional library days if not weeks to gather, process, and photocopy. Granted, mechanisms like ftp, gopher, and the Wide Area Information Server (WAIS) were hard to learn and difficult to use. And the Internet's information base tended to be pretty abstract stuff—scientific and academic papers, government reports, and the like. But Allard sensed all that was going to change. The types of documents published on the Internet were going to become more mainstream, even to the point of news and weather and sports bulletins. The types of transactions conducted over the Internet were going to become more broad-based. Allard was convinced that electronic publishing and shopping were going to explode over the next two years. Already by late 1993 commercial servers were starting to pop up, backed by forward-thinking, direct-market vendors like Land's End, L.L. Bean, and Victoria's Secret. You could order a music CD from the Virtual Record Store, browse the virtual bookshelves of Quantum Books, buy government surplus from Counterpoint Publishing, and even make a discreet stop at JT Adult Toy Store—all without having to leave home.

Internet connectivity was already a competitive advantage, in Allard's view. Within a year or two, any company, not just Microsoft, would be at a serious disadvantage if it lacked Internet presence. Microsoft was already well behind the eight-ball. On the server side, Windows NT was not even on the map. If you wanted to set up a server for publishing or commerce or whatever, you thought UNIX and Sun Microsystems. If you wanted a file and print server, you thought NetWare. The goal for the NT group, Allard felt, was to make sure future versions offered publishing and commerce servers better than UNIX out of the box, and file and print, as well as applications capability, better than NetWare. Doing so meant providing applications tools for software makers to tailor NT to their customers as well.

On the client side—the desktop and laptop computers people used to explore the Internet—Windows also lagged. The Apple Macintosh had gotten an early jump, partly because TCP/IP for the Macintosh, a program called MacTCP, had been available as early as 1989. At the most recent Internet Engineering Task Force meeting, drawing more than 500 participants, Allard had seen only one Windows laptop, and two Sun SPARC-Books but more than forty Macintosh PowerBooks. His own laptop was the only one running Windows NT. The leading edge on the Internet was decidedly UNIX and Macintosh. It only stood to reason: Windows tools for the Internet were crude and often lacking compared to UNIX and Mac. Microsoft had a lot of work if Windows was to catch up.

But it was not a hopeless challenge. Allard saw a soft underbelly to the UNIX-Mac beast. UNIX was hard to learn and use, and few PC users even knew what it was. The Mac may have been golden on the Internet, but it trailed far behind Windows on the corporate and home desktop. For every

UNIX and Macintosh computer in existence, there were at least five Windows machines being used. The primary reason UNIX and Macintosh held such sway on the Net had far less to do with user loyalty or customer preference than with the simple fact that they were prominent in the academic community, where most Internet users were based or had cut their teeth. Make it easier for PC users to connect and explore the Internet, Allard reasoned, and their natural orientation to Windows from working on desktop and laptop PCs would make them feel right at home with Windows on the client and server sides of the Net. Allard had clipped and photocopied a recent *PC Week* article on Web servers headlined: "Installing UNIX is the toughest part." To anyone who would listen, from Allchin on down, he showed the article as proof positive that NT had a golden opportunity.

Allard's stealth campaign to spread Internet awareness within Microsoft might have puttered along for months had not something dramatic happened that in an instant transformed the Internet. On November 12, 1993, in a move Internet Society pioneer Tony Rutkowski hailed as "a digital cannon . . . felt around the world," the National Center for Supercomputing Applications at the University of Illinois in Champaign-Urbana released its graphical Web browser, Mosaic, for UNIX, Macintosh, and Windows platforms. "Mosaic, A Killer Application," Rutkowski titled his piece, foreshadowing a theme Allard would adapt to Windows and the Internet. Allard had taken a look at Mosaic earlier that spring when it had first appeared on a UNIX computer, a Sun SPARCstation in his office. He liked it but saw limited potential. It ran on X Windows, and how many people were ever going to use X Windows to access the Internet? When Mosaic came out for Microsoft's Windows, though, it not only confirmed Allard's expectations of where the Internet was headed, it provided a far clearer and easier way to demonstrate the potential he saw for his company and its operating system. Now here was the old Cornell WORM—the computer virus that showed how one program could keep spreading and spreading throughout the Internet—in a positive form, Allard thought. Mosaic not only spread the good works of the Web, it underscored the importance of TCP/IP and Winsock and ftp and all the other arcana Allard and the Internet team had been working to evangelize for Windows. Without Winsock, Windows Mosaic would have faced lots of technical barriers to widespread acceptance. Winsock did for Mosaic what the movies did for actors. The star of the Net had been born.

Simply put, WinMosaic's breakthrough was to make the Internet as easy to use as Windows or the Macintosh. Instead of having to type long, arcane commands like "telnet 131.107.1.210" to get to a certain site, you could enter a more friendly URL like www.microsoft.com. Instead of having to do awkward and time-consuming ftp commands to remote sites and then go through directory searches, you could simply click on a "hot link" and *blam!* The file was displayed in front of you. Best of all, there were pictures and page layouts with Mosaic, using different fonts and styles in the manner of a magazine layout. To Internet minions used to plain white monospaced text on ugly green screens, Mosaic's displays were a revelation. It was like going from reading text produced on a typewriter to *Life* magazine.

In contrast to most early Web users, Allard does not list the day he first saw Mosaic on X Windows as the day that changed the way he looked at life. Most early Web users remember being blown away by Mosaic and the potential it represented for putting the Internet into the hands of the masses. They remember the day they first saw Mosaic the way other people remember the Kennedy assassination or the moon landing. Here was a new paradigm that would revolutionize the way people communicated, interacted, formed relationships, did business, and transformed society together. What most people could not tell you, though, was on what type of computer they first saw Mosaic — UNIX? Mac? Windows? Their focus was on the *browser*, not the computer displaying it or the server ferrying the information to the computer. They did not know how the whole infrastructure worked, nor did they particularly care. They just knew it was going to be big.

Allard, however, knew the iceberg below the surface just as well as he knew the tip. Mosaic, the tip, was not going to be a true force till its base consisted of Windows. When WinMosaic happened, the world changed overnight. In terms of high points of Allard's career, the day he downloaded Mosaic 1.0 for Windows was it. Nothing could ever touch it. It verified that Phase I of his vision had succeeded. Allard, Banks, Sanders, Treadwell, Thompson, Massa, Moore, Ostenson, and crew had managed to integrate TCP/IP and Windows sockets with the operating system. They had created an applications programming interface that enabled a couple of kids in a college basement to do something transformational for the Internet and Windows. They had done it quietly, without much attention or even support. Bill Gates had never stood up at a Comdex or Windows World and talked about Winsock. No pundit or commentator talked about Microsoft turning itself around on TCP/IP. But without Allard & Co.'s work, who knows what would have happened to Windows on the Web? The Macintosh might have remained the surfing computer of choice. UNIX might forever have been entrenched as the dominant server. And Microsoft would have been relegated to the increasingly niche status of a desktop software company, the Smith Corona of the new wired world. Had Microsoft come up with the concept of a browser? No. Would it ever be able to take credit for Mosaic? Of course not. Much as he would like to have been the guy who built the Web or invented the browser, neither he nor Microsoft had anything to do with it, Allard had to admit. But he and the band of Internet idealists from Redmond could take a measure of satisfaction in having contributed one undeniable factor to the looming Windows browser phenomenon.

They had *enabled it.*

Steven Sinofsky needed something to do. Something a little more challenging than setting up the CEO's computers and running the latest software demos. Sinofsky figured his new job, technical assistant to Bill Gates, could be as big or as small as he wanted. He wanted it to be big. For Gates and Microsoft, it was fortunate he did. As it turned out, what could have been bigger than the Internet?

Part of his job, Sinofsky figured, was to keep the Microsoft chairman and cofounder alert to subcutaneous computing trends. In the fall of 1993 Sinofsky saw that the Internet was starting to explode. As an undergrad at Cornell University in Ithaca, New York, from 1983 to 1987, Sinofsky had used the Internet a lot, mostly for e-mail and news. Starting in the 1970s, all incoming freshmen had been assigned computer accounts. In the early 1980s Cornell had become one of the first major BITNET (for Because It's Time Network) sites in the United States. As a top recipient of National Science Foundation and DARPA (Defense Advanced Research Project Agency) funding, the university had quickly evolved into a major Usenet node. These networks brought people together with mail, mailing lists, and newsgroups akin to the later forums on CompuServe and America Online. With your freshman orientation package you got a computer punchcard with a randomly generated e-mail address and password. Sinofsky's logon was tguj, his roommate's was something like z9vj. There was not even an attempt to be mnemonic or adopt a logon convention like first name last initial or first initial last name. . . . Alphanumerics were just the way things were done, and nobody questioned it. Mostly what you did with e-mail was communicate with students at other schools. Once you got to know someone at another school, you could start logging on to their computer, and they to yours, to exchange files. You ftp'd. As far as the Internet went, that was about it: e-mail and ftp. You didn't even think of it as the Internet, really. It was as if the two machines were in the same room, and you were running a cable between them. Security? Not an issue. Firewalls? What were they? Who was interested in your measly files anyway except some other undergrad at, say, velveeta.cs.wisc.edu at the University of Wisconsin (where the servers in the computer science department were, naturally, named after cheeses)? If by chance someone was interested, it was doubtful they were on the Internet anyway, or would know where to look if they were.

Sinofsky was born on Long Island but grew up in Florida after moving to Orlando at age ten. Growing up he was a dead ringer for Brandon Cruz, the kid actor in the hit TV series *The Courtship of Eddie's Father*, a resemblance that still carried by the time Cruz became editor of the late 1990s animated TV show *South Park*. When Sinofsky arrived at Cornell in the fall of 1983, the school was among the most computerized campuses around. It had several IBM mainframes running everything from class lists to CUInfo, a campus information network with things like movie listings and student phone directories. Sinofsky soon got involved with CUInfo and discovered the power of networking. Cornell used VT100 terminals like telephones. You'd call up CUInfo for a friend's phone number or a movie suggestion. His first semester, Sinofsky started working the Friday night 8:00 to 10:00 P.M. shift in computer services on a big IBM mainframe. People would come in and he would help them load punchcards—envelope-size cards where the computer read a series of perforations as instructions. Sinofsky's main maintenance task was to change the ribbon on the IBM floor printer. This involved pulling on rubber gloves that went up to his armpits, dipping himself in ink, and reinking the ribbon as well as he could while trying not to reink himself in the process. It was the way things were done. Nobody questioned it. This was back when computers were big, hot, closet-size things full of wires and switches, when they had to be constantly cooled by giant fans or piped coolant. When men were men, and computers were Big Iron.

Sinofsky went home for Christmas break that year and when he came back, whamo! The room had been cleared out and where VT100 terminals had been sitting there were now cowled little black-and-white monitors in sea-green plastic boxes called Macintoshes. Cornell had become one of the original Apple Macintosh consortium schools, getting big discounts on

Macs to help jump-start the Xerox vision, in the process of being popularized by Steve Jobs, of graphical computing. The user-friendly Macs opened
up computing to a whole new audience on campus and, as it would turn
out, hooked Apple into the Internet mind-set early on. Students who would
never have touched a punchcard in their life loved the Macs, even if they
used computers only to type term papers and letters home asking for
money. The Mac transformation taught Sinofsky something about himself,
however. He liked the computer for what it could do for the nonnerd. He
liked applications that broadened the computer's appeal to mainstream interests. On campus most of his friends were government majors, not computer science geeks. This perplexed Sinofsky from time to time, making
him wonder if he had missed his calling. But he decided he would rather
be a humanities guy trapped in a geek's body than a geek trapped in a humanities body.

After graduating from Cornell in 1987, Sinofsky attended a couple of
years of grad school in computer science at the University of Massachusetts
before getting bored and sending his résumé to Microsoft. How it happened
was typical of the randomness of life decisions that, given his control-freak
nature, was a particular anomaly for Sinofsky. He was attending a computer
show when he decided on a whim to enter a programming contest. A chem-
istry/computer science major at Cornell, Sinofsky had put together a graphical display of the Periodic Table for the Macintosh as an honors chemistry
project. He won. His prize: a copy of Microsoft Word for the Macintosh,
version 3.0. The software turned out to be a near disaster, suffering from a
bug serious enough to warrant a recall. But the box provided Microsoft's
Redmond, Washington, address. Sinofsky sent off his résumé with all the
right buzzwords—object-oriented this, C++ that—flew out to Microsoft for
an interview, then went back to grad school and took back up where he left
off.

Two weeks later he started getting phone messages from Bill Gates. At
least, that's what the messages said. Right, Sinofsky thought. A school friend
of his had grown up in Seattle, and Sinofsky had played enough practical
jokes of his own to suspect someone else's. He would leave the lab to walk
home and find a message waiting for him that Bill had called. The next
morning there'd be a note scribbled on the whiteboard: Bill Gates called for
Steven. After the third or fourth time, Sinofsky was muttering to himself,
Enough already! Finally a Microsoft recruiter, David Pritchard, actually
reached Sinofsky and said, How about setting up a time with Bill? Sinofsky
was shocked: Is this for real?! he asked Pritchard. The conversation with

Gates was a bit awkward. Gates let drop that he didn't really know what to talk about, he was just calling from a list. The recruiter later told Sinofsky that Bill wasn't supposed to say that—it detracted somewhat from the thrill. Not knowing what to suggest on his end, Sinofsky asked about the Apple lawsuit, which at the time was going badly for Microsoft and, let's face it, never made it to Gates's top 10 list of favorite topics anyway.

Nonetheless, Sinofsky got a job offer soon thereafter. He joined Microsoft in 1989 and went to work in Mike Maples's applications division, doing programming tools for software developers. Six months into his new job, Microsoft began working on an "application framework" for developers. Sinofsky's team and a similar group from Windows were united under Jeff Harbers, who had helped lead Microsoft's effort to develop applications for the Macintosh in the early 1980s. Their product was destined to become Microsoft Foundation Classes, a set of developer tools that made it easier to develop Windows applications and, later, adapt Internet features to Windows. At the time Harbers had the distinction of being the only guy at Microsoft whose e-mail logon was simply his first name, in violation of Gordon Letwin's original convention of first name last initial. Harbers was just Jeff. The team had a lot of veterans; at Sinofsky's first company meeting, five people got ten-year awards from Microsoft. All were in the development tools group. Microsoft Foundation Classes eventually shipped the same day as Windows 3.1, April 6, 1992.

By December 1992 Sinofsky had become Gates's technical assistant. The post, generally lasting two years, was meant to keep Gates abreast of industry trends and product developments—a key thing for the chairman, even if Gates always had mixed feelings about taking anyone off a product team for the job. Vision was important, vital, indispensable to Gates. But product was essential. Sinofsky was at the right juncture to fill the role. At twenty-seven, he was at a turning point in his own career, having earlier in the year finished his third product cycle. Sinofsky had been there as the leading programming language, C++, went from a text- (character-) based environment to Visual C++, a graphical version that broke new ground in the visual programming arena. It felt like a time to explore. The job came up, Sinofsky was available, and with typical serendipity he moved on. Within weeks he was casting his responsibilities for Gates on a bigger canvas that included pretty much everything the chairman was worried about at any given moment. Which was a lot, Sinofsky soon assessed.

Gates's many preoccupations did have a unifying theme. Information At Your Fingertips pretty much drove the corporate vision. Product groups throughout the company, from Visual C++ to Microsoft Word, were supposed to be thinking about how IAYF fit into their plans and goals. That was the beauty of the vision—it applied to so many diverse areas. Linking documents together. Easily searching databases and documents. Displaying them in rich text and layout form. Merging the creative process with editing and production. When Sinofsky saw all these disparate efforts and approaches trying to merge together, he thought of the Internet. If you looked at what was going on with the Internet, there were a number of parallels with Windows development. Ftp was like Windows Explorer for tracking down and opening files. Gopher was analogous to Microsoft's unified Help Index for things like Microsoft Developers Network support. Html, the layout and linking language for the World Wide Web, was like linking in Win-Help. Like IAYF, the Mosaic viewer (as it was then called, predating the term "browser") integrated the separate elements of the Net into a friendlier user environment.

The first Web viewers were beginning to appear, including one called Cello, hatched at the law school at Sinofsky's alma mater. They were not as widely used as Mosaic, but their genius was to integrate the various tools together under one roof, in the classic evolutionary track of software product development. Sinofsky set up a demo for Gates's fall 1993 Think Week in October. He demonstrated Usenet, UNIX mail, and the whole array of tiny tools developed for the Net. He telnetted to the CERN site in Switzerland where Tim Berners-Lee had developed the World Wide Web.

Gates was not particularly impressed. He was conversant with the Internet, having used it in part to work on the first BASIC for personal computers in 1975 with Paul Allen while still at Harvard: "I would ftp files up to this thing at Carnegie-Mellon University called the Data Computer. My [DEC] PDP-10 only had 64K of disk space. You'd have to spool your stuff onto DEC tapes. Well, instead I would ftp my stuff up to the CMU Data Computer."

Although there was no guarantee his work would still be on the CMU computer when he next logged on, Gates said it was—"I think every single time." Gates's heavy computer use eventually drew the attention of Harvard administrative authorities, who conducted an investigation. Although several disciplinary possibilities existed, including expungement (obliteration of his student record from university files), in the end Gates got off with a stern reprimand. "The only thing anybody ever questioned was whether I should have had Paul in the computer center as many times as I did," he says.

The Internet's tools had progressed considerably since his undergraduate days, but Gates felt the Net still had an insular, elitist quality with little mass appeal. Newsgroups like rec.art.startrek were still debating, years after Net users had first raised the theme, whether warp speed was technically feasible. It was not exactly the highest and best use of Internet bandwidth, nor computer disk space for that matter. Where was the business model? Gates wanted to know. UNIX—now, who was going to learn that? Who would pay for stuff like term papers and master's theses online? All this noise, everything free. Who would underwrite the kind of ramp-up the Internet needed if it were to reach a Windows-like critical mass, and who would then pay the ongoing costs to keep the system up and running?

The unsinkable Sinofsky was far from deterred. But he came away from the meeting knowing it would take something a bit more compelling than gopher to turn Gates's head. One problem was that anything having to do with IAYF and content to the masses inevitably had to compete with interactive TV in the Gates/Microsoft mind space. And ITV was hot. By mid-1993 cable giants like TCI and Viacom were announcing megadeals with telecommunications giants like Bell Atlantic and US West and entertainment giants like Time Warner and Sony. Set-top box makers were vying for their slice of the business. And then there were the computer powerhouses: Oracle, Silicon Graphics, IBM, Hewlett-Packard. In April TCI announced it would spend $2 billion to get fiber-optic cable to 90 percent of its 10.2 million subscribers by 1997. In May Microsoft announced a deal with Intel and set-top box maker General Instrument to get two-way boxes to 60 million cable subscribers. In July rumors were rife that Microsoft, Time-Warner, and TCI were entering the ITV deal to end all deals, dubbed "Cablesoft." Analysts predicted ITV would be in as many as 40 million homes by the year 2002. None of this materialized. But nearly everyone was inhaling the ITV herb.

Next to the neatly didactic vision of ITV, the Internet looked like an urban landfill. Lots of volume and movement in an atmosphere of pure chaos cluttered with junk. How many home consumers and corporate PC users, after years of gnashing their teeth over DOS, were going to bother to learn a whole new set of even stranger typed-out UNIX commands? ITV was sexy, easy to use, and cool. At the time Sinofsky demonstrated the Internet to Gates during Think Week, Microsoft was spending $50 million to $100 million a year on ITV. It had the backing of cable and phone giants, support from PC and television makers. Everybody wanted a chunk of this huge multibillion-dollar pie.

There was just one problem. ITV was expensive. The investment required to get the fiber-optic infrastructure in place for ITV was rocketing off the charts into the hundreds of billions. Even John Malone, the swaggering self-described Darth Vader of TCI, was turning his pockets inside out. To Internet mavens like Sinofsky and Allard, cost and infrastructural problems made ITV look like a money pit. Maybe the Net was not as cool, but it was here and now. It had been built from grass roots, a bottom-up user-supported decentralized collection of technologies that actually worked, as opposed to the top-down, monolithic, one-true-path approach of the cable/telecom giants.

Despite Gates's skepticism over the Net, Sinofsky knew the top guy liked to hedge his odds with side bets. Two months earlier, in an August 1993 press interview, Gates had waffled on his ITV commitment. There's no doubt we could bomb, he had said. I could take that, say, $50 million and it could all be wasted. An Internet server, on the other hand, cost hardly anything to set up and maintain, as Allard had demonstrated. Even Myhrvold saw potential in the Net, but only if something could be done to make it easier to use and to provide better content. The way Myhrvold saw it, the pipes were way too small on the Net to carry the real cool things like sound, animation, and movies.

The other problem was that Gates and Myhrvold also saw a far better, and time-proven, business model in commercial online services like CompuServe and America Online. In fact, Microsoft had committed millions to an unannounced project for its own online service. The online-services model was not unlike a typical newspaper or magazine: Build a community of subscribers, then sell advertising to vendors based on the community's interests and preferences. It had worked for others; why not for Microsoft as well?

Sinofsky knew he needed a better hook, but what? Something that would show how the Net was becoming more mainstream, more of a real-life representation of IAYF. As it turned out, he got a big assist from Mother Nature. It happened on a recruiting trip to his alma mater the second week of February 1994. Normally a recruiting trip was fly-in, see a bunch of earnest, fresh-scrubbed faces in back-to-back interviews, fly back out. Maybe a sandwich and Coke somewhere along the line. This time a huge snowstorm shut Ithaca down. It was total whiteout for two days. Sinofsky made eight trips to the airport and back, hoping to catch a flight out. He got to know the shuttle driver on a first name basis. On subsequent trips for years after they would reminisce about the episode and get caught up with each other.

Stuck on campus, Sinofsky started noticing changes in the way students were doing things since his departure seven years earlier. A huge transformation had happened. Computers practically ran campus life. There were DEC PDP machines in agriculture, vector processors in physics, a Prime miniframe in chemistry, Sun workstations in computer science, and Macintoshes in freshman writing. Walking across campus in the evening, Sinofsky noticed the glow of PC monitors from dorm rooms. It took a while to summon up the courage to ask about what was happening. As an undergrad Sinofsky had dreaded the returning Class of '60 alumnus who looked at the computer services mainframes and talked about how in his day they had made do with a few battered abacuses. But there was no other way to find out, so when he went to get a pizza Sinofsky screwed up his courage and said, Hi, I graduated here in 1987 and . . . he waited for the inevitable Ohh-hhhh, not one of those. Fortunately the place was deserted because of the snow and the guy had some time on his hands and was maybe looking for a job at Microsoft. So he gave Sinofsky his take. Later Sinofsky queried some students and it turned out that a lot of the kids brought PCs from home, or got them at discount from their parents' work, or had been given them as high school graduation presents or whatever. Cornell still had a lot of Macs, but PCs were on the move.

Sinofsky decided to check out his old computer services haunt and discovered from the managers there that the university was running a mishmash of heterogeneity. Macs, PCs, Sunstations, VT100 terminals. Gradually Windows machines were making curricular inroads. Cornell's world-famous Management and Hotel School was moving toward PCs using Excel. Human ecology and agriculture had PCs because of a big investment in MS-DOS courseware. There was even a battle at the School of Human Ecology, where selection of a new dean had come down to two candidates, one of whom favored PCs and the other Macs. Whether Mac, PC, or UNIX based, however, the computers managed to talk to each other. What let them communicate on campus and with the outside world, the glue that stuck them together, was TCP/IP. The one thing holding back Windows machines, in fact, was that Cornell Information Technology, which administered and coordinated the campus networks, was uncertain about using TCP/IP on Windows—and the fact that most Internet software tools for PCs were still based on DOS, not Windows. TCP/IP was approaching ubiquity. Two residence halls were conducting pilot programs with direct TCP/IP connections in dorm rooms, and other halls had clusters of basement Macs with access. Cornell Information Technology had set up a common front end, or opening screen to the university's network, called Bear Access, named after the school mascot. Through Bear any account holder could access electronic mail, Usenet news, gopher, CUInfo, library resources, a community directory called Who Am I, chat, ftp, telnet, and the campus store.

Sinofsky was blown away by how deeply networking had permeated his alma mater. What really drove it home was watching students during class break and lunchtime. They would rush to the first available Mac and insert floppy disks to pull down their e-mail. E-mail had taken the place of the between-class stroll or chat or random meeting. It had become an acceptable form of social interaction. Students even encouraged their parents to get Internet mail accounts on America Online or CompuServe, so they could write home electronically for money instead of having to buy a stamp and deal with ink and paper. Eudora was the program of choice to read and organize e-mail; students had to store their mail on floppies or risk losing it after sixty days because of space limitations on the campus's mail server. The focus on e-mail reminded Sinofsky of life at Microsoft, where the whole organizational structure was built around and depended on e-mail.

Right behind e-mail was Cornell Gopher, an adaptation of the University of Minnesota navigation tool. And coming up fast: the World Wide Web. Sinofsky figured the Web would replace gopher as the most popular access tool by the end of 1994.

Sinofsky's head was swirling. Still trapped at Ithaca, he put together a Valentine's Day e-mail message to Gates, Paul Maritz, and Brad Silverberg, with the heading "Cornell is WIRED!" picking up on the name of the Internet generation magazine characterized as the *Rolling Stone* of cyberculture. The next thing he knew he got an e-mail back from John Ludwig, a networking specialist who had worked on LAN Man and Windows for Workgroups and was starting to think about the next version of Windows after Chicago. Ludwig, who had been forwarded Sinofsky's mail by Silverberg, said, Hey, you've got to talk to Allard. The guy is hanging out there with all these great ideas. Sounds like you and he have a lot in common. Sinofsky sent e-mail to Allard, who sent him back a draft of the memo he had been working on.

Synchronicity! It was as if the ghost of Carl Jung himself had made the liaison. Allard's memo, dated January 25, 1994, two weeks before Sinofsky's trip, was a revelation. Around Microsoft, it quickly got circulated among the small in-house group of maybe a couple of dozen hardcore Internet advocates. For them it was like Martin Luther posting his ninety-five theses on the door of the Wittenburg Cathedral. Or, in a more contemporary analogy, here was Dylan's "Mr. Jones" adapted to Microsoft corporate strategy. Something was happening here, but we don't know what it is. Not yet, anyway. Running seventeen single-spaced pages, titled "Windows: The Next Killer Application on the Internet," the memo detailed a broad-based scenario for making the Microsoft operating system the easiest, most effective way to access the Net. "The Internet is very well aligned with our corporate vision of Information At Your Fingertips and serves as an effective infostructure to increase product group productivity and defray support costs," Allard put it. The Net had grown to more than 2 million connected nodes servicing 25 million users in 137 nations and was exploding at the rate of 5 percent a month growth. Not just government, defense, and corporate users were taking advantage, but homes, small businesses, and schools. The World Wide Web was starting to catch on as well. Although the Web represented just 3 percent of Internet traffic, compared to 41 percent for ftp, more than 700,000 copies of Mosaic had been downloaded in 1993. Allard figured that meant at least 1 million computer users had access to the Web. And Web servers, which had reached more than 600 in total, were growing at the rate of a new one a day. By 1998 the number would reach 4 million—twice the total number of Web *users* in 1993.

A revolution was happening, and Microsoft was in danger of being left behind. In terms of the company's history, the Allard memo felt something like the day in December 1974 when Paul Allen ran across Harvard Square to Gates's room after seeing a copy of the January 1975 *Popular Electronics* with the Altair 8800 on its cover. The word on the Internet, Allard pointed out, was that if you want to bring a server online, go with UNIX. If you want to get a cool Internet client, use UNIX or, better yet, buy a Mac. The best Internet navigation tools were X Windows on UNIX and the Mac running MacTCP. Windows sockets was helping to shoehorn the Microsoft system onto the Web. But Windows viewing and programming tools, including Mosaic, tended to be clunky, slow, and tone-deaf. Allard saw that the way to improve the situation was to offer Windows programmers—independent software vendors—a way to build the Internet into their software. The big win, he felt sure, would be to enable the massive numbers of Windows ISVs to make their Windows applications "Internet aware"—that is, adapt them so users could move back and forth from their PC over the Net as if the Internet were one big hard drive. Here was where Allard and Sinofsky became true blood brothers. The Jeff Harbers project, the Microsoft Foundation Classes, would enable the "Internetization" of Windows applications in the same way that TCP/IP and Winsock enabled browsers like Mosaic. When Internet capability got built into the MFC, it put Windows all the farther along toward winning the Web.

Predictably, Allard saw opportunity where others saw dead ends. He quoted from a recent discussion on Web authoring tools on the Net: "I think your idea is great, although I frankly think that the whole html concept needs to import some ideas from (gasp) Microshaft Word." And the response: "You don't want anything of the sort." It was an exchange that later burst with irony when Microsoft Word became the first mainstream PC application to gain Internet awareness with a product called Internet Assistant for Word. But the dismissal at the time was typical of the Internet's attitude toward Allard's employer. The Net community had little regard for Microsha, er, soft.

Microsoft's response, Allard figured, needed to focus on two additional fronts: To provide great Windows services on the server front, Microsoft needed an Internet information server for Windows NT. Teachers, journalists, researchers, and hobbyists had no interest in messing with the arcana of UNIX. They would much rather look to Windows first for their information needs—either Daytona, the version 3.5 upgrade of NT, or Chicago, which would become Windows 95. Second, to provide great Windows services on the client, or desktop, side, Microsoft needed what Allard termed an Internet explorer system. The Macintosh had a big head start. But then the Mac had had a big head start in the whole graphical-user-interface arena, and now Windows was outselling it four to one.

"In order to build the necessary respect and win the mindshare of the Internet community, I recommend a recipe not unlike the one we've used with our TCP/IP efforts," Allard wrote. "Embrace, extend, then innovate." By embrace, he meant figure out the needs of Internet users and how Microsoft's technology could best address those needs. By extend, he meant establish relationships with organizations and other companies sharing Microsoft's vision and offer well-integrated tools and services based on Internet standards. Then Microsoft could innovate—provide leadership with new Internet standards. "Change the rules: Windows becomes the next-generation Internet tool of the future!" Allard wrote. Microsoft had stood quiet too long, he warned. "By embracing current technologies available on the Internet, we position Windows as the choice system for interactive Internet services and prepare for the shift to the native IAYF technologies" offered by Microsoft's own next-generation products.

Embrace! Extend! Innovate! The words pealed through the corridors of

Sinofsky's consciousness like Paul Revere's clarion call of old. Sinofsky mailed Allard, whom he had never met, proposing the two meet and strategize. In the meantime he wrote up an extended report of his trip, titled "Computing at Cornell and the Internet," and sent it to Gates while cc'ing Microsoft's Net contingent. Sinofsky's eleven-page treatise told of his campus experiences in the spirit of an alumnus and cheerleader, but his point was that Cornell was not hugely different from what was going on all over the world in academic settings. And if the current campus generation was going to provide the Microsoft personnel of tomorrow, following the history of the company, then Microsoft had better get wired too.

The Net was just dangling there like a low-hanging fruit for Microsoft if only the company could respond, Sinfosky figured. Chicago could totally take over the university environment and productivity application use, and NT could make huge inroads on the server side as schools everywhere expanded online services. We've got to build TCP/IP into Chicago and Windows NT, Sinofsky urged. We could set up pilot TCP/IP projects at a couple of universities. Look into equipping Chicago with SLIP access for off-campus and remote dial-in services over the Net. Get news, gopher, and Web access on board. Look into real-time videoconferencing like Cornell's CU-SeeMe, which enabled computers equipped with microphone and camera to transmit speech and images of their users over the Internet like a video phone call. Look into Internet file formats and protocols for indexing Web content and viewing information on other platforms like Mac and UNIX. And make sure Microsoft content is compatible with Internet document standards like html.

A tall agenda, yes, but no more ambitious than Allard's blueprint. When Sinofsky returned from Cornell the two got together immediately. In terms of Microsoft's internal path to the Internet, their meeting was something akin to Churchill and Roosevelt, or Proust and Joyce. They knew something cosmic was at work when each noticed the other was wearing Puma tennis shoes. A footwear classic—Clydes—that had recently been reintroduced to the market. Both had worn them growing up. Shoes almost were more the topic than the Internet. The two came at the issue of Microsoft on the Net from different perspectives, as Allard tells it. Sinofsky, in school four years earlier than Allard and at the company a couple of years longer, understood Microsoft wholly and completely and saw the Internet as an opportunity. Allard came to Microsoft understanding the Net wholly and completely and saw Microsoft as an opportunity. The two perspectives complemented each other nicely. Allard was most impressed with Sinofsky's perception about how, in a campus atmosphere where the worst threat was a failed class, a culture even more efficient than Microsoft's had evolved using the Internet. How could it be that a bunch of college kids were farther along in their use of technology than one of the most sophisticated software companies in the world?

Allard and Sinofsky also both knew there was a ticklish political issue within Microsoft that eventually would have to be confronted: the online services project, at the time dubbed Microsoft Online Services, or MOS, soon to be code-named Marvel. Both took a conciliatory, common-ground approach to Marvel. Allard acknowledged the potential overlap between it and the Net but saw that the two efforts also could be complementary. Marvel had to begin determining a way to not just coexist with, but provide connectivity to, the Net, Allard insisted. It was fine for Marvel to provide whizzy content on its own, as long as that content could also be accessed over the Net.

Chapter 6

SCHISM

Allard's was not the only Internet memo floating around. In Microsoft's Connectivity Business Unit, a young agitator named Dave Pollon put together a strategic paper called "Microsoft and the Internet," dated January 26, 1994—a day after Allard sent the final version of his memo around. Pollon's memo was philosophically in tune with Allard's but held a more business-plan approach. Pollon saw NT as a way to displace UNIX "as the Internet server of choice." He felt Windows could provide "a well-integrated and easy-to-use interface" for Internet users, and he saw enhancing the e-mail component, code-named Capone, of the next version of Windows, code-named Chicago, as a way of spurring Internet newsgroup and mail users to upgrade.

"We want business users to buy Chicago because it allows them to utilize the Internet as a natural extension of their existing Microsoft desktop paradigms. We want individuals to buy Chicago because it's so easy to get connected to information that they want to see," Pollon wrote. Internet interfaces could also be extended to new Windows products, such as handheld devices, he suggested.

Gates's reading of Allard's and Pollon's memos did not particularly register. The chairman was still a skeptic, particularly when it came to a real business plan for the Net. And this was far from the first time a group of inside agitators had cried wolf at Microsoft. Sounding alarms was a daily occurrence at Microsoft, from Gates's view: "It is typical Microsoft fashion to say here's my idea, and by the way if you don't pay attention to it the company may go broke. Because we know we live in a world where such discontinuities happen all the time. We saw it happen to Wang, we saw it happen to Digital, we saw it happen to IBM. So the future of the company depends on being ultrasensitive to these things. Now if you're sensitive there's going to be some things like ITV or handwriting recognition that either come prematurely or never come . . . and when people look back they always remember the ones that turned into something. They don't remember all the noise about network computers will kill you tomorrow. Well, here I am!"

When Gates got hold of Sinofsky's memo, though, things began to click. "That had a huge impact on me," he recalled. "Sinofsky's not a the-sky-is-falling type guy. He's fairly measured in terms of how often he likes to push my alert button. But he definitely pushed it and got us really thinking."

It seemed apparent to Gates that there was enough buzz this time around to warrant a strategy retreat. "Understand—I'm the biggest advocate of retreats here," he said. They were a way to recharge the batteries, exchange ideas, get a ticklish issue out on the table. Best of all, they brought a bunch of smart people together. "I have a certain format I like for retreats that we used for this, where you give a lot of presentations, so you get the facts, and particularly the scary facts, so you have people with real expertise present. Then you have people break up into discussion groups and pick various topics, and you really mix people around. Not just people who understand that topic. Under what does this mean for Microsoft Online Services, you put one or two Marvel people, but you also put non-Marvel people and let them sit and talk about what does it mean for Windows."

When creative people came together, solutions that would never have occurred in a top-down management setting always presented themselves. Sinofsky reserved the Shumway Mansion, a twenty-two-room, 10,000-square foot house built in 1910 that overlooked Juanita Bay on Lake Washington in the Seattle suburb of Kirkland. It was a popular Microsoft retreat center, the rooms providing natural facilities for breakout groups. Shumway already had a storied role in Microsoft history—it had hosted the pivotal OS/2 networking session in 1990, the one that led to the tectonic shift in the Microsoft-IBM relationship that helped focus Microsoft's long-range strategy on Windows. Sinofsky prepared a three-inch-thick briefing paper on the Net, putting Allard's memo on top, for the twenty executives invited to the retreat. He knew it might be an uphill battle persuading some, starting with Gates and Myhrvold, of the need to jump on the Net. Neither of them, however, proved to be the toughest sell. That designation wound up going to the formidable protagonist of Microsoft Online Services, Russell Siegelman.

Like Steven Sinofsky, Siegelman was casting about for something new and challenging in the fall of 1992. The rapid-fire, bullet-headed Yonkers native had joined Microsoft in September 1989 fresh from an MBA at Harvard, where he was honored as a Baker Scholar. Siegelman had technical credentials as well. After getting his undergrad degree at MIT in 1984, he programmed for three years on artificial intelligence at an MIT spinoff called Applied Expert Systems. Pure science took him only so far. Siegelman liked building products.

At Microsoft, Siegelman found himself working in the Network Business Unit under Mike Murray, the original Macintosh evangelist for Apple who had just joined Microsoft after being recruited away from a potential executive job at Novell by none other than Steve Ballmer. Siegelman worked for a few desultory months on LAN Manager and was just getting restless after the 2.0 launch in 1990 when the big IBM "divorce" reorganization saved him. Artisoft's success with LANtastic and three-year run of 171 percent average revenue gains had spawned interest in a new networking market for PCs. Small offices and departments in corporations needed to link a few, not a lot, of computers together to trade files, schedules, contacts, and what have you. These were called peer-to-peer networks because they simply daisy-chained computers together. The opposite model, called client-server, was where PCs were hooked to a powerful, central computer like infants who suckled off the mother host.

Client-server was more powerful and efficient, but peer-to-peer was cheaper, as an expensive server wasn't needed. At Microsoft the word from above was clear: We'd better have a low-end networking strategy, and have it soon. Murray assigned Siegelman to work on it with another relative newbie, Jim Allchin. The two put their heads together and after a couple of months decided that Microsoft would build its own low-end networking product based on Windows. Siegelman moved to Silverberg's group to become lead product manager—marketing lead—of Windows for Workgroups 3.1.

WfW, as it was conveniently truncated to, got the usual splash of initial attention when it rolled out on October 27, 1992, with attendant predictions that Microsoft would soon crush all competition and dominate the peer-to-peer market. Microsoft was devoting 20 percent—a figure that eventually would rise to 60 percent—of its development resources to workgroup computing, Mike Maples told *Business Week*. In a $1 million rollout in New York City's Gershwin Theater, a skit-filled event designed to imitate a Broadway show, a bevy of Microsoft managers showed off the thrills of office connectivity. On the eve of his thirty-seventh birthday, Gates, who wore Blues Brothers shades and did a brief jumping-jack routine as part of the production, joked that most of the singing and dancing over Windows since 3.0's introduction had been done by lawyers—a reference to Apple's Windows lawsuit and the antitrust investigation by the Federal Trade Commission. Perhaps the most memorable line came after Gates, the production's natural focus, appeared mystified by a reference to a well-known pop song. "Bill, you need to get out more!" was the cast's response. In some ways it was true. The previous winter, after Intel's Andy Grove had called rival chip maker AMD the Milli Vanilli of the PC business, Gates confessed he had no idea who the lip-synching rock 'n' roll band was. Divining teen-culture analogies was one of the more recreational potentialities of Information At Your Fingertips. At the time, Gates good-humoredly went along with the WfW skit. But a year later he gave a candid assessment to *Forbes* ASAP magazine: "That was so bad, I thought Ballmer was going to retch."

Despite its high-profile debut, Windows for Workgroups 3.1 was not destined for the pantheon of Microsoft triumphs. It was not as easy to set up and use as LANtastic, and its designated market seemed perilously temporal. Small offices, divisional departments, and other groups of workers needing network capability would either discard WfW for an eventual client-server setup or skip it altogether on the way to a client-server system. The real problem was that information systems directors—the guys who ran the company networks—did not trust a peer-to-peer system. They did not really want users setting up their own shared files and accessing each other's computers on a one-to-one basis. It created the potential for bad things to happen to data, and besides, it was kind of like going around the boss to get something done.

In a way, the peer-to-peer approach was not even at the heart of LANtastic's success. A small office or corporate division would put the common programs and files on one computer—usually the secretary's, because she or he would need access to everyone else for scheduling, phone messages, e-mail, and so on. So the secretary's computer was the hub that everyone else fed off of. It was still a client-server model, even if technically it was called peer-to-peer and everyone could share everyone else's files. Psychologically, users needed one computer on the network where they knew they could find the files they wanted. It was yet another case of human nature, not marketing or labeling, dictating use of technology.

WfW also suffered from poor implementation. Disk access proved too slow. And a decision that at first seemed like a good idea—bundling network cards with WfW—turned into a disaster. Most PC users, especially in small offices, did not want to mess with opening up the case, finding an available slot, installing a network card, doing the software configuration, connecting the network cables. . . . WfW came in different packaging schemes, which confused software resellers, who did not know which would appeal to a specific customer. The network cards turned out to be the wrong model—they had the thin-pronged connectors instead of the phone-style connectors that were catching on. Jonathan Roberts, a marketing lead on the WfW project, was dispatched to Intel, which produced the cards, in an effort to see if the chip giant would take some of them back. No dice. Microsoft wound up with some $30 million worth of cards sitting in a warehouse. "It wasn't just net cards, it was T-Connectors and miles and miles of coax cable," Roberts recalled. "Oh yeah, and a bunch of little screwdrivers." Eventually Paul Maritz, calling on some buddies from his former employer, managed to persuade Intel to take back much of the load. But as of January 1999, Roberts still had some of the screwdrivers lying around.

It was obvious almost from the start that WfW was a work in progress. Rather than stay with the project through its next upgrade, Siegelman opted to cast about for bigger opportunities. Describing himself as a free agent, Siegelman let it out that he was looking to move. The decision caught the close-knit WfW team off guard. Siegelman had contributed a lot of energy and enthusiasm to the project, and now he was going to walk? It was not what you usually did at Microsoft, particularly with a key strategic product in obvious need of upgrading. The logical extension of eating your own dogfood, as Microsoft liked to call testing its own products, was cleaning up after your mess. Siegelman's abrupt departure left a lot of hard feelings with the WfW team: "It was clear we needed to change some things about WfW to make it successful, and the team perceived that Russ didn't have the perseverance to stick it through," one team member recalled.

Word of Siegelman's search soon reached Natalie Yount, a former librarian at Microsoft who had moved to human resources. Yount knew that Bill Gates's technical assistant, Aaron Getz, was moving on and Gates needed to fill the vacancy. Siegelman was more a marketing guy, but Yount thought Gates might want to split the post between a technical expert and a marketing specialist. Yount suggested Siegelman talk to Gates about the opening. Siegelman was his usual blunt self. He had an MBA, he had experience managing big projects, he wanted a career ladder move. Why don't you just go in for a chat? Yount persisted. If you don't like the way the job is currently defined, suggest something different. Maybe you and Bill can work something out.

So Siegelman thought, Fine, if Gates wants to interview me, I might as well see what's available. Siegelman had met with Gates only a couple of times since joining the company—never in a job situation—and did not know exactly what to expect. It took the Microsoft chairman less than a minute to break the ice. You know, you could do this job working as my assistant, he told Siegelman, looking him straight in the eye. But that's not what I have in mind.

What Gates had in mind was looking into a possible Microsoft entry to the commercial online services market. A rising player, America Online, was drawing quite a bit of attention, including a 24.9 percent investment from Paul Allen that AOL's board thought was big enough, thank you, leading it to impose a poison-pill provision to prevent a hostile takeover. If an outside investor (such as Allen) reached or exceeded 25 percent of the company's stock or tendered an offer to do so, AOL would distribute rights to existing shareholders enabling them to purchase 1/100 of a share of a new series of junior participating preferred stock, subverting the outsider's influence. AOL—especially its smart chief executive, Steve Case—had more than just chutzpah. It had a friendly interface and smart, hip attitude that was attracting a lot of new home computer buyers. Prodigy, a three-year-old entry from IBM, was plugging along despite a horrid blocky interface that looked like it had been designed on an

Etch-a-Sketch, confirming the Microsoft perspective that IBM could not design a user interface to save its soul. CompuServe, the old-timer who had three years earlier absorbed its pioneering rival, The Source, was doing best of all, drawing from a core group of industry hobbyists, information systems insiders, and online junkies. Microsoft already knew quite a bit about the online business from CompuServe, which hosted Microsoft's product support forums. Microsoft managers moderated the forums, where you could ask product questions, exchange messages with other users, download bug fixes and software updates, and otherwise tap into the Microsoft knowledge universe. CompuServe was more the techie space; America Online was the populist town square of online services.

If Microsoft could build its own CompuServe/AOL, it could set up an electronic product and services network that not only would feed customers directly back into the company but help Microsoft leverage the brave new online world, Gates reasoned. If online was going to happen, and Gates felt sure it was, Microsoft had to be a provider to know how its core technologies would benefit from being online. Gates had another fascination as well, echoing his original Information At Your Fingertips presentation. What about news? he asked Siegelman. You could add a lot of value to news by putting it online. Not only was the immediacy factor higher—no waiting for the hourly radio blurbs, evening TV hour, or newspaper the next morning—you could pull together customized clipping files for subscribers. You wouldn't have to wait for the medium to give you the news, it would come to you automatically. You could get the weather in the city you were flying to that day, find out what was going on there locally. Gates loved the efficiencies inherent in the system—savings on ink and paper, the ability to get the news you want when you want it. It was unclear how much people would pay for such a service when news was available from so many sources. But as an opportunity, it looked worth investigating.

Why don't you look over the online landscape for a couple of months, report back to me, and we'll go from there? Gates suggested. Siegelman eagerly accepted. It sounded great to him, something meaty in uncharted terrain. Something he could build from scratch and make a career bet on. In a way the whole thing seemed predestined. While slaving away on features in Windows for Workgroups, Siegelman had heard a little birdie whispering in his ear, What about AOL? What about the online business? Actually, it was not exactly a whisper or a little birdie—Steve

Ballmer was the perpetrator. Siegelman checked out AOL and was intrigued by its possibilities. The Gates imprimatur was all he needed to go find out more.

Starting in November 1992, Siegelman holed up in an office in Building 8 and spent the next six months coming up with a plan. For his new post, Siegelman reported to Nathan Myhrvold, the advanced technology guru. Myhrvold was staking a claim to the title of most colorful executive at Microsoft. Moon-faced and baby-cheeked, with a frizzy beard and roiled curls that gave him the look of a wood elf having a bad hair day, Myhrvold liked to write sometimes florid, sometimes bitchy memos postulating future technology trends based on a random thought or observation during the morning's commute. Myhrvold would send the memos to Gates and other executives as well as his own direct reports, but they invariably found broad distribution at Microsoft. Whether you understood the science or technology of a Nathan memo was almost beside the point. Myhrvold couched his treatises in such entertaining terms they could be appreciated on a lay level.

A Renaissance techie of sorts, Myhrvold stacked his office high with empty soda cans in geometric patterns, tinkered with classic cars, went fossil hunting across Montana in a Hummer, roasted barbecues in his stainless steel cooker while lecturing at length on the importance of different woods during the cooking process, and studied paleontology in his leisure time, investigating the unplumbed mysteries of dinosaurs' sex lives. Like other PC industry notables, Myhrvold had dropped out of college. Only in his case, it was decidedly farther along in the educational process—post-doctoral study at Cambridge University in England under one of the world's renowned quantum theoreticians, Stephen Hawking. Myhrvold, who liked to joke that he had more degrees than a thermometer, had finished high school in his hometown of Santa Monica, California, at age fourteen, had gone to Santa Monica Junior College, and then studied at UCLA, where he received undergraduate and master's degrees. From there it was off to Princeton, where he got another master's and a Ph.D. in theoretical physics for work on quantum field theory in curved space time and cosmology. Hawking, who had met Myhrvold after giving a speech at Princeton, asked him to a two-year program at Cambridge's Department of Applied Mathematics and Theoretical Physics. Myhrvold's research on quantum gravitational theory matched up well with Hawking's work. It was a career track that could eventually wind up with a prestigious professorship at any of the world's leading academic institutions, but Myhrvold got distracted. In the summer of 1984 he took a short leave of absence to work on a software project with his younger brother, Cameron, and some friends. By the end of summer the group was far enough along to form a new company, Dynamical Systems Research, based in Berkeley, with Nathan as president. DSR developed a clone of an obscure IBM software product called TopView, Big Blue's early stab at a menu-based, multitasking interface that never went anywhere. Nevertheless, in 1986, under pressure from the Armonk powers-that-be at IBM headquarters, Microsoft was looking for a way to make its nascent and still-klunky Windows 1.0 operating system compatible with TopView, and DSR caught Steve Ballmer's eye. Ballmer visited the gang in California and came back raving. These are our kind of guys, he told Gates. Microsoft purchased DSR in a stock deal valued at $1.5 million (with subsequent splits, the equivalent of $216 million by 1998), Myhrvold and crew moved to the Northwest, and the fidgety quantum physicist with the manic giggle began his rise through the executive ranks.

Reporting to Ballmer, Myhrvold was named director of special projects and helped with the development of OS/2 and Presentation Manager, then segued into work on networks. Product development was not really his cup of tea, however, and by February 1990 Myhrvold persuaded Gates to name him head of advanced research and technology at Microsoft. From that point on Myhrvold was Microsoft's designated information guru, the guy who would think deep thoughts and lead the company into the next millennium. The intellectual gadfly role suited him well: He liked to speak to techie audiences, was comfortable on TV and in print interviews, and had a bubbly affability that played well in groups as diverse as a chamber of commerce and the Association for Computing Machinery. But Myhrvold's public popularity was not always shared in-house. Like most intellectuals with diverse interests and restless minds, Myhrvold proved a distracted manager. The word from the rank and file was that he looked at budgets once a year, when it was time to sign off on them. Moreover, Myhrvold's analyses had an impetuousness about them that for all their charm tended to prove overly sanguine or flat-out wrong. He helped build the initial bandwagon for handwriting recognition in the early 1990s, an era full of effervescent predictions that within a couple of years keyboards would be replaced, or at least supplemented, by electronic pads capable of turning scribbled cursive into digital text. Early products like AT&T's Go pad and Apple's Newton bombed dismally and are now remembered primarily for being the butt of endless Doonesbury strips. Myhrvold also predicted that a surge in data transmission over phone lines would lead to free voice calls, a curious presumption given Ma Bell's long-standing tradition of giving away something only on the expectation she would soon be able to charge for it. (On balance, Myhrvold was correct in the sense that data traffic would overwhelm voice. And as competition among phone carriers heated up, giving away voice calls to gain the data business seemed a real possibility.)

By 1993 Myhrvold was absolutely convinced that the future was interactive TV. He liked to describe a world where the slick video content of Hollywood would merge with the interactive capabilities of the personal computer. You would be able to order up any content at any time: Watch *Seinfeld* when you felt like it, not at 9:00 P.M. Thursday night. Pull down the latest Tom Cruise or Sylvester Stallone epic to watch at your leisure without the inconvenience and time waste of driving to a video store and standing in line at the counter, only to find out the show you wanted was rented already. Call up his lifetime batting statistics and bio information when Ken Griffey Jr. stepped to the plate in the bottom of the ninth with the bases loaded. Renew your driver's license with a couple clicks of a mouse button. Interactive TV made such logical sense, there was no way it could not succeed. It was as if some technology genie had bottled up all the nuisances, hassles, and time sinks of everyday living and said, Here, we can fix everything with ITV. And all for the reasonable cost, Myhrvold calculated, of 50 cents an hour for downloads running 4 megabits per second, or three times as fast as a T-1 line providing high-speed Internet connections to large corporations. Myhrvold, ever the pragmatic visionary, even saw Microsoft or any other company getting a vig, or commission, on every ITV transaction. "Vig" was short for "vigorish," a Yiddish term for a bookie's fee. You would not have to charge much—you could even go with less than a penny—for vigs to start adding up to real money, given the millions of potential transactions. It was the old operating system model applied to the new medium: You did not have to make much money per sale if you sold in the hundreds of millions of units.

Myhrvold saw huge prospects for movies on demand but could never address the practical marketing question of which revenue stream Hollywood would risk—first-run theaters, video sales, video rentals, cable TV channels, network TV, and on and on—in order to make room for movies on demand. Even granted a ready and willing film industry, movies on demand comprised a dubious business model. Technology trials from Florida to California revealed little interest in the whole idea, even with minimal or no incremental cost to the consumer, and the concept slipped quietly into the scrap heap of great technological thoughts utterly lacking consumer interest. Microsoft frontline executives grumbled now and then about Myhrvold having little to show, particularly on Microsoft's balance sheet and its product lines, for his innumerable flights of fancy. But Gates liked him. Large organizations needed corporate gadflies at the executive level, Gates believed, to provide a point of departure, whether positive or negative. Whatever his administrative shortcomings and predictive insufficiencies, Myhrvold motivated the troops, even if their objective was mostly to prove him wrong. In his defense, Myhrvold hardly was alone in his stumbles. Intel CEO Andy Grove, Apple chairman John Sculley, TCI chairman John Malone, Gates himself, and leading telco scions were just as smitten by the vision du jour in the early 1990s.

Myhrvold's decidedly open-ended title gave him free rein to explore a variety of venues. His farsighted argument was that Microsoft would eventually need to provide the leadership in personal computing technology that AT&T's Bell Labs, IBM's Thomas Watson Laboratory, and Xerox's PARC (Palo Alto Research Center) had done for their industries. It was a lengthy commitment with no guaranteed payoff, but Gates saw it as a logical extension of Microsoft's long-term vision. Myhrvold's new position reported directly to Gates, which prompted Myhrvold to joke that his career ladder was leading to bosses with less and less formal education but more and more money: Hawking, then Ballmer, and finally Gates. By 1993, when Siegelman began reporting to him, Myhrvold's career options had been narrowed to a single individual—the Sultan of Brunei, the Saudi oil baron who was then one position ahead of Gates as the world's richest individual.

Siegelman, who had received his undergraduate degree in physics, liked watching how Myhrvold's mind worked. One day Myhrvold launched into a prolonged e-mail reverie explaining the physics of raindrops bouncing off his windshield on the drive home the evening before. He had worked out a mathematical calculation for splash patterns based on sines and thetas and the inclination of the rainfall versus the angle of the windshield. It reminded Siegelman of one of his problem sets at MIT. Of all the people on the "to" line, Siegelman mused, he was probably the only one who fully understood the theory behind the memo.

Although Myhrvold's attention was directed at the emerging interactive

TV phenomenon, he was keeping an eye on the Internet and online services as well. The problem with the Internet from his perspective was not just the lack of a practical business model for a free medium. It had to do also with ease of use and bandwidth. You were not going to make a mass medium out of UNIX commands and text displays on 9600 bps modems, he maintained. From his research into interactive TV Myhrvold understood the issues associated with moving large amounts of data interactively over phone or cable lines. For the Internet to get interesting at all, it would have to have much bigger pipes. So little appreciation did Myhrvold have for the Internet that, in an epic memo entitled "Roadkill on the Information Highway," Myhrvold did not once mention the Net, Ken Auletta noted in *The New Yorker*. The thirty-page treatise was distributed September 8, 1993, just a few weeks before Allard began work on his Windows-as-the-Internet's-killer-app memo.

As for online potential, Myhrvold had the notion of creating a Microsoft kit to sell to bulletin board sysops, or system operators. BBSes—small, locally owned basement operations where computerists dialed in for chat, forums, free software, and whatnot—numbered in the tens of thousands nationwide and were clustering into regional and even nationally affiliated networks. Myhrvold saw a potential for building a BBS business around Windows that would not only seed Microsoft's operating system and applications business but build potential new services, including software support, underwritten by online transactions. You could post Microsoft software, enable credit-card payment, deliver the goods electronically, and cut the BBS operators in on the sale, ultimately making higher margins by saving on distribution and production costs.

Siegelman was skeptical. BBS operators were strictly low-rent and independent-minded garage-shop types. They might spend a couple of grand a year upgrading their modems, but he suspected they had zero interest in becoming a channel for Microsoft. What they really liked was free stuff. In any case, there were not enough of them to make a real profit center. Maybe a quality package from Microsoft would sell, but not an integrated line. It looked to Siegelman like an example of Myhrvold's blue sky opening up into a black hole. It was fine if Myhrvold wanted to pursue the plan through someone else, as long as it was not on Siegelman's watch.

Myhrvold did have an intriguing technological proposition regarding the Net. If you could build Microsoft's linking technology, OLE (object linking and embedding), into the Web, you could enable Microsoft Office users and Microsoft developers to leverage their Windows content and programming acumen onto the Web. It would be a way of making the Web more useful to Windows users with lots of Microsoft Office–generated content on their hard drives. And programmers could write nifty applications that would run both on their hard disks and the Web.

Microsoft saw certifiable business opportunities in the online world. The choices were simple: partner, buy in, buy out. As part of his exploration, Siegelman met with CompuServe and America Online executives to discuss possible deals. CompuServe, happy with the Microsoft relationship as it was, showed little interest in modifying it. There was also the problem of what to do with H&R Block, which owned CompuServe and might want to continue a stake in a Microsoft merger. America Online was a different story. Steve Case & Co. were intrigued to talk to Microsoft, in part to try to fathom what the software giant's plans were for online services. Paul Allen's investment had gotten AOL's attention, and now Bill Gates had come calling. It was time for anti-Microsoft paranoia to kick in. In early May 1993 AOL made its move. In a meeting with Allen, Case and his associates made it clear they would fight any effort on his part to gain control of AOL. The same day they went to Microsoft to give Siegelman and Gates a similar message. AOL was convinced Allen and Gates were in league to take it over. Both deny it, and in fact during the years since his departure from Microsoft in 1983, Allen had almost never collaborated with Gates on a deal. The two were still friends and met regularly in Microsoft board meetings and for NBA basketball games featuring Allen's Portland Trail Blazers and Seattle's SuperSonics. But the tech titans had distinctly divergent business goals and styles.

Case and his AOL team and Siegelman and Gates explored everything from partnering with AOL to making an investment to buying AOL outright. The AOL side, as reported by author Kara Swisher in *aol.com*, recalls Gates saying, I can buy 20 percent of you or I can buy all of you. Or I can go into this business myself and bury you. The Microsoft side is distinctly different. Neither Gates nor Siegelman recall the term "bury" ever being mentioned, and all parties agree that discussions never got far enough to think about a price tag. To the contrary, the whole tone of the meeting, Gates said, was to explore relationships in a get-acquainted session. "We could not have been nicer in this meeting," Gates said. "We wanted to make friends with these guys. In no way did we have the chutzpah to believe we were a guaranteed success in this market. We did say, Steve, think about if you teamed up with us, you could achieve your vision in a broader way. We think you guys have done incredible work. There must be opportunities here for us to work together." Asked why he thought the AOL side reported things differently, Gates said with a smile, "Because it made a better story!"

Gates was clear that Microsoft intended to get into the online business, was clear about Microsoft having some natural advantages because at its core the online business was about software, and was clear Microsoft was going to make a strategic play to benefit Windows users. The whole point was to loosen up the AOL crew, Siegelman recalls. AOL did not appear to be in the right frame of mind for sweet-talking, however.

AOL counteroffered a partnership whereby it would create an online service for Microsoft, which would use Microsoft's own brand name, and offer a doorway to it on AOL for AOL users to jump onto the Microsoft service. AOL already was doing a similar deal for Apple Computer's forthcoming eWorld, a community-style online service with a uniquely friendly interface that never went anywhere. Under terms of the deal, Apple figured on paying AOL around $18 million in royalties and development fees. But the kicker was eWorld would save Apple around $30 million on AppleLink, a proprietary, service-oriented online system, used primarily for Macintosh support, that was costly to operate and maintain.

In its proposal to Microsoft, AOL's perk was obvious: It could lure customers interested in Microsoft's service and build its own brand identity along the way. The perk for Microsoft was not having to commit resources to building its own online service. But Microsoft had deep pockets and was never shy about going its own way. The AOL meeting convinced both Gates and Siegelman that the service was not for sale and had little interest in doing a deal.

It was not just big fish Microsoft pursued. Siegelman looked at a boatload of bulletin-board systems doing interesting things, some with databases, some with specialization software. Some used Windows in unique ways. In the end, Siegelman went to Gates and told him that.

Siegelman had written up his grand odyssey in a thirty-page memo covering competition in the online services market, the major players, profit potential. There were lots of great things happening, many good ideas, considerable money to be made, but no real single selling point. Looking forward, the growth potential was not entirely clear, but the trends indicated something big could happen. Microsoft could easily make some money by leveraging its name and products. There might be service and support benefits as well, a way to reach customers and build a community of Windows users. After the AOL meeting, Siegelman told Gates, We might as well do this ourselves. It's the only way we can get accurate, pertinent data: Be our own guinea pig. You're right, Gates replied, we're probably not going to end up buying anything. It was time to get moving on Microsoft's own technology.

The date is forever emblazoned in Siegelman's memory: May 11, 1993, his thirty-first birthday. AOL had told Paul Allen to butt out and had left its Microsoft tête-à-tête expecting a Cold War. Microsoft Online Services had been born. It was not just Siegelman's birthday but the birth of a new era in Microsoft online strategy.

Microsoft Online Services was Siegelman's big career play at the company. It was everything he had been aiming for: a huge challenge, something he could own and build and watch grow and flourish. Siegelman wanted a trophy, a thing he could point to and say "I did it." Marvel was his best and greatest chance. Siegelman assembled a core team of half a dozen managers and began putting together the pieces. The project got the de rigueur code name, this one Marvel, after the comics publisher. Things moved along well, with Marvel passing a Gates review in September. Gates gave the go-ahead to lab equipment and more staff. Hiring increased, coding began. Then, in November, disaster struck.

Over a weekend Siegelman was bothered by a headache but, with typical Type A bravado, decided to ignore it. It bothered him again on Monday, but it was not until he awoke in the middle of Monday night that he decided something had to be done. He rarely got headaches. This one hurt so badly it scared him. He made an appointment to visit his doctor the following afternoon. The next morning, before his appointment, Siegelman realized something was seriously wrong. Meeting with Myhrvold and some sales people, Siegelman would go to say something and sense that it was going to come out wrong. He stayed quiet throughout most of the meeting. His doctor could find nothing obviously wrong but directed Siegelman to have an MRI just in case. The MRI found massive bleeding on one side of his brain. The following morning Siegelman had emergency surgery for a brain aneurism. Caused by tangled arteries in the head that suddenly start to bleed, an aneurism can be fatal if not discovered and treated quickly enough. The surgery saved Siegelman, but the bleeding was over the part of his brain that affects speech. When he returned home after the surgery, his wife could barely understand him. Later Siegelman went back and looked at the e-mail he had sent that Sunday. It was full of dyslexic reversals of words, incorrectly used expressions, misplaced prepositions. Yet because the context made it clear what Siegelman's points were, nobody had gotten back to him questioning the mail.

No one knows what causes aneurisms, although they have been linked to blows to the head and congenital predisposition. Stress may or may not be a factor. If it is, Siegelman had all the pressure points. His wife was expecting. He had a new project, a new team, new quarters. Initially Siegelman's physician gave him some bad news: Cool it. Do not even think about going back to work for two years. The physician did not say it at the time, but whether Siegelman would ever speak normally again was in doubt. Faced with the dire edict, someone else might have taken his stock options and retired, or changed his focus, or called time out for a while. The classic Microsoft precedent had been set by Paul Allen. Stricken by Hodgkin's disease before he turned thirty, Allen resigned from Microsoft and, after the disease went into remission, spent a couple of years sorting things out before founding another software company, Asymetrix, and moving into other interests. Siegelman never thought twice about stepping aside, however. Instead he entered intensive language therapy and two months later returned to Microsoft. The astounding recovery was partly because Siegelman always had strong verbal skills but also because he ached so badly to return to his pet project. Within six months, no trace of the episode remained.

During Siegelman's rehabilitation, the man who had recruited him to Microsoft, Rob Glaser, visited the Marvel team with a different view of the online future. The previous spring, Glaser, thirty-one, had taken a leave of absence with the expectation he would not be returning. Before he was stricken, Siegelman had seen e-mail from Gates saying Glaser was around for consultation. Siegelman had liked Glaser from the day they had first met at Harvard five years earlier, and Glaser had persuaded him to take a look at Microsoft. So Siegelman sent mail to Glaser asking him if he would come and meet with the Marvel team.

A pug-faced technophile who talked in a machine-gun, robotic monotone, Glaser had worked on a lot of things at Microsoft, including the first version of Word, early CD-ROM development, networking, multimedia, and hand-held devices. During his leave he began thinking about a network project of his own, to be called Progressive Networks. The idea was to offer content for worthy environmental and civil libertarian causes, but Glaser did not see a commercial online service as his venue. Instead, what intrigued him was the Internet. When Glaser visited the Siegelman-less

Marvel team, he pitched the Internet hard. It was the first exposure of the Marvel team to what would become the great Internet debate within Microsoft.

The Internet movement, if you could call it that, at Microsoft was gaining momentum. Sinofsky had given Gates his Think Week briefing. Glaser was playing the role of outside agitator. And J Allard, the brash one, had started circulating drafts of his "killer app" memo to colleagues. There was noise on both channels at Microsoft: the online side and the Internet frequency. By the time Gates summoned executives to the Shumway Mansion on April 5, 1994, the setting was ripe for strategic tension between the two camps.

For nearly six weeks, Sinofsky had been lighting Internet fires among the ranks at Microsoft. After returning from Cornell and talking with Allard, Sinofsky decided he needed to know a whole lot more about how networking and the Internet worked. Sinofsky contacted Dave Leinweber, the head of networking services at Microsoft, and got not only a detailed briefing on Microsoft's network but an Internet tap as well. Once on the Net, Sinofsky downloaded Mosaic on both a Mac and a PC and started giving anyone he could collar what became known as the Sinofsky demos. Using WinHelp, the hyperlinked help software Microsoft had developed for Windows applications, as a reference point, Sinofsky showed how things like ftp and gopher and html were analogous to various parts of WinHelp—viewer, linking, search. The theory behind WinHelp was to try to direct users through a series of linked advisories that, it was hoped, led to the right answer or proper procedure. Using the Internet was much the same thing, you had to keep clicking and searching, moving through link after link, till you got the information you wanted. Even if a demo recipient had no clue about the Net, Sinofsky's analogy provided the aha! factor. Everyone at Microsoft knew WinHelp.

One way he got colleagues interested was to ask what school they had attended. Sinofsky would find the university's home page, click through to some of the popular Web pages on the site, maybe look up their favorite professor in the campus directory. Ironically, given its competition with Microsoft, Novell wound up in most Sinofsky demos. It had a good website—a long rack of red books with links to software documentation, help files, and so on. Sinofsky liked the book analogy—again, it helped the viewer understand how the Web worked. Another early classic was mtv.com, run not by the cable TV station but by Adam Curry, an MTV veejay who in the fall of 1993 put together a site with music news and clips. Curry eventually became embroiled in a legal snit with his employer and wound up relinquishing mtv.com, but his legacy as an early Web proselyte lived on. While showing the Web to a friend in Microsoft's public relations group, Kira Sorensen, Sinofsky ran across the mtv.com website. At first neither of them knew exactly what they were looking at. There was gossip about Michael Jackson and Madonna, and you could download an audio clip, even though it took ages. Wow, this is the coolest thing! Sorensen exclaimed. She did not really understand the things going on behind the curtain, but it hardly mattered. The fact it hardly mattered was what mattered. For Sinofsky mtv.com was a breakthrough as well. The Web could extend beyond e-mail, text, and written information. Cool content would be there too. "That was when it really clicked for me personally," Sinofsky recalled. "If there ever was an epiphany that the Web was more than just a cool computing infrastructure and was going to have relevance to normal people, this was it."

The demos led Sinofsky to a number of colleagues who got the Net. More than he had expected to find. But that was the magic of the Net; it was like some cabal whose members led conventional lives by day and got together with secret handshakes and occult rituals by night. Sinofsky's demos were the initiation rites. If the recipient lit up, showed some enthusiasm, glommed on to the whole concept, he or she was in the club. From his WinHelp demo Sinofsky compiled an invitation list to the Shumway retreat. Sinofsky bought a stack of Ed Krol's book *The Whole Internet User's Guide and Catalog*, the first truly useful Net handbook, published by O'Reilly & Associates, and distributed the books to executive staff and others. In preparation for the retreat Sinofsky put together his own catalog—a briefing paper with articles, news clippings, and other documentation that positioned the Internet and Web development circa January 1994.

Gathered for the session was a diverse sprinkling of twenty Microsoft executives from disparate disciplines at Microsoft. Besides Gates, Myhrvold, Siegelman, Allard, and Sinofsky, there were Brad Silverberg, Jim Allchin, and Tom Evslin—executives who would play key roles in formulating Windows strategy for the Web. Many of the others were midrange managers whose product or service might have Internet synergy—in customer support, for example, or an application like Microsoft Word. The retreat also was marked by the presence of a complete stranger to most of those in the room, although he was well-known in Internet circles. His name was

Bernard Aboba. In Berkeley, Aboba had pioneered an electronic bulletin board system e-mail connection with the Internet that quickly gained more than 10,000 accounts. His book, *The Online User's Encyclopedia*, had been published in December 1993 by Addison-Wesley. Aboba would not join Microsoft for another two months but had come at Russ Siegelman's invitation to offer a perspective on how a commercial service might incorporate Internet access as well. The Shumway retreat was an eclectic gathering of Internet idealists at Microsoft, each with a vision and agenda uniquely different from the other. Part of Gates's fascination with executive retreats was that one never knew, going in, where the conversations would lead, what ideas would come forward, whether history would be made—or at least incubated.

Chapter 7

VOLLEY

As was the custom at retreats, Gates led off the Shumway Mansion session with a positioning statement. He always gauged his opening remarks to set a framework for the day's discussion. They were meant to facilitate, but also to focus, the topics at hand. Despite the informality of the setting, a subliminal tension infused the gathering. For Internet partisans like Allard, Sinofsky, Evslin, and Silverberg, the key question was whether Gates would view the Internet as friend or foe. Sinofsky had witnessed Gates's skepticism firsthand with his Internet demo the previous fall. Allard figured Gates must have seen his memo by now but had no clue as to the chairman's reaction. And Microsoft in general was not exactly clambering onto the Internet bandwagon. An argument could easily be made that the Net threatened Windows' popularity.

Sitting across the room from Allard, Siegelman was just as curious to see how much Gates was going to buy into the Internet hype. Having read Allard's memo, Siegelman was worried about this thing turning into an Internet love fest. As he looked around the room, Siegelman saw more Internet zealots than online-services backers. Then there was Silverberg, whom

Siegelman suspected still carried hard feelings over the latter's abrupt departure from the Windows for Workgroups team. Siegelman was glad he had brought Aboba into the discussion. Aboba had unimpeachable credibility when it came to the Internet. He also knew how the Net and an online service could interoperate. You could have it both ways, Siegelman believed with all his heart. You could build an online service with Internet options. But it was going to take some persuading to get this group to buy into an online-services approach.

Surveying the gathering before him, Gates knew it would be folly to take sides or set too narrow an agenda. It was best to be as expansive as possible. Keep it wide open. Something was going on, something very, very significant, Gates pointed out. He had not really believed in Internet mania when he first encountered the hype, he said, but the label had turned out to be right on target. "The growth rate in use, clients, and servers is amazing," he told the group. "Perhaps greater than any growth we will ever see for any industry. Very few things grow exponentially as the Internet is clearly doing today." Doubling, doubling, and doubling, the numbers of users, computers, and servers on the Internet were astounding to behold.

So what did all this mean for Microsoft? That's what we're here today to talk about, Gates said. "Everywhere I go, people ask me about how Microsoft will be on the Internet. People want to know when we will provide support services on the Net. They want to know when Microsoft will have a program like Mosaic available, and they want to know how our future products, and our vision of Information At Your Fingertips, relate to the Internet."

So here's what has to happen, Gates continued. We need to build Internet consciousness into our strategy. We need to make the Internet part of our products and services. We need to embrace the Internet. And once we've absorbed the Internet into the Microsoft DNA, we need to extend the Internet with Microsoft technology. Embrace! Extend! Allard, sitting in on his first high-level strategy session, inwardly smiled. Gates had picked up on the lingo of his memo. It was a good initial sign. The chairman got it.

But wait. Gates was not buying into the Internet solution full bore. The Net had its limitations, he elaborated. A lot of people think of the Internet as the real-life digital highway. To his way of thinking, the Net was more a narrowband version. It did not have the capacity—the pipes, as Myhrvold liked to put it—to carry the real exciting stuff that interactive TV promised. The Net was still a place for simple character-based information. E-mail. News. Chat. File exchanges. They were great communications tools. But could they carry the Internet into mass-media status? How far could the Net progress as a commercial medium? Sinofsky nodded knowingly. The issue of how do we make money still overlaid Gates's thinking on the Internet. At each step, Microsoft needed to pay attention to the business opportunities, whatever they might be, inherent in the Net, Gates continued. And Microsoft needed to ensure that it got credit and recognition for its contributions as a player on the Net. Somewhere, somehow, economic opportunities would emerge.

After Gates's comments, the session separated into three breakouts, where the rubber met the road and intellectual jockeying for pole position began. "Exploiting Systems" investigated how Microsoft's expertise in systems software, including Chicago and Windows NT, could be used to further the Internet's presence and capabilities for personal computers. "Tools and Services," which included Word and Office, not just programming tools, examined the issue of how Windows applications might come into use for Internet development and how product support and other Microsoft services might be supported via the Net. While both had their share of yeasty issues, the pivotal session was the third, "Online Strategy." Online strategy was where Gates himself wound up, along with the two jousters, Allard and Siegelman. From their discussion emerged the greatest strategic divergence for Microsoft since the wrenching Windows-OS/2 debates of the late 1980s.

Gates had positioned the Internet as an opportunity, but Siegelman wondered about the impact of "embrace and extend" on the grand online strategy he had spent a year and half of his life putting into motion. How could Microsoft Online Services do anything representative on the Internet front in time for Chicago? The upgrade was supposed to ship by fall—October 1994, just six months hence. Attempting to recast the operating system or Microsoft Online Services for Internet compatibility would force a severe postponement. Any delay in Chicago would put Marvel farther behind in its ability to compete with America Online, CompuServe, and Prodigy. Moreover, and scariest of all, from what Siegelman could determine, every Internet capability you added to Chicago, you had to subtract from Marvel's value proposition to the Windows user. For example: If you added Windows support and services via the Internet, you diminished Marvel's opportunity to use support and services as a means of drawing online customers. If you made Internet connectivity a big thing in Chicago, what was to prevent a

Windows user from going into IRC—Internet Relay Chat—instead of one of Marvel's chat groups? If you offered a Web browser with Chicago, wouldn't that encourage Windows users to go to the Web instead of to Marvel for online information? Particularly if there were automated logon procedures of the sort Allard was evangelizing to make getting on the Net a simple matter of a few mouse clicks. And all this for a medium where no one was making money and that held few prospects for profitability in the future? Siegelman had nothing philosophically against the Internet. But Microsoft Online Services was a bird in the hand compared to the indeterminant qualities of the Net.

On the surface, Siegelman tried to remain cool-headed and well reasoned. Inside, he felt like someone was trying to pull his stomach down through his lower intestine. He had put months of brainstorming, evangelizing, and twelve-hour days including weekends into Marvel. His team was up to fifty people and still hiring. He was guiding Microsoft's Starship Enterprise into the Information Age, and now the Internet, on the strength of radicalized hype and a fringe-geek following, was threatening to sweep in and wreak havoc with his best-laid plans. Siegelman had seen the Net. He had seen Mosaic. He knew it was catching on: The previous fall he had been copied on an executive e-mail to Gates rhapsodizing over the wild download volumes for Mosaic. But the Internet offered nothing in the way of consumer content, ease of use, or commercial prospect. On top of everything else, it was slow.

Siegelman mentally rolled up his shirtsleeves. He knew he was going to have to make his case forcefully and explicitly or risk Marvel being run off the road by the Internet bandwagon. Rather than attempt to butt heads over the so-called promise of the Internet, however, Siegelman kept his argument on a rational level of robbing Peter to pay Paul. I'm not saying the Internet is not important, Siegelman told the breakout. But remember, everything you add into Windows to make the Web more attractive, you subtract from Marvel as a value proposition to the online community. The power of an online service lies in its ability to aggregate lots of different services and features into one system. Yet the Web is essentially *dis*aggregated. There are mailing lists here, and newsgroups there, but no one tells you where to find them. No one brings them all together in a consistent, easy-to-use way. Siegelman respected the lure of the Net. But what to do in a concrete fashion was clear as Mississippi mud. Siegelman could not justify revamping Marvel, stopping the whole development process, and telling his team, Hold on: We're going to build the whole thing on Internet protocols. First of all, it was not even clear what that would mean, and there was no easy or direct way to do it. And second, if Marvel did undertake an Internet re-make, it would, plain and simple, miss the Chicago release date. So if you are going to try to tell me to stop and do something completely different and get on the Internet platform, Siegelman told the group, his voice wavering with emotion, I will tell you fine. Do you want Marvel to have the Internet built in, or do you want to be in the Windows upgrade box? The answer was pretty damn simple.

There were other trade-offs, which Siegelman readily ticked off: ease of connectivity, Windows support and services, document publishing, chat, file searching and sharing. Microsoft Online Services would bring people to the Windows way of doing things, Siegelman argued. It would make pub-lishing and sharing electronic documents easier and more convenient than anything you could find on the Internet. Its chat would be more focused and entertaining than the Net's often-chaotic, sporadic chat mode. Things would be easier to find and gain access to in Microsoft Online Services. This was going to be Microsoft's signature service for the information su-perhighway. It was going to bring frustrated Internet users into the Windows environment. Doing things the other way—making Windows an entry point to the Internet—simply launched users into a vast, uncontrolled, non-Microsoft world, Siegelman argued. As he cataloged Marvel's game plan, he kept one eye on Gates's reaction. The chairman, after all, held the final vote in this election.

Sitting across from Siegelman, Allard tried to keep himself from jump-ing up and shouting. He had nothing against Microsoft's plans to do an on-line service. But to the extent Marvel might occlude Internet compatibility with Windows, it was absolutely wrongheaded. To Allard, the Net could exist side by side with the online world. It was perfectly fine to build a Mi-crosoft online service, as long as it supported Internet protocols and under-stood its mission to be serving the greater community of the Web. Yet the way Siegelman was casting things, the choice was essentially an either/or proposition.

Allard was the junior member of the breakout, one of the few without the word "vice" in his title. He was just there shaking the trees, a plumbing guy. He did not think it his place to try telling Siegelman how to run his op-eration, especially given Siegelman's close relationship with Gates. But if he let Siegelman's assumptions go unchallenged, and Microsoft started down a separate, non-Internet path with Marvel, Allard not only would find it difficult to live with himself, he would have to submit his resignation tomorrow. He could not work in a company in complete and total denial about the clear path of the future. He had to speak.

You know, he said, what would make the most sense for Marvel would be to use it as a vehicle to drive people to Internet. I'm a company guy, my loyalty to Microsoft is incredibly high. I want to see us succeed and I'm always looking to increase the benefit to our customers and to grow our business. So on goals, on values, I totally agree with Russ. But at the same time I'm so passionate about the Internet and the impact it's going to have on society that I'll stop at nothing to help get other people onto the Internet. The potential draw of Marvel would be to build a place where when people wanted to order an Eddie Bauer T-shirt or chat with someone in Stockholm, they would have to get on the Web. It was Marvel as a leverage tool for the Net. Making Microsoft Online Services a gateway to the Net would push PC software vendors of all stripes to make their products Internet-aware. As the Net grew, so would Windows grow.

Proprietary standards are a dead end, Allard asserted. Developing our own online protocols will put Marvel out in the cold. The big growth is on the Net. If you build on Internet standards, you will leverage a huge infrastructure and bring millions of people onto Marvel. Look at what you can do with product support—what we did with one little ftp server. We put just one product up on the server, DOS 6.2, and people were pounding down the doors to get in. Look at what is going on with e-mail on the Net. You've already got a universal protocol, SMTP, Simple Mail Transfer Protocol. It's right there, you can build all the services around it. Build our own e-mail protocol, and you're a step removed from the Internet. People will go somewhere else to get Internet mail because it will be faster, more efficient somewhere else. Come on, guys. Let's build Marvel on the Net, let's leverage that infrastructure, and people will come by the busload.

Siegelman, lips pursed, mouth tight, was shaking his head. You can't make money without adding value to the environment, he countered. And you need proprietary tools to do so. Sure SMTP was open, html was open, but what could you do with them? It was the old problem of the lowest common denominator. Can you build powerful directory services on SMTP? Not today you couldn't. How rich can your documents be in html? Not very. How could you differentiate your content from that of the guy down the street? Vanilla is a great flavor, but how often do you pick it when you've got thirty-one?

Wait a minute, Allard said. Think critical mass here. Think hands across the water, the ability of many many minds at work raising the bar. Eventually SMTP will be as powerful as anything proprietary. Eventually html will bloom into an incredibly full-featured, powerful, expressive environment. Nobody cares about plumbing. People care about the progress plumbing brings. How fast would the Wild West have been settled if each railroad had put in a different-size track? Everyone needs to use the same underlying infrastructure for real growth to happen. There's more money than you or I can imagine on the Internet, Allard said. It's growing exponentially. The whole infrastructure is in place already.

Yeah, but it's hard to get onto and navigate, Siegelman countered. When you control the environment, you can make the user experience much easier and more uniform.

Back and forth. Neither Allard nor Siegelman were much for backing down in an argument. And both could articulate their causes like '60s radicals at a campus sit-in. As their words got sharper and their necks turned more flushed, it became obvious the two would have to agree to disagree. Watching his lieges spar like a verbal version of Ali and Frazier did not faze Gates. He loved how passionate people got about Microsoft and its products. It was okay to disagree as long as no one got hurt and the results helped the company serve its customers. The truth was, in his heart Gates was divided on which path was the One True Way. He was an options tender; he liked side bets and fallback strategies. Tension was the yeast of progress. If everyone in a room agreed on a course of action at Microsoft, it scared Gates. It meant the company was sliding into complacency, just going through the motions.

But what's the economic model? he asked Allard.

Well, Allard said, it's kind of this community thing. It's like you can use my driveway to turn around in if you shovel my sidewalk; it's very communelike and very neighborly in many ways. It's difficult to articulate the economics of it because nobody has their head really wrapped around it. The economic model would grow, eventually, out of the community. No one knew, looking at a map of the Wild West way back when, that there was gold in the hills. The pioneers went out on faith that they could build something that would take care of them all.

So what Allard was seriously proposing was this: Let's bet the business on the commune. You help me, I'll help you. The only problem was, the commune wasn't interested in Microsoft Online Services and the commune wasn't interested in Microsoft's success per se. Allard could pardon Gates for being skeptical. Here was this kid out of college saying this commune should be the basis of Microsoft's business, and he's crazy! He's crazy!

Gates did not think Allard was crazy. But he did have his doubts about how the economics really worked. How do I know the connection from point A to point B isn't going to go down if someone decides not to pay his bill or not to bother with fixing the leak? he asked. Well, you don't, Allard said. But if this one guy doesn't pay his bill, there's this point a-c-b you could get through. And Gates was like, well, I still don't understand, somebody's gotta be paying for this, there's got to be some incentive to keep this thing up, and how do we come in and introduce new traffic and pay our part? Allard had to give Gates credit, he was really trying to understand whether Microsoft could count on this thing as an infrastructure. And at base, betting on the Net was really an act of faith. Allard had the faith, even if the more experienced minds in the room did not.

The Shumway parting was amicable. Siegelman wound up acknowledging to Allard that the Internet had great distribution. It was like a trucking company, it was all about delivery, Siegelman said. It would be foolish not to take advantage of it. Siegelman went back to work on Marvel, but in a new light. It was time to hedge his bets. He began putting in place a parallel development effort to build Internet compatibility alongside the online product. Marvel would need an Internet pipe. It would need an e-mail gateway onto the Net. It would need a way to publish on the Net as well as within its own confines. It would have to work with Allard's babies, TCP/IP and Winsock. Siegelman could not change directions, but he could bend his course a bit.

Siegelman hoped that the Net was not about to become a giant sucking sound for the online project. It seemed obvious that any Microsoft Internet offering would siphon off a certain percentage of potential Marvel customers. But there might be a way for Marvel users to take advantage of the Net when they needed to while still being captivated enough by the extras of Microsoft's environment. When over the course of proceeding months Siegelman was asked about Marvel and the Internet, he was careful never to say Microsoft's Internet strategy was wrong. Instead, he pointed out, you had to consider what you were losing when you talked about what you were winning from the Internet. Every time the Internet offered something better than MOS, Microsoft lost.

The difference between Allard and Siegelman following the Shumway retreat was simply this: Allard never for a moment thought that Siegelman was right about Microsoft's future direction. Siegelman, though, much as he would have hated to admit it, in his heart of hearts thought there was a pretty good chance that Allard just might be right.

On April 16, less than two weeks after the Shumway session, Gates issued a follow-up memo underlining the retreat's key points. Microsoft has decided to bet that the Internet will be very important, Gates wrote, with extra emphasis on the "very." At Microsoft, everyone knew that when Gates said "very," he meant "extra extra." Despite its trivial application in common speech, "very" was not a word used lightly around the company. "Product groups do not have to spend time studying the future of the Internet, or researching this phenomenon," Gates wrote. "We want to, and will, invest resources to be a leader [in] Internet support, fully understanding that if we are wrong about this it will have been a mistake."

It was important to move ahead on Internet protocols for Windows, Gates said. Get TCP/IP in there. Let's build in a quick, easy way for users to log on to the Internet. Let's make it easy for Windows users to obtain and share files over the Internet. Let's move ahead on Internet e-mail protocols. Let's enhance Microsoft Word to become a primary way for people to create and view Internet documents. Let's work on putting Microsoft support and Windows developer information onto the Internet, so our customers from all over the world can communicate with us via the Net. We need to think about security too, Gates noted. There had to be a way to prevent Internet hackers from using Windows to break into private networks. "There was a lot of discussion at the retreat about corporations wanting to let their users out onto the Internet without exposing themselves to arbitrary Internet traffic coming back into their corporate networks," Gates noted.

As for Marvel's compatibility with the Internet, Gates made the call: Siegelman's goal would be to make the online service a way to get onto the Internet. "There was a consensus that connecting our own online service, Marvel, to the Internet in a number of ways would be valuable," Gates noted. Doing so would enable Marvel subscribers to get the best of Marvel and the best of the Net. Marvel could even conceivably evolve into "supersets of the popular Internet protocols," Gates averred, suggesting that Marvel's stuff would do what the Internet did, only better, using the Net's infrastructure. Microsoft's pitch to Internet providers—the places where subscribers called in to connect up to the Internet—would be for Marvel to act as "Internet Plus." Siegelman was directed to evaluate possibly buying or licensing gateways—Internet service providers—to the Internet around the United States. The directive sent Siegelman and his team down a long and winding road involving talks with AT&T, MCI, and other phone giants.

What about something like a Microsoft Mosaic for Windows? Gates had raised the crucial issue at the outset of the Shumway session. The goal was to make it easy for Windows users to view Web pages and documents as easily as they would a Microsoft Word or Excel document. The first step, Gates said, was to make URLs—website addresses such as http://www.ford.com—the equivalent of OLE objects. Meaning that a Windows user could save a Web link just like a text file and put it in a folder or on the desktop, ready to be accessed with just a click of the mouse.

Gates directed Allard and Sinofsky to propose an "architecture and plan" for implementing the viewer strategy. Allard and Microsoft's networking team were told to come up with the features. "Since in many ways, J Allard is our public face on Internet services, I am asking him to act as a focal point for our Internet plans until we are ready to begin to publicize our on-line service, Marvel," Gates wrote. That was fine by Allard. It meant he would get to be Microsoft's No. 1 public evangelist for the Internet, a role he was already doing on an informal basis.

Viewing was the first step. Gates also wanted Windows users to be able to alter, cut and paste, revise, enhance, and otherwise edit Web documents right from Windows. Let's put an html editor in there as well, he directed. The suggestion would mean making html as universal a format as plain text, or ASCII. Web pages could pop up in Windows just as if you were using a browser. The move also implied that html might supplant Microsoft's own .doc Word format. That would be a tough sell, Gates recognized, pointing out later: "There's always this tension, should all text handling in the system be html or should you just have specialized things? . . . You don't want to have what you're looking at be any different than looking at a Web page. You want to have that standard edit control that wraps [lines of text in] mail and wraps everybody [else] in their applications. You want that to be an html control that includes links and everything."

No drumroll or fireworks accompanied the Gates memo, but history had been made. The Shumway directive marked the first official Microsoft initiative toward developing a World Wide Web browser. The path to the browser itself was still murky. Gates is not even sure the term "browser" was in play at the retreat. Mosaic was seen as in a class by itself: "I'm pretty sure what I said was we're going to put a Mosaic equivalent in. Because most of us when we talk about the terms back then, I don't think the term was browser. . . . Mostly they referred to Mosaic."

"Viewer" was the more descriptive term in Microsoft country. It drew on familiar multimedia territory—viewers were used to display graphics or video in products such as Microsoft's Encarta encyclopedia—and was a concept Microsoft developers could easily relate to. In a way, it was more accurate than "browser." Viewer suggested imagery and a window to a larger world. Browser related more to the activity of searching and retrieving, with or without accompanying imagery. Browsing was more in keeping with Tim Berners-Lee's original notion of the Web as a hyperlinked library dealing mostly in text. Viewing got at the magazine/TV metaphor better.

In any case, Gates later said, Shumway's key take-away was something that struck at the root of "Information At Your Fingertips." Whenever information was viewed, wherever it originated from, and however it got to the user, whether via the Internet or a corporate network or the computer's own hard disk, the operating system should be the vector. The only issue was how well it would get displayed. Would html, the vanilla flavor of document publishing, do the job? Or would Microsoft or someone else have to supply a more flexible and powerful technology? Later Gates summarized the pivotal consideration: "Understand, the idea that information viewing would be in the operating system, that was never a question. The question was: Is html an important enough protocol—as opposed to some that we would create ourselves, or other people would create."

When Allard saw the Gates mail, he was ecstatic. It was a crowning endorsement of the principles he had laid out in the "killer app" memo. Now it was time to get rolling. The imprimatur for www.microsoft.com, Windows' window to the Web, had been unleashed. Within days Alec Saunders, a young product manager from Ontario working on Internet support for Chicago, and a graphics designer named Rom Impas had put together what is considered to be the first Microsoft home page for general consumption. "Welcome to Microsoft's World Wide Web Server!" it announced in big bold letters. "Where do you want to go today?" Allard and Henry Sanders, the TCP/IP code captain, had the previous fall hammered together an earlier page heralding Microsoft's first built-from-scratch TCP/IP implementation. The TCP/IP project was code-named Wolverine, yet another play off a comic book superhero, and would not ship till August 1994. Allard and Sanders's page, featuring a logo for the project with the Microsoft slogan superimposed, came in the Web's infancy and got less attention, however.

The cherub-faced Saunders was yet another Sinofsky convert. During his demo run before the Shumway retreat, Sinofsky had pulled Saunders into his office while showing off his new shoes to a coworker. Check out these shoes, he said. They were white cotton canvas shoes, like something Elvis Costello might wear. The Pumas! Then Sinofsky ran Mosaic on a Macintosh. Saunders, an old hand at the Net, nonetheless saw Mosaic as a revelation. The Net was primarily good for e-mail; Mosaic took things another leap forward. Saunders immediately began teaching himself to do html programming. Soon he had put together a prototype for the first microsoft.com website.

The unusual graphic, a black half circle with a rising orange-yellow mid-section, earned the page the nickname "Death Star." Where did you want to go? There were not a whole lot of places yet. Saunders put the page together primarily as an advertisement/support tool for Microsoft software vendors and clients. In time everything from Microsoft TV to MSN and Employment Opportunities made it onto the page. Death Star stayed up till the launch of Windows 95.

Shumway would turn out to be the Internet rocket launch for lots of product groups. But the individual who walked away from Shumway most empowered, who walked away having gained the strongest enfranchisement from the Gates e-mail, was the king of Windows, Brad Silverberg. Silverberg's relationship with Siegelman had been rocky in the Windows for Workgroups phase, and Siegelman's departure had not helped things. Siegelman's effort to build a commercial online service suffered, in Silverberg's view, not just from its proprietary approach but from a key organizational problem. If you were going to put something in the next version of Windows, you had better well plan on working for Brad Silverberg. And Russ Siegelman did not work for Brad Silverberg.

By midafternoon April 5, 1994, the Shumway retreat was over and Gates was boarding a plane for Chicago, the city, where on the following day he would disclose an expanded vision for Chicago, the operating system. The coincidence was apt. After Windows 3.1 shipped, Brad Silverberg and the Windows team had conducted several design exercises aimed at figuring out what the next big upgrade would look like. At the time, the product looked as if it would dovetail with what Jim Allchin was doing with Cairo. Cairo was pretty exotic. So exotic, in fact, that people were not quite sure what it really was or did. Silverberg wanted to make the point that the next Windows was sort of on the way to Cairo but nothing close to mystical or ethereal. He and the Windows team brainstormed several code names, all having to do with other well-known cities geographically between Cairo and Redmond. There was London, New York, Boston, all the way down the line to Spokane, Washington. The closer a code name was to Redmond, the more modest the upgrade, with Spokane being just a .1 upgrade that would still be 16-bit. Silverberg's first choice was Cleveland, where he had grown up, followed by Detroit. Neither was quite glamorous enough, however. The city with the right combination of solidity and showmanship turned out to be Chicago. Silverberg had fond memories of the Windows 3.1 launch in Chicago, where Silverberg's impact on Windows development was first shown publicly. Windows 3.1 had improved on 3.0's memory management, cleaned up some nagging bugs, and sped up the operating system. It was an instant success. Silverberg hoped to top it with the next upgrade. "Chicago represented what I wanted that product to represent," he said. "Good, solid, heartland, steak and potatoes. This is software for everyman. Not New York, L.A., London, Paris."

Silverberg also knew that there was a Cairo, Illinois, not far from Chicago. But that was just a coincidence, he said. The Illinois town, for one thing, is pronounced differently (kay-ro). The main point was the working-class nature of the upgrade. The Chicago code name clicked well enough around the company to set off a long progression of "city"-related code names for Windows-related product upgrades: O'Hare, Capone, and Oprah for subsidiary Chicago technologies, and Daytona, Nashville, Memphis for further Windows upgrades. The other thing Silverberg liked about Chicago was that Interstate 90, which originated just a dozen miles southwest of the Microsoft campus, passed through the Windy City. "I told the team to get on I-90 and just keep going straight," Silverberg said. "No turns, nothing to think about on how to get there — just go." The marketing team had a jogging club that kept track of their mileage count as though they were running to Chicago.

Gates's goal in visiting the Windy City was to make sure the message got sounded: Windows and the Internet were headed for the altar. Chicago, which at the time most people thought would officially be named Windows 4.0 upon release, would include built-in Internet capabilities, Gates told columnist James Coates of the *Chicago Tribune*. It would have TCP/IP. It would provide access to the Internet through a service provider. All the plumbing to merge Windows with the Web would be there. Coates's subsequent article made national news. Within two weeks Gates was thumping Internet integration again, this time in a speech before the Annual Con-

ference and Exhibition of the Electronic Messaging Association in Ana-
heim. All the noise was starting to pique interest among Windows developers, prompting them to start peppering Microsoft with questions about its
Internet plans. Alec Saunders sent e-mail to Sinofsky asking "exactly what
it is we have committed to support." Similar queries were coming to him
from Christopher Lye in Microsoft's Developer Relations Group.

Saunders had good reason to query. There was a firestorm of interest
from developers who recalled how well the release of Windows 3.0 in 1990
had lined their pockets. Yet this time it was far from clear what Chairman
Bill was communicating in terms of developer opportunities for Windows
and the Internet. "We always end up with these situations where Bill will
announce something, and we'll all be running around like mad saying,
Man, we wish he hadn't said that!" Saunders explained. "Now what exactly
did he say?"

To get the word out over the Net about Chicago's forthcoming capabilities, Saunders set up a Chicago mailing listserv. Listservs were like virtual
birds-of-a-feather groups linked instantly by e-mail. Each piece of e-mail
one subscriber sent was delivered to all other members in a virtual roundtable discussion with no limitations of time or distance. Saunders had discovered the power of the listserv in 1993 while working for Microsoft
Canada in Mississauga, Ontario. As a way to save precious promotional dollars, he set up a mailing list for promoting Microsoft development tools.
Sales immediately spiked, "things were pretty successful, and it attracted a
bit of attention down south of the border," Saunders recalled. A year later
he had transferred to Redmond and was looking to repeat the strategy. His
Canadian success turned out to be a mere flicker compared to the bonfire
of interest sparked by the Chicago listserv. In the first twenty-four hours,
Saunders got 300,000 to 400,000 signups. The crush fried the server.

Bubbling developer interest sparked by Gates's pronouncements put
Sinofsky in somewhat of a bind. Microsoft did not want to discourage developers from beginning work on Internet applications for Chicago, but it
was too early to go public with specific Microsoft projects for the Internet.
Shumway had generated assignments for a number of attendees, but there
was little in the way of code or product yet. Saunders told Sinofsky that he
had decided to tell developers Microsoft was committed to providing Internet "plumbing" in Chicago, so they would not have to worry about supplying things like TCP/IP with their applications. Sinofsky told Lye to inform
developers that Microsoft did not have specific plans for something like
Mosaic or Cello, explaining in an e-mail: "Chicago is investigating possi-

bilities but nothing at all is public, and DRG should not be talking to anyone with the thought of including them in the box or resource kit—that is purely for Chicago/NT to deal with—though any interesting packages should of course be brought to everyone's attention."

Sinofsky's exchanges in 1998 drew the attention of the Department of Justice, which used them to suggest that Microsoft did not intend to integrate the browser with Windows. Saunders and Sinofsky later said there was no intent to foreclose Microsoft's doing its own Mosaic-type browser. Working from Saunders's cue, Sinofsky was simply trying to "avoid having our marketing evangelists specifically promoting having that capability in Chicago at that early date." Promising developers something still undefined could get the Windows folks into hot water very quickly.

As for Gates, he got reeled in soon enough. "I'm muzzled. I'm not supposed to go out and say the browser will get done for Windows 95, which I had been saying," Gates recalled. "People gave me a hard time for that!"

Gates may have been muzzled publicly, but behind the scenes, he was working the biggest stage of all—the Justice Department antitrust inquiry—to ensure Windows could integrate browsing technology. In early-summer negotiations with the Justice Department, Gates and Microsoft lawyers fought ferociously for integration rights. After a series of meetings in May with Microsoft, assistant attorney general Anne Bingaman had been ready to sue. "I didn't care what I sued them on," Bingaman later told presiding Judge Stanley Sporkin in an appeal of the decree. "I'd sue them on the licensing case. I'd sue them on vaporware. I'd sue them on anything I thought I could win the case. . . . Hey, I sort of like suing these guys." Microsoft got the message. During a frenzied three-week period in late June and early July, a legal team headed by chief Microsoft counsel Bill Neukom hammered out language for a consent decree that would avoid a Justice Department antitrust suit.

But Microsoft also wanted to ensure that it could integrate software such as a browser into Windows. On July 4 Neukom's team proposed that any settlement with the Department of Justice provide that "Microsoft will continue to develop integrated products like Chicago that provide technological benefits to end users." On July 5 the Justice Department's first draft of a proposed consent decree came back conspicuously lacking any language about integration. But Microsoft continued to raise the issue and by July 13 inserted language into a proposed decree enabling the company to develop "integrated products which offer technological advantages." At 10:30 that evening Neukom, Microsoft counsel Richard Urowsky, and other team lawyers held a conference call with Bill Gates to go over the wording. Gates was adamant that Microsoft accept no limitations on its ability to integrate. After all, just three months earlier Gates had told the world that Microsoft was integrating Internet protocols into Chicago. He was not about to jeopardize the grand plan for a consent decree based largely on complaints over ancient DOS licensing practices. Urowsky's handwritten notes of the conversation include an asterisk for emphasis next to "any integrated products"—a reference that Microsoft had to have the ability to integrate or it would lose its ability to innovate. Urowsky proposed return language to the department that the consent decree not prohibit Microsoft "from developing integrated products." Back came the response language: ". . . this provision in and of itself shall not be construed to prohibit Microsoft from developing integrated products, or necessarily to permit it to do so." The final clause, which seemed to contradict the intent of Microsoft's whole point, was dropped in the final version of the consent decree. The excision was vital, since it would have placed the kind of curb on integration that Gates specifically sought to avoid. Significantly, early on in the negotiations Gates also requested that the consent decree not cover Windows NT, a stipulation that stuck. The master chess player was still three or four moves ahead of the field. Three and a half years later the "integration" clause enabled Microsoft to win its first round against the Justice Department, when the appeals court ruled that Microsoft had the right to integrate its browser with Windows.

At the planning level, the browser remained firmly anchored on the radar screen. Six days after Shumway, Brad Chase, the DOS-Windows marketing executive who had not even been at the retreat, told the *Seattle Times* not to count the browser out of Chicago's feature set. "The big networking leap for Chicago is TCP/IP," Chase said. "The basic thing is that Chicago is going to have all the plumbing for you to hook up to the Internet. We're toying with additional things, we're always doing that stuff, but I think the key thing is that first we're going to have a protect mode version of TCP/IP, not just for hooking up to the Internet but for corporate accounts too. That means if you want to use a product like Mosaic, or any of the public configuration tools, you have the plumbing already in Chicago ready to go to do stuff like that to hook up to the Internet directly if you have an IP address." As for offering a browser, Chase said, "I wouldn't rule out our doing something like that. It's certainly something we're looking into. We recognize that's important to our customers. It's something we're exploring." Exploring. It was becoming the operative word for Microsoft's intimations at developing a browser. Brad Silverberg was on the move as well. Just days after Shumway he put together a series of slides describing the Windows group's three-year plan. One, captioned "Chicago Network Support," depicted "Integrated Net Browsing in Explorer." The group's goal, listed in another slide, was a "unified client" bringing ftp, gopher, and Web viewing together.

Eight hundred eighty-four miles to the south of Microsoft headquarters, a similar exercise in exploration—one destined to be characterized as navigation—was rolling into motion. On April 7, two days after the Shumway retreat and the day after Gates disclosed Chicago's broadened Internet-aware mission, documents were endorsed duly incorporating Electric Media, Inc., under the laws of the state of Delaware. Electric Media was meant as a placeholder for two Silicon Valley entrepreneurs, Jim Clark and Marc Andreessen, while they brainstormed the mission of their new company—the enterprise that eventually became Netscape Communications Corporation. Clark has consistently used the date April 4 as when the Silicon Valley law firm of Wilson Sonsini, under his direction, filed articles of incorporation for Netscape. But Netscape did not become the company's name till seven months later. On April 11 the same company was registered in the state of California as Delaware Electric Media, Inc. By April 12, Clark and Andreessen were in Champaign, Illinois, recruiting the original "rat pack" team of Mosaic makers from the National Center for Supercomputing Applications at the University of Illinois for their fledgling enterprise. Within a month they were opening offices in Mountain View, a faceless Silicon Valley suburb wedged between Palo Alto and Sunnyvale, under a new shingle: Mosaic Communications Corp. Clark, a legendary Silicon Valley entrepreneur who founded Silicon Graphics in 1981, does not recall being aware of Gates's Internet announcements. In any case, the timing of Microsoft's decision to build browsing into Windows gained dramatic significance four years later. In the spring of 1998 the Department of Justice, prodded by complaints from Clark and Netscape, charged that Microsoft's motivation for building the browser into the operating system was largely to crush Netscape—a company that did not even exist when the subject of browsing in Windows got on Microsoft's radar screen with e-mail, memos, and the Shumway Mansion retreat.

Chapter 8

UNDERDOG

he morning after Steve Pullner's "what think?" e-mail, Brad Silverberg read John Markoff's story in the *New York Times* about Mosaic being the treasure map to the Web. A name jumped out at him. It was not that of the NCSA's Larry Smarr, or Lotus 1-2-3's Mitchell Kapor, or even Tim Berners-Lee, although these were the most recognizable of the individuals quoted in the story. Instead it was Brian Reid, technical director of the Network Systems Laboratory for Digital Equipment Corp. in Palo Alto, who caught Silverberg's eye. Reid was a natural for Markoff to interview for a story on the Web. The two had known each other since Markoff and his then-wife Katie Hafner began researching their early study of computer hacking, *Cyberpunk: Outlaws and Hackers on the Computer Frontier.* About once a year Markoff and Reid would get together to talk over emerging trends. In late 1993 the trend Reid was most excited about was the World Wide Web.

Silverberg had been acquainted with Reid's work since the late 1970s, starting with a text processing/formatting program called Scribe that Reid developed as part of his doctoral thesis at Carnegie-Mellon University.

What made Scribe compelling was that, unlike other text processors of the day, it integrated a database and was descriptive in nature rather than directive. What that meant was that it was much easier to program a formatting command in Scribe. A descriptive term such as "header" would reference a set of commands stored in the attached database, saving the tedium of having to type out the complicated sequence. As an example, you could put the command @heading in a Scribe document, and when the document printed out it would automatically insert the header information. The header itself would be included in a database file that would list characteristics, such as 14-pt. Times Roman, centered, skip a line after, and so on. Then, if you wanted to change the title or its characteristics, you did it from the database rather than the document itself. Multiple text files could then use the same database to give a user's documents the same look and feel. The descriptive approach was to become a big deal for html, the formatting technology for Web documents. Somehow that connection clicked with Silverberg as an important contribution when he read Reid's quote, which was "Mosaic has given me a sense of limitless opportunity, which is the reason that I went into computer science." Markoff later said that he had emphasized the quotation in his article because it summed up why he had focused his journalism career on computer technology.

Limitless opportunity. Throughout his involvement with computers, Silverberg had approached any task with the view that his opportunity was wide open. Too many people boxed themselves in with preconceived notions of what was and was not possible, he felt. Anything was possible if you put your mind to it, focused, helped others and let them help you, and pursued the ultimate goal with the steadfast, battering obsession of a salmon on the spawn. Silverberg's sense of limitless opportunity had, by December of 1993, vaulted him and his teams to consecutive record sales of DOS 5, Windows 3.1, DOS 6, and Windows 3.11 releases. Now the biggest challenge of all was on his plate: Chicago, the next Windows upgrade. And suddenly the biggest opportunity of all had presented itself. Ballmer's "what think" e-mail and Markoff's "treasure map" article had created a new frontier for Windows exploration. E-mail. Chat. Newsgroups. Viewers. If the process went well, Chicago would literally become the window of Windows onto the Internet. Microsoft's long march to blend Windows with the Web had begun, and leading the phalanx was Brad Silverberg.

Born in Cleveland in 1954, Silverberg had grown up in the comfortably upper-middle-class communities of Shaker Heights and Beachwood. When he graduated from high school in 1972 he was ready to move on. Cleveland, famous as the place where a river, the Cuyahoga, caught fire at the height of the environmental awakening and for bitter race riots during the peak of racial tension in 1968, seemed an unlikely place to make a mark at the time. Silverberg had studied history and political science in high school and had an aptitude for math, but the usual career path in his social milieu was doctor or lawyer. What would he ever use math for? Silverberg looked eastward to the Ivy League and settled on Brown University in Providence, Rhode Island. What he liked was its flexibility. Brown lacked distribution requirements, a tradition it carries to this day, meaning you took whatever classes you liked. Silverberg doubted he would ever take a math or math-related class again in his life.

But after he had chosen his list of freshman year classes, mostly following on his preference for the humanities, Silverberg found he had one left-over course opening. Languages interested him, so he got in line for an entry linguistics course. Silverberg looked over the shoulder of the person in front of him and saw he was signing up for a course called AM51. Silverberg opened the course book and looked it up: Applied Math 51: Introduction to Computer Languages. Silverberg knew nothing about computers and had no idea they even had languages. On a whim he crossed out Linguistics 101 on his course sheet and wrote in AM51. He could always change his mind the next day.

Silverberg wound up going to AM51. A few classes in, he almost dropped the course. He was trying to write programs—the class had access to an IBM 360 timeshare system—but felt as if he did not click on the concept. Then one night he had a breakthrough. A doorstop inside his brain, some obstacle that was blocking his understanding of computer code, gave way and Silverberg wrote a program from scratch that worked, first time through. This was rare, especially for a beginner. Usually programming was a trial-and-error process, where a bug prevented the program from running correctly and you had to find and fix the bug by running the program several times. Now Silverberg understood the magic of the code, how it interacted with the computer, and was hooked. It was immediately addictive, the way a home-run hitter feels when he connects. He chafes to get back up at the plate and swing again. Silverberg completed the course, took a tougher class the next semester, liked it even more, and started wondering if he was doing the right thing, majoring in history when computer programming fascinated him so much. Right out of the gate his sophomore year he took the core class for the computer science major and sailed through. Suddenly he was spending all his spare time in the computer center, evenings, weekends, holidays, while interest in his major waned. "Clearly Brad was good at programming, and for some people it's practically addictive," said his professor, Andy van Dam. "You get to be creative and feel a sense of control at a much earlier stage than in physics, say, or biology." By the time he had Silverberg for a student, van Dam was already building an impressive slate of success stories in the industry. Ed Lazowska, eventually chairman of the University of Washington's computer science department; John Crawford, creator of Intel's market-leading microprocessors; and Andy Hertzfeld, one of the original Macintosh developers, all were van Dam proteges who went on to become leaders in their fields. Van Dam pioneered a process of using bright undergraduates for teaching assistants. Initially he drew criticism for pushing kids too early, but today the approach is common throughout academia. What Silverberg got from van Dam, he says to this day, was an early sense of self-confidence and an appreciation for intellectual rigor. Silverberg had been something of a slacker through high school. Brown taught him that perseverance and high standards were more rewarding than just getting by.

Silverberg felt guilty because his parents were putting him through school with the expectation of a professional career, and he had no idea what he would do with a computer science degree. He knew he could not follow a traditional trajectory and work for a monolithic computer company such as IBM or Digital Equipment. He was too independent, too small systems. Not a corporate drone. Fortunately, Silverberg's parents were understanding. Follow your heart, they told him. He switched his major to computer science, took on van Dam as his advisor, and began a structured programming project involving FORTRAN, an early mainframe programming language. The project was successful enough that in his senior year Silverberg and van Dam sold it to Raytheon Corporation, the defense contractor whose submarine work was done on Rhode Island. The pair split the $2,000 fee, giving Silverberg enough to take the summer off and tour the United States by car.

At van Dam's encouragement, Silverberg went to graduate school at the University of Toronto and got his master's degree. But he decided against going for his doctorate. He wanted to get out in the real world. After considering various geographic alternatives, he decided on going to California where he looked up fellow Brown alum John Crawford, already working at Intel. Crawford wanted Silverberg to go to work for Intel, but one thing held him back. Intel had an 8 o'clock rule. You had to be at work before 8:00 A.M. If you checked in between 8:00 and 9:00 A.M. you got a nasty note from your boss. In those days Silverberg was not a morning person. Crawford went on to develop Intel's breakthrough 386 chip, the first to handle Windows multitasking with any kind of aplomb, as well as ensuing X86 and Pentium chips. In 1992, he was named a prestigious Intel Fellow, the company's highest-ranking technical position.

Silverberg chose instead to start his career doing computer science research for SRI in Menlo Park, where he first became acquainted with the Internet. SRI was a developer of Arpanet, the Advanced Research Projects Agency Network established in 1969 that went on to serve as the basis for the Internet. In fact, SRI had been among the first to demonstrate TCP when it was first developed. Silverberg worked on a project requiring a connection to MIT. The Arpanet enabled him to link to an MIT computer as if he were sitting right in front of it—a remote terminal connection. Silverberg worked for SRI for about two years, and although he enjoyed the research, he discovered something about himself. He was a doer. He liked thinking about things, solving problems, discovering new connections. He held great respect for pure research and people who published in academic journals. But ultimately, conceptualizing was only half the fun. The real reward came with implementation.

After a brief stint at Exxon Office Systems, Silverberg was off to Apple and the job that changed his life. He worked on local-area-network projects and the Lisa, the pioneering point-and-click computer that preceded the Macintosh, but at $10,000 cost far too much to have an impact. During his LAN work Silverberg became a stalwart supporter of Internet standards. Apple, in the midst of developing a closed online network called AppleNet, was building from scratch protocols equivalent to those Silverberg knew were functioning already on the Internet.

Silverberg deemed it pure folly to re-create Internet protocols for Apple's network technology, but he had no authority to make the call. These were the Silicon Valley gods who had evangelized the Apple II into the hearts and minds of America. Silverberg thought it wiser to absorb and learn. But other instances of misguided thinking kept cropping up. While working on the Lisa, Apple decided to make its own floppy disk drives, dubbed Twiggy drives. Disk drives were hardly a core competency at Apple, however, and the Twiggys never worked right. Silverberg also watched in consternation as the Lisa team developed applications and hardware before the operating system was finalized. As a result, the project suffered acute planning overhang. The Lisa was designed to accommodate an operating system requiring 512K of memory; the actual system required a megabyte. It was supposed to be floppy-disk based; the actual system required a hard disk, virtually quintupling the price. The file system was far too slow. Separate teams working on various elements of the Lisa figured all the pieces would fall together when they were done. There would be a flash of light and *poof!* it would work like magic. In reality the project was a comedy of mismatches. The leg bone never quite connected to the hip bone, and in making the fixes Apple drove the price of the Lisa beyond affordability.

Silverberg had a couple of memorable encounters with the mercurial Steve Jobs. Although he spent most of his time on the Lisa, Silverberg was following Jobs's Macintosh project with keen interest. The Mac team was avoiding the miscoordination of the Lisa project, and Silverberg liked its small, compact approach. He also liked the idea of a cheap, end-user-oriented personal computer. Where the Mac was going to suffer, however, was in expandability. If it caught on, the Mac was going to have to grow with its buyers' needs. That meant it would need the ability to add more memory and data storage capacity.

Silverberg argued that the Mac, designed to run only on floppy disks, should have a hard disk. When, largely for cost considerations, that suggestion went nowhere, he told Jobs that the Mac should at least have a fast data port where an external hard drive could be added. That way at least you'll be building for the future, Silverberg said, and savvy customers will know they can beef up their systems. Jobs cocked his head skeptically and stared straight at Silverberg with his characteristic dark, fierce eyes. That's the stupidest thing I've ever heard, how could you even imagine something so dumb? he said, invoking the standard Jobs putdown. As for memory, Silverberg had the temerity to propose to Jobs that the original Mac should contain an extra row of sockets, so that when memory chips jumped from 32 kilobytes to 64 kilobytes, users could add enough memory to reach a then-whopping 1 megabyte, making the Mac competitive with IBM PCs and clones. Again the conversation was fairly one-sided.

All too quickly history proved Silverberg correct. Although he lasted only two years at Apple, he learned more there than in any other job. Mostly he learned what *not* to do. How not to act. How not to treat new ideas and innovative suggestions and fellow workers. And he learned to trust his instincts. To follow through on what he believed, even when it ran against the grain of accepted practice.

A Silverberg colleague at Apple, Eric Michelman, was leaving to start a database company with a friend, Adam Bosworth. Silverberg needed little persuading to go along. (All three eventually went into key product development at Microsoft.) The resulting company, Analytica, had a momentary hit with a flat-file database called Reflex. Reflex ran in memory, which meant it was fast. But its plus was also its minus. Running in memory limited the size of the database. Users were building bigger and bigger databases and were outgrowing Reflex's capacity. Analytica's venture funding ran dry before the team could address Reflex's limitations, and the company was purchased by Borland International. Borland CEO Philippe Kahn did his usual trip and dropped Reflex's price from $495 to $99. Sales briefly spiked, enough to more than recoup acquisition costs. After the initial spurt, though, Borland let Reflex wither and die.

Silverberg liked Borland, a young company with lots of esprit de corps. His most memorable time there came with the scheduled release of Quattro Pro, Borland's entry into the spreadsheet arena. On October 17, 1989, the day before Quattro was scheduled to be released to manufacturing (meaning the day it would be given to the warehouse for duplication and production), the Loma Prieta earthquake struck. Its epicenter was just two miles from Borland's Scotts Valley headquarters. The quake jolted the building Silverberg and the Quattro team occupied enough to rupture the main supporting beam. If the tremor had gone on two more seconds, a structural engineer later said, the building would have collapsed. Silverberg fled the structure and was standing outside when his heart sank. Still inside, he realized, were backup media—tapes and disks—containing all of Borland's intellectual property. They had to come out before an aftershock reduced the entire building to rubble.

Silverberg and a lead software engineer scrambled back inside and retrieved the backups, storing everything in Silverberg's Subaru station wagon. There was just one problem. Silverberg lived in Saratoga, over the hill and back down to Silicon Valley. The roads were reportedly a mess. Silverberg, an avid cyclist, had taken his bike to work that day and ridden at noon. While he could easily have biked back roads to get home, there was no way he was going to leave the intellectual property of a $700 million company unattended in his car. Silverberg drove the Subaru home, managing to skirt several roadblocks on the way.

The next day the Quattro Pro team was back at work. Computers, many of them waterlogged from the fire-sprinkler system and unable to boot, were hauled out into the parking lot to dry off. Some actually got up and running, and the team was able to finish the Quattro release. In commemoration of the achievement, they time-stamped the code 5:03 P.M. The earthquake was 5:04 P.M. The company had T-shirts made up reading "Borland:

The epicenter of software development," with bull's-eyes painted around Scotts Valley. This was the kind of kick-butt resilience that Silverberg loved, and Borland was brimming with it.

Despite its success in software languages, Borland had never been able to lay clear claim to No. 1 in a mainstream product. As a result, it played the perennial we-try-harder role. Kahn loved to fire up his troops with David versus Goliath comparisons. He would call Silverberg in and go off about what Microsoft was doing to persecute Borland. We're just this little company trying to eke out our fair share, make a decent living in the software business! We're just a bunch of immigrants off the boat! Have mercy on us! Silverberg himself would milk the Microsoft bogeyman for all it was worth. It got his teams motivated. During the Silverberg tenure, the underdog concept was institutionalized at Borland.

In February 1989 a headhunter called Silverberg on behalf of a "company in Redmond." Silverberg expressed interest and a few days later got a call at home from Gates himself. The two connected immediately. Really high energy, Silverberg later recalled. Gates made a persuasive pitch about the high level of responsibility Silverberg would be granted—a vice presidency, rare for an outsider to step into cold. And Gates impressed Silverberg with his command of technology and ability to articulate Microsoft's goals.

Gates had been impressed with Silverberg's accomplishments, particularly in programming languages that competed with Microsoft. "People knew Brad was good at working with developers and motivating developers," Gates later recalled. "After the first time I met with [him], the dynamic was totally what do we have to do to bring you here. It wasn't, Hmmm, are you the right guy to come here?" Microsoft had under way a database project for Windows code-named Omega—in the hope the Greek alphabetic reference would make it the final word in databases and not, as it was looking more and more to be, a complete and total dead end. Silverberg had the right blend of database background, team leadership capability, and out-of-the-box thinking to turn Omega around. As a sweetener, given Omega's checkered history, Gates was willing to throw in responsibility for Excel, the flagship Windows application and a proven moneymaker. Microsoft put the full-court press on Silverberg. In mid-1989 Ballmer, applications chief Mike Maples, president Jon Shirley, and Gates had several conversations with him. Gates even flew down to Silicon Valley to meet with Silverberg, who arranged for a private room in the back of an out-of-the-way restaurant. If anyone saw them together, Silverberg reasoned, the news would take all of twenty seconds to get back to Philippe. The valley was an incestuous Peyton Place of gossip and intrigue, and Silverberg did not want the rumor machine set in motion on his account.

Silverberg liked Gates. He had a warmth, charm, and sense of humor that seldom emerged in his public persona. Over the years Silverberg had gotten to know Gates and Ballmer a bit, mostly through competition in languages. Borland's languages usually beat Microsoft's in industry reviews and contests, including *PC Magazine's* annual Technical Excellence Awards given at Comdex. Silverberg found Gates and Ballmer gracious losers, curious about how Borland managed to be so successful, and complimentary of Borland's successes. It was obvious to Silverberg that Gates and Ballmer cared passionately about software and were involved down to the core in Microsoft's products and strategy. They admired technical achievement in others as well as their own products and, Silverberg thought, cared more about raising their own standards as high as possible than squelching competition. Still, Silverberg viewed Microsoft's relentlessness and obsession to do better with a mixture of awe and fear. No one combined the gifts of business acumen, strategic thinking, and understanding of technology as Gates did. People called him lucky, a beneficiary in the IBM deal of being in the right place at the right time. Silverberg thought of it as preparedness. Gates was always willing to try something new, to develop three or four strategies simultaneously and go with the one that panned out. Gates did not play just one hand. He was like the chess master competing on several boards at the same time. Gates had been involved in DOS, Windows, the Mac, OS/2, even UNIX. When the winner emerged, he was there, ready to take advantage. To a great extent, Silverberg thought, opportunity meant preparedness.

Most important, Gates offered no limits on opportunity. Silverberg sensed that although Gates might challenge you on an idea or question a suggestion, he was merely testing your ability to defend it and your commitment to follow through on it. If you stated your case and backed up your words with action, Gates was never going to stand in your way.

In the grand scheme of things, Silverberg also felt that Gates and Microsoft would make an unparalleled imprint on history. When historians recorded the twentieth century, there would be a significant chapter on personal computers and the information revolution. And Gates and Microsoft would be a major part of that chapter. Silverberg wanted to be able to tell his grandkids "I was there. I worked with that guy." Silverberg had been in the industry for fifteen years, had met and worked with some of the best minds around, but Gates was the pinnacle. The smartest guy.

Nonetheless, Silverberg felt torn by Gates's offer. Four award-winning years had given him a lot of loyalty to founder and CEO Philippe Kahn and the gang at Borland. Silverberg wanted to see the company go public in affirmation of the work he had done, and he was not finished building an organization strong enough to survive his leaving. But he also had doubts about Borland's long-term strategy. Even though the company was growing fast and doing well, it had a tendency to overextend itself. Software sold in cycles. One product had to be doing well while another one or two were under development or revision. Silverberg saw little planning for the down cycle. Borland would have a great quarter, hire lots of people, get excited about its press clippings, and try to be the next Microsoft. That led to budget crises, layoffs, having to refocus and scramble. It was no way to manage over the long term, and Silverberg, who endured the whole cycle twice, came to the conclusion it was endemic to Borland culture. Eventually, too many lean quarters would line up and Borland would collapse.

After getting some promises from Kahn on key management issues, Silverberg decided to stay at Borland. But the promises soon fell through. Within a couple of months he decided to eat humble pie and try Microsoft again. If you have the right job for me, I'm ready, he told Gates. Two days later Gates got back to him with an offer that made Silverberg think he'd died and gone to heaven. How would you like to head up DOS and Windows development? Gates asked. For Silverberg, the job not only addressed his interests and skills honed over the years in a variety of positions, it gave him the chance of a lifetime to build something really, truly high impact. As a Windows beta tester at Borland, Silverberg deemed it patently obvious that Windows was going to be a big hit, because it built on the huge DOS base of users and enabled a smooth upward transition from DOS. It had the right combination of familiarity, because of its DOS underpinnings, and newness, with its graphical interface, to get users to make the plunge. It was going to mark the next personal computing sea change, Silverberg was certain.

Even before Gates made him the offer, Silverberg knew in his own mind what Windows should look and perform like. Windows 3.0 was a great step, but he knew from his work on the Apple Lisa that Windows was only about halfway home. The next big upgrade—what would turn into Windows 95—was already in the back of Silverberg's mind. Now he was being given the chance to make his dream happen. Everything up to this point in his life seemed mere preparation for the challenge that lay ahead.

By early March 1990 Silverberg was ready to accept the Microsoft offer. Although he had his dream assignment with the DOS-Windows team, enormous challenges lay ahead. With DOS 5, Ballmer was proposing something new: retail sales. Previously DOS had been available only with the purchase of a new computer. This kept piracy down and made it easier to account for DOS sales, but it meant that the usual way to get a better version of DOS was to buy a new computer. But the rules of the game were changing. Digital Research, the company that had blown the chance to sell IBM an operating system for the original PC in 1981, was issuing an improved version of its DR DOS. Microsoft needed a retail product to compete. When Silverberg resigned from Borland on March 30, 1990, DOS versions 2 through 4 were running on PCs. A retail upgrade would not only present a huge revenue potential for Microsoft, it would get the bulk of PC users standardized on a single, current, updated version of DOS. That in turn would enable applications software vendors to upgrade their programs. It would be an all-around win for the industry.

Silverberg liked the notion of a retail DOS for another reason: It would get his team more pumped up about doing a high-quality product. Doing software for computer manufacturers was a perfunctory process with little feedback. All computer makers wanted was the code. Computer makers needed DOS because a computer needed a salable operating system. Apart from that, they did not particularly care what type of operating system they installed, who produced it, or how many features it had. The operating system was just a way of helping them get the computer out the door. On those terms it was hard to generate much excitement from the DOS development team. How could Microsoft's team get pumped up about a product when customers did not care what kinds of bells and whistles it had? It was kind of like working for the government.

With a retail upgrade, things would be different. You knew it had to be good or people would not buy it. And if it was good enough for people to buy, you knew you would be getting plenty of feedback, bad as well as good. But it would help you in the long run make a better product the next time around.

Silverberg took a couple of months to get moved and settled. In May he attended the Windows 3.0 launch in New York City but almost did not make it through security. No one recognized him; he did not yet have his official Microsoft ID. Here was the future brain trust of DOS and Windows, and he could not even get a pass to Microsoft's biggest launch ever! Silverberg was standing around with his hands in his pockets when Marianne Allison, a Microsoft PR liaison, happened by. Allison, containing her amusement at the irony of the situation, managed to get Silverberg admitted to the show. He officially began work in June 1990.

Silverberg brought a pensive, resolute, thinking-man's style to Microsoft. He was not the type, as many Microsoft managers were, to jump into the middle of an arms-waving debate with raised voice and agitated gesticulations. An avid bicyclist whose wiry build was perfect for riding up the long, winding hills not far from the Microsoft campus, Silverberg liked to take thirty- to forty-mile spins to sort out a problem or think through a plan of action. He made sure a course of action was right before he took it. Once he decided, he moved with the silent speed and power of a Stealth aircraft. Silverberg's penetrating blue eyes and raw, lean features, bibbed in a coal-black beard that offset advancing baldness, imparted a lock-tight focus and iron will that could come across as aloofness until you got to know him. Once you did, you understood that his intensity was merely an outward manifestation of his caring nature and appreciation for hard work, integrity, and dedication.

What Silverberg found upon his arrival at Microsoft did not particularly impress him. DOS 5 had just entered its first beta. Silverberg did not think it had enough features. I think we need to take a harder look at this, he told the team. We want to avoid a repeat of the DOS 4 disaster—the do-nothing upgrade that had flopped under IBM's stewardship. We want a product we can be proud of, that really moves the technology forward. To figure out how DOS 5 could be improved, the testing feedback loop needed to be bigger, Silverberg reasoned. Much bigger. Customarily, beta software was distributed among a few hundred testers—valued customers, friends, colleagues, and whatnot. Silverberg saw all those DOS 2.X, 3.X, and 4 computers out there with the potential for upgrading to DOS 5. To make sure the program would install and run correctly, however, the DOS 5 beta had to be tested on all those different makes of computer.

Silverberg foresaw the need for a huge beta test—not hundreds but *thousands* of testers. It was something that had never been done before, and he knew it would not be popular in-house. Managing a huge beta test would be orders of magnitude more work. To persuade his team of the need for better testing, Silverberg asked his programmers to spend a week manning a phone line for Microsoft Product Support and Services. In the wake of Windows 3.0, the company was being pounded by bug reports and unhappy users. Silverberg wanted his people to hear customer pain firsthand. (Besides, at that point the PSS crew needed all the help they could get.) The concept, accepted with much grumbling and skepticism, worked. It got the programming team to understand its challenge and take responsibility for the product's quality. The personal contacts gave a face and voice to the amorphous issue of software reliability. The more Microsoft's developers and designers could get in contact with customers, Silverberg reasoned, the better the company's products would be. Particularly useful for the beta feedback process were electronic forums on CompuServe. The forums not only let testers air complaints and offer suggestions, they enabled them to share and compare their experiences with the software. That led to a lot of informal swapping of workarounds and other solutions and built a core community of Windows users who could evangelize the product. CompuServe forums were populated by sharp, laser-witted PC users who were quick to point out Windows' shortcomings but would just as ardently defend its strengths. The forums taught Silverberg the value of the online feedback loop. He came to the same conclusion as Bill Joy. Joy's law held that no matter how many smart people you hired, most of the smart people in the world did not work for you. Silverberg's corollary read: The sun never sets on people trying to extend, or improve on, Windows. The large-scale beta helped draw more of those smart people into Microsoft's development process. Silverberg would spend two to three hours a day on CompuServe forums, monitoring feedback.

Silverberg continued the big-beta policy through subsequent operating system releases at Microsoft: Windows 3.1, Windows for Workgroups 3.1, DOS 6 and 6.2, Windows for Workgroups 3.11. The large-scale beta became a core competency of Microsoft, a huge and often overlooked strategic advantage in getting its software to be, on the whole, compatible with the vast and diverse constellation of PCs in use. Silverberg is convinced that without the broad public beta, DOS and Windows would have taken years longer to reach their relative maturation.

When Silverberg read the Brian Reid quote about limitless opportunity in December 1993, it triggered something that had been working in the back of his mind for some time. The ultimate goal of his stair-step DOS-Windows upgrade strategy was to leapfrog the Macintosh. One area where the Mac was clearly outdistancing Windows was on the Internet. Macintoshes had much stronger TCP/IP and networking support. At the time, Macs were also popular as servers on the Internet. So Silverberg played a mental game with himself. If I'm Apple, he asked himself, and I saw

Chicago coming down the pike, what would I be doing? I would be trying to identify the next paradigm shift and taking advantage. I would be trying to change the rules on Microsoft, to find the next paradigm and stay one step ahead in the innovation race. So I would try to remake the company around the Internet and establish in consumers' minds that Apple equals the Internet. It was clear to Silverberg that for the next big release of Windows, the one that combined DOS and Windows into a single operating system, Microsoft would have to match or exceed the Internet capabilities of the Macintosh.

Silverberg also saw Chicago as a breakthrough networking product for Windows. Since his arrival, he had pressed for networking to be built into Windows. This stuff should be part of the operating system, he told Gates in one of their first conversations. It should just be built in. Gates had no problem accepting that sentiment. Microsoft's shift away from OS/2 meant that its networking initiative needed to shift to Windows.

Silverberg chose the NetWorld conference in Dallas in mid-October 1991 to get the word out about Windows' new capabilities. His theme at the gathering: Windows Is Everywhere! "Windows Everywhere" was the latest wrinkle in the Gates-Microsoft slogan of a computer on every desk and in every home and a reiteration of a mantra Nathan Myhrvold had been talking up at Microsoft since 1989. At NetWorld, Silverberg noted that Windows had become, in just a year and a half since the release of version 3.0, the standard client interface, meaning that a majority of people were using Windows when they logged on to networks. Windows was starting to emerge as a networking force, posing for the first time a Microsoft challenge to Novell NetWare's dominance.

It would be a journey of many steps, however. Windows 3.1, a revision urgently needed to address memory-management issues, was released too early—on April 6, 1992—to accomplish a full network implementation. Waiting till the next major upgrade cycle in a year or more seemed too long. The solution was to go with an "enhanced" Windows—Windows for Workgroups 3.1—for networking support. On October 27, 1992, six and a half months after the release of Windows 3.1, Windows for Workgroups 3.1 entered the chute. A year later, on November 15, 1993, it was upgraded to Windows for Workgroups 3.11 and featured even more robust networking support. It was also a leap forward in Internet networking, featuring improved TCP/IP support. The fast revision track had Silverberg arguing for numerical differentiation. Going from Windows 3.1 to Windows for Workgroups 3.11, he thought, was as big, if not bigger, a jump as Windows 3.1

had been from Windows 3.0. So why not Windows 3.2? he wondered. Particularly since WfW 3.2 would have a 32-bit file system. Silverberg liked the idea of a numerical pun. In the end, Ballmer vetoed the 3.2 designation. It was a rare miscall, in Silverberg's mind, and wound up costing 3.11 a lot of sales because few users knew how beneficial an upgrade it was. Even so, WfW 3.11, with faster disk access as well as Internet compatibility, did land office business for Microsoft. Gates wound up calling 3.11 the most sensational .01 release in the history of software—in public, at least. In private he was more colorful, calling it the "most motherfucking .01 release."

The Windows 3.X run had been a long and successful one for the Microsoft systems team. But Silverberg knew he had to kill his babies. The next step for Windows had to be a dramatically clear leap forward with network and Internet support. By the time Ballmer sent around his "what think" e-mail, Silverberg was sensing a limitless opportunity built around Mosaic. It occurred to him that hyperlinking and page displays, usually performed by the browser, were functions that the operating system also did well. It seems silly, he thought, to have one method for things on my desktop computer and another method for the network. Just as Windows had made DOS easier to use, eliminating typed commands like dir c:\bin\forums\compusrv*.doc and the duress of having to remember hard-drive directory structures, the Web was liberating users from the complexity of networks—having to remember multiple drive letters, long file names, subdirectories, special-purpose applications. Networks usually contained a wealth of information, but no one used it because they did not know where it was kept or how to reach it. It was like having an itch that you could not reach to scratch. Somehow the user's experience with Windows and with the Web ought to be united into one seamless experience that took advantage of both worlds.

By the time of the Shumway retreat, Silverberg was convinced that the next version of Windows had to have profound Internet support and that the Internet would help drive adoption of the new upgrade. The Shumway debate convinced Silverberg all the more that the Internet was the way to go for Microsoft's online services. He harkened back to Apple's not-invented-here syndrome, the insistence that network protocols had to be invented all over again. A proprietary online service was doomed to failure, Silverberg was certain.

For Silverberg, Shumway was a good summation of where the company stood regarding the Internet and online services. It was a bonding experience for the Internet idealists within Microsoft. And it was a good mechanism for Gates to be exposed to the Internet side of the online service argument. Silverberg sensed that because of Gates's close relationship with Siegelman and Myhrvold, the chairman had been hearing a one-note song. Nevertheless, for Silverberg, Shumway was hardly an earthshaking occasion. He listened to the debate of online versus the Internet with interest. It was an intriguing psychological dynamic for Microsoft, but it had little impact on his thinking. His mind was made up. Shumway merely reaffirmed the need for him to keep moving down the trail he had already been blazing. As far as he was concerned, the debate could continue without him. The Windows effort could not afford to sit on its hands, waiting for an elusive consensus to emerge. By then it would be way, way too late.

So Silverberg started the Chicago team down an Internet path that was in many ways parallel to the goals of Siegelman's online effort. Chicago was firmly in the camp of supporting open Internet protocols for things like e-mail, security, and dialing up from home. Marvel was building its service from the ground floor up, on its own e-mail and publishing and dial-up protocols, with the hedge that if users wanted Internet access, they would be able to get there from Microsoft's online service.

The Siamese-twin approach had enormous inefficiencies in development and personnel overlap. It was the kind of budget drain most executives and big companies would never countenance. Choose one or the other, they would direct their managers. But Gates saw benefits to multitasking the online strategy. It gave him the chance again to play two hands at once, as Microsoft had with parallel OS/2 and Windows development. Competition was important, even if it was internal. And Gates was loath to discourage entrepreneurialism within his ranks. Creative tension was needed in an organization for it to thrive and move forward. Gates was not going to stand in the way of a process that would save Microsoft from becoming a Wang or an Apple or a Lotus or an IBM.

Gates also was caught in the bind of the Silverberg-Siegelman personality conflict. It too was nothing new in Microsoft's competitive, ego-driven culture: "It's just another thing you have to manage," Gates said later. In this case, he saw benefits to a macro, not micro, managed approach. He had given Siegelman the green light well before the Net was a factor. And at the Shumway retreat he had made it obvious that Silverberg was to integrate the Internet into Windows. Gates was like the basketball coach having two point guards play one-on-one to see who would get the starting assignment.

After the Shumway retreat, Silverberg met with Phil Barrett, a lead systems manager who had just joined the Windows 95 development effort. Silverberg asked him to look at how Internet capabilities could be woven into Chicago. Included on the list were Allard's initiatives regarding TCP/IP, ftp, telnet, WAIS, auto dialer, and other Net access features. Silverberg added another item to the laundry: browsing capability. Should we include a browser with Chicago? he asked Barrett. What would be the browser's role vis-à-vis Chicago connectivity with the Web? Should we build it ourselves, from the ground floor up? What would that take, in terms of resources and time? Would it be better to license or buy existing technology and improve on it? Silverberg did not want to rush headlong into a drain on Microsoft resources. There were lots of browsers out there, after all, and little discernible demand. There was still plenty of time, it seemed, for Microsoft to make its play in the browser sweepstakes.

Barrett hired two part-time program managers and by midsummer had a college intern on hand to help out with product management. But his primary focus was on Chicago, not the Internet. "Everyone was focused on getting Chicago out," he recalled. "Bill may have said the Internet is very, very important, but organizationally, I don't think that took right away at all." Barrett took on the assignment, but for him the Internet was not a huge action item. As for the browser, Barrett had heard nothing about integrating it into Windows at the Shumway retreat, and he felt little urgency to pursue the issue.

For Silverberg, however, browsing in Windows was a top priority. The Windows three-year plan he presented after Shumway specifically outlined "integrated Net browsing in [Windows] Explorer." He was not sure what form it would take, but browsing needed to be there. On board as well was John Ludwig. "It was clear from Shumway that we needed to Internet-enable our operating systems much, much, much more, and that a browser was the most important part of this," Ludwig later recalled, even if all the t's were not crossed or the i's dotted.

Six weeks after the retreat, Silverberg attended Windows World at Spring Comdex in Atlanta, with an eye toward finding out what Windows vendors were doing with the Internet. Sinofsky was there with a similar goal in mind. The two hooked up and strolled the floor together. In a tiny booth tucked away on a side aisle they found gold—or at least some glitter. Book-Link Technologies, Inc., a small software developer based in Wilmington, Massachusetts, was showing an early iteration of Internetworks, browsing technology that integrated tightly with Windows. Silverberg and Sinofsky had learned of BookLink from Allard, who knew one of the company's principals, Bill Hawkins, through various Internet conferences. Hawkins, who struck Allard as a super-bright guy, had been telling Allard how well Book-Link would work with Windows in a browser. You guys really need this, Hawkins said. It's a great way to leverage Windows on the Web. Allard agreed, even if after a preliminary look he had concluded that BookLink's technology was a better Windows application than Web browser—almost the opposite of Mosaic, which was a much better browser than Windows application. But Allard thought highly enough to nudge Silverberg and Sinofsky BookLink's way.

What particularly caught the pair's eyes was BookLink's use of Windows OLE—object linking and embedding. OLE put data produced by Windows applications together into richly formatted documents, then made it available for group use and live revision right from the whole document without having to call up each separate application. So a chart from Excel and a text file from Word and graphic from Paint could be manipulated and edited right within the annual report, say, or company brochure itself. As Ballmer had suggested in his "what think" message, OLE's implications for the Web were formidable: Windows documents and data stood to become the standard way Web users published their information.

There was another appealing aspect to BookLink's approach. Internet-works was componentized. You could build its browsing capability into an application you were doing for the Web. This made accessing the Web faster and easier. No going through the browser separately to get to a certain link or provide a certain page. No having to use the browser's interface for your application. It made the application feel "Web ready." And it kept the application's look and feel intact, even when the user was accessing Web material. Componentization provided application developers with a lot more flexibility, in other words, when building Web access into their software products. It also saved them a huge amount of work by not having to write their own browser code. Again, the Ballmer notion of integration with the Internet was manifest.

The two Microsoft executives had a chat with the BookLink booth-minders and agreed to continue the discussion. "We were impressed with their implementation of Windows technology," Silverberg recalled. At the time he and Sinofsky had no way of knowing just how long the discussions between the companies would continue, or how consuming a challenge Microsoft's quest for browser technology was destined to become.

Chapter 9

BLUE

Peter Pathe walked out of the Shumway retreat with rockets in his shoes. As the recently appointed head of Microsoft Word development, Pathe (pronounced path-hay) was adamant that Word should be the way Internet users created documents for the Internet. For more than four months, since assuming responsibility for Word over the 1993 holiday season, Pathe had been making the rounds, telling everyone who would listen that Word had to be the publishing tool of choice for the Net. Not everyone was interested. Even those who were tended to greet Pathe's pitch with a sideways glance, a knitted-brow, or a blank stare. Some thought he was chasing butterflies, others that he was wasting his time. The most frequent comment he got in response to his crusade was a single word: Why? The Word team had enough on its table just adding features and capabilities to the next up-grade. Why complicate things with functionality that looked to be margin-ally necessary at best and a drain on resources at worst?

Pathe had the sort of disarming persistence that can plow through the most daunting obstacles, however. Keep talking it up, and eventually you'll strike a chord, he figured. One person he mentioned his idea to lit up like the Christmas tree in Rockefeller Center. Yes! Steven Sinofsky exclaimed. Great idea! You've really got to do this! Sinofsky was in the process of putting together his invitation list for the Shumway retreat. Boom: Pathe was on it in an instant. You've got to come to the Internet brainstorming session. Pathe needed little persuasion. It looked like a great place to bring along his soap box.

In assuming responsibility for Word, Pathe had followed in august footsteps. Chris Peters, a popular Microsoft longtimer, and his team had taken Word to new heights of functionality, adding things like autocorrect, which corrected a typo like "teh" to "the" automatically and made the first letter of a sentence upper case. Peters had spent hours studying Word usage in Microsoft's usability lab and was intent on reducing the drudgery of document production. Autocorrect turned out to be a killer feature, one that anyone who spent lots of time at a keyboard instantly appreciated. Word 6 also had AutoFit, AutoSelect, AutoFormat—all designed to automate functions that previously took lots of clicks and drags. In all, Word had gained more than 170 new features. It was a triumph that, for the first time, put WordPerfect clearly behind in the power-user race for word processing. Now Peters was moving on to take his usability brilliance to the entire Office set of applications—which in addition to Word included Excel, PowerPoint, and Access. Pathe could not have had a tougher act to follow.

Peters made it as easy as he could on his successor. When it came time for the changeover, Pathe paid Peters a visit. They exchanged pleasantries, and Peters said, Okay, it's transition time. He got up from his chair and said, Here's your desk, that's your chair, here's your computer, there's the phone, let me know if you need anything. And then he took off down the hall. Peters was basically telling Pathe: This thing is all yours, do with it what you will. Do not worry about carrying on someone else's vision. Do your own. It may mean accepting full blame for anything that goes wrong. More likely you will get to claim full success for whatever goes right. For someone with only a couple of years under his belt at Microsoft, the handoff was a welcome affirmation of Pathe's instincts and a confirmation that Word was all his baby.

The first thing he needed to do, Pathe decided, was to get his baby up and crawling on the Internet.

Pathe had barely settled in when two applications managers, Eric LeVine and Michael Cockrill, stopped by to say hello. It turned out they were working with sgml, which stood for standard generalized markup language. Sgml could translate different document formats, making it a great tool for environments like the Internet that had to handle a variety of formats. Sgml's approach harkened back to Brian Reid's work with Scribe that had so impressed Brad Silverberg, using a descriptive approach to reference complex formatting commands. In the case of Word, sgml held potential application for making Word's .doc format sympatico with the Internet. Pathe brightened immediately, which took LeVine and Cockrill aback, as they were used to headscratching responses. You have to do this, it's just the right thing, Pathe told the pair. Cockrill and LeVine exchanged surprised glances, smiled a bit sheepishly, and said, No one has ever said that to us before.

As it happened, Pathe knew all about sgml. While he had doubts that it was the right thing for what Word needed to accomplish vis-à-vis the Internet, he knew it was important to get the Word team thinking about Internet integration. Said Pathe: "A few weeks after that I asked Eric and Michael if we could add some Internet protocol software to the project and enable it to load and edit html directly from the Net, including the ability to follow hyperlinks. They said sure, and that's when I knew that somehow or other we were going to make this happen."

Pathe instituted another ploy for getting Word onto the Net. With Reed Koch, head of Word product planning, he put together a project called "Word Everywhere" that promulgated the notion of Word being a universal reader of documents, whether paper based or digital, whether printed out or on the Internet. At heart it looked like a master plan to overtake Word-Perfect, which as of early 1994 was still the No. 1 word processing program. But Pathe thought a horse race was too shortsighted. The Internet held far more potential growth than WordPerfect's user base. Use Word to read Internet e-mail. Use Word to compose and display Internet documents. Use Word for interoffice communications over the Net. Wherever you used words on the Net, use Word. Koch's team put together a slick demo, demonstrating concepts that were to become cornerstones of document handling and display on the Net. Several were not fully realized until Office 2000, released in beta in late 1998.

Word's makeover as the default Internet viewer for text documents had begun.

Born in Boston, Pathe had grown up in Ashland, Massachusetts, and graduated from high school there. Somewhere in high school, he does not remember exactly how, Pathe picked up the unlikely nickname of Blue. He did not particularly care for the moniker, but it stuck. He tried to shake it when moving cross country to continue his education at Cal Tech, but mail kept arriving at his dorm addressed to Blue. There is nothing blue about the way Pathe acts or his color choices. He does not even have the kind of bluish fluorescent skin tone afflicting many a computer geek; his most distinctive personal feature is his crown of thick, straight, jet-black hair. Nothing about his tastes in music or art suggest blue. Nor is his insistently buoyant disposition anywhere close to the common synonym for depression. If anything, he's the antonym of blue. Perhaps the contradiction is what made the nickname stick. It turned out to be a popular choice at Microsoft, where Pathe eventually adopted it for his logon: blue@microsoft.com. And then had to endure constant kidding. Sinofsky asked Pathe "if he would call me, like, Beige."

Pathe got his degree in engineering and applied science from Cal Tech but missed the East Coast and soon afterward moved to Cambridge. In 1977 he signed up with a mainframe systems company called Intermetrics. Intermetrics was strictly big iron—mainframes and minicomputers—but what Pathe remembers most is its work on global positioning systems. Some day, the vision went, a soldier in the field would be able to find his unit just by carrying around a backpack-size GPS. Wow, Pathe thought, to get all that electronics capacity down to the size of a backpack, that would be something. By the mid-1990s GPS units fit easily in the palm of a hand.

Pathe's work at Intermetrics got him interested in computer graphics, languages, compilers, and printers. This was the dawn of the personal computer era, though, and he was feeling restless with big systems. A friend at Intermetrics knew some people at MIT's Architecture Machine Group, destined with half a dozen other research groups to form jointly the school's renowned Media Lab. Pathe paid a visit. It blew him away. The group was doing some radical thinking on the notions of document production and publishing, and Pathe was sold. He signed up for a master's program and jumped into a project for group leader Walter Bender. Over a weekend the two built voice and gesture commands for a Rubik's Cube animation Bender had put together. Subsequently the two worked to develop a customized information service called NewsPeek. The goal was to take news from online databases—Dow Jones News Retrieval, Nexis, XPress, wire services, and TV news—and turn it into a thinking machine that created custom newspapers automatically, without the user having to do any searching or browsing or even thinking about what he or she wanted to read that day.

News services sucked information from hundreds of leading newspapers and journals into a giant text archive, which they licensed back to news providers, Wall Street, research institutions, and others needing in-depth research data. Many, like Nexis, were treasure troves of information. But their user interfaces were like some kind of encrypted hieroglyph out of an Edgar Allan Poe short story. You needed special instructions to access their material, and even trained specialists hated the thing. The NewsPeek team wanted to put the Nexis database to good use without exposing people to its interface, so they hooked Nexis into an Interdata minicomputer with a graphical interface, touch screen, speech recognition, gesture recognition, and a keyboard and mouse pointer as well. You could access the data in any number of ways. It was all pretty whizzy for its time. What Pathe liked most about it, though, was the notion that the NewsPeek system would monitor your preferences and start to feed back items of potential interest, based on the content of what you had been reading in the database. It was an early manifestation of intelligent agenting—the concept that a robotlike genie would go out and troll a network or database, gathering stuff of interest to its master. The user filled out profile information — likes and dislikes—to get started, and NewsPeek took it from there.

NewsPeek actually worked pretty well. Every morning it created a customized newspaper from the database. Pathe's piece was to try to adapt different fonts, or typefaces, such as Bodoni and Courier and Helvetica, onto the screen, to give NewsPeek's displays a little more flavor. The notion of getting screen displays to look exactly like printed output, taken for granted today, was still problematic then. Pathe's work took him into the realm of font technology, digital typography, and electronic publishing at a time when, on the other side of the continent in Seattle, a former Atex publishing executive named Paul Brainerd and his associates were creating the concept of desktop publishing and the original killer app for the Apple Macintosh, Aldus PageMaker.

After getting his degree, Pathe worked for a number of start-ups, including a brief venture called Javelin, where he met his future wife, Louise Cousins, before it folded soon after the Black Monday stock market crash in October 1987. Pathe and Louise moved to Bitstream, a well-known font maker for personal computers, which was working on fonts for equipment manufacturers including Apple Computer. At the time, in 1989, Apple was looking for potential alternatives to Adobe PostScript, the only fonts that reproduced on a printer exactly as they displayed on a screen. PostScript was high quality but very expensive to license. Apple approached Adobe about lowering the price, Adobe said no, and the search for an alternative was on. In a showdown at the annual Seybold Desktop Publishing Conference in San Francisco on September 20, 1989, Adobe was upstaged by none other than Bill Gates, who announced that Microsoft was going to work with Apple on a forthcoming font technology called TrueType as an alternative to PostScript. Competition is good, said Gates. Two is a good number. Following Gates's demonstration, a furious John Warnock, Adobe's founder, lashed out at what he called garbage, mumbo-jumbo, and snake oil. A dominant company threatened with competition does tend to react emotionally, Gates later pointed out. Microsoft's entry into fonts with Windows 3.1 is often cited as one of personal computing's rawest power grabs, but consumers wound up the real winner. Microsoft offered a TrueType Font Pack carrying forty-four fonts for $99 retail at a time when a single Adobe font set would run $100 or more. Font prices plummeted and text displays on computers became richer. An argument can be made that without Gates opening up font technology through competition, the ability of the graphical Web browser to display magazinelike text and formatting would have been delayed.

As Microsoft developed TrueType for Windows 3.1, Pathe got a call from an old Cal Tech dorm mate, Steve Shaiman, who was heading up font strategy for Microsoft. Would you like to do some contracting work? Shaiman asked. Pathe signed on. The TrueType business blossomed quickly enough for Shaiman to offer a permanent position. The font flap and general industry buzz about Microsoft—good company, mediocre technology—gave Pathe pause, but Shaiman was persuasive and Pathe decided to give it a dry run. Still finishing up on his contract work, Pathe made a couple of trips to Redmond and met with Shaiman's crew. Wow, I've found the one smart team at Microsoft, he thought to himself. Buried among all these mediocre people was the shining light of the TrueType team. Then Pathe coordinated some work with the Windows systems group, and he thought, Hey, another bunch of smart guys. Two in a row! It occurred to him that he needed to do a little reset here. Maybe Microsoft was not the dull, derivative-technology machine as he had been led to believe. There was a method to its success. The people were cool, energetic, hardworking, and, in their own way, innovative. When Shaiman repeated his pitch, Pathe jumped at the chance.

Pathe joined Microsoft in December 1991 and worked on typography technology for two years, basically doing accessory products piggybacking on Microsoft core products that needed font or image enhancements. He put together the "Microsoft Scenes" line, three sets of forty-eight images each of impressionist paintings, outer space images, and Sierra Club photos that could be used as screen savers or background images for Windows. One of Pathe's screen savers showed the current satellite picture of North America on a real-time basis. Installed on an Internet-connected computer, the software would grab the photo off the NASA website at periodic intervals. Pathe had used the Internet since his Cal Tech days, when he was a regular on the Arpanet and did a lot of e-mail as well as occasional remote terminal sessions. He had seen Mosaic for the first time on a UNIX machine at the SigGraph conference in 1993. Or maybe it was at the Media Lab during one of his periodic visits in the 1993 time frame. He does not quite remember. As enthusiastic as Pathe was about most things, he had not felt the earth move the first time he saw a Web browser. It was a neat idea, he recalls thinking, but not a world beater. There were other neat things going on: gopher and ftp and WAIS. The browser's graphics were pretty crude to Pathe's trained eye. Instead he focused on its convenience as an integrated package. That's what you did with software, you brought pieces together to form a greater whole. It was clever how the browser combined html, http, ftp, and other components. The browser as a distinct entity in and of itself did not really capture Pathe's imagination till he saw Sinofsky's "Cornell is WIRED!" memo the following February.

When Pathe began pulling down the NASA satellite image for his screen saver, most of those he showed it to thought it was pretty cool, even if they did not understand the technology. The guy who really jumped on it was Nathan Myhrvold. Pathe grabbed Myhrvold from a hallway conversation one day in the fall of 1993 and said, Hey, look at this. Excitable in any setting, Myhrvold got especially giddy at the NASA image. The quantum physicist in Myhrvold appreciated its cosmological aspects, but what intrigued him most was the underlying principle: grabbing stuff off the Net on a real-time basis and repurposing or otherwise cleverly using it. Myhrvold and Pathe talked a lot about the potential for such a technology, which in many ways was a crude precursor to what would become the hot topic of 1997—PointCast and the whole move to "push" on the Net.

It was Myhrvold who asked Pathe to lead Word. Chris Peters is moving over to Office, Myhrvold said, and we need someone to take over his job. Pathe, somewhat chary of following a legend, instead pitched Myhrvold some ideas he had for expanding the Scenes business, but Myhrvold persisted. You're the perfect guy for this job, he said. At the time, Pathe had no way of knowing the new directions word processing would take with the

Web. His first thought was, what more could any mere mortal do with Word? Okay, he told Myhrvold. If that's the way it is, well, I guess I'm ready.

Once in tow, Pathe began thinking about Word and Web documents. When Cockrill and LeVine came to visit him to talk about sgml, Pathe already was starting to think in terms of text formats on the Web. He had first worked with markup languages at MIT, becoming involved in programming on screen due to the lack of a printer. Pathe worked on enhancing documents, improving typography and screen displays through fonts, letter spacing, typeface styles, and the like. He would complain to Nicholas Negroponte, the lab's director, that he needed a printer to show output. Hard copy, Negroponte replied disdainfully, was a crutch. Over time Pathe began to believe him. There was really no reason, especially as screen technology improved, to resort to paper for displaying anything. That was a fundamental premise of the Media Lab's work.

At first glance, sgml seemed an appropriate focus for Word. Sgml was a sophisticated text formatting standard, one approved by the International Standards Organization headquartered in Geneva. Sgml had a lot of momentum behind it and a rich history. But it also was a fairly high-level language, requiring users to be comfortable with programming. The Web was for generalists just looking for quick and dirty ways to get stuff posted. It was apparent that html, Tim Berners-Lee's hypertext markup language, was on its way to ubiquity. If you looked at the Web, even in its early days in 1994, html was the driving force. As a simpler, more direct language, it could not match the richness and subtlety of sgml. It also lacked the power of sgml, particularly when it came to linking text with database files, a factor that would become increasingly important as Web transactions and commerce grew. But html's charms far exceeded its warts. It was easy to learn, easy to use, and easy to edit. It was, Pathe liked to say over and over, simple, simple, simple. Just about anybody could put together a Web page, however crude, with a few html commands. Nothing along the lines of a four-color brochure, but a calling card that, in the new, cool medium, got you up and running with a minimum of pain. Pathe talked the situation over with Sinofsky, who confirmed Pathe's intuition. Html was the way to go, for the sake of popularization.

Pathe approached the subject of html compatibility in Word gingerly. The situation was this: The Net obviously held a lot of potential for Microsoft, but it also posed a certain type of threat. If html were to be the document standard for the Web, what would that do to Word's own .doc format? Microsoft had worked long and hard to make .doc a powerful format for creating rich documents. If html became the word processing flavor of choice and the Web the preferred medium, would people just chuck their copies of Word and use html for all their document production? It was a delicate line to walk for Pathe. Word documents needed to be compatible with the Web. They needed to "talk" to html commands. Otherwise Word stood the risk of being made obsolete by the Web. Yet if he went around hyping html, Pathe figured, he would get a pretty cool reception from the Word team and others at Microsoft. Persuading others to see his point of view was, in a reprise of Pathe's original let's-get-the-Net crusade, a daunting challenge. Those who avoided resorting to the knitted-brow or squint wondered why he did not simply let sleeping dogs lie. Word was obviously a better environment than html. Why give html added recognition by making it a target? If html did become the standard, wouldn't it undermine .doc's influence in the galaxy of document publishing and by extension jeopardize Word's market share?

So it was with some trepidation that Pathe pursued his vision: Make Word an html editor while continuing to enhance the .doc format. The next good tool for Word had to be a browser, Pathe started telling people. It does not have to be a brilliant browser, but Word had to have the capability. We are not going to do it with sgml, he said. Look at all the stuff on the Internet in html. It's just going to fly. You're looking at the future of word processing.

Pathe had another motive for evangelizing html. Ultimately, he thought, there had to be a document standard for electronic mail. If html was going to do publishing on the Web, and people were going to trade documents and text files and work in progress—or not even trade, but share live documents for group editing in real time—there would have to be an editing standard. It looked as if html would be the logical candidate. Word would always have the sophisticated, mature features for document processing. If you could get users to produce their documents in Word and save them in html, it would keep them from leaving Word as their editor of choice. Separately, Pathe had arrived at Allard's notion of embrace, extend, and innovate. Incorporate html into Word, build on their synergy, and create a best-of-both-worlds approach. Make the global network one big Word document creation and transport mechanism.

When Sinofsky invited Pathe to the Shumway retreat, Pathe knew immediately what his pitch to the others would be. Word for document processing and e-mail on the Internet, incorporating html and browsing functionality. Pathe's concept was summed up in his name for the technology:

Internet Assistant for Word. A helping hand, a butler of sorts, for producing text of all kinds in the Web environment. In his breakout session Pathe negotiated the opportunity to present to the full group in the closing plenary session. It helped to have Bob Frankston, the spreadsheet cocreator who already had his own Internet domain, frankston.com, in the breakout. The gnomelike Frankston, a cerebral techie with mad-scientist fly-away hair, could be a little opaque sometimes, but no one doubted his instincts. Frankston has been on the Internet more than two decades previous and had done his master's thesis at MIT in 1973 on microtransactions, which he considered more akin to paying for phone service than to the vig, or "tax," envisioned by Myhrvold. Frankston considered the Microsoft Online Services proposal to resemble "CompuServe warmed over" and argued from the get-go for Internet connectivity.

When he made his pitch, Pathe was unprepared for the response he got. Gates immediately endorsed Internet Assistant. It was like a snap of the fingers, and Yes! No explanation required. Gates got it! Pathe was stunned. Gates not only understood wholly and instantly what Pathe was proposing, he was saying, Go do it, you *have* to do it. Cool! How often does a middle manager get direct support from the very top like that? It energized, inspired Pathe. It was completely empowering.

The next step was to come up with browsing technology for Word. In his pursuit of that goal, Pathe was fortunate once again to have Sinofsky on his side. Once Sinofsky and Silverberg looked over the BookLink booth at Windows World five weeks after the Shumway retreat, Microsoft was on its way to licensing technology for Internet Assistant. By early summer 1994 Pathe brought Lydja Williams on board as program manager and Quentin Clark as tester, and the two began the Word Assistant project. BookLink's Internetworks had components that would fit into Word easily, if not downright seamlessly. Pathe thought it obvious that browsing capability would one day be part of everything you did on a PC. It would have to be. When you wanted a file from your hard disk, you did not call up a viewer called "Disk Navigator." When you wanted a file from the local area network, you did not use an application called "LAN Navigator." Why, then, did you need a "Web Navigator" browser to look at files on the Internet? Just build the browser into the PC via the operating system, and you were home free.

For now, he needed some code quickly, something he could just license and plug right into Word. Pathe just wanted to be able to say: Okay, I can open a file over my local file system, right on the hard disk, or over my LAN or over http. I can pull stuff off the Web and put it right into a Word file. And I can put stuff from a Word file onto the Web.

Pathe's quest got a big boost from the ever-vigilant Steven Sinofsky, by then in the process of winding down his two-year tenure as Gates's technical assistant. During Gates's fall Think Week Sinofsky had been back on the demo bandwagon, this time showing how electronic publishing via the Web would transform the way people thought of documents. Sinofsky showed Gates how html pages were created, how the glue of html and http worked. And he arranged for Gates to get a demo of Internet Assistant for Word's html conversion capability from Clark, a wet-eared recruit just six weeks out of college who was a new tester for the Word team. Sinofsky loved the ensuing dynamic, the rookie with the master: "And Bill was like, That's really cool! Quentin was so scared he was shaking. I mean, he couldn't move the mouse, and he was hyperventilating, and I realized we're doing this with a nineteen-year-old. And Lydja Williams [his boss] who was not much older to Microsoft was also shaking like a leaf. I felt so bad for them, but I was so excited because it actually was very, very cool."

Sinofsky took Gates back to his office, then returned to thank Williams and Clark. The latter, cheeks flushed, eyes sparkling, was on the phone to his mother, talking nonstop about the meeting with the chairman. When he got off, Sinofsky discovered Clark had just graduated from the University of Massachusetts, where Sinofsky had gone to graduate school. Later Lydja Williams called her mother too, a rural Idaho homemaker, and told her of the meeting. "Sounds very exciting, dear," her mother responded. "Now, who is this Bill Gates fellow?"

To Sinofsky, the episode illustrated the best aspects of working at Microsoft. You were always discovering things, making connections, and closing the circle on technological change.

You were also constantly evolving on a personal level. By the time Sinofsky had finished pushing a Microsoft publishing solution for the Web, he had a new job: joining the Office team to make Microsoft's suite of applications—Word, Excel, PowerPoint, Access, and whatever—Internet-ready. After two years of preaching as Gates's technical assistant, it was time for Sinofsky to do a little practicing. The result would be a product transformation unlike anything outside the systems business ever for Microsoft, or any other software company for that matter, culminating in the grandly ambitious Office 2000 suite.

Internet Assistant was yet another example of classic Microsoft: Start modest and build from there. It was slow because of the way it interacted with Word. But it was a start, and better than nothing, which is what Word users had until then.

By the fall of 1994, the major components of Microsoft's Internet strategy were firmly in place. More than 2 million Internet users had ftp'd to Microsoft's Internet site, encouraging J Allard mightily. On September 8 Paul Maritz announced that more than 60 million copies of Windows had shipped and that the next version would be named Windows 95, not Windows 4 as had been anticipated. On September 21 Windows NT 3.5, code-named Daytona, was released and BackOffice, nearly a year in planning, was officially announced along with NT 3.51. Allard was rolling into action with a sweeping Internet server business plan that would lead to Microsoft's Web server, Internet Information Server, or IIS. Slivka was assembling the O'Hare browser team. On October 6 Bill Gates issued another of his Think Week memos— this one called "Sea Change Brings Opportunity."

"Sea Change" was one of Gates's more subtle explorations. Although it referred to the World Wide Web by name only once, its entire 750-word message encapsulated the opportunity the Web posed for electronic publishing with Microsoft's Office applications. Instead of outputting data, files, and information to printers, Gates noted, private and public networks would be the target of more and more publication: "Word must become a great authoring and reading tool for electronic documents. Excel must blow away the competition in being a viewer for corporate data by tighter integration to databases, and extensions of features like pivot tables. We need to make sure public networks include lots of documents best viewed with Office. The product approach for this is complex and multifaceted, including things like supersetting Internet features and providing free subset readers."

In other words, Microsoft's popular applications would have to be as useful over networks as they were on desktop computers, Gates was saying. And the biggest network of all? The Internet. "Extended Web viewers from start-ups will grow to provide Word with new competition. These competitors will ridicule the number of commands and features Word brings from its past and suggest it is not the right tool for the new usage model"—Web viewers being browsers.

Gates's thinking in part was influenced by a long message from Brad Silverberg, in response to a Gates inquiry about browsing documents on the PC's hard disk. On October 3, 1994, in an e-mail time-stamped 8:49 P.M., Gates messaged Silverberg and two other executives:

> One question that I am thinking about may sound totally vague: How should hyperlink browsing with documents and nice visual screens be blended with [Windows] Explorer type browsing? It seems like over time they shouldn't be totally separate. The desktop is like a page, with hyperlinks which the user can set up very easily.

By 8:06 the next morning Silverberg had responded. The Windows 95 team was on the case, he noted: "We've been thinking about this already—we had a meeting with Paulma [Maritz] on the Internet yesterday where we discussed it." Essentially there should be multiple ways for the PC user to access information with Windows, Silverberg suggested. The standard tree view, like the old DOS directories and subdirectories. A query-based view, like you would perform with a database (find all files with "Windows" and "Web," for instance). This approach was being pursued by Jim Allchin and his Cairo team. Another means would be document-based, as with the Web, where live links and things like icons and graphics could be clicked on to surf through pages or documents. "Further, we could index documents so that they can be searched, too," Silverberg suggested. "Bill, you've commented on what a mess our Net organization at Microsoft is! Imagine how much nicer it would be if we had document-based browsing internally!" Silverberg added that within three months after the release of Windows 95, then still scheduled for the following spring, Windows users would have ftp, gopher, and Web access built right into the desktop shell. As it turned out, Windows 95 did not ship until August 24, and shell access was included (on new PCs, and in a separate upgrade Plus! Pack for Windows 95).

Whatever direction it took, the sea change to electronic information sharing "is a particularly important one because it will bring us closer to our customers," Gates concluded in his memo. But be forewarned: The Internet would also "bring our competitors and free software closer to our customers." Time to panic? No: "I don't think new entrants will be able to redefine the categories enough to take Office out of the mainstream. The value of having the best software will be even greater because of the new scenarios." This was a key point often lost in the debate over the Internet's evolution. If Microsoft kept supplying the best software solutions, Gates was saying, it had nothing to fear from the Net. The company would simply sell more of what it had been selling before. The Internet was not a rip-and-replace threat to Microsoft's traditional strengths, no matter how the company's competitors might position it as such.

At the time of "Sea Change," BookLink looked to be all wrapped up as Microsoft's browser of choice. When Russ Siegelman left the Shumway retreat pondering Internet compatibility for Marvel, he quickly came to the conclusion that the Microsoft online service would have to have Web browsing capability. Word of the BookLink technology got back to Siegelman, and Allard, who was handling the BookLink connection, passed the baton. Allard had been unable to muster much support for a broad deal and could not justify the expense of licensing BookLink simply for publishing and proxy server projects. Siegelman figured he could, and entered talks to purchase the company or broadly license its software. Discussions were cordial but complicated. Siegelman did not have a lot of money to work with—$1 million or so, max. A more realistic approach looked to be a partnering/licensing arrangement, where BookLink would give Microsoft rights to use its software in return for promotional considerations on Marvel—product positioning, an icon on the desktop, co-op advertising, what have you. Siegelman entered extended negotiations with Dave Wetherell, BookLink's president. "Extended" was somewhat of an understatement; they went on for weeks. Gates himself got involved, asking for a demo of BookLink at the mid-September Informat Trade Show in Barcelona—Spain's version of Comdex. A deal seemed imminent.

As the fall progressed, the issue of publishing on the Internet got hotter and hotter. Browsers were seen as the vehicles for publishers to market their wares on the Net. BookLink wanted to license its browser but also had its relationship with its parent company, CMG Information Services, to think about. CMG provided services to publishing and finance industries. Book-Link wanted to be able to control Microsoft's licensing of Internetworks technology to potential CMG competitors. At one point Siegelman said, Okay, carve out a list of publishers you think might be potential competitors. Wetherell sent him a list of some 5,000 publishers, and Siegelman protested, Dave, that's not a carve-out! It's a white-out! Even the *Wall Street Journal* was on the list.

Finally they agreed on principle, had a contract drawn up, Siegelman signed it, and got ready to send it off to Wetherell. On November 7, 1994, Seigelman called Wetherell to thank him for all the hard work and Wetherell dropped a bombshell. I sold the company, he told Siegelman. To America Online. Siegelman was not sure he heard right. To AOL? It was his worst nightmare. Not only was Microsoft losing a choice technology, a competitor was gaining it instead. In Microsoft's early days, Gates used to warn about the double jeopardy of losing a deal. You not only fail to get something valuable, you all but hand the thing over to one of your competitors.

Wetherell later told author James Wallace in *Overdrive* that Microsoft had delayed getting the contract to BookLink, giving AOL an opening. "No way," responded Siegelman. "Dave dithered." Siegelman was speechless, till he heard the terms of the deal. America Online had picked up a tiny company with a still-in-testing product for $30 million. It was a stock deal — one that turned out to be highly lucrative to Wetherell — but the valuation nonetheless broke the sanity bar. No one could have conceived browser technology would be worth $30 million. At that point, most browsers were easily obtained for free over the Web. Internetworks had been, admittedly, trying to change the paradigm. Throughout the fall BookLink had said it was planning to charge $99 for Internetworks. BookLink had after all planned to spend more than $1 million promoting the technology to software vendors as an add-on or Web enhancement to their technologies. Two days before the AOL deal was made public, partly in response to the success of Netscape's beta, BookLink announced it would distribute a limited-feature version of Internetworks for free over the Net. How could a company intending to give away its only product be worth $30 million?

AOL considered BookLink the golden gateway to the Internet. Steve Case had heard about Microsoft's interest and had taken a look at Internetworks as well. It would be a great tool for America Online advertisers and content providers to get their stuff onto the Web. Perhaps best of all, Microsoft would not get it first. For about a month after the AOL acquisition was announced, the Microsoft licensing deal stayed alive. The AOL takeover was not supposed to be completed until December 31, leaving a bit of time for negotiating. But Siegelman held out little hope. Doing business with a company owned by a fierce competitor would be just a little too complicated, especially given the predatory nature of AOL's maneuver. He doubted there was much opportunity for a Microsoft play.

The AOL acquisition was announced November 9, just four days before the start of Fall Comdex in Las Vegas. Case made hay. We intend to establish the Internetworks technology as the de facto standard in the Internet world, he told Heather Clancy at *Computer Reseller News*. AOL would create a new open standard, Case proclaimed, forming a global consortium consisting of major media, communications, and software companies. Open standards already existed, as did a global decision-making body by the name of the World Wide Web Consortium, but never mind. Case was feeling his oats; he might as well talk big while he had the microphone.

Microsoft's best-laid browser plans, in the meantime, had gone awry. The skids that had been greased for a triumphant Microsoft online/Internet strategy announcement at Comdex now were ludicrously gummed up. The Marvel announcement could still take place, but sans browser. At a time when browser awareness was starting to heat up, Microsoft was coming up empty at the biggest showcase there was. Except for one thing: The deal to license BookLink's software for Internet Assistant for Word was still a go. And one worth milking for everything Microsoft could. Pathe, who had been pushing for fifteen minutes of fame at Comdex to promote Internet Assistant, had newfound leverage. He got a meeting with Gates and told him, I'm ready. Let's launch. Give me a few moments before the Marvel announcement, and I'll get people itchy for this thing. Pathe had even primed the pump with a preview a couple of weeks earlier to industry legend Jonathan Seybold, publisher of a widely consulted newsletter on publishing technology.

When Seybold saw Internet Assistant he was aghast. This is great! he told Pathe. But does Bill know about it? At the time the publishing patriarch was engaged in a long-running dispute with the Microsoft cofounder over the legitimacy of Marvel. Seybold deemed online services doomed—as publishing media, at least. There might be some money to be made in gateways—providing access to the Internet through commercial services. But Seybold thought Gates was pouring money and resources down a sinkhole. Yes, Pathe assured Seybold, Gates knew.

Seybold raised his eyebrows. He could not understand how Pathe's project could be sanctioned while the Marvel team was working on a publishing tool of its own, code-named Blackbird after the Lockheed SR-71 surveillance jet, fast enough to fly in 1990 from Los Angeles to Washington, D.C., in sixty-five minutes while taking high-resolution photos covering 100,000 square miles. The idea behind Blackbird was to make Marvel the best place for advertisers and vendors to go if they wanted to reach an online audience. To provide the extra pizzazz to publishers, the Blackbird team was working on a proprietary tool called the Blackbird Markup Language, or bbml. It hardly needed competition from a maverick in-house product based on lowly html. What Pathe was doing was tantamount to an act of subversion! Seybold thought. To Seybold, it was a firsthand lesson in Gates's affinity for making multiple bets.

Blackbird had come to Marvel via a small Seattle company, Daily Planet, which Microsoft had purchased for cash and stock. As its name suggested, Daily Planet was developing tools for newspapers to publish electronically on the Internet. Blackbird's cofounders, Pat Ferrell, John Shewchuk, and Steve Millet, had in mind a customized news system, somewhat along the lines of Pathe's NewsPeek of old, that would ship news automatically to electronic subscribers based on their preferences. Later a Silicon Valley start-up called PointCast would make the technology, called "push," all the rage. By then, Blackbird would be all but forgotten in the pantheon of New Media.

Okay, Gates told Pathe, you're on for Comdex. There's this lunchtime press meeting we're doing at the Mirage, can you be at that? I'll introduce you, and take it from there. Pathe planned for one of the side conference rooms, holding maybe fifty people or so. Instead he showed up to find the event scheduled in a huge auditorium, with a big stage, overhead projector, and more than a thousand attendees in the audience. Whoa! With no time for stage fright, Pathe got up, led the demonstration, and found himself the hit of the show. Little had been disclosed about Internet Assistant before then. The roomful of scribes had some real news on their hands. Afterward Pathe was approached by Walt Mossberg, personal technology columnist for the *Wall Street Journal*. Thanks, Mossberg told Pathe, for giving me something to write about.

The overall purpose of the noontime press session had been to update Microsoft's commercial online strategy—that is, to announce MSN. Now it was official: Microsoft had an entry in the online sweepstakes. Without the browser piece of the puzzle in place, however, Microsoft seemed to have flubbed a golden opportunity. AOL, not Microsoft, was going to set the Internet standard, Case had promised. It was a masterful stroke of one-upmanship.

Nonetheless, word had been building about Marvel for weeks, and Microsoft needed a rejoinder. First, Gates felt compelled to issue a disclaimer. The Microsoft service would not be named Marvel, was never planned to be named Marvel, he told the gathered throng. Instead, it was going to be called the Microsoft Network. Marvel had been strictly a code name, one of thousands in use at any time in the computer industry. Code names were, as the term implied, supposed to be secret, known only to product team members and executives, in order to disguise the nature of the project. In the case of most popular products, however, they soon leaked out. Attorneys for Marvel Entertainment, the comics conglomerate responsible for the Fantastic Four, Spiderman, the Incredible Hulk, and other memorable figures of America's male youth, had issued a cease-and-desist letter accusing Microsoft of potential trademark infringement. Silly as the flap seemed, it was not an isolated example. After word got out about a new Apple technology code-named Dylan, attorneys for the folk-rock singer filed suit. Apple eventually prevailed, but thereafter chose the names of dead composers—Copland, Gershwin—for code names of projects that ended up equally moribund.

It was an inauspicious start for MSN—perhaps a hint of misfortunes to come. But Pathe had salvaged some credibility with Word Assistant, while also driving a stake, or at least a 10-penny nail, into the ground for Microsoft's Internet strategy.

As it turned out, Microsoft was not the only software company experiencing name indigestion at Fall Comdex in 1994. Over at the Las Vegas Convention Center, a start-up called Mosaic Communications Corporation had been forced, just before the show opened, to assemble a new booth banner with a different ID. Hours before Comdex began, MCC had settled a dispute with and decided to drop its lawsuit against the University of Illinois over use of the term "Mosaic." Hard feelings would remain for years over the bitter clash, but it was time to move on. Eschewing all reference to Mosaic, the company had decided to change its name to reflect the newfound popularity of its flagship product—a World Wide Web browser called Netscape.

Chapter 10

REVOLUTIONARY

The BookLink fiasco sent a message to the Internet partisans at Microsoft. Things were moving along more quickly than they had suspected, and at a far higher valuation than they thought conceivable. After the deal fell through there was predictable finger-pointing from all factions. Silverberg reopened his rift with Siegelman, simmering since the latter's abrupt departure from the Windows for Workgroups project two years earlier, by suggesting that the latter had failed to act decisively enough. Siegelman was quick to the defense: If you'd told me I had $30 million to work with, hey, BookLink would have been crawling all over me to sign the dotted line. Thirty million in 1994 was a big outlay, even for a company with $2-plus billion in the bank like Microsoft. A deal of that proportion required a lot of due diligence, lawyer involvement, technology vetting. Siegelman had his hands full with a dozen more important deals and action items for Marvel. To Silverberg, Siegelman's complaints sounded like excuse-making. You did the deal you needed to do. If something like money got questioned, you could always apologize. Besides, if Siegelman had acted decisively months earlier, before browsers and publishing got hot on the Internet, price would not have been as much a factor, Silverberg argued.

For Silverberg, long the Marvel skeptic, the problem was that the browser, and by extension the Internet, was too low a priority for Marvel. Siegelman had simply blown a huge opportunity, and now Microsoft was back to square one. Silverberg was determined to have browser technology in Chicago. It looked like his team would have to develop or obtain it themselves. John Ludwig, the networking veteran who was "blue-skying" future opportunities for Windows for Silverberg, agreed: We had better reassess where we are in the browser game, he put it to Silverberg. We need to decide whether we are serious about this stuff, in which case we had better start moving faster and more decisively. Or we need to cut bait. It was a short conversation. As far as the Internet goes, Silverberg said, we're as hardcore as Microsoft has ever been about anything. It was more than a year before Bill Gates, on December 7, 1995, would say the same thing to the world at large.

Tall, gentle-mannered, and cerebral, Ludwig brought keen analytical skills and a calm rationality to the browser project. Ludwig monitoring a project was like a submarine tracking a target. He preferred working below the surface, unnoticed, while tirelessly and unflaggingly plotting strategy, honing in on challenges and charting progress. Silverberg and Ludwig made a great alliance. Both hated ego-boosting or self-aggrandizing schemes. Both practiced a subtle form of leadership where they enabled those around them either to make the right choice or to learn from mistakes — miscues neither of them might have committed, but which were necessary as lessons learned. Both drew more satisfaction from watching those around them succeed together than from calling attention to their own contributions. From mid-1994 on Ludwig was a critical part of each significant strategic decision Microsoft made on the browser front. Yet, innumerable articles and analyses of the browser competition almost never identified him.

There was an almost audible shifting of gears going on for the Redmond gang. Through early fall of 1994, browser development had more or less meandered along as part of the Chicago effort, but not a huge part. It was not so much that the browser was considered unessential or insignificant. The Shumway retreat, and Gates's mobilization e-mail immediately following, made it clear that integrating browsing capability into the operating system was a vital goal for the company's Internet effort. But it seemed unrealistic to expect that a browser could be cobbled together in time for Chicago's release, at the time still scheduled for the upcoming fall of 1994. Integrating an entirely new dimension would mean lots more coding, debugging, testing, coding, debugging, testing—the seemingly endless programming cycle. If you altered one line of code in a program as complex as Windows, Silverberg was wont to point out, you usually stood the chance of introducing a bug or glitch that would have to be fixed, introducing the possibility of yet another bug or glitch, and so on down the line. Software development at its heart was a mind-drubbing, Sisyphian chore of debugs and fixes. Microsoft's ability to persist to the bitter end in ferreting out as many bugs as possible and in addressing user needs helped explain its successes where others had run out of ideas, steam, or initiative.

The previous spring, Barrett had been assigned to look into a browser, but with attention focused on more pressing issues in the Chicago upgrade, he had not put it on the front burner. Over the next few months he talked to a few people, looked over the field—then consisting of a wild assortment of browsers that did one or two things well but overall were slow, underfeatured, and immature—and drew up some preliminary specifications. But no team got assembled, no product description or business plan got drawn up, and no code got written. Neither did any alarm get sounded. The BookLink discussions were progressing along a normal path, after all. With most browsers available for free, there was no real commercial pressure on Microsoft. Once the Internetworks code became available, the thinking was, the browser effort would be able to ramp up production quickly.

When the BookLink deal fell through, everything changed.

As luck would have it, and Microsoft often did have luck, a coding maniac by the name of Ben Slivka had other ideas. Bearing a striking resemblance to Anthony Edwards—Dr. Mark Greene on the TV series *ER*—Slivka combined a studious demeanor with alacritous energy, stamina, and will. Starting the previous summer, Slivka had agitated Ludwig's next-generation Windows team to do something like Mosaic for Windows. Although it was not true that, in order to be part of Microsoft's Internet effort, your last name had to begin with "S" and feature some combination of "v," "i," "n," or "l," Slivka was a perfect fit for the company's aborning browser development. A veteran of the OS/2, DOS 5, and DOS 6 projects, Slivka had a ton of code under his belt and was known as a just-ship-it kind of guy. He liked impossible challenges, particularly if he could drag his friends into them as well.

Ludwig, looking for a programmer to start prototyping browser technology for Windows, asked Slivka onto the team. At that point, the Internet was just one aspect of the blueprint for Memphis, as the leapfrog upgrade of

Windows—the one following Chicago—was code-named. The whole idea of projecting an upgrade ahead was a new twist for the Windows team. It harkened back to Silverberg's conviction that software development had to happen in incremental iterations rather than one shot only. Besides the Internet, on the Memphis team's plate were things like wireless communications, game machines, PCs in the home, the eventual merging of Chicago with Windows NT. Permeating the effort philosophically was the Gates vision of Information At Your Fingertips, approaching its fourth anniversary. How would the Windows of three or four years hence continue the IAYF vision? Ludwig thought about the question every day.

After joining Ludwig's team in July, Slivka initially was interested in the notion of indexing all the content on the Internet. It seemed a natural extension of the IAYF metaphor. In order for the unthinkable amount of data on a vast interconnected network to be useful, it would have to be indexed in a way that gave meaningful access to users. Ironically, by that point, the summer of 1994, Slivka had not even gotten a home connection on the Net. He knew next to nothing about the Web. He hadn't seen the Allard or Sinofsky memos. He hadn't attended the Shumway retreat. Of all the eventual architects of Microsoft's Internet presence, Slivka was undoubtedly the last to the starting line. But in terms of producing actual code, Slivka was first out of the blocks.

Ludwig loved this about Slivka. Ben is not a patient fellow, Ludwig would say. When he identified something that needed to be worked on, Slivka was like a woodpecker, tapping, tapping, tapping till he got to the meat of the matter. "He'll come at you every day with ten things you ought to be doing," Ludwig put it. "Some percent you already are doing, he just didn't know about it. Some percentage are just shooting from the hip, he hasn't really thought through. But some percentage are dead on and you should listen to him. I let him have his say, and he tells me how to do my job, and then I throw away the nine things I don't want to hear about. The one thing he says that's accurate, I say, That's a good idea, I'll try to do better on that one."

First Slivka tracked down a Microsoft technician and browbeat him into providing an Internet tap to Slivka's office. As of the summer of 1994, getting an Internet line at Microsoft still was not a trivial procedure, where security concerns about the Net still kept it from being widely accessible. Once he got on the Net and downloaded Mosaic, Slivka spent twelve hours straight surfing. He would get on a home page, then click to a link, then go to another URL, then find a dozen more links. It was revelation after revelation. This was as close as Slivka had seen to an actual manifestation of IAYF in all its original intent.

After his tour of the Web, Slivka did not just *feel* the world had changed, he set about making sure it had—at least, his world. He started sending around e-mail, asking questions, communicating with programming teams. He asked Silverberg and Ludwig where the company was on the browser. Shouldn't we be developing something for Chicago? From the standpoint of programming, the browser did not seem to be a monumental challenge. Even if we can't get it in time for the Chicago release, Slivka told the Windows team, we ought to have it ready within a few months afterward. Directed to consult with Barrett, Slivka became even more convinced that Microsoft needed to move more quickly. What he found was pretty bare bones. Barrett had "already decided this was nuts. This is going nowhere, and I don't particularly want to be in an enormous company." To his mind, Microsoft did not get the Net and was not likely to soon. It was time to move on. By August "I'd already made a decision to leave," Barrett recalled. Knowing he was a short-timer, Barrett ignored the Internet project.

Oblivious to Barrett's disenchantment, Slivka spent little time puzzling over the situation. Microsoft would get a browser, he decided, if he had to write every last line of it himself. Slivka's first step was to take a comprehensive look at Mosaic, break it down feature by feature, figure out how the stuff worked, and where Microsoft had the opportunity to improve. What was the competition in the browser space? Who were the players? What were the feature sets? What problems do users encounter with surfing? One of Slivka's first assumptions was that browsing—at the time still being referred to as "viewing"—would supersede gopher and ftp. This despite the fact that at the time, gopher and ftp were by far more popular ways of navigating the Net than any of the browser technologies. Our focus should be on the Web, Slivka told Ludwig and Silverberg. That's where our resources should go.

Like Ludwig himself and Silverberg, Slivka was a systems guy, which meant he thought in terms of platforms. How could Microsoft use a new technology to benefit Windows users? How could the company get thousands of software developers to use Microsoft technology? That was the key question to platform guys. At the time, the Memphis team was well aware of parallel efforts to incorporate browsing into other Microsoft products. Pathe had the Internet Assistant project going for Word. Evslin headed the effort to make browsing a part of Microsoft's Exchange e-mail project. No, no, no, the systems guys were saying. Browsing—viewing, exploring, whatever—should be a part of Windows. Not that Pathe or Evslin were misguided in wanting to make browsing a key part of their end users' experience. But writing a browser for Word, and another one for Exchange, and yet another one for Windows would waste resources and create a lot of redundant code.

On August 22, in an e-mail time-stamped 5:10 P.M., Slivka notified the Memphis planning team that he had gotten started on the user interface design for what he termed Microsoft's "WWW Explorer"—there was that word again. Slivka had cataloged the entire Mosaic user interface—at least as far as http was concerned; ftp and gopher mechanics were still awaiting assessment. To a crack systems programmer like Slivka, Mosaic was a collection of pieces, as its name implied. There was an html piece, a user interface component, a caching element—caching referring to the process where things like Web pages, or URLs, were stored on the local machine for ready reference by the browser user or the browser itself. Caching made it much easier and faster for the browser to call up previously displayed URLs. Slivka thought it was done pretty poorly on Mosaic, and it became one of the WWW Explorer team's top priorities and early triumphs. From his initial analysis, Slivka concluded that the process of Web browsing was pretty similar to network browsing and hard-disk browsing. It was all exploring, he thought at the time. Slivka started a list of what changes and improvements the Windows team could make to Mosaic, but a key design question also needed to be addressed: "At this point, I'm not sure if I want to be *TOTALLY INTEGRATED INTO THE CHICAGO EXPLORER,* or if we want a separate window for the html viewer." The reference provided another benchmark in Microsoft's plan to blend Windows with the Web. Eventually Slivka would have it both ways. The html viewer—browser—would start off as its own window but gradually, with the release of Internet Explorer 4.0 in September 1997 and Windows 98 the following June, meld with the Windows Explorer.

Slivka's persistent questioning of the browser effort got back to Silverberg. He looked into the situation, found it wanting, and told Barrett he was not happy with the progress he was making. Silverberg was a patient manager as long as progress was evident. It looked to him as if Barrett did not understand what the browser did and what Microsoft needed from the technology. Barrett was in no frame of mind for second-guessing. By the first week of October, he told his supervisors, "I'm quitting and I've got four weeks of vacation. See you later." Within days Ludwig was paying Slivka a visit. How would you like to be in charge of the browser effort? Ludwig asked. It was an entirely rhetorical question. Slivka did not even bother to ask what happened to Barrett. As it turned out, Barrett took about a month off and then joined Rob Glaser's Internet start-up, Progressive Networks, as vice president of software development.

It was fitting that Slivka found himself on the cusp of Microsoft's biggest paradigm shift since DOS-to-Windows. Everything in his upbringing and career path had pointed toward a day when he would tackle something worthy of his talents. Since childhood, Slivka had been self-driven toward programming achievement. One of twin boys born in 1960 in Seattle to a public librarian mother and Seattle Symphony percussionist father, Slivka grew up playing with a variety of electronics. His first-generation Russian father, Meyer, put together a Theremin, a rare electronic musical horn whose "wooo wooo" sound changed tone when one's hands passed over its surface. Meyer also built an oscilloscope and TV set from Heathkit and, in the mid-1970s, put together his own electronic music synthesizer. Assisting him, young Ben got handy with a soldering iron. It was his mother, Enid, however, who introduced Slivka to programming. In the early 1970s she took a course on programming in BASIC, and Slivka got intrigued by what you could do with computer code. He was still a little on the young side to do much on his own, but a seed had been planted. When Hewlett-Packard came out with its programmable pocket calculators, Slivka would go downtown after school, a half-hour bus trip, and program display models for an hour or two at Seattle's leading department store, Frederick & Nelson. The salespeople, amused at what a kid could do and figuring it might attract buyers, were tolerant.

Slivka learned early on the value of hard work and independent thinking. His working mother had the two boys helping out almost from the time their younger sister was born. "The poor things never knew what it was like to sit still and have someone wait on them," Enid Slivka recounted. As a result they learned to speak their minds when they wanted something, a trait heartily encouraged by their mother. Enid Slivka had read a book about the Compton family, which produced two university presidents and Nobel Prize–winning physicist Arthur Holly Compton. "The way their [Compton] children were encouraged to investigate things for themselves made quite an impression on me," she said. Ben eventually drew the admiration, not to say awe, of Microsoft coworkers for being able to repeatedly challenge a boss named Bill Gates, and take the return heat without flinching.

Slivka eventually outgrew the calculators and discovered bigger terrain. Near Green Lake in north Seattle, a treasure trove called the Retail Computer Store had opened. It was a longer bus trip, an hour and a half to two, but offered a bigger reward. Slivka, bringing his own floppy disk, would spend entire Saturdays at the store, hacking away on a Processor Technology Sol 20, one of the earliest personal computers. He'd type in a BASIC game, play it till he pretty much had it mastered, then type in another one. Again, he got to use a floor model. His parents, unable to afford a computer, got Slivka an HP 25C pocket calculator. The nice thing about it was it saved programs in memory when the unit was shut off. At Seattle's Garfield High School, Slivka played around with a programmable desktop calculator, a Litton 1880, which lacked a display but would print out on adding-machine tape. The school let students submit batch programming jobs on punch cards to an IBM mainframe at the district's central office. Slivka did FORTRAN programming. It took once-a-day bus trips to and from the headquarters to report back results, however—which Slivka found frustrating. By 1977, at age seventeen, the computer prodigy had gotten his own account on a University of Washington computer and was doing some computer consulting for several graduate students to fund his hobby.

Slivka's first real job came when his father, who primarily played the tympani, became involved in contract negotiations with Seattle Symphony management. Young Slivka got salary and career data on all the musicians and wrote a FORTRAN program to analyze the statistics and project the workers' financial needs in retirement. It was the kind of thing that today, in Excel, would take an hour or two, but this was before the first commercial spreadsheet, VisiCalc, was even on the drawing board. For his efforts, Slivka earned the munificent sum of $1,500, every penny of which went to paying for computer time. His father was less beneficially rewarded. As a result of his union activities, Meyer Slivka was fired from the Symphony.

In 1978 Slivka headed to Northwestern University in Evanston, Illinois, intent on a career in programming—so intent, in fact, that he selected his dorm on the basis of it being closest to the campus computing center. During freshman orientation week Slivka ran into a computer center worker. They started talking, and Slivka's mastery of FORTRAN paid off again, this time with a ten-hour-a-week student consulting job working with other students, faculty, and staff. Slivka not only held the job all four undergraduate years at Northwestern, he also did summer work on systems programming at the university. In 1982 Slivka graduated with bachelor's degrees in computer science and applied mathematics and was the recipient of the Hewlett-Packard Senior Award. He also married a Northwestern freshman, Lisa Wissner.

Right after graduation, Slivka went to work for IBM in Poughkeepsie, New York, on a secret high-speed computing technology that never saw the light of day. Over a year's time, he wrote an assembly language manual, rewrote more than 7,000 lines of code in REXX, a scripting language, and took a three-month system programmer training course. Slivka discovered he was a poor fit. IBM was too big and bureaucratized, and he saw little future in big iron, the slang term for large, centralized mainframe computers that were IBM's bread and butter. Lisa, who had transferred to Vassar, was equally unhappy. The couple decided to move back to Northwestern so Lisa could finish her degree. Slivka got a job as staff programmer at the campus computing center. Although working full time, he, at Lisa's urging, decided to get his master's in computer science. Might as well, Lisa told him; the school will practically give you a free ride. In 1998 the couple returned the favor, donating $2.1 million to Northwestern's computer program.

While back at Northwestern, Slivka started playing around with a Macintosh. Northwestern was one of a few dozen schools, including Sinofsky's alma mater Cornell, chosen to be part of Apple's University Consortium. Slivka leveraged his programming job into being sixth or seventh on Northwestern's list to get a new Macintosh. In March 1984, three months after the Mac's debut, his machine arrived. It was the most exciting moment of Slivka's early programming career. He put the Mac in his car and drove straight home, praying he did not get hit on the way and die before he had the chance to use it. Over the next two days Slivka spent every spare moment playing with the Mac, exploring its menus, testing its features. And then it was: Is that it? There was nothing yet available to program the Macintosh. MacWrite, the word processor, seemed to work, so Slivka wound up starting his master's thesis on his Mac. The program ran entirely in the Mac's memory, however, and at one point it crashed, taking Slivka's deathless prose with it. Slivka went out and bought a copy of Microsoft Word. Although he was from Seattle, Slivka recalls Word as his introduction to Microsoft software. Four years later Word would lead Steven Sinofsky to Microsoft.

After Slivka and Lisa graduated from Northwestern, it was time for the young couple to move on. On a lark Slivka decided to try for a job at Microsoft, then a well-known but still-emerging software company of 775 employees. In the literary equivalent of a cold call, Slivka on December 5, 1984, wrote a letter of introduction to "Sir or Madam" at Microsoft, presenting "my credentials as a computer scientist and programmer." Slivka went over his qualifications in excruciating, acronym-laced detail, let it drop that he was from Seattle and would be visiting his parents over the holidays, and waited to hear back. Twelve days later he had a return note signed by recruiter Jo Ann Rahal, asking him for code samples, design documents, user manuals, and other examples of his work. Slivka sent back samples the same day, with a reminder that he would be in Seattle and could visit then. As it turned out, he did not hear back till January 9, and a day of interviews was scheduled for February 1. Microsoft flew him out for the interviews, but Slivka stayed with his parents to save the company money. February 1 turned out to be the date of one of the Northwest's worst snowstorms of the decade. Snow-wimpy Seattle curls up in a fetal position when the white stuff strikes, but Slivka, possessing a rental car with front-wheel drive and an adopted midwesterner's haughtiness toward snow, drove to campus without a hitch. Hardly anyone else was there, however, and impromptu interviewers had to be scrounged up. The interviewers may have been as impressed with Slivka's snow-handling skills as his programming acumen. In any case, he wound up being offered a job verbally at the end of the day. In a follow-up letter signed by Steve Ballmer, Slivka was offered a position at $31,000 annual salary, with 1,500 shares of Microsoft stock at $3 a share, vestable over eight semiannual installments. Because Microsoft had not yet gone public, there was no way of knowing whether the stock options would be worth anything. Slivka didn't even know what options were. Rahal told him they might be worth as much as $20,000 one day. By 1999 they were worth about $17.5 million. For Slivka, the salary offer was good enough on its own. Once he had sent back his acceptance letter, Slivka got a February 21 telegram from Western Union, signed by William H. Gates himself. "We believe good people like working with others who are as capable, energetic, and dedicated as they are," Gates wrote. "Part of the uniqueness we have is because of our care in selecting people to join Microsoft." For Slivka, going to work at Microsoft was like fire meeting oxygen. Slivka, the manic coder, had met the fast-track company with the hardcore executives of his dreams.

Although Ballmer did not identify a specific position for Slivka in his offer letter, it did not take long for the newbie to find a niche. The next-generation DOS team—in charge of what would become the OS/2 quagmire—was ramping up and looking for talent. Slivka slid right in with some of Microsoft's ace programmers at the time, guys like Mark Zbikowski, Anthony Short, Gordon Letwin (one of the original Bellevue employees when Microsoft made the move from Albuquerque in 1979), and Ray Pedrizetti.

The group's daunting task at the time was making the equivalent of a circus bear ride a unicycle: get DOS to run several programs simultaneously on an Intel 8088 chip in 640K of RAM. They got it to work, dubbed as MT (for multitasking) DOS version 4. But IBM poisoned the waters for anything going by DOS 4. As part of its continuing tug-of-war with Microsoft over DOS, IBM had assumed primary responsibility for DOS 4.0 development (the upgrade from DOS 3.3), but DOS 4 was buggy and uninspired. The only place MT DOS sold was in Europe — primarily to the French post office. It required more RAM than most computers had and, at the end of the day, tried to do too much with too little. In addition, Microsoft had tagged Windows, not DOS, as its multitasking solution and had little enthusiasm for widely marketing MT DOS. Slivka's first assignment was to do screen-display technology, which he finished in three weeks. Short was impressed. You're done already? he said. Okay, well, how about helping out on DOS compatibility for OS/2?

Over the following five years, until rumblings of an IBM-Microsoft divorce became real with the two superpowers' realignment in the fall of 1990, Slivka worked on several projects to smooth and enhance DOS interaction with OS/2. His task derived from an early manifestation of one of Gates's cardinal rules about upgrading: The old system had to work with the new system. You did not under any circumstances give your existing customers an excuse to go to a competitor's product. At a time when the Macintosh was building momentum and UNIX provided a high-end alternative, Microsoft deemed it imperative that OS/2 provide a smooth transition track for DOS users. The same principle was applied, with greater eventual success, to the DOS-Windows migration path.

From 1988 to 1990 Slivka worked on defining feature sets, writing code, and leading team efforts on future versions of OS/2. At one point he spent a three-week stretch working on finishing OS/2 version 1.1 at IBM's Boca Raton, Florida, plant and led a team putting together a virtual DOS machine enabling multitasking of several DOS programs at once for OS/2 2.0, or 386 OS/2. A virtual machine, or VM, allowed a user to boot up several DOS applications at the same time and switch among them as the need arose. It was as if each program were running on its own separate computer. Previously, users needed special memory-management software to call up multiple DOS programs, but only one program ran at a time and each took up the full screen when it was being used.

Ultimately, Slivka's initial experience with IBM in Poughkeepsie was a better alarum than enabler. IBM was still IBM, and no amount of code wizardry from Slivka or Microsoft could overcome its plodding, Kremlinesque ways. In the way that two people will look at a distance down the road and call it a short jog or a long walk, the ultimate truth of the Microsoft-IBM experience with OS/2 will always vary according to the teller. From Slivka's standpoint, IBM simply overengineered and micromanaged the software process to the point of stultification. Microsoft's method was to code, test, debug, rethink, then code again. Features and capabilities were added as the program matured. You never knew at the start exactly where the process would take you—that was part of the miracle of software. It was a creative, fluid, reactive process, a work of art, really, expressed in recondite, abbreviated lines of poetry that only its authors and the microprocessors that ran it fully appreciated. For IBM, years of producing software for big mainframe systems that had to be secure, robust, and mission critical had resulted in an inviolable step-by-step procedure that was top-heavy and front-loaded from the word go. There were huge teams, with no one, really, ultimately in charge; they were all supposed to do their own piece of the puzzle, report back, merge the code. And it would all come together in the end. It was all hierarchical and structured. IBM would start out and draw up a features list, define which features were practical, how many lines of code they would take. There were arguments over each step. IBM would draw up the initial programming functional specification, the IPFS, then the final programming functional specification, the FPFS. There was no flexibility, no room for adding or subtracting along the way. No adapting to suggestions from testers or adding a cool feature you happened to discover in the process. Iteration was a dirty word.

This process had stood the test of time and given IBM its reputation for rock-solid quality and reliability, but the personal computer was still an emerging, fast-changing, and unpredictable platform. You had to do things differently or you just never got anything done.

Ultimately, Slivka characterized his IBM-OS/2 experience this way. Two people get in a car and start driving cross country to the East Coast. One wants to go to New York, and the other wants to go to Florida. They take turns at the wheel. As a result, they never get anywhere. Slivka had four people on his OS/2 team, IBM had nine on its parallel team. Slivka's team wrote five times as much code as its IBM counterpart.

When the OS/2 relationship blew up, Slivka moved over to the DOS-Windows side. It was a new era for the systems group, with a new boss, Silverberg, and a mission to make DOS great while keeping its pas de deux with Windows choreographed to the benefit of both platforms. Slivka was project lead for Win 32—32-bit Windows, the early basis for what became Chicago and Windows 95—from 1990 to 1992. Then he took over DOS development for versions 6.0 and 6.2. It was on DOS 6 where Slivka executed the data-compression innovations that led to the first of his patents. One of DOS 6's big drawing cards was a technology called DoubleSpace. In the early 1990s, hard disks were expensive to upgrade, and, with programs growing in size, disk capacity was at a premium. Data compression programs, particularly an effective product from a tiny California company called Stac, surged in popularity. Microsoft decided to add data compression to DOS in the form of DoubleSpace; Stac complained and sued for patent infringement. In a rare black mark against Microsoft's court record, Stac prevailed in a $120 million jury award issued June 10, 1994. By then Slivka had redesigned DoubleSpace's compression algorithm twice—the first time, in a two-month sleepless jag, in response to the lawsuit's filing, the second time in response to the verdict. He was deposed in the suit and called to testify as well. Slivka learned more about software patents and lawyers than he ever cared to. He also filed nine patents, four of which were granted by 1999. By the time the DOS 6 dust settled, Microsoft had invested in Stac; hard disks had gotten faster, bigger, and way cheaper, and disk compression was no longer a big deal. DOS 6 sold more than 6 million retail units in its first year of distribution. Although just an incremental upgrade, DOS 6.2 gained its niche in Microsoft's Internet history when J Allard used it as code bait to get Netheads to visit Microsoft's stealth ftp server. Slivka never knew of Allard's clever ploy.

Slivka's final assignment before Ludwig plucked him away for Windows was a DOS 6.2 project involving improved data compression to pack more code onto floppy diskettes. Slivka negotiated rights to Quantum compression technology, 10 to 15 percent better than the standard PKZIP utility. He and Mike Sliger worked on expanding the data capacity on floppy disks used for read-only setup programs (i.e., the diskettes Microsoft customers used to install programs on their hard disks) from the standard 1.44MB to 1.68MB, for 17.7 percent more space. Microsoft Office 4.2, for example, dropped from twenty-five diskettes to eighteen. The bottom-line savings to Microsoft, once most of its programs converted to Slivka's algorithm, was $60 million to $90 million in fiscal years 1994 and 1995.

By the time Ludwig put the arm on him for a browser, Slivka had established a reputation for getting a lot done in a hurry. To do so, however, pretty much required that he work with small teams, light on their feet and unfettered by bureaucracy. Slivka knew how to perform due process—to make requests in writing, fill out forms, convene meetings, draw up proposals. It was just that he pretty much hated it. He liked to plunge right in and turn on the jets. When Ludwig asked him to take over the project lead for Microsoft's still-amorphous Web browser effort, Slivka took it as a green light to the Autobahn. By October he had shed the vestiges of his DOS and data compression work and was ramped up for the Web. On October 6, 1994, in an e-mail time-stamped 2:58 P.M. to Silverberg, Ludwig and Evslin, Slivka disclosed details of what he termed the Internet client, but what would actually become the Web browser, for Chicago. His goals for the initial features included making it easy for Chicago users to sign up with an Internet service provider for instant access to the Net, providing e-mail and newsgroup access and what Slivka called "shell-integrated" Web browsing via http, html, ftp, and gopher. A potential service provider at the time was MCI. Bob Frankston, Slivka noted, knew Vinton Cerf, one of the fathers of the Internet who had been hired by MCI to develop an Internet-provider business for the telecom giant. The reference to "shell-integrated" harkened back to Slivka's August e-mail, where he discussed the trade-offs of a separate viewer window for browsing versus building it into the Windows Explorer, the system-navigation software for Windows. Apparently the door was still open for either. And Microsoft was still counting on the Book-Link deal to go through. As Slivka assessed in his e-mail, "Should have deal signed in a week or two."

With typical fast-track aggressiveness, Slivka projected the new effort's deadline for beta testing to be February 17, 1995. At the time, the date also represented the scheduled release-to-manufacturing date for Chicago. The browser would then ship "no more than three months" after Chicago in a "frosting version 2" upgrade package, putting the browser's release around June or July 1995. In keeping with the Chicago theme for the next release of Windows, Slivka code-named the browser "O'Hare." O'Hare Airport was Chicago the city's gateway to the physical world. A browser would be Chicago the software's gateway to the world of information.

Slivka had no way of knowing for sure, but in the back of his mind he gave his new team an outside chance of making Chicago's initial release. There was still lots to be done on the next Windows version—too much, Slivka intuited, to have the program ready in February. Although the basic elements of the new Windows interface were in place, the guts of the system still needed polishing. As it turned out, a month later, on November 15 at Fall Comdex in Las Vegas, Silverberg announced a third beta version of Chicago, by then officially dubbed Windows 95. About 400,000 users would get the beta some time in January. Given that test cycle, Slivka felt certain that Windows 95 had no prayer of getting released before summer.

It was time to motor. Five days after he wrote the memo outlining the Windows Internet client effort, Slivka and three other members of his new-born browser team were at a Seattle rollout for IBM's new version 3 of OS/2, called Warp in reference to its faster speed. They stayed more than two hours. When he got back to the office, Slivka put his take-aways in a message to the team:

> Overall, their message was "time is important, Windows 95 is not here yet, so take what you can get—OS/2 Warp." Each presenter mentioned the Internet and getting onto the info superhighway, and most of them also got a dig in about the delay in Windows 95. . . . They spent most of the time *talking* about Warp, about Getting Warped, but very very little time actually demoing the product itself.

The last point was a telling sign to the crank-it-out coder in Slivka. "If the product was good, wouldn't they have demo'd it more?" he asked rhetorically. For all the jokes about Windows 95's tardiness—one IBM executive said her flight from New York to Seattle was delayed in Chicago—Warp did not appear ready for prime time. Overall, Slivka concluded, "OS/2 seemed sluggish, had way too many icons and menu items and dialog box entries (eight or nine tabs on one dialog box)—it seems like a grab bag of stuff." Windows 95, with its focus on ease of use, single-click access, and an un-cluttered opening screen "is definitely a win over Warp."

Maybe . . . but he was not about to count chickens. Slivka, along with everyone else associated with Windows including Steve Ballmer and Bill Gates, saw Warp's Internet software as a potential OS/2 reviver. Although it had been four years since the Microsoft-IBM ship had first wrecked on the shoals of OS/2 development, and although Windows in the interim had outsold OS/2 by roughly forty to one if not better, Gates made sure no one at Microsoft took anything for granted. It was another replay of the IBM-is-out-to-replace-Microsoft paranoia. Any operating system that outfeatured or otherwise offered an alternative on personal computers to Windows was a threat, no matter what its track record.

OS/2 thus became, ten months before the release of Windows 95, the first personal computer operating system to come with its own built-in browser. Big, stodgy, laggardly IBM had managed to integrate Web brows-ing at a time when Microsoft was still trying to come up with its first set of viewer code. "We've bundled all the pieces together in a full suite," crowed IBM vice president of communications John Patrick to Talila Baron of *Communications Week*. "There's automatic connection, so getting hooked in appears seamless to the user." Bundling? Automatic connection? The words sounded straight from the Internet Explorer and MSN business plans. Worse, IBM had productized Microsoft's favorite metaphor for Web viewing: Warp's browser was called WebExplorer.

Within a week of the OS/2 pep rally, Slivka had made an in-depth analysis of two other browsers—beta version 0.9 of Mosaic Communications Corporation's NetScape, released just five days previous, and beta version 2 of the BookLink Internetworks technology. In a long, detailed e-mail dated October 18, addressed to browser team members and called "Thoughts on Web Browsers, Win 95 TCP/IP and RNA," Slivka laid out the foundation for O'Hare—what would become Internet Explorer 1.0, Microsoft's initial browser. Among Slivka's early suggestions: Make it easy for users to copy Web information to their hard drive. As long as the Internet and PCs had worked together, the procedure had been awkward and time-consuming. Slivka talked up what would become a popular Internet Explorer feature: the ability to define and drag a URL to the desktop in order to create a shortcut to the chosen page. From then on a user could simply click on the screen icon and the page would display—in fact, as it turned out, IE would automatically log onto the Internet for the user, simplifying the process immeasurably. Slivka also talked about being able to load multiple pages at once, a feature that, as Bob Frankston had pointed out in a previous e-mail, NetScape offered but in a way so complex that users could easily lose their place and not know which windows they had called up first.

At the time, when modem speeds were just 9600 or 14,400 bps, pages took a long time to draw. The original Mosaic drew a screen line by line, as if the page were a curtain slowly dropping, an agonizing procedure at low speed. NetScape vastly improved on the process by displaying text first, then grabbing images. Internetworks downloaded text and used placemarkers for images but redrew the text as the images appeared, giving the screen a jumpy, herky-jerky aspect that made reading text difficult. Slivka suggested a nice compromise: Grab the text first, fill the screen, then draw the images one at a time without reflowing the text. And he added another wrinkle: If the user wanted to keep scrolling down the page and reading text without looking at the images, O'Hare would simply keep drawing all the text, even if image sizes were not immediately known. To speed the redrawing process for a favorite page or site, Slivka proposed caching images in a given document on the hard disk. Doing so greatly sped up display of a repeated graphic—a 3-D bullet, for example—that most browsers loaded over and over again as the document displayed it. Another nice touch: Slivka suggested showing the download file size and estimated time. This gave the user a notion of whether the page was worth downloading in the first place and also decreased the pain of waiting for the download (caused by not knowing how long the process would take). Finally, Slivka suggested keeping a history of URLs that had already been visited and making it persist through multiple sessions. NetScape, Slivka noted, kept track of visited URLs, but only for the current session. Slivka thought users would want to keep an ongoing record of visited sites, although for space considerations it would have to be limited by a maximum number or maximum amount of disk space, or perhaps by how long it had been since the user had gone back and looked at a saved URL.

The persistent "favorites" list—NetScape dubbed them "bookmarks"—would, Slivka noted, enable Microsoft to institute another user improvement. NetScape cleverly differentiated links to URLs that already had been visited by making them a different color, alerting users to the fact they had already seen the linked-to site. An unvisited site link was aqua; the visited site was purple. If O'Hare kept track of visited sites over multiple sessions, the Microsoft browser also could keep on displaying the links of previously visited sites in a different color—taking the NetScape feature one step further.

Although Slivka's memo did not mention it, he liked BookLink's componentization approach. It meant that a software vendor marketing a program or application could plug Internetworks' browsing technology right into the software without having to write a browser from scratch. It was a great way to ensure widespread adoption of a browsing technology, and it was a big reason why AOL was willing to fork over the $30 million. AOL would earn that back in no time from advertisers and content providers wanting to grab potential customers off the Internet as well as from Internet providers wanting access to AOL's growing customer base. There was nothing particularly inventive or original about componentization's appeal. Microsoft had long understood, from its BASIC and other programming-language origins, that you built success by appealing to developers. When developers embraced your programming tools and used your technology, they helped make it a standard. In the new paradigm of the Web, developers were people building websites, putting together advertisements, and doing content. They were a whole new crowd. But the tools approach would work just as well with them as with desktop applications developers. The BookLink developers understood this. And because they thought the way Microsoft thought, their approach appealed to the Microsoft browser builders like Slivka.

Fortunately for Microsoft, losing the BookLink deal did not mean sacrificing the componentization approach. Down the road, making Internet Explorer modular would pay huge dividends in Microsoft's quest of the Web. But a lot of code would be written before IE could make componentization a big win for Microsoft.

In assessing the browser landscape before beginning the work of actual code for O'Hare, Slivka was doing what Microsoft did best. The company was habitually criticized for not being innovative in the strictest sense of the term. Microsoft had not invented BASIC or DOS or the graphical user interface or the word processor or spreadsheet or any other "killer app" for desktop computers. But it had succeeded time and again by analyzing existing technology, combining the strengths of the field, and then improving through its own unique blend of features, ease-of-use enhancements, and improved usability. Microsoft's innovativeness—creativity, ingenuity, or whatever other term might apply—came in taking existing technology much farther than its creators were capable of taking it. Other factors, such as pricing it lower or giving it away or bundling it with other Microsoft products, ignored a critical consideration: Until Microsoft beat the competition on the merits of its software, none of its other marketing ploys made a whit of difference. In the latter 1980s Microsoft gave away thousands of copies of Windows and Excel in an effort to evangelize the graphical interface on a PC. Both were slow and clumsy and looked almost comical next to Excel on the Macintosh and the Mac's graphical interface. The early versions of Word came with a mouse bundled free but lacked key features of Word-Perfect, the market leader. Word did not become the leading word processor until its Windows incarnation, in the capable hands of Chris Peters, added a powerful set of ease-of-use and intuitive features. Microsoft products that failed to improve on existing technology—MS-Net, Access (its original communications program, not the database), Word for Windows 3.1, Money (in its early years), Bob, At Work, Pen for Windows, and any number of other bombs—could not overtake market leaders no matter what Microsoft did to distribute them, including offering them for free.

Perhaps the most significant point of Slivka's October 18, 1994, e-mail browser assessment, however, was to provide a benchmark for Microsoft's awareness of a new browser on the scene. NetScape, still a product (of Mosaic Communications Corporation), not yet a company, had made it onto Microsoft's radar screen. It was still a test version, not yet the leading choice in the browser field. There was no way of knowing that it would become a huge hit. To Slivka, it was just one of the bunch. It had some good features and some bad; like all the browsers, it was immature and unpolished. But it was good enough to get his attention, where the academic browsers such as Cello, Viola, Midas, and Berners-Lee's original were not.

Shrewdly, in fact, Slivka chose to focus his evaluations on the three browsers that ended up having commercial impact. Mosaic was already bringing in revenue, in the form of licenses with a host of software vendors, notably IBM and Spry. BookLink intended to charge for Internetworks once it released a version to the public, although it had dropped the price from $129 in early fall to $99 by the time Fall Comdex rolled around in mid-November. And although NetScape was still in test form and would continue to be offered for free for some time, it became the leading browser moneymaker of all time. The mercenary commonality of Slivka's troika was strictly a coincidence of history. His choice of browsers did not imply that Microsoft planned to charge money for O'Hare. Slivka, the platforms guy, just assumed browsing would become part of the operating system.

Once his game plan was on record, Slivka wasted no time recruiting the best talent he could find. He brought on Chris Franklin, who had worked on the Lisa at Apple, moved with Steve Jobs to NeXT, had written the first visual shell for the NeXT cube computer, and, after spending some time at a start-up, joined the Microsoft At Work project. At Work, or MAW, as skeptics abbreviated it, had been a promising Microsoft effort to set Windows as an office machines interface standard starting in 1993. Even if you did not think Microsoft should be the standard-setter, it was a laudable idea—devise a single universal interface for fax machines, programmable telephones, copiers, printers, scanners, and the like. But getting vendors to agree on a universal standard, especially one they would have to license from a third party like Microsoft, was an impossible task. Microsoft At Work did a huge announcement, lined up some top-name business machine vendors such as Sharp, Compaq, H-P, NEC, Ricoh, Xerox, Sanyo, Philips, and sixty others to make a pledge of support, and then went into virtual hibernation. At Work turned out to be proof that just because Microsoft tried to set a standard did not mean that its technology would stick. Franklin put in a heroic effort, as Slivka saw it, to build html for Microsoft's first browser and come up with a technique for progressive rendering—a means of displaying text quickly while more data-intensive graphics downloaded over the modem. Progressive rendering was a key, early Microsoft advantage in the browser feature wars. Slivka also brought on board John Cordell from outside Microsoft to do the user interface programming and additional html programming.

In a hurry and not particularly mindful of hiring protocol, Slivka in some cases got people on board and working before getting HR approval or funding clearance from Silverberg. His philosophy, like Allard's and others' before them at Microsoft: Apologizing was better than asking for permission. At each turn Slivka waited for the inevitable second guess or put-on-the-brakes e-mail. It never came. Instead, Maritz, Silverberg, and Ludwig all said go. Go, go, go.

By November 7, 1994, Slivka had made sufficient progress for Maritz to shoot an e-mail to Gates promising that Windows 95 would ship a standard initial-access and WWW browsing package (code-named O'Hare) by mid-1995. The package would be based on work Slivka was in charge of delivering, a Web viewer and a means of making it a snap to log on to an Internet service provider through Windows. Silverberg, too, liked what he saw from Slivka's new team. Barrett was gone, Siegelman was off in MSNville. In Slivka, Silverberg had a guy he knew could produce, and do so fast, decisively, with little need for care and feeding. For the first time since he had envisioned browser capabilities in Windows 95 a year earlier, Silverberg felt confident it would happen in a timely and effective manner.

The loss of the BookLink deal was bad enough strategically for Microsoft. For Slivka, however, strategy was well down on the list of why Book-Link was vital. He had been working from the start on the assumption that Microsoft would license at least some browser code to serve as the basis for O'Hare. Microsoft was after the best way to gain html and http compatibility in a browser. BookLink's use of OLE had been its key attraction. Now it was back to the drawing board for the next best browser. Slivka wanted some code. And fast.

Part 3

ENACTMENT

Chapter 11

GWEEP

he day America Online announced its purchase of BookLink, Microsoft Windows strategist Thomas Reardon picked up the phone and renewed acquaintances with Mike Tyrrell, marketing chief for Spyglass. Rail thin and pale-skinned, with the sculpted features of a young Irish poet, Reardon had an approachable vulnerability about him not usually found among Microsoft denizens. It came in handy in delicate deal making and conflict situations. Spyglass, a tiny Illinois company with a provocative name, was the window to the quickest way out of the BookLink mess, Reardon knew. The previous August, shortly after joining John Ludwig's what's-next-for-Windows team, Reardon had done a survey of promising browsers. Curious about what it would take to license Mosaic, Reardon called up the National Center for Supercomputing Applications at the University of Illinois, where Mosaic had been developed. At the time, the university was being inundated with interest in Mosaic from other large enterprises, including IBM. On August 24, 1994, university officials, feeling overmatched, awarded Mosaic licensing rights to Spyglass. Cofounded by NCSA alum Tim Krauskopf four years earlier, headquartered in nearby Savoy, Illinois, Spyglass was considered a company the university could trust. Reardon and university officials at first discussed dealing directly with Microsoft. But Spyglass, getting wind of the talks, pressured the university to send Microsoft its way. Reardon called Tyrrell and chatted a bit, feeling him out as to licensing terms, cost, availability. Then he moved on down the list.

Reardon's survey took him to Mosaic Communications Corp. in Mountain View, California. He was unprepared for the reception he got. Mosaic Communications' marketing director, Paul Koontz, called back to say, basically, forget it. Nobody here likes Microsoft, Koontz told Reardon. So there's no reason for us to be having this call. See you later. Reardon puzzled over the brush-off—what had Microsoft ever done to this unknown start-up?—but thought, There are plenty of other fish in the sea. I'll just go pursue other opportunities. Besides, with negotiations still proceeding on the BookLink front, it looked as if Internetworks was the debutante of choice.

Behind the Reardon brush-off was Mosaic Communications cofounder Jim Clark. When Koontz approached him about Reardon's inquiry, Clark let loose with both barrels. I don't want to deal with Microsoft, I just don't trust them, Clark said. They're going to screw us somehow. I don't want to have anything to do with them. Clark had heard too many stories about Microsoft offering to partner with or license technology from a start-up company with a good idea, only to develop its own version of the technology subsequently. He was not about to let Mosaic Communications become yet another straw man for a Microsoft grab for glory.

So when BookLink fell through, Reardon saw little point in trying Mosaic Communications Corp. again. Instead, he was back knocking on Spyglass's door.

Just as great wars start with border skirmishes that suppurate into international conflagrations, Reardon's renewal of talks with Spyglass precipitated the software clash eventually known as the browser wars. Reardon had no idea of the rivalry he was igniting. He was merely trying to get browser code the fastest, most efficient way possible. Inevitably, however, word of the renewed Microsoft-Spyglass talks got back to Jim Clark. With the terrible sinking sensation that only a veteran entrepreneur with best-laid plans for a glorious IPO can feel, Clark realized a Microsoft-Spyglass alliance around Mosaic could leave his fledgling enterprise in the digital dust. Suddenly the Microsoft-basher in Clark had a change of heart. Maybe he could find a way to jump into the middle of the Microsoft-Spyglass talks. Maybe he could find it in himself to become Microsoft's friend. Let's see, he thought to himself. Who among his executives knew someone high up at Microsoft . . . ?

Reardon cared less about the politics of browsers than about the code. What he wanted for a Microsoft license was one thing: compatibility. Whatever code Microsoft used as a basis for its browser had to be compatible with the Web standard, particularly html. From where he sat, Mosaic was the standard.

For Reardon, compatibility was king. His crowning moment at Microsoft, a triumph that was to change the nature of competition in the PC networking field, had been based on getting compatibility with Novell's NetWare into Windows. The lesson had been driven home the previous March, in fact. At Novell's annual BrainShare conference, he had demonstrated a technology that was the culmination of more than two years of tedious, painstaking, mind-numbing grunt work. At a private meeting with key customers, Reardon had shown Chicago running pretty much a clone of the market-leading NetWare network operating system. With the technology, Microsoft had proven it could do everything on a computer network with Windows that NetWare could do. For Reardon, this meant Windows had won. And that was worth celebrating long into the night, even if it meant lying comatose on a lumpy bed in a cheap hotel the next day in Salt Lake City, the last place on this spinning green pill anyone would want to be. We have to fly back tomorrow for a Bill review, Ludwig had told him. And Reardon quickly said: I will be there. You bet. No way will I miss that. But that was before they went bar-hopping and saw this hilarious British funk band and had too many drinks too late into the night . . .

For Reardon, computers had always lent themselves to a magnificent obsession. Growing up a loner in an Irish Catholic family with eighteen children (eight adopted), Reardon found in computers a refuge of orderliness, predictability, and isolation. His parents were strictly working class—his father a bartender, his mother a waitress who wound up working in a plastics factory. He thought of his family as a beautiful mess. As the youngest kid, he was left pretty much to his own devices. More often than not, his device of choice was a computer.

Reardon grew up in Nashua, New Hampshire, a Boston suburb. The best thing about Nashua, in his eyes, was Digital Equipment Corporation. Long before the information superhighway was barely a glimmer in Al

Gore's eye, DEC was wiring schools and public places with computers. Its early minicomputers, the PDP (Programmed Data Processor) series, were the accepted standard for logging on to mainframe computers via time-sharing accounts and on to the Internet long before the advent of the PC. Just about every pioneer of the PC revolution, including Bill Gates and Paul Allen, spent much of his early computing career pounding on a DEC PDP-8, PDP-10, or PDP-11 terminal. DEC was responsible for getting PCs called DEC Rainbows (interesting because they ran both CP/M and MS-DOS) into the schools Reardon attended. DEC also helped fund a local children's museum, which had computers the kids could program on. Reardon hung out with half a dozen other inner-city, working-class kids who grabbed computer time wherever they could. The adults called them gweeps. The term, spawned out of DEC culture in the late 1970s, was a slang expression for hacking, or writing computer code, on the early PDPs. The hackers went late into the night and tended to have the rough-edged social skills and monomaniacal lifestyle later connoted by the terms "nerd," "geek," "wirehead." Gweep was a similarly disparaging term, but for the computer kids of Nashua, it was a compliment. It meant acceptance into an elite, if not well understood, circle of Wild Ones who ate, breathed, and lived computers. When they should have been sleeping, they were off gweeping. None of the kids Reardon hung out with had parents who worked for DEC. None had home computers—still a rarity but not, with the advent of the Apple II and IBM PC, an impossibility. At age eleven, Reardon and four other gweeps formed a partnership called Quadrasoft and tried to adapt a sophisticated program called TRON, The Realtime Operating system Nucleus, to the Apple II. They did not get very far. But eventually they all did wind up in computer careers, amazed that they would get paid actual money to do what they had considered pure unadulterated fun while growing up.

For the Nashua gweeps, the network—DECNet—was god. It was the way they communicated with one another when they were not together. It was the source of most of their software and information. They played games against the computer such as VT Trek, a Star Trek game, via the network. They dreamed of a day when they could play against each other, from their homes, over the network. They differed from the first wave of computer pioneers, the Gateses and Allens and Jobses, in that they felt they had power over the network, rather than the other way around. In the early timesharing days, any computing was done off a big, centrally controlled mainframe at a business or institution. Logging on to the computers was expensive, and in most cases the public (read random kids) was not allowed access. But it was the only way to use a computer. When personal computers arrived, they were seen as a liberation from the centrally controlled behemoths—one reason that even today Gates emphasizes personal empowerment as one of the PC's enduring appeals. But it worked the opposite way for Reardon and the gweeps. The standalone PC, the Apple II and IBM PC, was taken for granted. The PC was the norm. The magic was in connectivity—in linking PCs together. The network was their key to the kingdom of computing.

By age fifteen Reardon, who already had taken a couple of programming classes at MIT, was ready to try college. It was an unusual and daring step—none of his seventeen sisters and brothers had gone to college. It was not considered in the realm of options. Reardon enrolled in the University of New Hampshire with high hopes. But after two aimless years, he decided he was not cut out for academia and headed south with a friend to North Carolina. It was there, at Duke University in 1987, that he started learning the ins and outs of Novell NetWare. Reardon landed a job in information systems at the university medical center's radiology lab, where PCs were just starting to be recognized as a means of distributing mainframe tasks. The goal: to integrate patient information with medical research in an ongoing archival database with the potential for providing disease patterns and possible clues to remedies and cures. Radiologists were intrigued by the notion of being able to access national databases in real time for a patient record or research on a specific disorder. Information sharing in the medical community began pushing Duke toward use of the Internet, and by 1990 Reardon was spending all his time doing Internet programming, mostly for e-mail, tying the university's network to the Net. He familiarized himself with SMTP, the Internet mail standard, and other Internet protocols and for the first time began to think about how to set up information systems that would span organizations. If the information could be accessed from portable, hand-held computing devices while physicians made their rounds, that was all the better. Searching through folders of papers, which had a tendency to get misplaced or disheveled, was the bane of physicians on the go.

While at Duke the lingering gweep in him prompted Reardon to start a network software company called PropellerHead Software, specializing in add-on applications such as backup software and file management utilities for Novell's NetWare. Reardon learned everything he could about NetWare programming on the server side. It was an esoteric pursuit: Not many people wrote server code for NetWare because of its idiosyncrasies and complexity. The company lasted less than a year but was not intended to make it on its own. Reardon's ultimate goal was to become valuable enough in a niche area that a bigger fish would come along and swallow PropellerHead.

At the Fall Comdex in Las Vegas in 1990—the Comdex where Bill Gates gave his "Information At Your Fingertips" address—Reardon was manning the PropellerHead booth when Ann Winblad stopped by. Winblad was a talkative, pixieish blonde who had until the year previous been Gates's girlfriend but in industry circles was known equally as well for her technological acumen and her venture capital firm, Hummer Winblad. Winblad loved to roam the side aisles of the giant trade show, looking for interesting little companies with unique products. She saw the potential for PropellerHead's expertise to mesh with the strategic goals of an Oregon PC utilities seller named Central Point Software. At the time, Central Point saw considerable potential in adapting its software tools to networks. Winblad, who was on Central Point's board, pitched Reardon on joining forces, telling him a story about a drive up Oregon's Mount Hood with Gates. The road up the mountain was long and switchbacked. With each new vista you thought you had reached the top, only to discover another more breathtaking outcropping the next turn. Gates told Winblad he thought of the connected world the same way: Every time you thought you had figured out all the possibilities of interconnected PCs, you would round another turn and discover a whole additional capability. It was like turning into a bright white light; there was always a new, unexpected insight you had never contemplated. Reardon liked the story, even if he thought it a little on the corny side. Within weeks he was packing up and heading for the green hills of Oregon.

Reardon did not last long at Central Point, which was losing its luster in the battle over PC utilities against Norton's array of tools and not moving deftly enough to compete against other network utility providers such as Cheyenne. Winblad liked Reardon's idiosyncratic, ruminative style and occasionally nudged him to consider Microsoft, which was still somewhere out at sea when it came to networking strategy. In 1991 Reardon hooked up with Ray Pedrizetti, managing development of networking for Windows 3.1. By the time Windows for Workgroups 3.1 shipped in October 1992, Reardon had joined the Windows networking effort with the intent of doing something about Novell's dominant position in networking. Because of Novell's overwhelming market share, Microsoft had to ensure that Windows worked with NetWare. But Novell, led by a crusty, gruff Microsoft basher named Ray Noorda, had become increasingly more difficult to work with. Noorda had been deriding Microsoft from the time desultory merger negotiations between the two software powers broke off in the spring of 1991. When Novell acquired Digital Research and with it the MS-DOS clone DR DOS, in July 1991, Gates and Ballmer interpreted the move as a shot across Microsoft's bow. All the while, Noorda continued to poison the relationship with anonymous accusations to industry players and the press. Noorda liked to write bits of doggerel about "Pearly Gates"—Bill Gates—and Steve Ballmer. One promised you heaven and the other prepared you for the grave, as author Wendy Goldman Rohm reported Noorda saying in *The Microsoft File*. Gates was taken aback by the personal nature of Noorda's attacks: "Noorda was just vicious! I mean, frankly, I'm trying to think of anything quite as poisonous that people have said about someone else in the industry. I can't think of anything as strong as that Noorda stuff was." Nonetheless, the two companies continued to work together. They had to. NetWare had to work with DOS and Windows to make networked PC users happy. For the same reason, DOS and Windows had to work with NetWare.

Also helping drive a stake through the heart of the Novell relationship was Windows for Workgroups 3.1. Microsoft had licensed IPX, Novell's Internet network protocol, for use in Windows 3.1, released April 6, 1992. When IPX also showed up in Windows for Workgroups 3.1 six months later, a surprised and outraged Novell complained bitterly that Microsoft had taken liberties. The Windows 3.1 license, Novell asserted, did not cover networking versions of Windows—to wit, Windows for Workgroups. The dispute, combined with Novell's increasing march into Microsoft's operating system territory, gave a clear signal to Silverberg, Ludwig, and the Windows networking effort that they would not be able to rely on Novell for future support. Not only that, Novell obviously had ambitions of building its own personal computer empire—operating system, desktop applications, all network-linked. Microsoft could compete easily on the first two fronts. But how was it going to make a dent in NetWare's hegemony on the networking front?

Reardon thought he knew the answer: NetWare compatibility. As things stood, Windows was having a rougher and rockier time of running on Novell networks. A Windows user never knew, as he installed his or her machine onto a network, whether things were going to work all right. Enough problems arose to give rise to a new expression, the black screen of death, referring to a Windows 3.X computer's tendency to crash on a network. No warning, no applications lockup. Just a blank, inscrutable monitor. With MS-Net, LAN Manager, and Windows for Workgroups 3.1, Microsoft had tried to supply an alternative to NetWare, offering equal but separate technologies to accomplish the same networking ends in hopes network administrators would choose them instead of NetWare. The strategy did not work. NetWare was holding firm, and Windows was having a harder time running on it.

You're doing it wrong, Reardon told Pedrizetti. You need to love NetWare. You need to make Windows the highest and best use of NetWare. Without using the actual terminology, Reardon's notion was a precursor to J Allard's embrace and extend strategy.

Okay, Pedrizetti responded. Can you clean-room NetWare? The expression referred to the ability to replicate, or clone, a software program without seeing or otherwise being exposed to its actual source code. Programmers figuratively worked in a "clean room," untainted by knowledge of how the product they were cloning performed its magic. Reardon said he would try. Cloning should be possible, he said. After all, DR DOS aka Novell DOS was birthed a clone. If MS-DOS could be cloned by Digital Research/Novell, surely NetWare could be cloned by Microsoft.

So Reardon began the painstaking process of putting NetWare compatibility into the next upgrade of Windows, Windows for Workgroups 3.11, code-named Snowball after a Calvin & Hobbes comic strip. Snowball was also a play off the code name for WfW 3.1, Winball, which in turn was a play off Pinball, the code name for a disk-formatting system, HPFS, developed by Gordon Letwin. To Reardon, Snowball also implied a gathering momentum for networking in Windows.

For the next two years Reardon did everything he could to perform a Vulcan mind meld with NetWare. He set up a NetWare network and ran simulation after simulation. He would have the PC do something on the NetWare network—send a file, print a file, copy a file—and then watch what the PC said to the NetWare server—in other words, what the spaceship said to Houston control. This was called sniffing because you really did not get to see any inner workings but did get a whiff of what was going on in the interchange. The process happened fast. Reardon would have to repeat it again and again, day after day, week after week, until he learned the magic. "We would run a simulator to the client that would use the Novell software, talk to the Novell software. Then we would watch the traffic on the wire and we would see what the server and the client would say to each other. And we would say, Okay, if I read 500 bytes from a file, this is what happened on the wire. What was actually going on, we tried to decompose packets on the wire and see what kind of commands they were sending."

It was a devilishly slow, frustrating process, a little like giving someone all the words to James Joyce's *Ulysses* jumbled together and saying, Now go write the book. Reardon compared it to learning a foreign language without a translation dictionary. You had to look for patterns in certain situations and then figure out that a certain set of commands translated as a certain functionality. What emerged was a set of protocols for Windows 95 that emulated NetWare functionality and then some. For network administrators having to wrestle with arcane configuration problems and the black screen of death, the promise of Windows 95 was simple: Add a Windows 95 machine to your NetWare network and it will boot right up automatically.

Ultimately, the NetWare triumph would extend beyond Windows 95. Win 95 was client software, meant to reside on PCs attached to a server. The majority of servers ran on NetWare. If the same protocols were built into Windows NT, however, then NetWare compatibility would reside on both the client and the server side. What this meant was that network administrators, faced with adding a new server to their network, would have a choice. They could go with NetWare or Windows NT. If Microsoft made NT more attractive in other ways than NetWare, then all-Windows networks would start to creep into large connected organizations, Reardon was convinced: "It's a lot easier to introduce a new server machine—it's just one addition to ten [on a network]—than it is to go change a thousand [client PCs] machines," he said. "With those thousand machines out there, with Microsoft software already running on them, and that [network] redirector being able to talk to NetWare or Windows NT, equivalently, without discrimination, then installing an NT server next to a NetWare server was a no-brainer. Up till that point it was a big problem. So as we allowed that to happen and as that organic upgrade [to Windows 95] happened at the client, it opened up a huge opportunity that wasn't there before on the back end [server]."

It was going to be a slow burn, Reardon knew. Networks get built in increments. No one was going to replace NetWare servers. Corporations hated throwing out anything. But as networks grew, they had to add servers. If Microsoft made it easy, or otherwise attractive, to add an NT server, then over time all-Windows networks would start to emerge: "It was one of those things Microsoft does really well," Reardon said. "Sort of qui-etly invest and provide compatibility, generate adoption, and then the competition wakes up three or four years later and is sort of like stunned at how pervasive the Microsoft solution is. And then they have to turn around and support us."

Strategically, Ludwig saw NetWare interoperability as the perfect of-fense. It gave Novell, for all its acrimony against Microsoft, nothing to come back with. "What could be bad about us doing work to support users of their products?" Ludwig observed. If Novell tried to block NetWare compatibil-ity either politically or technologically, "they would be hurting their own customers who liked our work," he added.

Ultimately this strategy would pay huge dividends. With the Chicago gang building networking into Windows desktop and laptop PCs, and with the NT gang building Windows into a robust server environment, it was be-coming easier to think of Windows as the network itself. There was no need to think of a separate network operating system like NetWare. The killer app of the network was, as Allard had put it, Windows. By extension, Win-dows was the killer app for the global network of networks, the Internet. It would take years for the impact of Reardon's grand inspiration to reach full bloom. When it did, the shift to NT was tectonic. By 1996 the server mar-ket began to segue from NetWare to Windows NT, and in 1997 new NT in-stallations surpassed NetWare for the first time.

Reardon took to calling the NetWare cloning procedure the lesson of Snowball. When he got the call to license browser code for Windows 95, the first thing he did was apply the lesson of Snowball to his search.

Ludwig had turned Reardon on to the potential of the browser. After the NetWare compatibility coup, Reardon joined John Ludwig's life-after-Chicago team. Ludwig had spent much of the early spring and summer working with market research analysts, doing customer visits, and conduct-ing focus groups on the future of Windows. The results pointed him in the direction of integrating Windows with communications networks—with the telephone, with online services, and with e-mail. But how? Could there be a consistent interface for e-mail and something like gopher? What would a voice phone look like on Windows?

Then Ludwig saw Mosaic and everything suddenly made sense. Nor-mally low-key and analytical, Ludwig went upside down and backward over

Mosaic. Look at this, he told Reardon. Look how easy it is to use. Can we make Windows this easy? Reardon found Ludwig on another jihad every other morning. One morning it would be navigation: Look how easy Mosaic makes it to move back and forth among screens, the e-mail would cry. The next morning it would be histories: Can we keep a trail of where a user has been, what that user has done, so the user can just click on a line in a list to reenter a recently used program or page? How about "back" and "forward" buttons for Windows file management? Can Windows files be indexed and hyperlinked the way Web files are? Ludwig's campaign gained momentum in August 1994, when IBM announced browsing capability for OS/2 in Warp. Ludwig saw no reason to panic—IBM was still IBM, after all, and would find some way to botch the browser. Still, it was a sign the world was continuing to move ahead. He brought Slivka on board to initiate an actual coding strategy for browsing in Chicago. As for possibly licensing some browser code, Ludwig knew the guy for the job: Reardon. Can you look at the various browser products available—Mosaic, Cello, Viola, Midas, BookLink, and whatnot—and see where Microsoft might do a license or acquisition? Ludwig asked his pal. With Allard and, subsequently, Siegelman already exploring a BookLink deal, Reardon mainly window-shopped. And waited for an opening.

Along with Ludwig and Silverberg, Reardon believed the way people should get to Marvel was through the Internet. Siegelman was holding out for people getting to the Internet through Marvel. What Reardon really balked at was the notion that Blackbird, the enhanced publishing platform for Marvel, could somehow become the publishing vehicle for the whole Web. It was obvious to Reardon that html would serve that role as it grew, matured, and flourished: "The idea that html would just be a control set of Blackbird, and that Microsoft would only allow interaction with this OLE environment called Blackbird and this design tool for Blackbird, with html just a little thing inside of it—well, that was just upside down. In fact the browser would be the overall experience. Microsoft would have controls inside of it, not the other way around."

So Reardon chafed while the BookLink negotiations dragged on. When America Online bought BookLink and everything blew up in smoke, he was ready to rock. The AOL acquisition may have seemed like a disaster to Siegelman, but to Reardon it was a classic opportunity. Reardon called Spyglass and renewed talks. Clark got wind of the deal, and suddenly Netscape was pounding on Microsoft's door.

At the time, the University of Illinois, Spyglass, and Mosaic Communications were enmeshed in a bitter dispute over the rights to Mosaic. When Mosaic Communications announced on September 12, 1994, at the Net-World + Interop 94 trade show in Atlanta that its new browser would be called NetScape and its server line NetSite, there was enough confusion between Mosaic Communication's browser and the original NCSA Mosaic browser that the University of Illinois and Spyglass cried foul. The university still had a bad taste in its mouth over the defection of much of the original NCSA Mosaic team to Clark's venture. Now Clark was trying to steal the name as well. And maybe even the product. University and Spyglass officials were convinced there was latent Mosaic code in NetScape. Early NetScape users reported some striking similarities in certain functionality between it and NCSA Mosaic. The university collected the notifications, said Marcia Rotunda, associate university counsel, adding, "There were error messages that would mention NCSA or something. I can't remember if they said the actual word Mosaic or what, but they were things that pointed back to NCSA. They weren't major but indicated there was a little bit of shared code there somewhere."

Although the campaign consisted mostly of whispers and implications, it cast grave doubt on the legality of any deal with Mosaic Communications. When browser customers came the university's way, its legal staff let them know that Mosaic Communications had not licensed the real article—NCSA Mosaic—and was not likely to either.

Soon enough, word got back to Clark, who had been working on a big deal with thirteen high-profile Japanese customers to license Mosaic NetScape. Then things turned chilly all of a sudden. How can we be sure you are able to license your browser, they asked, when the University of Illinois and Spyglass say you do not own rights to Mosaic? Clark was beside himself. The uncertainty was costing him crucial deals in the short term and the dream of a successful IPO in the long term. Wall Street would never back a company whose lead product faced a potential intellectual property suit. Clark's first step was to hire a software expert to compare NetScape with its predecessor. The expert gave NetScape a clean bill of health, and Clark was confident enough to offer the university the opportunity to look over NetScape's source code. The university never did, however. Rotunda said the issue was moot—the Mosaic brand was a more pressing issue than borrowed code: "They offered at one point to have us compare the code, and by that time we didn't think it would be helpful. It would not give us any kind of answer that would tell us anything. They proposed to have someone analyze the code and see if there was duplication.

That's kind of the first step in that process. By then the trademark side had gotten more important so we were kind of focused on that."

Prodded by Spyglass, university executives began making noises about possible legal action. On October 13 a *Wall Street Journal* story quoted NCSA director Larry Smarr as saying that the university was "considering its options" with respect to legal infringements. That was followed by a letter to the editor published in the *San Jose Mercury News* on October 24, stating that Mosaic Communications did "not have a license to the university's software or trademarks." The next day, in a cease-and-desist letter, the university alleged that Mosaic Communications' software was "an inherent misuse of our intellectual property" and demanded that the company withdraw NetScape from distribution.

Clark knew he had to get the matter resolved to move his promising enterprise forward. He faced further motivation as well. His primary candidate to lead his new company as CEO, Jim Barksdale, had stated that he would not consider the job unless the naming issue was cleared up. Barksdale had grown revenues from $1 billion to $7.7 billion as chief operating officer of Federal Express and, after moving to McCaw Cellular, had negotiated its big $11.5 billion sale to AT&T. He was considered to have a golden touch. He had even been contacted by a Valley headhunter, David Beirne, for the COO post at Microsoft. Barksdale expressed little interest in the job, but Microsoft kept after him, going so far as to invite him through an intermediary to "come over and have a bowl of pasta with Bill and talk about it." Ultimately Barksdale declined: "I couldn't picture myself being surrounded by all these guys who'd built this marvelous company—what influence could I have on it? I would have been the sixth wheel on a one-wheel car," he said. "I was really thinking about retiring." Retiring? At fifty-one? Unlikely, associates say. The factor that really kept him from going to Redmond, they suggest, was Microsoft's hardball reputation. It wasn't because of pay or other issues, said one longtime Barksdale friend. It was because he didn't think he could work for Bill. It was an assessment shared in some Redmond quarters: The word inside Microsoft was that Gates and Ballmer would have eaten the genteel Southerner alive.

Gates later said he merely, at the suggestion of his friend Craig McCaw, had wanted to meet Barksdale, not necessarily hire him. The dinner invitation had nothing to do with the COO position, Gates said. The job subsequently was filled by Procter & Gamble executive Bob Herbold.

Headhunter Beirne came back at Barksdale with another proposal: There was this little Internet start-up in the Valley that was looking for somebody. Which one? Barksdale asked. Mosaic Communications, Beirne said. Barksdale had never been on the Net and didn't know Mosaic from bathroom tile, but the name rang a bell. Two weeks earlier he had been reading an article in *Fortune* magazine about twenty-five new companies to watch, including Mosaic. He had even mentioned the story to his wife, Sally, something way out of character. A sign? Some ascribe such synchronicity as part of a grand scheme, Barksdale said later; he considers it just random particles intercepting. Whatever, he decided to follow up. I have heard of them, Barksdale told Beirne. I'd like to take a look.

Clark and Doerr, whose venture capital firm Kleiner Perkins had invested $5 million in Mosaic Communications, flew to Seattle for a visit. The three hit it off. Barksdale agreed to join Mosaic Communications Corporation's board but said he would not take over the CEO slot till the company had settled its differences with the University of Illinois.

Doerr somehow got Colbeth's car phone number. "That's what I like about John. I didn't even know the guy. I knew who he was but didn't know him. He got my car phone number from somebody. To this day I don't know who. And he said, let's get this thing settled. We met, had a big pow-wow in downtown Chicago. We couldn't resolve it. But you know, we [at Spyglass] were the country bumpkins. They thought they could just throw $100,000 at us and be over with it."

The next day Clark was in court, filing suit against the University of Illinois and Spyglass for trade libel, unfair competition, and business infringement. Clark's suit, filed in northern California federal district court to ensure venue, asked for a determination of noninfringement on the NCSA Mosaic copyright. The suit also asked for monetary damages to be established later.

Reardon had no inkling of the hornet's nest he was stirring up when he called Spyglass to inquire about licensing Mosaic. When word got back to Mountain View, Clark went ballistic. A deal between Spyglass and Microsoft would give both Netscape competitors a lot of visibility and momentum, he reasoned. As much as he disliked the thought of dealing with Microsoft, Clark hated the notion of a big deal going Spyglass's way even more. A thought occurred to him: His head of OEM relationships, Ram Shriram, had been a neighbor of some Microsoft executive. Who was it? Brad Silverberg. The head of Windows 95 development. Clark thought he had hit paydirt. He asked Shriram to call Silverberg and warm him up to the idea of licensing Netscape. Silverberg, cognizant of Reardon's talks with Spyglass, was noncommittal. His message to Clark: "We did not want to license Navigator because it was under a legal cloud with the University of Illinois and the NCSA; there were many rumors floating around that were very damaging to Netscape . . . [and] We were very close to the deal with Spyglass."

Clark turned up the burners. He called Silverberg repeatedly, sweetening the pot with talk of a Microsoft "equity position"—a 10 percent or higher investment—in Mosaic Communications as well as a board seat. He asked his executive circle to explore a deal. "Clark pleaded with me to invest in Netscape and sit on the board," Silverberg asserted. Clark was not happy with his Hobson's choice. Cozying up to Microsoft was so far out of character that he later denied the whole thing. Only when pressed in an interview did he confess the full extent of his campaign: "I probably made a pretty impassioned plea for them to consider licensing our stuff, and probably in that context I suggested taking an equity position. As a possible way, a quid pro quo, for them to license with us instead of Spyglass."

Clark had gone after so many pressure points, Silverberg thought it was getting a little comical. Particularly after Mosaic Communication's rudeness in the earlier contact. Curious, Silverberg asked Clark why Microsoft had been rebuffed the first time around. Despite having directed Koontz to cold-shoulder Microsoft, Clark professed not to know about the earlier incident, told Silverberg the marketing manager had been acting on his own, and blamed Koontz's attitude on anti-Microsoft sentiment at SGI, where the manager had previously worked. Anti-Microsoft bias, Clark said, was one of the reasons he himself had left SGI. We want to be a good partner with Microsoft, Clark told Silverberg. But Silverberg remained suspicious. He had read recent comments in a *WIRED* magazine article about Mosaic where Andreessen belittled and disparaged Microsoft. Andreessen saw Microsoft as "one of the forces of darkness," author Gary Wolf wrote, quoting the Mosaic prodigy as saying, "The overriding danger to an open standard is Microsoft."

Is that any way to talk about a potential partner? Silverberg asked Clark. Clark responded that Andreessen was just a young pup shooting his mouth off, and he would talk to him about it.

Partly to assuage Silverberg's concerns, Clark moved forward to settle once and for all the Mosaic dispute with the University of Illinois. His initial offer had been for 50,000 shares of stock in his start-up, if the university agreed to relinquish all intellectual property rights to Mosaic—the name *and* the product. The university, which had already licensed Mosaic to a number of vendors, turned the offer down flat. Accepting the offer would have left Mosaic licensees without rights to the software, creating a potential legal headache much worse than anything Clark could pose.

Clark also did not want to license from Spyglass, which was asking a per-copy royalty, from 55 cents to $1 depending on volume. The rule of thumb with software, practiced earliest and most steadfastly by Bill Gates and Microsoft, was to pay flat fees instead of royalties. If a program hit big, you would be much farther ahead than anything that could be calculated based on present worth. Clark had another reason for avoiding a royalty: He was not sure how much he would be selling the NetScape browser for. Pricing, always a black art in software, was even murkier in the free-for-the-taking world of the Internet.

Gates had rattled Clark at a panel the two of them appeared on at the CMP Publications–sponsored Networked Economy conference in Washington, D.C., just three weeks before the release of the first Netscape beta in mid-October. "I think every operating system will build in the pieces that let you easily get onto the Internet with TCP/IP," Gates told the session. "And I think every shell that's done will have the html protocol, the Web Mosaic protocol support built right in."

At the time it was a natural assumption for Gates to make. IBM already had announced its OS/2 Warp was coming out with a built-in browser, WebExplorer, included at no charge. Apple Computer was talking about similar capabilities for the Macintosh. Given those precedents, Gates figured that Microsoft or anyone else would have a hard time charging for a browser in Windows. But the Gates declaration scared Clark, who heard Gates saying, "I hope no one plans to make money on browsers, because I am sure all the operating systems vendors will incorporate this technology into the OS." Clark decided "then and there I would make Netscape free," he recalled. His memory was somewhat of an oversimplification. When it first announced NetScape as Mosaic Communications, the company made no mention of charging for its browser. Instead, it planned to make money charging for servers. Initially it announced pricing for its NetSite communications server at $5,000 and commerce server at $25,000. Those would come down to less stratospheric levels, but the financial model remained in place. The Gates comment may have settled the issue in Clark's mind, but Mosaic Communications had never announced plans to charge for its browser.

No matter what he stood to make on servers, Clark had no intention of paying 55 cents a copy in royalties for a product he was going to distribute for free.

As a show of good faith, Clark decided to change the company name, a move he hoped would lay to rest the brand concerns from Spyglass and the university. On November 17 and 18 he had the company's name officially changed in Delaware and California, respectively, to Netscape Communications Inc. The upper-case "S" was no longer applicable. The switchover had created some excitement for the Mosaic now aka Netscape Communications Corp. gang the previous Sunday, as they set up the start-up's booth quarters at Comdex in Las Vegas. The booth got delivered with the legend Mosaic across the front. "We went out there with masking tape and effectively changed the company's name to Netscape on the Comdex floor," recalled Greg Sands, employee No. 21 and a server specialist. "Everything that said Mosaic, we put sticky tape over and wrote Netscape."

The name change did not, as Clark hoped, quiet the intellectual property rumors. Nor did it satisfy Barksdale. It was back to the negotiating table. After a lot of back and forthing, the two sides on December 20, 1994, agreed to flat-sum payments that turned out to total, with increments of $725,000 on two subsequent anniversaries of the agreement and payments of $500,000 in 1995 and $250,000 in 1996, in the neighborhood of $2.7 million. Later Andreessen pointed out that, had the university accepted the stock offer, it would have been $6 million to $9 million ahead (during the stock's heyday, at least). But, the university countered, he conveniently omitted mention of what the university would have to give up: the value of the Mosaic brand name. The university believed it got the better of the deal.

As part of the settlement, the principals agreed not to discuss whether Netscape's code contained any of the original Mosaic code. Doubts remain to this day. A possible objective source is Chris Wilson, who wrote the original Windows Mosaic with Jon Mittelhauser but wound up at Spry in Seattle instead of Netscape. Wilson, who subsequently was hired by Slivka at Microsoft to work on Internet Explorer, doubts that actual Mosaic code wound up in NetScape. But he believes it would be impossible for the original Mosaic team to produce a similar product without to some extent emulating its predecessor, saying: "I don't think they took any source code and copied it. I'm not sure if they looked at the source code to remind themselves of how anything was done either. But if you took most of the core development team of the project, and said go sit in the room and write software that does exactly what you just wrote, you're going to end up with large chunks of it the same, conceptually at least if not in detail. I don't necessarily think there's anything illegal about that but I know they [Netscape] have a lot of the same limitations that Mosaic did. Their whole rendering engine [the way pages get displayed] is very much based on the same models that we were working with on with Mosaic."

In any case, the settlement was too late. For all the sturm und drang over Netscape, Reardon considered Mosaic the better product. It was the standard. Other browsers, Reardon noticed, were not necessarily Mosaic-compatible. They did things just differently enough, even though their goal of rendering html into Web pages was the same, to set off alarms. Reardon figured that for Microsoft's browser to be successful, it would have to be compatible with Mosaic. "We realized early on that that kind of visual compatibility was going to be critical. So we wanted to stay with Mosaic, because we thought that was the law of the land in terms of how to render." Spyglass, moreover, was intent on improving Mosaic. When Spyglass obtained the rights to Mosaic, a team of eight programmers led by Krauskopf hammered the code into shape for commercial use. When Slivka looked at the Spyglass code, he was pleasantly surprised. There was quite a bit to do in terms of integrating it with Windows 95, but the Spyglass team had pretty much eradicated the sloppiness and inefficiencies Slivka expected.

There remained the issue of pricing. When Reardon had made his first round of inquiries regarding obtaining a browser, he had been tossing around the figure of $1 million for a flat-fee, paid-up license. Spyglass, however, countered with the dreaded royalty. It was not that much: $1 a copy, down to 55 cents for large-volume commitments. But it was a royalty nonetheless.

Reardon suspected Gates would never go for a royalty. After all, Gates faced the same dilemma as Clark. If Microsoft was going to give away the browser, it would be hard to justify paying someone a per-copy fee—particularly if the units got into the tens of millions. Colbeth initially stuck by the royalty approach. But Spyglass had the flexibility to negotiate any deal it wanted, and Reardon, joined by John Ludwig for the negotiations process, held the leverage of being able to walk if he wanted. As long as Clark was out there begging Silverberg to do a deal, Microsoft knew it had a bargaining chip or two.

Reardon also let it be known that Microsoft could, if it chose, develop its own browser from scratch. In fact, Reardon was getting pressure from J Allard all the way to Bill Gates on that score. It's absolutely stupid to buy a code base, Allard told Reardon every chance he got. We could just do our own from the ground up. It had worked with TCP/IP—in fact, Microsoft had wasted a lot of time and money, in Allard's mind, licensing other stacks when ultimately it was forced to do its own. When the contract numbers started filtering up to Gates, he had a similar reaction. You mean we're having to *pay* for software developed at a university? Gates asked, incredulous. The irony of his having, with Paul Allen and Monte Davidoff, done the original Microsoft BASIC on university equipment while an undergraduate at Harvard was probably not lost on Gates, who despite outward appearances could enjoy a joke on himself as much as on the next guy. Neither did the hypocrisy of his position keep him from grumping to Reardon.

Colbeth did not take too seriously Microsoft's threat to roll its own. His guys, particularly Krauskopf, had let him know that browsers were a lot harder to do than they looked. It was one reason so few really effective knockoffs of Mosaic existed. For Microsoft to come up with something that had no suggestion or overtones of Mosaic would be nigh to impossible.

By December 9 the two sides, which had started talks on an offer of $200,000 from Microsoft, agreed to a fee totaling $2 million, licensing Mosaic for Windows 95 and Windows NT. Microsoft saw little reason to license for other platforms—Macintosh and UNIX—where Mosaic already was entrenched. As for Windows 3.X and Windows for Workgroups, there was no point in dragging them into discussions. It would be a tall enough order to integrate the browser into Windows 95. The Windows 3.X versions were soon to be outmoded—at least, everyone assumed so—and the added cachet of a built-in browser would be one more incentive for Windows users to upgrade to Win 95.

Tyrrell signed the contract, dated his signature December 9, and sent it to Microsoft. With talks still proceeding with Netscape, Microsoft was in no hurry to ink the deal. Monday passed, then Tuesday and Wednesday, without Gates's signature. Tyrrell was turning apoplectic. As a vice president of sales, he was always expecting Murphy to tap him on the shoulder. Reardon had a week of phone hell from Tyrrell, who knew all too well what was going on with Netscape: What's happening? Why hasn't Gates signed? Tyrrell spent much of the Spyglass Christmas party on December 14 on his cell phone, going back and forth with Reardon, Ludwig, and voice mail. Reardon felt sorry for Tyrrell but could not give him the real reason for the delay: "It was just unfortunate that we had asked Spyglass to sign it first, because we knew we would have to sell it to Bill . . . and he pissed and moaned about $2 million, and why can't we do this internally?"

In the end, Spyglass prevailed. Reardon was intent on getting the code that the Web had standardized on. So far that was Mosaic, not Netscape— although that would change remarkably fast. Spyglass also struck the Microsoft contingent, including Silverberg and Ludwig, as a better potential partner, given Netscape's mixed messages in the press versus in private.

After the Mosaic settlement, Clark gave Silverberg a final try, in an e-mail sent December 23 and again at the noteworthy hour of 3:01 A.M., December 29. "I'd like you to reconsider using our Netscape client," Clark wrote. "Microsoft is the de facto standard 'client' software company, and we have never planned to compete with you, so we have never considered a 'client' as being our business. Our business is adding value on the back-end in the form of vertical applications, currently using Oracle databases. We intend to do this primarily on NT and BackOffice very soon." Sweetening the pot, Clark offered "an equity position in Netscape, with the ability to expand the position later." Given the "worry that exists regarding Microsoft dominance of practically everything, we might be a good indirect way to get into the Internet business," Clark added.

The e-mail was as forthright an invitation for Microsoft to invest in and/or partner with Netscape as could be stated. When it was made public four years later in the Justice Department suit, Barksdale explained it away as "a moment of weakness." Netscape's counsel, former Federal Trade Commissioner Christine Varney, added that it was the end of the year, the company was running out of money, it was late at night, Clark was acting on his own in desperation. In actuality, Clark had conducted a multiweek campaign aimed at winning over Microsoft to the detriment of Spyglass and Mosaic. All to no avail. It was too late. Gates signed the Spyglass papers on December 16, a week after Tyrrell had signed them. The contract wound up being dated December 12, effective December 9, 1994.

The gweep had gotten Slivka some code. Now the real work could begin.

Chapter 12

AFRIKANER

In the fall of 1994, Microsoft was making strides on the client side of the Internet—what users saw on their screens. But what about the server side? Server technology, the software engines that whirred and clicked and ground away on high-end workstations (mostly, at the time, Sun Microsystems' SPARCstations) and beefed-up PCs, was still second fiddle to the desktop stuff at Microsoft. The viewer side of the Internet—mostly embodied by the browser but also reflected in gopher, ftp, WAIS (search), and other functionality—got all the glory. The server side was all the guts.

Allard had a little personal crusade going to change all that. Why shouldn't the plumbers and electricians and masons get a little of the credit, instead of all the attention going to the architects, designers, and Big Thinkers? Allard and a merry band of steel-driving men had been busting their butts to push, push, push Microsoft onto the Net. They had hammered TCP/IP into shape, gotten Winsock rolling, demonstrated the power of a Net address for ftp, for corporate identity on the Net, for product distribution and support. The browser stuff, that was the cake and icing. The server folks, guys like David Thompson, David Treadwell, Henry Sanders,

Mike Massa, Keith Moore, John Ludeman, and Jawad Khaki, they were the meat and potatoes. Heavy lifters—that's what Allard called them.

As far as Allard was concerned, you could talk all you wanted about things like Mosaic and Word Assistant and html and sgml. You could jump up and down about how the Web was going to transform publishing, advertising, and media. About how it would eliminate the middleman—disintermediation, that was called—and produce a "vig" or "bookie's fee," for each transaction. And break down time and distance barriers between messenger and receiver. You could evangelize all you wanted; unless there were servers capable of handling it all, of managing files and organizing data and tracking transactions, it was all whistling in the dark.

When talk started turning to publishing on the Web, Allard saw a huge opportunity. Make NT the way people managed rich information on the Web. This would accomplish several things at Microsoft. It would give NT technology, which had stumbled out of the gate with an ill-defined mission that led to doing many things poorly, a specific goal. It would open up a huge market to NT. It would create a synergy between Microsoft's client software—Windows 95 and whatever browsing and Internet access technology it came up with—and the high-end NT networking system. It would give Microsoft a competitive wedge against NetWare. Mostly it would create an upside for NT, which was hurting. It had fallen far short of even 1 million units its first year out the door. It needed a killer app. It needed a dynamite platform. It needed credibility. Heck, it needed a *plan*. Off in his little corner of Internet evangelism, Allard was thinking, Hey, we can do that!

NT had another true believer, a big and loud one. At the company meeting the fall of 1994 inside Seattle's Kingdome stadium, Steve Ballmer took the stage with laptop in hand. "O ye of little faith!" he bellowed to the gathered throng of 10,000 or so. "Here in my hand, I have NT! And we will keep driving till we make this thing a standard!"

It was time once again for Allard to make Ballmer's pain go away. What he had in mind was an Internet server for NT. In typical Allard fashion, he broke the concept into components and plumbing. The first step was to build what he and Treadwell, who was instrumental in the plan as well, liked to term the PBX—the exchange businesses used to manage telephone services—for local area networks. "I thought it would be a palatable way to talk to medium and large businesses, as well as the [distribution] channel, about an opportunity to sell a new and exciting service, the Data PBX," he recalled. "You understand PBXes, right? Well, this is a data PBX. It doesn't cost a whole lot, and you can manage your internal network, it gets you out onto the external network [Internet]. And you can put these à la carte services on top."

It was the kind of thing tailor-made as an add-on capability to NetWare. But Allard felt sure Novell was missing out. Novell had a formidable sales and support channel, everything from huge corporate accounts to mom-'n'-pop outfits on suburban corners selling NetWare to small businesses. It had a broad fleet of certified engineers trained to handle networking problems. It was the gold standard. But Novell was not minding the store. Since merger negotiations with Microsoft had fallen through in 1991, it had been bent on trying to be another Microsoft. Novell had held prolonged and fruitless discussions to purchase Lotus and had put together a deal, announced March 21, 1994, to buy WordPerfect, which was about to be unseated by Microsoft as the No. 1 word processor, for $1.4 billion and to purchase Quattro Pro from Borland for $110 million, tossing in an additional $35 million for a bundling deal with WordPerfect and Borland's Paradox database. It had expended a lot of time and energy on pushing the Federal Trade Commission to take antitrust action against Microsoft based on what it saw as unfair practices against Novell DOS, née DR DOS. By early 1994 all of this had left its core business exposed and in disarray, even though Novell's market position remained strong. On April 5, 1994, the day of the Shumway retreat, Novell's sixty-nine-year-old empire builder, Microsoft-basher Ray Noorda, resigned. Named to succeed Noorda was genial Hewlett-Packard executive Bob Frankenberg, who realized "rather quickly that his first job was to undo all that Noorda had done in his last two to three years," as analyst Mark Anderson put it. One of Frankenberg's first actions was to meet with Gates on July 7 at Microsoft. The conversation went amicably, with the promise of a new era: "He [Frankenberg] said, 'Look, I'm in charge now and all that hateful stuff that Noorda kept saying [is past] . . . I'm really going to fix this, and I'm going to get some focus,'" Gates recalled.

By the summer of 1994, Allard and Treadwell put together a strategy to build an Internet server that would enable corporate networks to publish, manage, and control documents and files over the Internet. The key was to make NT the easiest, most effective way for corporate networks to interact with the Net. There was still the issue of how to make money on any of this, but lack of a business plan had never stopped him before. Allard started assembling a team, beginning with John Ludeman, a veteran systems programmer, and came up with a name for the new approach: Internet Information Server. The name was an unintentional, even unconscious echo of Allard's "killer app" memo the previous winter. Only when he went back later and reread the memo did Allard realize the parallel.

IIS would turn out to be a seminal product for Microsoft on the Internet, but it was just one step on the NT server ladder. The announcement of BackOffice, a cleverly amalgamated suite of products designed to raise NT's visibility and usefulness, went hand-in-glove philosophically with Allard's Internet goals. The play off "Office" provided an instant association with what Microsoft was trying to accomplish. Front Office tasks, files, documents, records, and other data could be shared through the BackOffice network administration capabilities. Whether the catchiness of the name itself belonged to Ballmer, as Rich Tong recalled in a *PC Week* story by Steve Hamm, or to Tom Evslin, as Ballmer himself credited, the concept eventually catapulted NT to the top of PC networking for large enterprises.

The "Sea Change" memo, Slivka's browser development, Marvel's BookLink negotiations, Pathe's Internet Assistant for Word, J Allard's Internet Information Server . . . the Microsoft machine was cranking into gear. The Internet was driving more and more product development, perhaps not yet in a broadly coordinated fashion, and certainly not in any public forum. To the naked eye, Microsoft was still an Internet nonentity. At Stewart Alsop's Agenda conference two weeks before the "Sea Change" memo, Gates had talked about Microsoft's plans for Marvel. In the audience was Dave Winer, a pioneer software developer known by one and all as much for his opinions as his UserLand Frontier code. Incisive and acerbic, Winer had a quick trigger finger and Hemingway's built-in bullshit detector. What he took away from Gates's comments at Agenda was simple: Microsoft was hopelessly out of touch.

Winer already had his own website, called DaveNet, which he used as a kind of Dear Diary to the Internet at large. On October 18, he confessed to his readers that he had intended to write some code that morning, "but I'm having trouble concentrating. There's another essay lurking in my head!" Nothing lurked inside Winer for very long, and the result was "Bill Gates vs. The Internet," a ten-paragraph jeremiad on Microsoft's inability to fathom the Web. "The old software industry is struggling (even flailing) to not be random idiots," Winer declared with typical forthrightness. Upcoming versions of Windows, Mac, and OS/2 all were pledging Internet clients, but "none of the platform vendors had any say in the definition of these standards!" The Internet had simply happened of its own accord, catching Gates flat-footed. Winer had understood Gates to characterize Marvel as a bet-the-company move: "Bill is scrambling. He understands the stakes, and is doing the only reasonable thing he can do." After all, Gates did not want to become the next Ken Olsen, nor did he want Marvel to be the DEC Rainbow of online systems, Winer observed, unaware of the irony in at least one aspect of the comparison: Thomas Reardon, the archetypal Microsoft Internet renegade, had gotten his start using Rainbows in school back in New Hampshire.

"Marvel can't compete with the Internet," Winer concluded. "Once users take control, they never give it back."

Winer could not have known the extent of Internet development inside Microsoft, but Gates decided to set him straight anyway. In return mail, Gates called Winer's mail "stimulating," but added, "why the demagoguery?" Marvel was not a bet-the-company thing at all. "The Internet is a great phenomena [sic]," Gates wrote. "I don't see how the emergence of more information content on a network can be a bad thing for the personal computer industry. Will it cause less [sic] personal computers to sell? I think quite the opposite. Less copies of Flight Simulator or Encarta?" Keep your eye out for Internet support in Windows 95, and Microsoft's website, Internet Assistant for Word, and Internet server technology in NT, Gates advised. "We want to do our best on all of this and welcome additional ideas."

By the time Gates wrote about a sea change caused by electronic publishing, Mosaic Communications was exactly one week from releasing its browser over the Internet and watching the downloads mount up like the burger sign at McDonald's. On October 13, 1994, Mosaic Netscape (by now the capital "S" had been lowered) version 0.9—still a beta offering—was released. Among avid Web watchers, Netscape was getting a lot of attention, if only because of the talent behind it. At Microsoft, it was just another browser. Slivka and his team were evaluating it, along with BookLink and Mosaic. But Slivka was preoccupied with OS/2 Warp and the potential competition posed by its WebExplorer browser.

Warp's big splash was expected at Fall Comdex in Las Vegas, and by the eve of the big show, Maritz was weighing in with a characteristically succinct analysis of options and strategic game plan. In an e-mail dated 11:52 A.M. on November 7, addressed to Gates, Silverberg, Allchin, Ludwig, Myhrvold, Siegelman, and Evslin and headed "Internet access and issues,"

Maritz offered a proposal on moving forward with Internet access re Marvel and Windows 95:

> I think we [Microsoft] have the following important objectives: A) Ensure that Windows is very well-connected, in particular ensure it's straightforward for a user to get connected to the Internet, and ease and ubiquity of connection do not become differentiating attributes of Macintosh or OS/2. B) Enable Marvel to become the preferred one-stop shop for online access to both Marvel and Internet content, both over a dedicated network and over the Internet. C) Leverage the Internet phenomenon of a public high-speed WAN network to unseat Novell and Notes wherever possible.
>
> The issue is to ensure we don't do something that automatically prevents one of the above and to put us on a path that achieves all three.

The last line was classic Maritz: Make sure, whatever you do, that you are neither proscribing your options nor shooting yourself in the foot. Gates once commented that Maritz's particular gift was to reduce complex challenges to their core essence, addressable in one or two action items.

At its heart, the Maritz memo was an attempt to define a best-of-both-worlds approach to Microsoft's internal schism over the Internet. The Windows 95 team would get its wish of easy, built-in, point-and-click Internet access. The Marvel team would protect its raison d'être by being the door through which all online content and Internet access proceeded. Strategically, it was a reasonable approach. Technologically, it was more problematic. If the Windows team was going to blend browsing capability with the operating system, users were going to have to be able to jump right from a Word file to the Internet, Marvel notwithstanding. Silverberg, Ludwig, Reardon, et al., still hung on to their conviction that Windows, not Marvel, should be the way PC users got onto the Internet.

Maritz saw "good news" on the Marvel front, however. BookLink negotiations for browser technology were proceeding. Evslin was talking with MCI to provide a dial-up network for Win 95 users to log onto automatically. And Microsoft's support divisions were working with the Marvel team to provide Internet access and signup software for Win 95, Windows NT, and Marvel. As for Lotus Notes and Novell, Microsoft's Business Systems Division—NT—needed to get cracking on leveraging Internet access against its two prime competitors, Maritz urged: "I and lots of others have

some thoughts on this, but BSD really needs to pick up this ball. It is a closing window and a once-in-a-lifetime opportunity to leverage a protocol vs.
Novell." When Maritz said once-in-a-lifetime opportunity, it was not a
cliché. What he meant was, once and only once. Pretty much forever.
There would be no second chance.

Gates wasted little time responding to Maritz, with a wrinkle. Writing
after midnight, at 12:19 A.M. on November 8, Gates noted:

> I agree with all of this except one thing. Based on my modest understanding, the
> deal with UUNet which would be equity would be preferable over the deal with MCI.
> Whoever is looking at this needs to sit down with Russ and discuss it and if they
> don't agree, send some mail to us and get us to resolve it quickly.

UUNet? It was a collection of companies, based in Falls Church, Virginia,
that sold Internet access. With annual sales of just $13 million, UUNet
was small trying to get to big. It offered Internet access in twenty-five cities
via a local telephone call but aimed to expand the world over. Talks with
UUNet had gotten under way on an eastern swing by Bernard Aboba, the
Berkeley author and online services guru hired by Russ Siegelman for
MSN. Aboba figured talking to a small carrier for Net access beat going
with one of the big telcos. He had been told by PSI Net, which had purchased a then seemingly promising service called Pipeline, that Microsoft
would never get anywhere on the Internet. When he knocked on UUNet's
door, Aboba found paydirt. "Within five minutes I knew we were going to
do a deal with them," he recalled. John Sidgmore, UUNet's steely chief
executive, laid out a point-by-point plan for building up to 11 million ports
for MSN. "They needed money and that's basically what we decided that
we would provide," Aboba said. "We take a stake in the company, and they
would spend all their waking and sleeping hours building Internet dial-
up."

The Palindrome Man (his name has the rare trait of being spelled the
same backward as forward) brought years of Internet savvy to MSN. The
son of an Egyptian immigrant father and American mother, Aboba had
grown up in the Bronx and gotten his first exposure to computers on an
IBM 1620 mainframe at the Bronx High School of Science. In 1975 he left
for Harvard University, got an Internet account, and studied engineering
and applied science with the thought of "doing something with computers." He never met Gates or Ballmer, but did know Bob Greenberg, one of

the original "Albuquerque 11" of Microsoft's early years. Greenberg was a math teaching assistant at the time.

After Harvard, Aboba continued to pursue postgraduate computer-related study at Stanford University. He learned UNIX system adminstration and did AppleTalk networking at the School of Earth Science, from which he received a doctorate in 1990. Then it was off to the University of California at Berkeley, where Aboba enrolled for an MBA "to see if I could make something like [Internet services] a commerical business on a large scale." At Berkeley Aboba became a systems god for one of the nation's leading hobbyist groups, the Berkeley Macintosh Users Group. BMUG ran an electronic bulletin-board system that included Internet e-mail access. Partly to solve the problem of endless support questions involving the Net, Aboba wrote a book, *The BMUG Guide to Bulletin Boards and Beyond*. Aboba drained his bank account to self-publish 5,000 copies. When they arrived, "I was pretty nervous. They filled up half the office, and I had my whole life savings in them." They sold out in three months. Aboba was shocked: "I didn't understand what was going on. I was asking, Why are people willing to slog through all this stuff about the Internet? And there would be this woman who wants to use it to talk to her child who she hasn't talked to in twelve months who lives in Israel or whatever. She's willing to spend a week of her time learning how to do this so she can talk to her kid. . . . I realized for the first time I was underestimating the commerical potential of the Internet."

Still in school, Aboba picked up a contract programming job with Borland to do work on the spreadsheet Quattro Pro. He also wrote a sequel, *The Online Users Encyclopedia*, this time published by Addison-Wesley. While noodling around with Winsock and TCP/IP in 1993, Aboba came across the logon of J Allard. "I came to understand that Microsoft had a pretty good handle on building their TCP/IP implementation." At a conference early in 1994 in Seattle, Aboba ran into Russ Siegelman, who invited him to the Shumway retreat. Aboba joined Microsoft in June with the notion of helping Marvel get Internet access, but with little realization of the monumental effort it would require.

At first Siegelman and Aboba held little hope that Marvel could get Internet capability. Marvel was calculating that it would need access for 1 million users right out of the gate. The duo soon discovered that there were not enough ports in existence to guarantee the numbers. "I called carriers and I called my friends asking, Who's got the ports?" Aboba recalled. "It added up to a pitiful number. In the thousands. I wrote a memo to Bill saying, if we bought them all, we could supply the first five minutes of signups (on Marvel) and that would be it."

It looked like Marvel would stick with the AOL model and offer e-mail and newsgroup access to the Internet but nothing else. That could be done through the x.25 protocol, where plenty of ports were available. When AOL bought BookLink and made noises about becoming the new global Internet standard, the pressure was on Marvel to respond. Aboba started making the rounds to find a partner who could supply Internet access, and eventually wound up on the doorstep of UUNet.

The UUNet proposal still had to compete with one of the Big Boys—MCI. Bob Frankston, the spreadsheet pioneer and an early Internet visionary who at the time was working for Microsoft and had been at the Shumway session, had brought Tom Evslin together with legendary Vinton Cerf, one of the Internet's original creators who had been hired by MCI to develop its Internet business. Evslin had in mind enabling Windows 95 users to log into the Net via MCI, bypassing MSN altogether. A deal with MCI would bring Microsoft a high-profile player, lots of technology, and instant visibility as a big Net player. But MCI had lots of things on its mind more absorbing and demanding than supplying Microsoft with Internet service. Aboba remained skeptical: "I have enormous respect for Vint and for MCI, but I thought, 'This is a major carrier. How much are they going to commit to doing this?'" Siegelman minced no words either: "I am vehemently against this proposal," he wrote in e-mail dated October 13, 1994. Siegelman felt permitting an alternate way of getting into the Internet via Windows 95 would dilute MSN's appeal. "The real issue is that we want Microsoft to be the service provider—this means we sign up the accounts, not MCI."

In the end, Gates made the call in favor of UUNet. "Basically we presented the two deals to Bill," said Aboba. "And he chose the one we had because he thought it made more sense from a financial point of view, and also from the commitment point of view." Not that finances were a big problem: On December 25, 1994, cable giant TCI and its fearsome CEO John Malone turned Santa, putting a $125 million investment under the MSN tree. The deal, a 20 percent stake, made MSN worth over $600 million overnight. On January 5, 1995, Siegelman sent e-mail that Gates had decided to put Microsoft's Internet marbles into the MSN box. Instead of accessing the Internet through a Windows 95 browser, as Silverberg, Slivka, and the Net agitators wanted, users would get to the Net through MSN. "Billg will make, state, and reinforce this new message" within the next week, Siegelman wrote.

At first, Silverberg balked. Even with Internet access tacked on, a proprietary online system was the wrong way to go, he believed. "I fought it for a while, but then eventually it came down to Bill saying, 'Hey we're going to ship it,'" Silverberg recalled. "I stopped fighting it and tried to help them." Silverberg asked Slivka to tackle putting TCP/IP support in MSN. The code name for the project, Rome, may have unintentionally implied (in keeping with the team's geographical implications) the likelihood of the product making it into Chicago. Although as MSN Internet strategist Anthony Bay put it, Rome also "wasn't built in a day," the next eight months were going to be a mad dash. The MSN team was panicked over security—what if hackers got into the system via the Net? Slivka had an inspiration: "I'm like, what if you cut all that stuff? They were, oh, okay. Then it was not much work at all. I accelerated that schedule a little bit."

Slivka's breakthrough was to enable access from MSN to the Internet, but not the other way around. The decision reduced much of the server security work. It also meant, however, that MSN cut out a huge amount of early Web curiosity-seeking access. Slivka was not particularly bothered by that aspect, either. A flood of Webheads hitting MSN the first day or two would simply overburden the system, preventing anyone, pay customer or freeloader, from having a good experience.

On January 13, 1995, the UUNet deal was announced at a Washington Software Association Online Advantage conference in Bellevue. Microsoft made what over the course of the year amounted to a 15 percent investment, $26 million, and got in addition a board seat—to be served by Rosen, at Sidgmore's invitation. It was an exception for Microsoft, whose executives seldom served on other corporate boards. Rosen was the first at the product-unit level to take a board seat elsewhere. For added drama, Microsoft announced, a month after the deal was sealed, its licensing of the Spyglass Mosaic browser.

With the UUNet deal inked, the enormity of the task facing MSN started to sink in. When he looks back today, Aboba says even knowing what he knows, "if somebody asked me to do that, I'd say you're out of your mind. We had to build the world's largest Internet online service in six months." UUNet had been plugging away, adding lines and designing the system for several months. But a lot of leg and hip bones had to be connected. UUNet's collection of systems, remote-access servers from Ascend Communications, dial-up and browser software for MSN and Windows 95, a new data center . . . "I have never worked so hard in all my life," Aboba recalled. "There were a lot of eighteen- and twenty-hour days." The MSN effort had its own jihad, as much guts if not ultimately glory as the Windows 95 quest.

With MSN pursuing its Internet path and Slivka & Co. building Internet access directly into Windows, Microsoft's browser strategy was not just bifurcated but muddled. On November 5, 1994, Jim Allchin threw his hat into the Internet access ring with the understated observation to Silverberg, Ludwig, Allard, Evslin, and Muglia that "Today we have many 'explorers' being created." By "explorer" Allchin was still referring to a viewer—the equivalent of, in the argot of the Web, browser. Allchin ticked off five viewer strategies on the Redmond campus alone, including the Win 95 shell, the e-mail client Capone, and Marvel. Then he noted, to protests from no one, "This is a mess." No one believed another Explorer should be created just for the Internet, Allchin pointed out. To the contrary, maybe it was time to start focusing on one "explorer" for everything. Perhaps that process should start by answering which "explorer" should be the Internet one.

"It seems to me we have two choices," Allchin wrote: Windows Explorer or the e-mail interface. Allchin's instincts told him that the latter—code-named Capone—should serve as the "explorer" model for the O'Hare browser. Microsoft at the time had a project code-named Ren to tie together e-mail with appointments, contacts, and to-do lists. Ren ultimately became Outlook, Microsoft's personal information manager. Allchin elaborated that "Perhaps Ren will create world peace and that will solve all our problems, but until peace comes I think we should have a strategic bet between us. My initial bias (assuming performance, etc., isn't an issue) is to put it into Capone. However, I don't think I have thought through all the issues to arrive at a final opinion."

World peace? Not likely given the tensions between the NT and Windows 95 sides. The guy who *had* thought through all the issues and *did* have a final opinion was John Ludwig. Within forty-eight hours of Allchin's note, Ludwig had fired off return mail. It was a pretty obvious call to him: O'Hare, the Windows 95 browser, should be a one-size-fits-all interface for Windows. Performance was an issue, yes: "Capone is several times slower than the current BookLink beta for common operations like startup," Ludwig related. Besides, what did integration with e-mail buy you? It "doesn't really provide any advantage for Web browsing," Ludwig added. "Web browsing is nonhierarchical." With e-mail you wanted folders and directories and threaded tree structures. With browsing it was a lot simpler: You just wanted to jump from page to page. Backward and forward. Keep track of your trail, yes. But e-mail viewing and Web surfing were like swimming and bicycling, two completely disparate activities.

Which "explorer" mattered? The Windows team helped answer the question by moving to give O'Hare an official name. The team compiled a list of several candidates that included variations on Mosaic, e.g., Microsoft Mosaic. Contractually, the naming was permissible, and several licensees had adopted the convention. But in the end, the decision to go with Explorer rested on the browser's synergy with Windows. Windows 95 had its own Explorer, or viewer. It made sense to adapt its capabilities to the Web as well. At an Internet World demonstration of Windows 95, browser team member Alec Saunders showed how "you could access information wherever it was, whether on your local hard disk or on your network or on the Internet, all using the same browsing metaphor. We saw Windows 95 as a tool you could use to access information anywhere." Explorer it was, but without any conscious reference to J Allard's initial use of the term in his "killer app" memo of January 1994. After all, who would remember to check?

Unifying products by metaphor was one thing. Getting Microsoft's separate product teams to align was another. The O'Hare, Marvel, and NT projects all were proceeding along similar Internet paths, sometimes parallel, sometimes perpendicular, and, occasionally, even merging. It was a managerial nightmare that only someone like Bill Gates, who understood the benefits of internecine rivalries, could appreciate: "You have two worlds, Windows 95 and Windows NT. A lot of the Cairo ideas became part of the Windows 95 shell. So there was a bit of a challenging process taking the Cairo shell guys and transferring them under Windows 95. Would that group embrace them? A lot of angst about that!"

The world peace guy, Allchin, set out to merge the Windows 95 and NT paths as best he could. It was an uphill battle: "The Windows 95 team decided NT is for the server, NT is irrelevant. I don't care if I ever support you, I only care about Novell. So it was the longest time of me trying to convince the Win 95 team and others here that they should do things to support NT. I remember being told several times to just go away."

Tensions first erupted when, in 1993, members of Allchin's Cairo team were transferred over to the Win 95 effort to implement object orientation in the Win 95 interface. It was a great idea technologically, a good idea strategically, a bad idea politically. The Cairo and Windows 95 teams philosophically shared the same goal. They wanted the user interface to be simpler and easier and to have files and folders be clickable objects that could be opened or copied or moved or deleted by using a mouse. But while the

Cairo team was off in the ether designing the world's most perfect interface, the Chicago team had been moving ahead, making concrete decisions based on the hard realities of computing life. Silverberg kept a 386-33 MHz computer with 8 megabytes of RAM as his personal machine during the Windows 95 development effort. As time passed, his configuration fell further behind the newly shipping 486 and Pentium designs. The Chicago development team grew to hate the old rust bucket. But Silverberg knew there were a lot of 386 computers still being used. Besides, if Windows 95 ran on a 386, it stood to run all that much better on a 486 or higher chip.

The Cairo team's "angst," David Cole recalled, probably stemmed more from their cherished project's loss of initiative than from differences with the Chicago vision. "We just looked at it as some developers and a (project) lead coming to help us," Cole said. "Perhaps there was some angst just about that issue." The Chicago effort already had decided on several file management options, based on Silverberg's old ironsides. Methods for making shortcuts and cut/copy/paste of files were in place in Chicago, where the Cairo team was still experimenting with alternatives. And Windows 95's signature Taskbar—the across-the-bottom-of-the-screen selection menu—and Start button were already in place. Cairo's vision included similar goals but, with the expectation of running on NT, required more memory and system resources. When the Cairo team split off, in fact, it left NT without the user interface advances of the Chicago effort. Allchin and Maritz, reckoning that the typical conservative, corporate NT customer wanted the tried-and-true, decided not to put the Windows 95 interface on NT. Silverberg thought this to be pure folly and argued strenuously that *any* customer would want Windows 95's user advances. Silverberg, surprisingly, found an ally in curmudgeonly David Cutler, the NT god, who actually liked the Windows 95 interface. In the end, Silverberg and Cutler proved right. Demand for the Windows 95 interface on NT ran high. But NT users had a painful wait till version 4.0, which shipped more than a year after Chicago, before they got it.

Any time two groups merged at Microsoft, Cole pointed out, you could expect competitive friction. As it turned out, the Chicago group managed to fold in a number of the object-oriented features of Cairo without altering its system requirements or becoming an entirely object-oriented system. Silverberg saw the arrangement, despite its initial rockiness, as ultimately beneficial: "Yeah, there was angst with the Cairo UI team coming over. But it worked out fine in the end for the company and the product. . . . It made no sense for the company to have two separate and similar but different shell efforts. . . . My group had responsibility for more of the 'presentation level' technologies like the shell, multimedia, Internet client, mail client, while the NT group was more focused on some of the underlying shared components, like protocols, OLE, and so on."

Angst aside, Windows 95 was slipping behind schedule. Throughout summer and fall of 1994, Silverberg had pushed, pushed, pushed the Chicago team to hold to a March or at the very least a first-half 1995 release date. But the feedback he was getting from the beta 2 cycle led him to believe the program still needed wider testing and more thorough debugging. Windows 95 was Silverberg's baby, and if it was going to ship with his name on it, it had better be as rock solid as humanly possible.

One might have assumed that the Internet plumbing work was delaying Chicago, but really the problem was the same old hobgoblin that haunted any system upgrade—compatibility. In yet another reiteration of the perennial systems battle, DOS applications absolutely had to work with Windows 95. Yet loads of new features in Windows 95 played havoc with DOS compatibility. Long file names was one feature: Windows 95 would make it possible for Windows users to move beyond the 8.3 limitation—eight letters in the file name, three letters in the suffix, such as 2MOMNDAD.LET. Instead the user could write: Letter to Mom and Dad. Moving Windows from a 16-bit environment to 32-bit—faster, bigger, better—was another feature. And there was Plug and Play. The term, popularized on the Macintosh, referred to the ability simply to attach a peripheral, or add-on device, such as a printer or external hard drive or scanner, and have it work all by itself without going through a brutal and mysterious installation routine. In Windows 3.X versions, users often had to go into DOS and enter configuration lines in CONFIG.SYS and AUTOEXEC.BAT files simply to get something like a sound board or CD-ROM drive to work. Then there was the whole issue of networking, not one of DOS's strong suits. Silverberg wanted NetWare compatibility and TCP/IP and dial-up networking in Windows.

As daunting as these challenges were, they paled in comparison to making Windows 95 compatible with the vast array of software applications and devices available for Windows—hundreds, thousands of them. Silverberg knew compatibility would be hard. It turned out to be so hard it was almost evil. The popularity of Windows had spawned a huge third-party industry. Sound cards, video cards, joysticks, games, multimedia. Sound and video card manufacturers, competing to stretch Windows as far as they could, were upgrading their equipment on almost a monthly basis. They had no idea from one version to the next how the two differed. The Windows team wound up hiring experts from MediaVision and Creative Labs because they were the only ones around who knew how their boards interacted with Windows.

DOS games were a special headache. Many installed their own device drivers in DOS, altering configuration files in a process that tended to crash Windows. Yet Silverberg knew that the games market attracted the leading-edge techies, who had to jump on the Windows 95 bandwagon if the program was to succeed. At one point he got so fed up with the DOS configuration quagmire that he told his son he was not going to buy him any more games. He was sick of hassling with memory managers and disk load utilities and whatnot. Silverberg didn't care if he never saw another DOS game as long as he lived. Yet he would go into the office every day knowing that Windows 95 had to do DOS games.

New stuff was coming out so fast that in the time it took to test a beta version of Windows 95, a whole new round of software, hardware, and peripherals would appear. Microsoft had to supply test suites of Windows 95 features to software and hardware vendors so they could test their products against it. By the time Microsoft settled on a test suite based on the existing product landscape, refined it, and got it in the hands of vendors, the whole world had changed. One day Silverberg and David Cole were commiserating over the situation when Silverberg came up with an idea. The issue was, with so much new stuff out there, how do you tell what's really important to the customer? Silverberg said, Why don't we just go to the local Egghead store in Bellevue and tell them we want one of everything? You're kidding, Cole said. One of everything in the entire store? Silverberg was in no way kidding. You have to figure that if Egghead stocks it, it must be selling, he said. Cole hopped in his pickup and drove over. The store manager's reaction was about the same as Cole's initial response. What do you mean, one of everything? You heard me right, Cole said. It took four hours to get everything loaded up. The store manager was beside himself with delight until he figured out it would blow his monthly quota. There was no way he'd match that month's sales the following month. When Cole got back to Building 6 with the software, Silverberg wanted to know if he'd gotten a deal.

"A deal?" Cole asked.

"Yeah, you know, a volume discount. Or something."

The next step was a loan-to-own program. Cole posted a list of everything they'd purchased and offered it free to developers to take home and keep, as long as they installed it and submitted bug reports. Then there were Boy Scout days, where local troops were invited to a community college or other facility and given the chance to pound on Windows 95 betas and various applications. There were "Install Fairs," where people would bring their machines to Microsoft on weekends. Silverberg would hit up anyone he ran into to test Windows 95. And he invited them to get back to him personally. Send me an e-mail with a bug, suggestion, or comment. Here's my address. The top guy was not above the feedback loop. Silverberg loved contact with average users; they were the reality check against the somewhat insular and ingrown techie culture that had little relation to how the millions of Windows users interacted with their software.

An obsessive personality with perfectionist tendencies, Silverberg became consumed with making sure Windows 95 was going to be a hit. Improvements would occur to him in his dreams. He would wake up at two, three in the morning with a couple of great ideas. At first he told himself he would write them down in the morning, when he got up. But he found he could not always remember them. Sometimes he could prompt himself numerically. If he told himself "three good ideas" when he awakened in the middle of the night, then he would work at it the next morning and concentrate until he remembered all three.

Sometimes he simply could not conjure them back up, though, so he started keeping a notepad next to his bedstand. When he woke up, he would jot down the ideas on the notepad, then go back to sleep. That worked, as long as his handwriting was not too scrawled as to be illegible. Other times the ideas would come to Silverberg when he did not have ready access to a pen and pad, as when driving to the store or riding his bike. In that case, he tried various mnemonic devices, such as the first initials of an idea or the numerical trick. In any case, he wasted no time sending off the ideas for feedback. He got to be pretty famous for e-mails at odd hours, when a flash of insight simply could not wait.

For Silverberg, Windows was a 24-by-365 job. Every hour of every day, all year long. It was the only way he knew to inject the passion and spirit of excellence required to make great software into the entire product-building process. He believed that there was an emotional component to software that took it beyond just a tool, something people used to get things done. There had to be a coolness factor, little things that made people smile with pleasure or exclaim with delight. Ultimately, the end user is what made software important. End users were the boss. If you did not keep that point in mind and meet their needs, someone else would come along to do it in your stead. That notion kept Silverberg, and by association, the Windows team humble, motivated, and scared. It was the classic underdog mentality. Silverberg ran as scared at Microsoft as he ever had at Borland or Apple. And the Windows team ran with him.

Early on, Cole found a way to motivate the rest of the team to keep up with Silverberg's manic pace. A test manager approached Cole with concerns that even though the Windows 95 project had detailed specifications, vision statements, and team agendas, "nobody knew what the key aspects of the project were." Cole did his own poll and was surprised to find it true. To keep the team focused on specific goals, Cole came up with the idea of the Ten Commandments. Everyone had to memorize them, he said. "I said that I'd come around and test people." The Ten Commandments were:

1. New, easy-to-use user interface
2. Complete, integrated protect mode system
3. Plug-and-play hardware
4. Win32 API
5. Complete and integrated network connectivity
6. Compatibility
7. Performance
8. Size
9. Robustness
10. Date (of shipping)

"Which varies," he might have added to the last. Nonetheless, the scheme took root overnight, "and the commandments became part of the culture immediately," Cole said. Most of the team committed them to heart. Some wrote them on their palms in case Cole happened by.

At one point rumblings got back to Cole about the toll Win 95 was taking on families of team members. The team itself was not complaining, but those close to them were. Cole came up with the idea of having team members bring families in on weekends to help test. He and Silverberg would cook breakfast for everybody—omelets, pancakes, and the like. "A lot of running the project was an exercise in motivation and inspiration," Cole said. Over Christmas break in 1994 Cole had office relights—hallway windows—painted to read "Every day we're getting closer to changing the world." The background, clouds on pastel blue, mimicked a default background for the Windows 95 test desktop.

Windows 95 was getting closer, but Silverberg concluded that the program would not be ready in the first half of 1995, as he had promised just weeks earlier at Comdex. The week before Christmas he had to face the music and tell Gates: "It was one of the worst days of my life. I had been pushing the team pretty hard to hold to that first half of 1995. There had been lots of speculation about would it slip, but I'd held hard to the first half. And then right before Christmas I knew we were not going to make it, even though it would be close. So I had a review with Bill, and I told him, no, we aren't going to make it, and man, that really hurt. He was good about it. He didn't scream at me, didn't yell about it. Just having to tell him was hard enough."

Driving home that night, Silverberg heard the news broadcast on his car radio. "I thought, 'Oh God.' That was really, really painful." There was a good chance the team might have made the end of June. But it was too close to call. Silverberg felt more comfortable with a postponement than with shipping not-quite-ready code. As it turned out, Windows 95 code went to shipping in mid-July. Silverberg never regretted the decision to delay.

More pleasant circumstances greeted Allard and Sinofsky in their year-end review with Gates. Sinofsky had wanted to gain closure on the year's efforts with Gates, and the review seemed an ideal time. He had to talk Allard into coming along but thought his partner in conspiracy undoubtedly was curious to hear Gates's assessment. A lot had happened since Allard first floated his memo nearly a year earlier. Sinofsky had gone to Cornell; the Shumway retreat had mobilized the company. There was a new development thrust, built around the Internet, to Windows 95 and Office and NT and Marvel and Exchange and NT Server and . . . well, a lot had happened. Sinofsky felt pleased. "J and I put together a two-hour meeting with Bill in the board room which was just a checkpoint, and what we did is we took all the things we said we'd do six months earlier and said, Well, where do we stand?"

When they were done with their presentation, Gates's response was something Sinofsky would cite as having made everything worthwhile: "Well," the chairman said, leaning over and nodding Allard's way, "a retreat that really made a difference!"

The UUNet deal was still fresh in Dan Rosen's mind when he ran across an old AT&T buddy, Jim Barksdale, at a Hambrecht & Quist conference in

March 1995 at Snowbird, Utah. Rosen, an AT&T lifer who had left the telecom giant at Nathan Myhrvold's behest to work on Microsoft online strategy the previous fall, had been tangentially involved in discussions with Netscape during Microsoft's search for a browser. When Jim Clark had presented his after-midnight late December e-mail proposing an equity investment to Microsoft, he forwarded it to Rosen to pass on to Silverberg. Rosen had the affable let's-do-a-deal air of an old pol and the smoky voice and graying hair that bespoke a lot of midnight bargaining. After giving back-to-back talks at the conference, Rosen and Barksdale met in a lounge and had a couple of drinks. Barksdale, true to his word, had joined Netscape in January as president and CEO once Clark got the Mosaic rights issue cleared up with the University of Illinois. For his services Barksdale received 4 million shares of stock exercisable at granting for 11 cents apiece. "Them's the price 'a eggs," he had told Clark. The last thing in the world I want to do starting up a small company is fight a battle with Microsoft over plumbing, Barksdale told Rosen. I want to find a way to work with you guys.

Barksdale asked if Rosen had a model in mind for the two companies to work together. Rosen mentioned the UUNet arrangement. UUNet was preparing for its May 25, 1995, stock offering, where it would bolt from the gate at $76.1 million—then the third most successful IPO in Wall Street history—and Rosen suspected Netscape was headed in the IPO direction as well. Rosen, taking it for granted that Clark's e-mail offer still more or less stood, had every reason to believe Netscape was interested in a variety of deals. He was not sure what would work between the two companies but felt the market was wide open enough to find some areas of synergy. Nonetheless, it was not an easy time to be bringing Netscape's name up at Microsoft. Articles were hitting the trade press about Netscape, Clark, and Andreessen, making inevitable comparisons with Microsoft. Clark and Andreessen were not the only ones fanning the flames. Most of the articles quoted analysts comparing the two companies and pronouncing Netscape the Microsoft of the Internet and Andreessen the next Bill Gates. Rosen got a different message from Barksdale: "I have to admit that the culture in his [Barksdale's] company at that point did not reflect his attitude. There were a number of people like Jim Clark among others who even during that period were saying to the press that Microsoft was the evil enemy and we gotta kill 'em. And Jim [Barksdale] would call me up and say, 'I just read this in the paper and I'm sorry. Don't let that dissuade you.'"

All the attention got Netscape on the radar screen of the wrong guy at Microsoft: Paul Maritz. Microsoft's master strategist spoke softly, in his distinctive Afrikaner brogue, and carried a big stick. At face value, he was one of the more serene, ideological, and contemplative executives in Gates's inner circle, the emotional antithesis of Steve Ballmer. Maritz processed silently, made slow, short, measured movements, and when he spoke, in clipped, spare phrases, he made very few words communicate extremely broad messages. There was never a mistake about a Maritz plan of action. He left no contingency unaddressed, no vagueness unclarified.

Maritz was born in 1955, the same year as Gates, Apple legend Steve Jobs, and numerous other industry pioneers, in Rhodesia, later to become Zimbabwe. He grew up in the African bush, gaining a love of African wildlife and culture he never relinquished. After studying math and computer science at the University of Natal and University of Cape Town in South Africa, he left for a job with Burroughs Adding Machine Co. (later Unisys) in Britain and also taught at the University of St. Andrews in Edinborough, Scotland. He had come to Microsoft in 1986 by way of Intel, which had hired Maritz in 1981.

The first wave of rhapsodic publicity over Netscape had gotten Maritz to thinking about the potential of a browser to become a network platform— a Trojan horse of sorts that ultimately could provide a wedge for Internet domination. Maritz had seen this happen to a PC market before. When he joined Microsoft as general manager of the XENIX group—Microsoft's UNIX division—PC network strategy was on Maritz's plate. The focus quickly became formulating a networking component for OS/2 with IBM. The result was LAN Manager, which Maritz eventually headed up. Putting Microsoft's eggs into IBM's basket made a lot of sense. IBM was the dominant force in enterprise computing. Nobody ever got fired for buying IBM, the saying went.

It all made perfect, logical strategic sense. It just did not happen that way. While Microsoft remained locked in its IBM partnership, Novell came out of left field and started growing the PC networking market entirely apart from Big Blue.

Maritz had watched in pain as NetWare built an empire under Microsoft's nose. He was unwilling to have history repeat itself at his expense. Yet Netscape had the potential, with its browser-server strategy, to build a new networking platform. If the Internet became the primary way people used their PCs in the future, Netscape could dominate Internet connectivity the way NetWare had risen to power via corporate networks.

Everyone from Gates on down through the organization had justified the Spyglass deal on grounds that Mosaic was the prevailing standard for viewing, or browsing, the Web. Few challenged the notion at the time. But Netscape was winning all the reviews based on speed, ease of use, speed, compatibility with html, and speed. Speed was why Navigator, officially released in December, had been downloaded by more users in its first three months than had downloaded Mosaic in all of 1994. There was a real possibility that Netscape, not Mosaic, would become the new Internet standard.

If that were the case, it was easy to build a scenario where Netscape would begin to create enhancements for its browser-server duology that made it clearly superior to others. Two possibilities immediately presented themselves. Netscape could extend html with functionality that not only enabled Navigator to show richer, more compelling Web pages but also locked out other browsers from showing the information at all. A page that in Navigator might look like a page out of *Esquire* or *Vanity Fair*, with multiple typefaces and fonts, type over colored backgrounds or photographs, pullouts, and other features, might in another browser just display plain monofont typeface or a black box where a graphic was meant to appear. Then there was the area of security. If Netscape dictated the standard for Web security, it could give its server leverage over e-commerce, at the time expected to be as much as a trillion-dollar market by the year 2000.

The technological savviness of Netscape, combined with the public comments of Clark and Andreessen, gave Maritz pause. Paul was disturbed, a colleague later put it, using the same tone he might have used to say a hibernating grizzly was disturbed.

Chapter 13

SUPERTANKER

The role of the Internet, meanwhile, continued to loom larger for Microsoft. Slivka's team was beavering away on Internet Explorer code. On April 18, 1995, at the World Wide Web conference in Germany, Thomas Reardon showed IE for the first time publicly. This was a tough hall: UNIX heads, academic types, Net purists. Reardon's trip report was glowing: "Based on applause they were blown away by the integration and 'prettiness' of our UI [user interface]," Reardon wrote. "A lot of people were expecting (or afraid of!) some very nice stuff from us, and they got it. While people expected pretty & sexy, they did not expect to see all the integration. They were blown away by links into/out of MSN." A month later, the first public beta of IE was issued. IE was starting to get noticed.

In mid-May Gates went off on yet another Think Week. The result was yet another memo, "The Internet Tidal Wave," dated May 26, 1995. "Tidal Wave," which would not be made public, and then only in excerpted form, till the following fall, was easily the most impressive of all Gates's Think Week memos—at least, of those to escape the confines of Redmond Central. Gates led off the nine-page call to action with a sweeping observation:

Microsoft's vision for its first twenty years was to see that "exponential improvements in computer capabilities would make great software quite valuable. Our response was to build an organization to deliver the best software products." The Internet, Gates suggested, was simply another venue for software—one that was going to continue to elevate the importance of software in driving human activity into the twenty-first century. "In the next 20 years, the improvements in computer power will be outpaced by the exponential improvements in communications networks," Gates elaborated.

The Internet was the single most important development to come along since the IBM PC, the chairman noted. Later he acknowledged the statement was intended to turn heads: "When I say something like 'This is the biggest change since the IBM PC,' that gets people to really wake up, because I'm saying it's even bigger than, say, the move to graphical interfaces." Gates had gone through several stages in his view of the Net's impact, he noted, but "Now I assign the Internet the highest level of importance." The pronouncement was not as cataclysmic as it might seem. Only other targets on his radar screen had kept him from top-rating the Net earlier. The Internet had, after all, been "very important" to Microsoft after the Shumway retreat a year previous. As to why he had not given it No. 1 emphasis earlier, Gates responded with a glint of sarcasm: "If you'd caught me on the street and said, what's my highest priority, I might have said, 'Well, we might ship Windows 95 sometime! Might get that out! That's my highest priority!'"

It was time to bet the company again. "All work we do here can be leveraged into the HTTP/Web world. The strength of the Office and Windows businesses today gives us a chance to superset the Web." In other words, Gates saw no reason why the Internet should not be an extension—a subset—of Microsoft technology. It was an audacious claim, akin to John Lennon declaring that the Beatles were more famous than Jesus. But Gates had already proved how important the Net was to Microsoft. The month before, on April 10, he had sent dyspeptic mail to the interactive TV squad, including Nathan Myhrvold: "I admit I find it hard to focus lots of resources on trials [tests] and things when the Internet is taking away our power every day and will have eroded it irretrievably by the time broadband is pervasive." Gates needed hint no more. The once shining light of interactive TV had been snuffed out under the Internet bushel.

"Tidal Wave" showed how scrupulously Gates had followed the Internet since first logging on as a Harvard undergraduate and how precisely he understood its implications. This was not a case of old school versus new school. Point by point Gates analyzed the impact of the Internet on Microsoft's core products and strategies and divined appropriate challenges and opportunities for his legions to address. There was the issue of Microsoft's online offering. For users logging on to the Internet other than through Microsoft Network, "we will have to make MSN very, very inexpensive—perhaps free," Gates acknowledged, to attract Webheads to the Microsoft service. There was that word again—free. J Allard's legacy lived!

Gates had little doubt that the Internet would be very good for the PC business: "Virtually every PC will be used to connect to the Internet, and . . . the Internet will help keep PC purchasing very healthy for many years to come." Bingo: The Internet spawned the biggest boom in PC sales ever, doubling annual unit sales from 1996 to 1998. Gates's favorite sites? "Of particular interest are the sites such as Yahoo! which provide subject catalogs and searching. Also of interest are the ways our competitors are using their Websites to present their products. I think Sun, Netscape, and Lotus do some things very well." Ironically, by the spring of 1998 the ensuing Internet boom made the founding Yahoos, Jerry Yang and David Filo, self-made billionaires at an even younger age than Gates, who reached the distinction at thirty-one in the spring of 1987.

Then there was Windows NT. The platform should be molded to offer "the highest performance http [Internet protocol] servers," Gates wrote. Music to Allard's ears. If NT servers did the best job of catapulting files and links around the Web, it would only serve to increase Microsoft's presence on the Internet and spread sales of its products. What of server and browser maker Netscape? To compete, Gates called for integrating the browser and MSN into Windows and "working with"—pursuing business relationships with—Netscape customers, including "MCI, newspapers, and other [sic] who are considering their [Netscape's] products." Picking up on Maritz's Netscape-as-NetWare theme, Gates advised: "A new competitor 'born' on the Internet is Netscape. Their browser is dominant, with 70 percent usage share, allowing them to determine which network extensions will catch on. They are pursuing a multi-platform strategy where they move the key API into the client to commoditize the underlying operating system."

Later, Department of Justice investigators would seize on this observation as indicative of Gatesian predation. But its context was more warning than threat. Gates was telling his troops: Wake up, guys! If we don't answer the Netscape model, we will become dinosaurs and die. In a single paragraph, Gates articulated the primary Microsoft concern about Netscape, the browser, and the Internet—that they could make Windows irrelevant.

The concept would go on to gain wide distribution among Microsoft competitors, Internet pundits, and industry analysts later that fall. It was not until the full "Tidal Wave" memo was publicly released more than two years later, however, that it would become apparent that Gates had beaten his competitors to the punch in foreseeing the browser's threat as an alternative platform.

Microsoft needed to get its technologies moving onto the Web, Gates urged. For example: OLE, the object linking and embedding technology that enabled users to open a spreadsheet within a Word file, had plenty of applications for the Web. "Browsing the Web, you find almost no Microsoft file formats," he noted. "After ten hours of browsing I had not seen a single Word .DOC, AVI file, Windows .EXE (other than content viewers) or other Microsoft file format"—an observation that was at least as revealing in what it said about Gates's surfing tenacity as his product loyalty.

Almost everywhere he looked, Gates saw competitors with better, more advanced technology. Where is our answer to Acrobat? he asked. Acrobat, from the font maker Adobe Systems, enabled richly formatted documents to be transmitted over the Internet and then viewed on a person's PC. Sun's Java, announced just three days before the May 26 date of Gates's memo and already endorsed by Netscape, was a major competitor: Let's figure out a way to download programs over the Net to PCs the way Java does, while making sure there is a "security approach to avoid this being a virus hole," Gates admonished.

"There will be a lot of uncertainty as we first embrace the Internet and then extend it," Gates wrote. Embrace! Extend! The words echoed J Allard's "killer app" memo precisely. "Tidal Wave" not only summed up Microsoft's strategic deployment on the Internet, it marked the clearest signal the rank and file had received from Gates that the Internet's time was nigh. Justice Department investigators focused on the grand total of four references to Netscape as indicative of Microsoft's targeting the browser company, but "Tidal Wave" was a broad, multifaceted call to action that addressed many other competitors and a raft of other challenges. In addition to making the Internet Microsoft's No. 1 priority, Gates reshuffled his best and brightest to pursue Net challenges. "I want every product plan to try and go overboard on Internet features," Gates noted. Myhrvold and Office overlord Pete Higgins would head up the applications and content efforts, including protecting and growing Microsoft Office. On the Windows side, Maritz would be the key executive. "Paul Maritz will lead the Platform group to define an integrated strategy that makes it clear that Windows machines are the best choice for the Internet," Gates wrote. "This will protect and grow our Windows asset."

Of the three men, only Maritz wound up having an indelible impact on Microsoft's Web jihad. The Windows platform strategist was to spend little time pondering his boss's directive. It was time for another offsite retreat. Unlike Shumway, this one would involve more of the in-the-trenches development folks. And it would be focused not on blue-skying but updating progress—and elaborately mapping the future—of various Internet pursuits at Microsoft. Setting the date for Friday, June 2, 1995, in the Phoenix Room of the then Bellevue Hilton, Maritz listed the goals: Get a status check on where we are today versus our competition and raise awareness on how the Internet affects "the critical issues we need to solve as a company." On the agenda were Sinofsky, Pathe, Slivka, Allard, and Anthony Bay, the latter for Microsoft Network. Suggested reading included a Sinofsky monograph entitled, "Using Office Documents Online and on the Web," a Pathe memo called "Application Strategies for the World Wide Web," Slivka's "The Web as the Next Platform," a Darryl Rubin opus entitled "Unifying the User's Navigation/Viewing Experience," a Maritz memo called "A Linked, Active, Queryable World," the post-Shumway memos from Gates and Sinofsky, and two Gates Think Week memos, "Sea Change" and "Tidal Wave." Only a week had passed since the latter Gates memo had hit the executive ranks. Maritz liked to move fast.

Acting on a number of Gates's action items, the Maritz session explored Microsoft's competition in the Internet realm and drilled down on specifics with regard to proliferating Microsoft technologies on the Web. Netscape, Novell, and Sun were identified as leading competitors. So were America Online, Spry/CompuServe (three months earlier, on March 14, 1995, CompuServe had purchased Spry for a cool $100 million), and Quarterdeck, which was marketing its own soon-to-fade browser at the time. Significantly, as many Internet *technologies* were targeted as there were companies. SSL—Netscape's security protocol—http, gopher, and ftp were listed among Maritz's slides. Heading the list was lowly html.

Html was still seen as a weak format compared to Microsoft's .doc or the grand plans for Blackbird in MSN. But Slivka saw html's limitations as both temporal and fixable. His experience at IBM had included a stint using gml, or generalized markup language. Gml offered ways of tagging paragraphs and doing scripts to perform formatting commands. It was a way of giving a document some razzmatazz. When Slivka saw what html could do, "the things I had done at IBM kind of made me get a little more excited about it." He saw it as the basis for something a lot richer, the clay for a Rodin. The Blackbird project should forget about its own publishing protocols and simply focus on html, while leaving browser work to Slivka's O'Hare team. Ironically, Blackbird team members silently agreed with Slivka. "We actually thought you should do it that way [with open Internet protocols]," said John Shewchuk, a Daily Planet cofounder who went to Microsoft with the acquisition and helped lead the Blackbird development team. "But Siegelman didn't. He prevented us from going the Internet route."

Slivka's html talk unsettled Pathe, who was still struggling with the html-versus-Microsoft dilemma. Pathe loved html, as long as it stayed simple, unfancy, plain Jane html and did not evolve into something bigger and better. That way, Web users would want to import html documents into Word to dress them up. If they could dress up the documents in html, they might forget all about Word. To Slivka, Pathe was in denial of the obvious: Html was going to rule no matter what the Word team did. On May 5, just weeks earlier, Slivka had fired off a message to Maritz, copying Ludwig, grousing, "Do I have to write a rejoinder memo to refute Peter's misconstructions and misconceptions? I don't want to be unnecessarily confrontational, so you be the judge." The note was in response to a Pathe missive declaring that html would go the way of UNIX, rendered asunder by lots of companies doing lots of differing versions. Nope, Slivka retorted: Leadership by Microsoft and Netscape would product a rich standard. In Slivka's view, Internet Assistant was a "lousy" html authoring tool. Painfully, excruciatingly slow. Its browser was equally lame. If Microsoft continued down the Word Assistant path, Slivka warned, it would be tantamount to ceding html to Netscape — "a major, major mistake." What really rankled Slivka was Pathe's insistence that the Internet was a "huge, shared, distributed file store" and not a "new, interactive computing environment requiring a fresh start from a clean slate." Slivka considered that attitude "an interesting bit of paranoia": "I'm a software design engineer, looking for ways to solve problems and make Microsoft successful. I see html and the Web as a way to deliver information more quickly and more easily to customers. . . . I apologize that Word doesn't seem to fit the bill, but it's not because I'm trying to upset the status quo, I'm trying to build great products."

At the Maritz offsite, Slivka proposed adding editing and extended capabilities to html in order to get people to use O'Hare. Pathe again got a bit nervous. Slivka held his ground: "So Peter was trying to get Bill in this meeting, saying, Bill, could you tell Ben not to add any new features to html? And Bill sort of said Ben, you shouldn't add too many features to html. And I sort of ignored him."

Slivka thought the notion that his six-person browser team could kill a billion-dollar worldwide business like Microsoft Word pretty . . . "well, I guess it was flattering. But I think there were other people who could've killed the Word business a lot easier than I." Slivka had been given fifteen minutes to make his presentation and wound up talking for an hour and a half. It was a tour de force for one of the frontline guys generally not known for vision statements. But Slivka's essay, "The Web as the Next Platform," had been distributed before the session, and "there was just all this stuff floating around in my brain," he recalled. "I'm not taken to like being this big thinker, this memo writer type guy. I figure Nathan Myhrvold's paid to do that, I should work on shipping products." Nevertheless, Slivka's memo wound up reflecting Microsoft's ultimate Internet strategy more accurately than any of Myhrvold's essays.

Slivka laid out for the first time a plan to componentize the O'Hare browser into pieces that other software companies and developers could use to make their applications Web compatible. The idea basically was that new, unforeseeable applications were going to spring out of the Web just as they had at the invention of the personal computer. Not productivity applications, like Word and Excel, but content and service applications. Such as Virtual Vineyards, the wine-shopping service. Or 1-800-FLOWERS, the electronic flower-sending service. Slivka "just did a projection, like these [were] things my mom was going to care a lot more about than Excel. My point was that the Web was a platform for delivering these applications. It looked better than Windows, because it was targeted at that content and that interactivity. It was a distributed application platform, if you wanted to get nerdy about it."

The problem was, there was no indication yet of how Microsoft could make money on any of this. Whereas there were suspicions it might lose a business or two. Undaunted, Slivka forged ahead. He took the opportunity to discuss some new features to the O'Hare browser, including support for specifying different fonts in html. It was a nifty little touch, enabling Web authors to choose preferred fonts instead of the same old Times standard. Because Mosaic and Netscape were cross-platform, they lacked font capability. "So I was like, let's give away TrueType fonts so people can have cool, sexy websites that look best on Internet Explorer," Slivka said later. "What the heck, right? And Bill was like, What are you, a communist? Those fonts cost money! Why would we give those away?"

At one time or other Gates had called just about all the Internet idealists at Microsoft communists. It was almost a joke around Microsoft—one that the chairman was fond of perpetuating. In 1993, when he faced a showdown with the Federal Trade Commission over antitrust allegations, Gates had reportedly used the term in a behind-closed-doors meeting with the commissioners. Since then it had gained a mythic quality at Redmond. It was almost a badge of honor to be so designated. Slivka, in a ninety-minute rap on how the Internet could turn Microsoft's revenue stream on its ear, had set a new standard. But as a measure of how much weight Gates assigned the derogation, within three years he had totally forgotten the encounter.

Slivka was on the Java case as well. Within a couple of days after Sun rolled out Java at SunWorld on May 23, 1995, Slivka had purchased a Sun SPARCstation 5 and installed it in his office. Once he got his TCP/IP connection up and running, he downloaded Java from Sun's Internet site and began playing around with it. There was an animated demo of Duke, the tooth-shaped Java mascot, dancing around the screen. Slivka also pulled down HotJava, a browser written in Java. He found it interesting technology. We need to pay attention to this thing, he thought. When he demonstrated Java at the offsite, the reaction was: Not ready for prime time but bears watching.

The Maritz session got product groups mobilized on several fronts. It would be six months before the impact of "Tidal Wave" and the Maritz offsite would be demonstrated publicly—in Gates's climactic Pearl Harbor day session with media and analysts on December 7, 1995. But the critical components of the company's future triumphs—as well as its eventual federal scrutiny—were set in place.

On June 21, 1995, three weeks after the Maritz summit, Dan Rosen's team met with Netscape at its Mountain View headquarters for a summit session of sorts between the two companies. Rosen had decided to accept Barksdale's invitation to hold the meeting there: "Jim [Barksdale] said it'd be easier to get all the right people in the room . . . and I also thought it was a good gesture on our part," he said. "The bigger company typically would assert its privilege and have the small company come visit it. I was really trying to send the signal that we were going to behave reasonably in this process."

Leading up to the meeting had been a flurry of e-mail from key Microsoft browser players, including Silverberg and Gates. The discussion focused on Microsoft's protocol for secure electronic payment, STT (for Secure Transaction Technology), and how Netscape's server strategy might benefit NT. On May 31 Gates expressed a willingness to help Netscape out in its server products—where the company expected to make actual money—in return for Netscape supporting Windows NT. "Clients [browsers] make no money," Gates noted. "Servers will make money. For the next 24 months we can help Netscape with servers, without hurting ourselves in any large way. We don't have a large forecast for servers. We want them to focus somewhat on NT servers, but it doesn't have to be exclusive."

Gates saw little revenue potential in the short term for Microsoft on Web servers. Internet Information Server was going to be free; Microsoft was not developing much in other server areas Netscape was focusing on—mainly commerce, security, and applications. Gates saw sharing "our server and our technical work" and helping Netscape "market their server" as potentials for synergy. "This kind of deal could be a big win win," he concluded. "I would really like to see something like this happen!!" Yes, the two companies eventually would bang heads on servers, he acknowledged. In the meantime, there was a lot of potential for working together to grow the server market.

Rosen pulled together a diverse group in hopes of a variety of collaborations. "I said, the only way to pull this off is to get a group of people at Microsoft who have responsibility for each of the things that might be important, and get them together with a group of counterparts at Netscape who were going to have things that might be important, and put them in a room and see if there was any chemistry and any possibility of getting to a win-win," Rosen recounted. On the Microsoft side, that meant people like Reardon; Allard; Barbara Fox, a former VISA executive who was working on transaction—e-commerce—protocols; Chris Jones, a lead program manager on the Microsoft O'Hare browser; Anthony Bay, representing the Microsoft Network; and Richard Wolf from the Office group. On the Netscape side were Barksdale, Andreessen, and Mike Homer, head of marketing, replacing Paul Koontz, who had given Reardon the browser brush-off.

Three years later this meeting gained notoriety when Justice Department investigators pointed to it as an attempt by Microsoft to intimidate Netscape from doing browser development on Windows 95. The allegation, which Justice enforcers say was revealed in typewritten notes Andreessen took at the meeting on his IBM ThinkPad, was that Microsoft offered to stay out of Windows 3.X, Macintosh, and UNIX development if Netscape in return avoided developing Navigator for Windows 95. It sounded like carving up the market. It could just as easily have been a misunderstanding of intent. The fact was, Microsoft had little interest in any of the non–Win 95/NT platforms. In the wake of the Win 95 rollout, it expected—incorrectly, as it turned out—that Windows 3.X would fade quickly. The Microsoft side also figured that Netscape wanted to make a deal. Finally, Microsoft believed Netscape saw little revenue potential in the browser and was focusing on the server. "In every meeting we have," Reardon wrote in e-mail time-stamped 1:51 A.M. on June 1, 1995, "they emphasize that they realize there is no money in the client business." Maritz four days later took slight issue with Reardon, writing in mail that it was clear Barksdale, at least, viewed the browser "as a key place to make money." But Barksdale also held a "rather strange view of the market," Maritz said, adding, "I wonder if he speaks for all of Netscape."

At the historic meeting, the Microsoft team talked up what a partnership would give to Netscape. You'll get early looks at Windows upgrades. You'll be able to work closely with us developing APIs—programming tools—for things like dial-up networking and DocObjects. Dial-up networking was a breakthrough for Windows 95 that eliminated much of the complexity of starting an Internet access account. DocObjects enabled Office documents to pop up in Web browsers without having to call up each separate application, like Word or Excel. The notion had the touch of Office's new Internet agitator, Steven Sinofsky: "We thought, this is kind of cool because the whole idea is links of documents and it didn't matter what format they were in." The two companies could collaborate on issues of security and transaction protocols. As they could on NT, which could benefit from Netscape server work.

But every pitch Rosen & the Microsoft gang made ran up against Netscape skepticism. Homer's background at Go Corp., the pen-computing start-up that like other pen computing software never went anywhere, and Apple Computer before that had left him wary of promises from the Redmond empire. At Go, Homer had watched as Microsoft visited with the proposal of licensing Go's software, gotten a look around, and then announced later it was going to build its own pen operating system instead—in Windows. Homer was not interested in a redux. "Of course we're going; I smell a rat," he later said. "By implication they were saying, If you don't [play along], then you won't have all these things and we'll have all these things, and we're going to beat the crap out of you, basically."

Andreessen was equally dubious: "I studied this stuff. I read all the books. I talked to people who dealt with them in the past. Everybody says . . . Microsoft is a sponge when it comes to information. They will make this approach to you as a small company and say you know, Tell us everything. And most small companies say, Oh, you betcha! We'd love to do that! They go through everything and Microsoft says, Hmmm, that's interesting. Six months later Microsoft builds it into the operating system and puts them out of business. Our theory was, Okay, let's not do that."

Barksdale, too, indicated a measure of wariness. Before the meeting, he was concerned about documenting the proceedings, Andreessen said: "We were going to this meeting and Jim's like, I wonder what they're going to say. They're probably going to say stuff that is kind of, a little strange, and wouldn't it be great if we had a record of the meeting. And you know it's like, well, let's see. We can't really tape it, because it's illegal to tape it without their knowledge. And if we taped it legally presumably it would change their behavior or whatever. Plus we didn't have a tape recorder set up. So Barksdale said, All right Andreessen, take notes. So I'm sitting at one of the tables, they're talking, and I'm sitting with my little IBM ThinkPad with the butterfly keyboard and I'm typing just as fast as I can. And they're sort of looking at me funny, but they just keep on talking. The biggest amazement to Jim about the whole thing was they said all this stuff while they knew I was taking notes."

It probably would have served historical rectitude better if Netscape had taped the meeting. Andreessen's presumption that Microsoft would have altered its behavior knowing it was being taped in fact was disproven by his own acknowledgment that his obvious transcription had no impact on the proceedings. Whatever the rationale, Andreessen's notes wound up conflicting diametrically with notes taken on Microsoft's side. Andreessen also was not just note-taker. In several instances he inserted his own asides and commentaries. Describing Rosen's pitch, for example, Andreessen notes: "(Quoting Rosen) Would you be interested in having a partnership where NS gets all the non–Win 95 stuff and MS gets all the Win 95 stuff? If NS doesn't want to, then that's one thing. If NS does want to, then we can have our special relationship. THREAT THAT MS WILL OWN THE WIN 95 CLIENT MARKET AND THAT NETSCAPE SHOULD STAY AWAY."

The capitalization emphasis was Andreessen's, and the aside marked a stepping out of his role as stenographer. The "special relationship," by Rosen's account, referred to the general partnership and client/server co-operation. It was hardly a threat; it was a pitch to do business together, Rosen said.

At one point, Barksdale asked if collaboration on the APIs and Doc-Objects was dependent on Netscape accepting the Microsoft proposal. Andreessen recorded Rosen's response as "It certainly isn't independent." Andreessen saw the response as Rosen basically trying to have it both ways. "He appeared to be reluctant to actually come out and say what he was trying to say, so he kept trying to like qualify it," Andreessen recounted. "But he was making a point, which was you need to do this, or otherwise . . . " As Andreessen saw it, the way Microsoft "had set it [dial-up networking] up, it appeared to not be technically possible to install an alternative dial-up method and have it reliably work. Which is what we would have done, otherwise." It was a charge Microsoft hotly disputed: America Online had put together its own dial-up procedure for Windows 95 with no help from Microsoft, Ludwig asserted. And Microsoft had offered Netscape code to help build its own implementation—code it did not have to use—but Netscape "tried to turn it into a federal case."

Hefting a monumental chip on its shoulder, Netscape interpreted each Microsoft gesture to collaborate as a threat to compete. Where Microsoft wanted to team up on servers, Netscape saw an attempt to peek at its technology with the intent of co-opting it down the road. Where Microsoft proposed to take ownership of the Windows 95 browser space so Netscape could concentrate on building its money market, servers, the Netscape contingent saw an attempt to strongarm it away from an important strategic product. The entire offer to partner was a source of contention to Andreessen: "We didn't take it seriously at the time. We didn't take it seriously because we thought they were full of shit, we thought they were lying, we thought they would never do it that way, we thought they would screw us."

Listening with interest but saying little through the session was J Allard. After about two and a half hours, Barksdale turned to him and said, You've been awfully quiet—what do you think about all this? It was a pertinent question. Allard was the server guy, the man behind the curtain who was taking NT's power and scalability onto the Web. Netscape was showing off a broad line of server technology, some of which would be ideally suited to running on top of NT, others of which would compete head-on with server offerings Allard had in mind for Microsoft. It seemed perfectly logical to Allard that the two sides should put their heads together and understand where they were dancing and where they were boxing.

Yet Allard did not know what to think; there was not enough on the table for him to have an opinion. Here we've been pretty open-kimono on our side, he was thinking, and on the Netscape side they had just been chatty. Very chatty. They had handed out some nice glossy Silicon Valley start-up promos, multicolor trifolds, brochures that talked about all their products. They had fourteen of them. Allard said, "Well, Jim, I think I'm just confused." Then with a flourish he spread out the glossies like a huge playing deck. "Look at these," he said. "You've got more products than developers. I don't understand what business you're in. The only reason I came down here is to understand where we're going to compete and where we're going to complement each other so I can go back and do my job. And understand a little bit more. And I don't feel like we're getting there in any rational way."

At one point the two sides took a break and Rosen and Barksdale talked some more. Rosen told Barksdale that he had talked to Gates, and Microsoft was willing to make an investment. And that would be really good for Netscape, Rosen suggested, because when it went public it would have the Bill factor on its side. What's the Bill factor? Barksdale asked. Rosen was referring to UUNet's successful road show for its IPO, he told Barksdale: "I had heard from Goldman Sachs that during the road show for the UUNet IPO they were absolutely astounded by some of the buy-side investors coming to the road show. They were coming in and saying how much can we get. Well, don't you want to hear the presentation? And they said no, if it's good enough for Bill it's good enough for me."

In the end, Netscape's wariness killed any possibility of a deal. Ludwig later scoffed at Andreessen's "sponge" criticism: "We don't learn anything in these meetings with small companies that is a totally new, unheard-of idea. The real value in the software industry is not the idea—it is the implementation—the follow-through." Officially the talks were put on ice. But a major distraction was brewing for Netscape. Although no one told Rosen and his crew, two days before the Microsoft summit—on June 19, 1995—the Netscape board had officially authorized the company to pursue its initial stock offering. The Internet investing craze was just getting started, with previously unthinkable valuations going to companies like BookLink, at $30 million, UUNet, at $76 million, and Spry, at $100 million. When Rosen got word that Netscape was going public, his hope for a deal sank: "They were getting all the press, and testosterone took over, and testosterone overwhelmed reason. . . . I just sensed their position becoming increasingly unreasonable. [They were] saying they really did want to compete."

For all of Netscape's putative enmity, it still found a way to do a deal with Microsoft on one significant front. Microsoft wound up licensing Netscape's SSL. On the security side, the two companies actually began partnering to move the technology forward.

Moreover, at the time nothing sinister was seen in their discussions. In an Associated Press story dated September 27, 1995, three months after the meeting, Homer acknowledged that Netscape "wanted early access to Microsoft's Windows 95" in return for an equity investment. The talks were described as typical of software partnering discussions in the computer industry.

Ultimately the question remained: If Netscape was so distrustful and wary of Microsoft, why invite them to the meeting at all? When the Justice Department got involved three years later, the answer may have been revealed. The night after the Microsoft meeting, Andreessen was in touch via e-mail with Netscape attorneys, who forwarded his observations to the Justice Department. The next day, Justice investigators issued a civil investigative demand for documents about the meeting. Within twenty-four hours Andreessen's notes were forwarded to the department by Netscape attorney Gary Reback. Microsoft attorneys later said the sequence of events suggested that Netscape orchestrated the meeting in an effort to incite Department of Justice interest. Andreessen's asides and the fact that Netscape discussed how to document the session added fuel to Microsoft's assertion that the meeting was a set-up. Moreover, Microsoft was not told of Netscape's concerns over the meeting, and the Justice Department made no equivalent civil investigative demand at the time for Microsoft's notes of the session.

Despite all the scrutiny, a Rashomon quality to the session lingered. If the meeting held antitrust overtones, why under terms of its consent decree did Justice Department investigators not ask Microsoft for information about it at the time? (Justice later declined to respond to an e-mail query asking about the delay.) Finally, if the meeting was as significant as the Netscape side later made it out to be, why did no Microsoft executives on the level of Barksdale, Homer, and Andreessen attend?

"We weren't marketing executives," recalled Reardon. "We were twenty-five-year-olds in a room with the CEO and three critical executives of a company [Netscape]. We were nerds, not managers." Reardon compared the session to Microsoft telling WordPerfect that with Windows, the Word-

Perfect programmers would no longer have to write nonrevenue utilities such as printer drivers. Microsoft would be doing WordPerfect a favor, not "asking it to divide the market," Reardon complained.

When Brad Silverberg read Rosen's trip report from the June 21 meeting, he brushed the session aside as a routine mid-level product-planning meeting: "If this meeting were really significant to the future of Windows, I would have been there. I had seen the meeting notice, and it did not look like anything I needed to be at."

According to the trip report, Barksdale had told the Microsoft team that Netscape was not interested in the client, or browser, side of the Internet software business. It was a reiteration of Clark's late-night e-mail assertion. Instead, the server was the focal point. Silverberg had shaken his head at that. You'd have to be crazy or a fool to think that was true. Granted, they were confused about what business they were in, and where the market was going. But to say they weren't in the client business, well . . .

Compared to the upcoming Windows 95 launch, the Netscape talks were strictly small potatoes to Silverberg. But then, compared to the launch of the century, everything was. When he had given Gates the "final-final" ship date of August 1995 the previous December, Silverberg had consciously built in a two- to four-week buffer to allow for last-minute fixes. The problem was, everybody from Gates on down knew that Silverberg put the buffer in. So they calculated that buffer into their development schedules. In software code deadlines, a buffer never really was a buffer.

In any case, Windows 95 was ready to "go gold" on time—July 14, Bastille Day, 1995. Going gold meant that the code was done, fini, frozen, and RTM'd, or released to manufacturing, to be pressed onto disks and distributed to computer makers. It was the final watershed event for any product, and it had been a long time coming for Windows 95—nearly three years from concept to completion, and nine months later than initially anticipated. Bastille Day, the anniversary of the start of the French Revolution in 1789, marked the freeing of the prisoners from the Parisian jail. Silverberg intended the symbolism. It was time to celebrate. At Building 6 the Windows 95 team convened for the long-awaited ship party. Champagne was on ice. Cake, strawberries, whipped cream, and chocolate were on hand. The normally reserved, all-business Silverberg was in the midst of his introductory remarks when, without prompting, he picked up a bottle of Dom Perignon and poured it over his head. The gathered hundreds of team members took it as a cue. Silverberg got doused like the winner of the Tour de France. Leading the way was David Cole, who had filled his fabled pickup truck, the one that had carted the Egghead software stash to Microsoft for compatibility testing, with twelve cases of Dom Perignon. One hundred forty-four bottles. "They disappeared so fast I couldn't believe it," Cole recounted. The rule was, you had to drink them there. Cole caught some contract programmers trying to sneak off with a case and said, Uh-uh. Let's open those bottles up right here, guys.

The Windows 95 crew knew that Building 6, their Bastille for the build years, was scheduled for renovation in two months. A little knowledge was a dangerous thing. Everyone went wild, running through halls, spraying unsuspecting coworkers with champagne. In the lobby someone had stretched ladders of bubble wrap down the second-story stairwell. People were actually climbing up and down the stuff. Cake, strawberries, whipped cream, and chocolate fondue made for unusual assault weaponry. Some workers got so smeared with the goo they had to wash off in the campus fountain. A few got necessarily indecent in the process. Someone was driving a motorcycle through the halls of Building 6. Cole, disputing witness accounts, denies it was he but said he was a passenger at one point. "The rate of speed scared me," he recalled.

At one point the Windows 95 team hauled Silverberg's bucket of bolts, the 386-33 test machine, into the lobby for a ceremonial tribute. After team members expressed some sanctimonious calumnies about how much they had grown to love, respect, and rely on the PC throughout the development process, they enthusiastically administered a series of sledgehammer blows to serve as final rites.

And that was only the stuff that they talked about. The Win 95 launch broke the mold for postship revelry and inspiration. "It was the wildest RTM party the company had ever seen," Silverberg said. "That one really set a new standard for how creative the team was." By evening around fifty celebrants were still hanging tough. Cole made sure they had taxi vouchers to get home. What really blew him away was the next morning. Mary Hoisington, Silverberg's admin, had suspected the incipient bash and lined up cleaning services to come in after hours. The place was spotless. Cole walked around, thinking, "Did I really just dream all that?"

The Win 95 team may have been having fun, but the breakdown of talks between Netscape and Microsoft had led to an increasingly chilly relationship. Through the summer Steven Sinofsky was making what he considered routine courtesy calls to Netscape to talk about DocObjects, the cool Windows technology for enabling Office documents to pop up in Web browsers automatically. No having to save the file to disk, open Word or PowerPoint, then open the document back up again. Microsoft was putting together a software developers kit for DocObjects, and Sinofsky thought Netscape might want to have some input. Lotus had already picked up on the technology and was working to build it into Notes. Sinofsky, who had not been involved in the Netscape negotiations and knew little of the history between the two companies, expected the same reception from Netscape: "I called up Netscape and said, Do you guys want to do this? Here's how. We'll just send you the how-to, and it's not a money thing, it's not a deal thing. It's just evangelism."

Sinofsky simply wanted Netscape's browser to be able to handle the Doc-Objects approach as well as Microsoft's. The next thing he knew he was talking to Roberta Katz, Netscape's new chief counsel. "I'm sitting here, I want to talk to some programmer about how to do this, and I end up dealing with their counsel. I was puzzled beyond belief," Sinofsky recalled. Not long afterward, in September 1995, Netscape announced plug-ins, an idea similar to DocObjects. If you called up a Word file over the Web, a Netscape plug-in would open up the copy of Word on your hard drive automatically. The difference was, plug-in technology had Netscape's name on it. Sinofsky felt played. Nothing he could prove, but the two events seemed too coincidental. "That was the first time I realized the kind of environment that the Internet Explorer team was dealing with," he said. "I was very naive, I guess personally, to the venom in those feelings."

The O'Hare team too was butting heads with Netscape. As Rosen recounts it, relations were strained to the point where Netscape was not only withholding its plans from Microsoft, it would not share anything having to do with its Windows 95 Navigator. "They wouldn't tell us what their product looked like at all. And they wouldn't give us any beta code of their product to test out against our stuff." It was typical of major developers to work with Microsoft before a major launch to ensure compatibility at ship time. Not so in Netscape's case: Just days before the Windows 95 code was "frozen," or set to ship to manufacturing, Dan Rosen got a frantic call from Netscape.

"They wanted some changes to some of the APIs," Rosen recalled. The dial-up issue had resurfaced, with Netscape claiming Microsoft was withholding critical access. The Win 95 team, under the gun to get the code out by July 14, "had no cycles to spend" on Netscape's cause, Rosen said. He managed to twist the arm of one Win 95 developer to do "some special things at night," but the code was clearly not robust and Netscape complained mightily. Jim Clark, by then having rescinded his e-mail equity offer to Microsoft, was not pleased. "I said this seems like something the Justice Department ought to get involved in somehow," he recalled.

Rosen called the problem a timing issue. Netscape needed the APIs so that its browser could be shipped, already installed, on new machines. That meant Netscape needed the APIs earlier than it typically would in order to ship a standard shrink-wrapped piece of software with the Windows 95 launch. "There wasn't a person at Microsoft who knew they [Netscape] were going after an OEM [computer maker] market," Rosen said. At the time, he said, "Homer was sort of embarrassed by it. He knew the truth." Rosen said the incident "hurt me pretty personally. I think if anything, as a sign of good faith, we did more for them than we did for anybody else."

The extent of Microsoft's support for Netscape eventually emerged in an e-mail from field marshal Maritz to Rick Schell, dated August 15, 1996. Maritz asserted that Microsoft had provided the dialer and remote network access APIs to Netscape "just as fast as we could stabilize and document them." Windows 95 developers had provided direct technical support, preliminary versions of the APIs, and other help to Netscape starting in July 1995, he added. "We received positive feedback in mail from Netscape at that time on the support we were providing." Moreover, Microsoft had been thanked by no lesser a force than Andreessen himself for providing an early prototype of Internet shortcuts, the automatic linking technology that proved a boon to Windows 95.

Thinking back, Brad Silverberg's eyes flash when the subject of withheld APIs comes up. It may seem strange to consider, he says, but the "killer app" for Windows 95 was Netscape Navigator. Silverberg knew Internet Explorer, for all its hurricane of activity and improvement over the original Mosaic, was no match for Navigator's speed, power, and popularity. "We did everything we could to help those guys," he said. "It would have made no sense for us to keep a developer off of Windows. Our job is to get all the developers we can on Windows. It was total posturing on their part."

Chapter 14

PEARL HARBOR

hat Netscape and Microsoft were experiencing was a failure to communicate not witnessed since Paul Newman's inspirational truculence in *Cool Hand Luke*. Perhaps the most public signal of Netscape's point of view came in the prospectus published for the company's celebrated stock offering on August 9. In two sections of the sixty-one-page document, under "Risk Factors" and "Competition," Microsoft was identified as a leading competitor that could make life miserable for Netscape if it chose. The Microsoft Network and Windows 95's browser might increase the size and use of the Internet, but "it will likely also have a material adverse impact on Netscape's ability to sell client software," the prospectus stated. From there a long litany of ifs and maybes ensued:

> *Because the Company's [Netscape's] client software products will not be able to access Microsoft Network, [they] may be at a competitive disadvantage versus Microsoft's browser. Further, Microsoft may choose to develop Web server and applications software as a complement to its product line and to support the Microsoft Network, which could mate-*

rially adversely affect Netscape's ability to sell server software or inte-grated applications. To the extent that Microsoft's browser gains market acceptances, Microsoft will be better positioned than the Company to sell Web server and applications products. Microsoft has a longer oper-ating history, a much larger installed base and number of employees, and dramatically greater financial, technical and marketing resources, access to distribution channels and name recognition than the Com-pany. Moreover, to complete development of Netscape Navigator for Windows 95, the Company must obtain certain technology from Mi-crosoft. There can be no assurance that Microsoft will make such tech-nology available to the Company on a timely basis, on commercially reasonable terms or at all.

Netscape chief financial officer Peter Currie said later the prospectus warn-ing was a standard advisory meant to inform potential investors of possible risks. Bill Gates saw it as a tossing down of the gauntlet: "They slam us. They use their IPO to do negative PR against Microsoft. It has this thing about how they could bundle, we wish they wouldn't, they probably shouldn't but they could, Oh No! They could do this and they could do that. Well, hello!" Gates, remembering his browsers-will-be-free admoni-tion to Clark at the Networked Economy conference the previous fall, saw little need for Netscape to state the obvious in a prospectus: His feeling was that "there's a lot of value in the browser just because you get the traffic, and so browsers are essentially to the users always going to be free. Because if you look at the research and development cost of the browser versus the value of having that search button and default home page, it's way greater than the engineering cost. So there's never a case where people pay to buy browsers." Gates's point was that the value of the browser was in drawing Web users to your home page and, presumably, the advertising and content contained thereon. It was like giving away free raffle tickets to get people to come to a charity ball. You wanted the visitors, the customers, the buyers. Gates's view was an early expression of the rationale for "portal" sites on the Web for aggregated content that linked elsewhere.

The circumstances of Netscape's storied IPO are well known. Five mil-lion shares were initially offered at $28, rose in early bidding all the way to $75, then settled back to $58.50, creating a $2.2 billion enterprise literally in a day. It was an unbelievable coup that had Wall Street agog, and it was a culmination of the year's hugely successful Internet-related initial public offerings.

Even the IPO had an anti-Microsoft undertone to it. Coming two weeks before the long-anticipated rollout of Windows 95, it sent the message that the technology universe was shifting. The Internet, not the desktop, was the new focus of computing. The World Wide Web, not Windows 95, was where the money was. Microsoft, by implication, was missing the boat. In Mountain View, Barksdale acknowledged there was rhyme and reason to the IPO's timing. It was not exactly meant to thumb Netscape's nose at Microsoft, he said. But "it did occur to us" that might be the effect, he said later with a slight smile: "Sure, it occurred to us that it was two weeks before the big rocket launch. I do remember saying, It's good to get out before [Windows 95] rather than after. We were in sort of the glow of technology interest at the time, because you couldn't read the paper without seeing something about Windows 95."

In the wake of Netscape's explosive IPO, Barksdale recalled the Dan Rosen pitch at the June 21 meeting and chuckled to himself. Gee, he mused, I wonder what it would have been like *with* the Bill factor?

Although computer product launches had gotten increasingly burlesque since the Steve Jobs extravaganzas of the mid-to-late 1980s and the Windows 3.X and NT bashes through the early 1990s, the Windows 95 launch dwarfed anything before or since. On August 24 the epicenter of the known computer universe became Redmond, Washington. An advertising budget characterized as $200 million included the reputed $12 million purchase of rights to the Rolling Stones song "Start Me Up." The figure mystified Brad Chase, head of Windows marketing. "While I can't tell you the number, trust me, it's nowhere in that vicinity," he allowed afterward. "But before you knew it, it was gospel." Whatever Microsoft paid, Steve Ballmer decided to get his money's worth. The night of the Windows 95 rollout, Ballmer, Microsoft sales chief Jeff Raikes, and Jay Amato, CEO of Vanstar, a Windows NT support supplier, toured software outlets doing "Midnight Madness" sales. Ballmer had "Start Me Up" on continuous replay at top volume in Raikes's BMW. "We spent all this money for this song, we might as well enjoy it!" he exclaimed. It was like the scene in *Wayne's World*, where Garth and Wayne are listening to Queen, Amato recalled. The reference was to Windows 95's distinctive "Start" button, a prime ease-of-use feature put together by Daniel Oran, who had done graduate work in psychology at Harvard and applied some of the principles of working with chimpanzees to design issues in Windows. While studying a Boeing engineer's confusion over where to start with Windows 3.1, Oran had the inspiration that led to the button. At first it was in the upper left-hand corner of the screen. Oran also created the "Taskbar," Windows 95's display of all open programs along the bottom of the screen. Both were breakthroughs for new users trying to understand how their computers worked.

The front yard of Microsoft's sylvan headquarters was festooned with tents, balloons, and banners. A big top teemed with Microsoft frontline executives, press, analysts, wellwishers, and returning heroes. For the main show Gates teamed with Jay Leno in a propeller-head version of Leno's standard warm-up routine. "I'm kind of a computer virgin here, Bill," he said. "As we go through this I hope you'll be gentle." Gates's best rejoinder: Windows 95 was so easy even a talk-show host could use it.

The Microsoft marketing machine was cranked to the limit. A fifty-two-page press kit, known as a "Wagg-Ed Bomb" after the Microsoft PR firm, provided inexhaustible fodder for industry scribes. Waggener-Edstrom was matching Microsoft hours minute by minute. The night before the launch Karla Wachter, a PR specialist in charge of third-party support for the event, woke up around 3:00 A.M. and rattled off the names of all her assigned companies, locations of their booths, and contact personnel—scores of them—then went back to sleep. The next morning her roommate, Claudia Husemann, told her, "You know, you take your work soooooo seriously."

The Internet was there for the curious, but you had to look. For one thing, IE 1.0 was scarcely a barnburner. The interface was "Generic Browser, circa 1995." Slivka's team had spent much of its energy getting the browser mechanics to mesh with Windows 95's infrastructure. The result was a few nice touches—fonts were one—and one noticeable plus called progressive rendering, the Chris Franklin feature. The browser crew at Netscape looked at IE 1.0 with curiosity and respect. "We could see they were doing some interesting things," recalled Chris Houck, one of the original NCSA hires. But the Mountain View browser makers felt they had about a year's lead technologically over IE. Especially given the fact the media and analyst community thought Microsoft was clueless on the Internet.

IE 1.0 would have slipped by largely unnoticed had it not been for a flap over winsock.dll. When users of an existing Windows browser upgraded to Windows 95, Internet Explorer's winsock.dll took the place of the previous browser's file by the same name. To get the previous browser to work right, a user had to reverse the process manually. Marc Andreessen was there to fan the flames: "In effect your Internet account gets nuked," he declared. It was an exaggeration but got big play on the Web. Reversing the .dll installation, which simply meant renaming the previous .dll "winsock.dll" and moving the Microsoft file elsewhere, was not a difficult procedure, but it did create headaches for users and browser makers alike, who complained that Microsoft was trying to lure users to switch to IE by default rather than hassle with changing the .dll back. David Pool, the Spry innovator whose Internet in a Box had spread Mosaic's popularity partly by its ease of installation, was quick to complain to the Justice Department about unfair competition. Pool eventually had a meeting with Ann Bingaman, who had headed the department's investigation of Microsoft. He did not get very far. "When you don't understand how the government works, you think the government works," he later explained. "I presented [it] to Ann Bingaman, I did the demo of them [Microsoft] overriding the winsock.dll. But the reality is, if you look at it from Ann's standpoint, she's going, 'Well, you're probably right. It screws up a few people. But doesn't it help people in general get on the Internet quicker, the fact that Microsoft has this stuff in there?'"

Silverberg said Microsoft tried to work with Spry but could never get Pool to respond to his requests for information. "We said, 'David, what are your issues? Let's fix them.' And he would never respond to me." Microsoft had notified browser developers before Win 95's release of the winsock.dll issue. Browsers like Spry's Mosaic put slight variations on the file to better enable Internet connections, but that made conflicts inevitable. A Spry programmer at the time, Chris Hopen, said he doubted Microsoft meant to harm other Winsock vendors but felt the company ignored potential conflicts in the interests of jamming Windows 95 out. "They should have gone out to TCP/IP vendors and said, Look, here's what we're planning on doing, let's work through the situation and make sure it works well for everybody. With all the pressures of the date sliding and everything else, it was just one of those things they had to do." Microsoft did try to alert vendors, Slivka countered, but developers had implemented mutually incompatible Winsocks, and something had to give if Windows 95 connections to the Internet were to be made easy and painless for PC users. Microsoft said it heard about several companies being subpoenaed in a Justice Department investigation that presumably had to do with the winsock.dll issue, but the company itself was never contacted. The issue later died as vendors put in workarounds.

IE was ready in time to ship with the retail upgrade of Windows 95. But Slivka and Silverberg the perfectionist were uncomfortable with the less-than-exhaustive amount of testing IE had undergone. If the browser created a problem with the retail upgrade release, a support nightmare would ensue. Silverberg decided to play it safe. Let's release the browser separately, he told Slivka. Then whatever problems the browser might cause on installation can be dealt with wholly separate from any issues raised by the Win 95 upgrade. Silverberg did give the okay for IE to go out to computer makers for installation on machines carrying Windows 95. That was more straightforward: The computer maker would test the machine before it went out the door, and Microsoft could work with the manufacturer directly to eliminate any glitches.

There were legitimate reasons for doubting the browser that had nothing to do with the team's programming. One was the sheer onslaught of users expected to sign up for Internet access through MSN. The initial surge of Win 95 upgrades could overwhelm MSN, Slivka theorized, if every upgrade pack contained easy dial-up access to the network. If Microsoft put IE in a separate package, it would slow the uptick.

So the solution was: Give IE to computer makers for installation on Win 95 machines. Keep IE out of the Win 95 upgrade package. Make IE available via download over the Internet. Include IE in a separate enhancement package, sold at retail, called the Plus! Pack. "We thought it [including IE] could help sell the Plus! Pack and we thought that people wouldn't buy as many Plus! Packs as Windows 95," Slivka recalled. In short, IE would have some breathing room to iron out glitches.

And so would MSN, Bernard Aboba agreed. For Plus! Pack, MSN jumped from version 1.0 to 1.05 and included Internet Explorer on installation. That allowed MSN to include TCP/IP dial-up but in a slower ramp-up. "We only had thirty POPs [points of presence] so we thought if we give IE to everyone and they want the Internet, we will just overload and make everyone unhappy," Aboba pointed out. Points of presence refers to regional phone access lines to MSN. Waiting for more might smooth the ramp-up but would risk delaying shipment of Windows 95: "And people didn't want that." Especially people with first initial B and last initial S . . . or G.

As it turned out, even with the Plus! Pack's delayed impact, MSN had its hands full as onliners signed up by the tens of thousands. The Win 95 team may have been able to take a deep breath after the launch; the MSN side merely shifted into hyperdrive. Aboba was firmly strapped to the wheel: "I remember thinking when we turned on MSN and shipped, it was very different from anything I'd been involved in. Because before when we shipped we thought, Aaah, I get to rest. Couple of support calls, couple of bugs to fix, but I'm done. With MSN we realized, Oh my God. This is just the beginning."

In more ways than one. Not long after MSN's debut, Aboba got a piece of e-mail that drove home the real meaning of his years of computer toil. Over the years, he had purchased PCs for his father, who despite a technical background as a Univac field engineer had never caught on to the mysteries of DOS or Windows. Now, at age seventy-eight, the first thing his father had done with Windows 95 and MSN was to send his son an e-mail. It simply said "Hello!" But a sweeter greeting Aboba had never seen. Aboba's eyes mist and his speech breaks when he relates the episode: "It's made a big difference, actually, because [before] I would call him on the phone and very often he'd be out or he wouldn't talk much. And now he sends e-mail all the time. I sent him pictures of the family and the house and all that stuff. So again it's confirmation that ordinary people use the Internet and they find this is a very important part of everyday life. It's not something I would have suspected because you look at all this arcane stuff, who would've thought that a seventy-eight-year-old man would get on the Internet to do all this stuff?"

By November MSN reached 550,000 subscribers and was on its way to No. 2 status behind America Online. It was clear from monitoring MSN that "Internet traffic was dominant to a very large extent," Aboba said. "We realized we'd built this MSN service, and it was being used as an Internet service." Fully three-fourths of the logins were going straight to the Net. Silverberg and the IE crew had been right all along: Windows 95's big online draw would be the Internet. For his leadership in the Windows 95 effort Silverberg received *PC Magazine*'s "Man of the Year" award—the industry Oscar—at fall Comdex. Windows 95 also took Technical Excellence honors. Accepting the awards, Silverberg brought David Cole onstage as well: "It was important that people there got to see and meet David and give him credit," Silverberg recalled later.

The Windows 95 launch left Microsoft in a morning-after stasis. Much of the Win 95 team took off on vacation, although the two Brads, Silverberg and Chase, stayed on the case to see through any after-launch cleanup. In September Silverberg went to Europe to assist in several of the European

Windows 95 launches and do postlaunch marketing. At the Stuttgart airport on his way to Munich, Silverberg, who speaks German, encountered some "very serious and capable-looking German soldiers, not like the somnolent rent-a-cops here in the States." One, armed with an automatic rifle, asked him to boot up his laptop. When the Windows 95 splash screen came up, the guard broke into a smile: "Ah, Windows Funf-und-Neunzig!" he said, and waved Silverberg through, not having a clue whom he was addressing. Silverberg preferred it that way—he got the honest reaction. "That was a cool feeling, to see the worldwide awareness of Windows 95 at launch, even among German soldiers," he recalled.

Back on campus, Allard, Reardon, and friends were working to keep alive the bonding experience of the Windows 95 IE launch. And what better way to do so than with the primal male ritual of poker night? The idea was hatched by Steve Linowes, who had headed online marketing efforts for Windows 95. Linowes figured the strategic synergy between the Internet Information Server and Windows 95 efforts would be well-served with once-a-month get-togethers over $2 stakes. David Treadwell, Chris Jones, and Bill Gates's technical assistant, Brian Fleming, also were part of the original set. They called it Internet Geek Poker Night and met the third Thursday of each month.

Reardon had a game called Field Goal that, on Poker Night No. 2, got the server guys in trouble. Under rules of the game, each player was dealt two cards, which provided the goal posts. The object was for the third card to fall in value in between the first two, scoring a field goal. Losers had to match the pot, which quickly raised the stakes. At $64, Treadwell got dealt a king and a 7. It seemed a pretty good bet. Instead, the third card was a 5. The pot went to $128.

This time, Allard looked to be a surefire winner. He drew a queen and a 3. With only a hint of swagger, Allard asked for the third card. Back it came: a deuce. A couple of weeks later, Allard was on an Internet chat session talking about NT. In came a question, "I heard last week you dumped $128 on one hand of cards—is that true?" The question had been submitted by Brian Fleming, rubbing it in.

In September 1995, Jonathan Seybold paid a visit to the Redmond campus. Seybold, a tech patriarch with a keen eye for human observation, noticed something about the company. "Microsoft had kind of gone into the doldrums. There was no focus for the company, and political infighting had grown tremendously. The place lacked energy. It was the first time I'd seen these symptoms at Microsoft." Another industry veteran, Bothell, Washington-based Traveling Software's Mark Eppley, saw the same malaise. Microsofties he'd known and worked with for years were leaving the company simply out of boredom, he noticed. "Windows 95 had conquered the world. There was nothing left in Microsoft's gunsights."

Neither of them had encountered Ben Slivka and his rogue corps of browser desperadoes. The Windows 95 launch meant only two things to Slivka: Work harder, work faster. Microsoft had its toe in the water; now it was time to swim or sink. To engage in full catch-up mode to Netscape, Slivka's team immediately threw itself into not just version 2.0 of IE but version 3.0 as well. It had to. Parallel development on Microsoft Hours was the only way Microsoft was going to catch Netscape on Netscape Time. Within days after the Windows 95 rollout, Netscape announced version 2.0 of Navigator. Included would be the technology that was rapidly becoming the watchword of the Internet revolution: Java. Navigator 1.1 already had tables, a technology that Slivka dearly wanted to include in Internet Explorer. There was more: Navigator Gold 2.0 was coming out, a version of the browser that Webheads could use to put together Web documents, sort of like a word processor or supercharged Internet Assistant for Word. And Netscape announced LiveWire, a collection of website management tools. Netscape was turning up the burners big time, keeping the heat on the feet of the Redmond giant.

Slivka set out to tart up IE 2.0 as much as possible. First up: tables. Tables made it easy to display data on a browser page without having to set up tabbed spacing or some other kludgy approach. Slivka had wanted tables in IE 1.0 but there just had not been time. To get tables and frames—ways of displaying a page-within-a-page in a browser—in IE 2.0, Slivka again called on Chris Franklin and John Cordell. He also went after http "cookies"—technology that lets websites track a browser's fingerprint down to the .com address (nothing about the individual, in other words). And IE 2.0 added SSL, licensed from, of all places, Netscape. Slivka's team also put in a few of its own html wrinkles, including marquee effects—scrolling sideways text, like the stock market readerboard in Times Square—background sounds, and something called in-line AVIs. The latter were animations that called up Windows "movie" effects. Later .gif files did the same thing.

In injecting such features, Slivka's goal was to mimic some of Java's cool tricks. No one was going to argue that Microsoft wasn't doing clever Windows programming to match some of Java's appeal. Still, the IE 2.0 effort was important for a precedent it established: extending html to do things beyond simple linking, layout, and page display. Html was not just a text format anymore. True to Slivka's predictions, it was becoming a special-effects technology as well. Before the html extension battle between Microsoft and Netscape played out, the Web almost split in half in 1997 as each company's browser tried to differentiate itself.

Slivka shrewdly foresaw Microsoft's need to come up with a response to Java buzz, which was getting to white-noise levels. Concomitant with Win 95's rollout, *Forbes ASAP* magazine published in its August 28 issue a long essay under the cover line, "Netscape's Marc Andreessen: George Gilder Thinks This Kid Can Topple Bill Gates." It was a call to arms from techno-pundit Gilder, a wiry fitness freak whose deep-set dark eyes and toothy half grin recalled a George of another era—McGovern—although the men's politics would never get confused. After watching a particularly animated Gilder speech, one wag said Gilder combined the arm movements of Ross Perot with the speech mannerisms of George Bush. In the coming software shift, as Gilder termed it, Windows 95 would be practically irrelevant. Forget "Information At Your Fingertips!" Instead the new world order, the Telecosm, would use Java, Java, and more Java to run a variety of devices hooked to the Internet.

Java's particular sorcery was the promise of one program running on any type of computer. The concept had bewitched but also bedeviled technologists since software incompatibilities first surfaced, requiring a given program to be rewritten to operate on a given computer. The most common example was the IBM PC and the Macintosh. Programmers had to rewrite their software for each platform. Throw an IBM mainframe and a DEC minicomputer into the mix, and you had a real nightmare getting the same code to operate in the different environments. The notion behind Java was to offer programmers the ability to write one program that ran everywhere. Sun Microsystems, whose star coder James Gosling had put together Java in the early 1990s, called the philosophy WORA—Write Once, Run Anywhere. It was the holy grail, the fountain of youth, the ultimate buried treasure. When the Internet hit, Java all of a sudden had instant cachet. Any computer connected to the Internet, from a mainframe on down to a lowly DOS clone, could communicate with another via e-mail and newsgroups. With Java, the computers could share data, files, and programs as well. At least, that was the vision circa 1995.

Gilder's piece set industry tongues wagging, but it was far from the only hair in Gates's soup. At the European IT Forum on September 4, 1995, Oracle's smooth operator Larry Ellison was in prime gunslinger mode. Out of the blue he announced, "The personal computer is a ridiculous device."

Too hard to use. Too expensive. Too flaky. The alternative? A machine that substituted the Internet for a disk drive . . . that plugged into the Internet (or corporate network) like a lamp into a wall and drew data from the Net as easily as a toaster draws electricity. No hard drive to crash, no system software to reboot. And all for just $500, at a time when the typical PC ran $2,000 or more. Ellison's term for the vaguely defined device: Internet Appliance, later dubbed Network Computer, or NC. Following Ellison on the program, Gates—not wanting to pour gasoline on a brush fire—kept his response low key. PC sales during the next ten years would easily outstrip sales over the previous ten, Gates averred.

Could the decline and fall of the Microsoft Empire be nigh? Was Bill Gates like some misbegotten railroad baron, scratching his head at the Wright Brothers' magnificent new machine, an NC running Java? Even though the previous quarter had blown off the doors, with Win 95 orders increasing profits by 58 percent, to $499 million, on $2.02 billion in sales . . . even though industry trend-watcher Dataquest had just reported that Microsoft's share of the personal computer software market rose from 37 percent to 42 percent from the first to second quarters of the year and was expected to leap again in the third quarter with Win 95 sales . . . even though Microsoft had, if you rolled back the clock and gave the company the benefit of the doubt during its early privately held years, twenty years of consecutive quarter-to-quarter growth . . . somehow doubt was being cast on Microsoft's invincibility. All because of the Internet.

By November Microsoft was mounting a sporadic defense. Maritz accused Rick Sherlund, a leading Goldman Sachs analyst who had downgraded Microsoft stock because of "vagueness" in the company's Internet strategy, of "potentially overreacting. These issues will have an impact, if they have an impact, over a long period of time." Gates tried to quell the rising din with deferential nods to the Internet as the next big thing. In early October he told a Gartner Group conference in Lake Buena Vista, Florida, via satellite, "The Internet will drive PC volumes higher," adding without elaboration that Microsoft was "investing very heavily in this area." On November 10 Microsoft released to major news media Gates's May "Tidal Wave" memo, assigning the Internet "the highest level of importance" and calling it the most important single development to come along for Microsoft since the introduction of the IBM PC in 1981.

Strong words, yes. But, for competitive purposes, huge portions of the memo, where Gates detailed his company's sweeping deployment of Internet technologies and plans for Windows on the Web, were excised in the released version. The result was a three-page "treatment" of the original nine-page epiphany that for wired observers read like a rehash of one of Gilder's books, explaining how various Internet and online technologies would create new computing and telecommunications opportunities. All mentions of Netscape, Java, the Word html strategy, the MSN strategy (including the word "free" and Microsoft's growing NT server strategy) were eliminated. Comparing the excerpted version to the full memo, eventually released in Justice Department documents, gave dramatic evidence not just of how broad and deep Microsoft's Internet strategy ran but how precisely the company understood competitive issues that it felt needed to be protected from the public eye.

Particularly aberrant, in retrospect, was Gates's release of his vision statement for the information highway, *The Road Ahead*. In the book, released in late November to great fanfare, the Web received only four index mentions, and it was treated as a functional appendage of the Internet. Netscape and Java were nowhere to be found. And nothing about Microsoft's interest in leveraging Web technology for Windows was addressed. None of this was particularly shocking, giving the generalist tone of the book and its target audience of undigitized America. But the book did nothing to enhance Gates's or Microsoft's reputations for Internet awareness, and in fact fed the skeptics.

No matter. The full frontal assault was on the way. As early as midsummer Microsoft's inner circle had decided "we had to let our customers know that this [the Internet] was an important part of what we were doing," said Brad Chase. "So we decided to have this Internet day on December 7." Why not go before then? Chase denied it had anything to do with Windows 95 or the Gates book tour. "I think it's just that's when we thought we could be ready . . . there were big issues about whether we should show that [Windows integration with the Web] stuff then, because we knew we wouldn't have it for a while." The December 7 briefing in Seattle before media and analysts turned out to be auspicious in more ways than one. Not only was it the anniversary of the Pearl Harbor bombing, it marked the second anniversary of Steve Ballmer's "what think" memo.

Ballmer wouldn't have missed this briefing for the world. In a coffee hour before the morning briefing began, he was floating like a butterfly and stinging like a bee. The Internet had galvanized Microsoft, consumed the company, he said. Focus! Focus! Focus! Pounding his palm with his fist. Bobbing and weaving as he worked himself up, his voice rising from a near whisper to a truck horn's bray. "You will see this company be transformed!" he promised. "This is our jihad!" Microsoft's holy war. Ballmer had used the term before, back in 1991, characterizing his company's then-confusing, two-pronged campaign to push Windows and OS/2 3.0, the product that became NT. No one was second-guessing the success of *that* strategy now.

If the wartime symbolism of December 7 had escaped notice—and none of the invitations to the event had touched on the Pearl Harbor day parallel—Gates soon made the room aware of it. Leading off the events, Gates noted that in researching the original Japanese bombing, he had noticed that the most intelligent analysis of the attack had not come from Wall Street or indeed any analyst. It was from Admiral Isoroku Yamamoto, leader of the raid, who said, "I fear we have awakened a sleeping giant." Depending on how you interpreted it, the remark was an in-your-face to the crowded room: Benighted analysts who had pounded on Microsoft's lack of strategy had completely forgotten about the giant's prowess. Gates paused at the end of the remark, and light laughter tittered across the room. The comment showed how much the combative Gates had returned, and for the assembled group, that was good. Gates had not needed to look far for the quote. In yet another example of Microsoft eating its own dog-food, the citation was prominently featured in the Microsoft Encarta and Bookshelf entries under the heading "Pearl Harbor Day."

If the occasion was historic, so was the address. Always in his element in front of analysts, Gates not only laid forth a detailed platform strategy for Microsoft's triumph on the Net, he defied the widespread expectation that it would take a counterattack to do it. Instead of fighting the Internet, Microsoft would join it. Everything Microsoft was doing, Gates disclosed, was aimed at building the Internet into its corporate consciousness and product line. "You will hear from us that we're not forming an Internet division. To us that's like having an electricity division or a software division. The Internet is pervasive in everything that we're doing."

Microsoft would build Internet standards, and Java, and scripting, and whatever else the Web crowd demanded into Windows-based products. And it would do so without, in many cases, charging a premium. Why? Gates had a litany of reasons. First off, he took issue with the concept that the Internet, where software and publishing/subscribing was free, had changed the rules of competition. "Have we ever seen people giving away software before? Well, the price that we made MS-DOS available to IBM for was about $80,000, was a zero royalty deal, and they could use it forever, do whatever they wanted, and could get it out there and hopefully make a standard of it." Whoa! That was the kind of bombshell Gates tended to let drop offhand, delivered in a way that only a few in-the-know antennae would pick up. Gates had never given a figure for the DOS deal with IBM publicly—but doing so had never served his purpose before. Now he was citing $80,000 as the moral equivalent of free. It was an arguable point. In 1995 eighty grand seemed like pin money, especially for a piece of software that had earned Microsoft billions over the years. At the time of the deal in 1981, however, it was a bucket of coin to pay for something like an operating system on a toylike computer with no track record or proven market. Still, the money was chump change to IBM and a nanofarthing when it came to DOS's eventual revenue stream, which peaked at nearly $1 million a day in the early 1990s. As with browsers, there had been numerous DOSes—Gates cited the figure fourteen—at one point. But Microsoft had prevailed by continuing to improve the product beyond what others, including IBM itself, could offer.

"When we were developing the spreadsheet," Gates continued, "we didn't sit down and say what's the world's best spreadsheet. We understood that the market was a market for 1-2-3. People knew 1-2-3, they had 1-2-3 macros. The only thing people were interested in buying was a better 1-2-3." With Excel, Microsoft embraced Lotus's macro language, embraced Lotus's extensions, and did extensions of its own. In a warning salvo to Netscape, Gates noted it was one of those cases where the clone had gone on to conquer the market.

Embrace the Internet . . . and extend the Internet! The language of J Allard's "killer app" memo, repeated in Gates's "Tidal Wave" memo, became the public watchword of Microsoft Internet strategy for the first time. Embrace and extend Java. Embrace and extend html, Javascript, and whatever else the Web community served up. "This is exactly what Netscape does," Gates pointed out in one of his few references to the browser maker. "They support all the standard protocols."

A demonstration of IE midway through Gates's talk showed how Microsoft was building standards into its browser. "And what do you think we'll charge for it?" Gates asked the demo-giver. Presenter Steve Guggenheimer's reply: "Like all the others, nothing."

Free! Like a Johnny Browserseed, Gates was going to plant free copies of its browser on hard drives everywhere in hopes of gaining share on the Web. There was nothing novel in the approach: The original browsers, developed in academic settings, all had been given away over the Net as part of the ethic of sharing code under development for peer review. With the same thought in mind, Netscape had given away Navigator in its test and early release stages. You could still download Navigator from the Netscape website for free, which gave the widespread impression was that it too was free. But Netscape wanted it both ways: Navigator was free, yes, but only to educational and nonprofit institutions. Everyone else was asked to buy or license. Gates himself later corrected Guggenheimer's suggestion that "all the others" were free: "When we say a browser is free, we're saying something different from what other people are saying. We're not saying you can use it for ninety days, or you can use it unless you're a corporation, or you can use it and maybe next year we'll charge you a bunch of money. We're saying it's free."

There it was: The core of Microsoft's browser strategy. Free, and, it was implied, free forever. Seated in the audience, Spyglass executives Mike Tyrrell and Tim Krauskopf exchanged a disbelieving glance. At first there was euphoria: Microsoft would be paying royalties for a piece of software that, offered free, would be used by millions. Ludwig noticed Tyrrell look at him and say, "Ka-ching!" "He knew we would be paying him for all those free copies," Ludwig said. Then something occurred to Tyrrell. Feeling himself go prickly with trepidation, Tyrrell reached down and pulled the amended contract from his briefcase. The contract, effective the day before, added Win 3.X, UNIX, and the Macintosh to Windows 95 and Windows NT as browser platforms Microsoft could use Spyglass Mosaic code to build. Tyrrell wanted to make sure there was no language exempting Microsoft from paying for browsers it distributed for free. Later Tyrrell compared his surprise at the giveaway to that of an author who was being paid a royalty on each printed copy of a book. If the publisher said the book was being given away, the author might well wonder where his royalty checks were going to come from. It was all but unprecedented: Bill Gates hated to pay royalties, because you never knew when a product might take the world by storm. Microsoft had gotten away with a flat-fee, paid-up license for $2 million the first time around for Windows 95. But that was when it was still talking to Netscape about licensing its browser. Spyglass needed Microsoft back then. This time Microsoft needed Spyglass. No royalty, Tyrrell said, no Windows 3.X. No Mac. No UNIX. As he liked to point out: "Microsoft understands leverage better than anyone, and they apply it better than anyone, like any good businessperson should. Once you have them in a position where you have some leverage, you can apply it back."

Spyglass's standard deal for a commitment to 1 million or more browsers was 55 cents a copy. Ludwig told Tyrrell, We can go lots higher than 1 million copies; how about a break on the royalty? Tyrrell dropped to 50 cents and drew the line. "They got the best royalty deal by a nickel," Tyrrell said. Microsoft also got a royalty cap—a maximum amount it would pay. The cap never was a factor, however, Tyrrell said. Instead, after Microsoft's browser began to be adopted by Internet Service Providers like America Online and software vendors, the two companies had to reset terms in early 1997 over the royalty amount owed. After some talks, Spyglass accepted a one-time payment of $8 million that bought out all current and future royalties due on Internet Explorer. All told, by the time the contract between the two companies expired in 1998, Spyglass received $14 million from Microsoft in return for technology it used in a free product.

As he pored once again over the contract language, Tyrrell noticed Brad Silverberg and John Ludwig, seated on either side of Tyrrell and Krauskopf, exchange sideways glances in reaction to Gates's pronouncement. "They looked at each other like, 'He said WHAT?!'" Tyrrell recalled. Ludwig was not as surprised at "free" as he was at *how* free: "The breadth of the free was a surprise. Covering all platforms [free] was a surprise. Because while on the Windows platform I do have this product called Windows that I can include Internet Explorer in, and do my math, and justify our investment and say yes, we make money overall in the totality of this investment because we get this much money for Windows and the Internet Explorer business is part of Windows—on the Mac platform I don't have that, there's nothing to give me any air cover." The same was true for UNIX and Windows 3.X. Revenues from those platforms were not going to justify sticking in a browser. One other thing took Ludwig aback: "The commitment to forever being free was kind of a surprise." Products often were given away free, especially on the Internet, with the expectation that once demand had been built, you could charge for them. Apparently that was not part of the game plan with Internet Explorer.

Had Gates gone off-script? It seemed so. The free-forever declaration came in response to pointed questions from analysts who were trying to figure out revenue streams and business plans. Ablaze with competitive fire, Gates had embraced and extended his Internet renegades' "communistic" model further than anyone ever might have expected. To his mind, however, he was merely following through on his initial analysis of a browser's real worth: It lay in the eyeballs—the Webviewers—and traffic it brought to your software, not on the retail stand: "When I said, okay, it's going to be part of the operating system, built-in and free as far as future versions of the operating system [went], everybody knew that. . . . The fact I said it was free on Windows 3.1 and the Macintosh was kind of a last-minute decision there, really, the night before. So there were people at Microsoft [who were surprised]."

The most surprising relationship would be with Java, the programming language most Internet insiders figured Microsoft would prefer to strangle. Throughout the fall, Myhrvold and other executives had been bad-mouthing Java to Gilder and others. Microsoft had been down the Java path to glory before and found a dead end. In the early 1980s Charles Simonyi, a brilliant young Hungarian émigré who had come to Microsoft by way of Xerox's pioneering Palo Alto Research Center, had put together a cross-platform system for Microsoft applications based on pseudocode, or p-code. Applications written in p-code theoretically would run on any computer. Simonyi came up with a Multi-Tool Interface that enabled similar commands to be used for different applications. But p-code programs ran more slowly and were more difficult to use than those written specifically for a type of computer. The noble effort taught Microsoft a lesson no amount of product hype could sway. Myhrvold himself had marshaled a project in 1988 to develop OS/2 into a portable operating system to compete with UNIX, based on the Mach kernel developed at Carnegie-Mellon University. It was called Psycho because, Myhrvold explained, people thought they were crazy and because they could substitute the lyrics of the Talking Heads song, "Psycho Killer," with "Psycho kernel, q'est-ce que c'est?" The project, dismissed by Dave Cutler in favor of building from scratch what became NT, wound up more like Janet Leigh in the Hitchcock movie.

The only way Microsoft could teach the world at large the same lesson, though, would be to license Java. In the previous night's wee hours, Microsoft and Sun had finalized language of a letter of intent. The deal culminated days of long-distance faxes, cell phone marathons, airport conversations. At one point Eric Schmidt, Sun's chief technology officer, cracked up when Paul Maritz, talking nonstop on his cell phone, had to walk through an airport security device. Maritz, asking that Schmidt please excuse him, handed the device to the security guard, walked through the detector, then picked the phone back up and renewed his conversation on the way to the flight gate.

Schmidt had started the Java ball rolling with Microsoft in early October, four months after Netscape first announced its intent to license Java. Both moves were part of a definite Sun strategy hatched by Scott McNealy and Schmidt: "We made a list in May of the companies that we would like to license, and the question was do you go to Microsoft first or last? And the conclusion was, go to Microsoft's competitors first, starting with Netscape, which was very primed. . . . We decided to wait till we had created a wave before we contacted them [Microsoft]. Then over the summer we knew we were creating a wave, we were getting deals and I was watching Microsoft's behavior."

At a conference at his alma mater, Princeton University, Schmidt found the opportunity to make his move. Also on the agenda was Nathan Myhrvold, who had caught the attention of Stephen Hawking while doing graduate work on quantum field theory at Princeton. The two agreed to meet. Schmidt was immediately impressed with how much Myhrvold knew about Java. Myhrvold also was curious about the Netscape scripting language, called LiveScript, that was gaining popularity on the Web. "He asked me all sorts of competitive questions," Schmidt recalled. "They were very worried about LiveScript." Microsoft saw LiveScript as an avenue to the hearts and minds of the Web programming community as well as potential competition to Microsoft's OLE technology on the Web. Make developers happy, Microsoft had long ago learned, and you control the platform.

Myhrvold told Schmidt that Java was not exactly his area of responsibility, but he would check further and report back. By Monday morning Microsoft's head of developer tools Roger Heinen, an Apple Computer import, called Schmidt and asked to visit. Heinen wanted to know contract language and licensing terms. Schmidt sent a Sun Microsystems team up to Microsoft within two weeks to provide technical disclosure. Then the two companies spent another couple of weeks hammering out contract language. By the first of November Heinen and Ludwig visited Sun to talk money.

When Schmidt had first raised the issue of what to charge for Java, McNealy told him, "I want what Microsoft gets for DOS!" Call it Scott's revenge. In 1992 McNealy, under pressure from several big clients including the Boeing Co., sought a Windows license that would enable him to put applications like Excel and Word on corporate desktops running Sun workstations. Sure, Gates told him, for a price. At the time, McNealy characterized the asking fee in colorful terms: "Gates is absolutely willing to sell us anything for a reasonable tax. As long as I get up every morning and work the first few hours of the day for him, he's very happy. And if you notice, all the companies that have gotten up every morning and started work for Bill Gates have found they're out of money. They're broke."

Down, boy, Schmidt told his boss. This is the Internet era. A lot of stuff is downloadable free right off the Web. Furthermore, Schmidt pointed out,

Netscape gave its products away! No one was going to pay $20, $30 a pop for Java. Particularly not Microsoft. Oh. Well, okay, McNealy said. Most Java licenses were a negotiated annual fee based on volume and expense. Even for large customers, Sun had to keep pricing in the seven-figure range. Otherwise, a company might simply clone Java. Schmidt said: "You go, okay, now how much is it going to cost me to build a clone of Java? I need how many programmers—ten, twenty? I need libraries, that's another ten. So now you're up to thirty, so that's like $4 million. You're not going to pay me more than what it would cost you in theory to do it yourself." Schmidt had in fact heard that Microsoft was working on cloning Java. Ludwig later confirmed it: "We concluded it was a good thing to have, so they went out and did it," he said. Shades of Reardon and NetWare! Another clean-room experiment had worked.

As Schmidt characterized the negotiations: "They [Microsoft] said how much do you want for this? And we had constructed a financial argument which they said was ridiculous. Which was about what we expected. And the next forty-eight hours we negotiated numbers." The numbers turned out to be pretty good for Sun, considerably more than they were getting from most other licensees. Microsoft wound up licensing Java for $17.5 million over the five-year duration of the contract.

Schmidt said money was not the key Sun concern in the Microsoft negotiations. "The final issue involved what leverage we had over Microsoft concerning product evolution," he said. "In other words, could we stuff 'em." Sun wanted to draw explicit boundaries around how Microsoft used Java. In particular, it wanted to ensure that Microsoft could not make Java run better on Windows than on other platforms. "Think of it as a defined box. Now, around that box Microsoft can do whatever it wants. It can add stuff, it can layer stuff. It can do AFC [application tools for developers] . . . it can innovate on top. But it had to respect the box." At least, that's how Schmidt characterized Sun's goals later. The actual contract language left enough latitude for interpretation that Microsoft came away from the deal understanding it could create enhancements for Java under Windows as long as it met certain baseline parameters. After the letter of agreement, it took Sun and Microsoft lawyers three and a half more months to come up with contract language satisfactory to both sides. Even then, when Ben Slivka saw the license, he thought, Oh, no. This will never work. Under the terms he saw, Slivka considered it inconceivable that both Microsoft and Sun could abide by the contract's intent. And Gates took heated issue with Schmidt's assessment that the money was irrelevant: "We ended up paying a fair amount of money in that thing, just to make sure we had the latitude" to do things Sun later claimed were outside the contract's bounds.

Sun's licensing of Java to Microsoft stunned the Internet world. It was like turning over a winning Lotto ticket to the family's black sheep. Schmidt's ears were burning for weeks from Silicon Valley colleagues questioning Sun's sanity: "Many, many people said it was what they thought of as one of the biggest business mistakes they'd ever seen. The argument was that you were licensing the candy to your competitor, because Java was such a competitive advantage. But Scott had been clear: License to everyone. Anyone who studies the history of Sun and of Scott would know that's the only way the company could react."

The week before the Pearl Harbor day briefing, Mike Homer got wind that Microsoft was in the process of licensing Java. It was time to preempt. Netscape announced JavaScript, an enhanced version of its scripting language for the Web. In reality, it was simply renaming LiveScript. JavaScript had nothing to do with Java, but the buzzword was so hot that all you had to do was whisper it and venture capital began floating down from the rafters. Gates considered it one of the great scams of software history: "LiveScript becomes JavaScript. It has nothing to do with Java. Nothing whatsoever! They just say it to be cool." And to steal some of Microsoft's we-have-Java! thunder. But not much, as it turned out. By lunchtime in Seattle Netscape's stock had dropped $33.25. Microsoft was up $4.25. In San Francisco, Netscape CEO Jim Barksdale was asked during a talk to an accounting conference what his company intended to do to counteract Microsoft. Barksdale replied that "there's still an enormous business from people who don't want to be tied into one company." The questioner persisted: What are you going to do? Barksdale said there was a big market in enterprise software, and "we don't compete in all those areas against Microsoft, just in BackOffice and Exchange." Again the questioner asked, what was Netscape going to do? "I said, Well, we're going to fight hard, we've got a great young team, fine young engineers, plenty of money. Fine reputation, good customer relations. And he said, Yeah but what're you gonna do? I said, in the final analysis, it's going to be a dogfight, but we think God's on our side."

The God quote. While Barksdale later stopped short of saying he regretted making it, the God quote was what got reported universally as Netscape's response to Microsoft. Barksdale later said he meant it as a tongue-in-cheek remark to close the Q&A to an amused audience. Nonetheless, it was taken seriously in a number of quarters, generating e-mail asking what Barksdale thought he was doing "bringing the Lord's name into this." Barksdale, possessing a humanist's command of history and literature, was actually lampooning the notion in the vein of the epic film, *The Longest Day*, about the invasion of Normandy. Whose side was God on? "The Germans all say, Ya, ya, ya, God's on our side," Barksdale noted. "And the Americans say, Yeah, yeah, yeah, God's on *our* side."

Taking the podium after Barksdale, veteran industry analyst Dave Coursey framed the issue in starker terms: "What this means is that Netscape is dead," he declared.

Given the breadth of the Pearl Harbor day address, it nearly escaped notice when Gates demonstrated how, in the next version of Windows, Microsoft would build the Web into the Windows desktop. Steven Sinofsky showed how bouncing back and forth from Windows to the Internet would involve just a click or two of the mouse. The buttons in Windows would look like Web icons; the folders on the hard disk would act like Web pages. Windows married with the Web. Steve Ballmer's "great front end to the Internet." J Allard's "killer app." Brad Silverberg's "gateway to the Information Highway." They all were coming together publicly for the first time. The Sinofsky demonstration was the unveiling of a strategy that had been in motion for two years. The events of the day were universally characterized as the time when Gates began to turn the supertanker around. In reality, it had been full rudder right for some time.

Pearl Harbor day was hailed as the beginning of a new era for Microsoft. In reality, it was the end of the company's Internet planning and strategizing cycle. December 7 on marked the era of execution, as Silverberg, Slivka, Sinofsky, Allard, Ludwig, Reardon, and associates moved into action with the decisiveness and force of a Dust Bowl tornado.

And Barksdale aided the cause too. When Silverberg saw the God quote, he made copies and posted it on hallway walls, in bathrooms, on office relights. Disrespect, Silverberg knew, was one of the greatest motivators around.

Chapter 15

THE OTHER BRAD

n the fall of 1990, Microsoft applications chief Mike Maples approached a young product manager by the name of Brad Chase to ask a favor. The systems team, headed by recent arrival Brad Silverberg, needed someone to head up marketing of DOS 5. Chase, who was marketing chief for both the Macintosh and Windows versions of Microsoft Office, demurred. He liked what he was doing, and he was not sure DOS was really a step forward. "I'll talk to him," Chase told Maples. "But the whole world is moving to Windows—and you want me to work on *DOS*?" Chase did not know much about his would-be boss. Silverberg seemed like a nice enough guy, but he had been with the company only since June. The whole thing struck Chase as kind of a gamble, when by contrast the Office gig was guaranteed . . . manifest destiny.

Chase had to go to Paris on business but promised Maples to give it some thought. The next thing he knew, Silverberg was on the line, calling long distance with his pitch. Silverberg told Chase, You're a savvy marketing guy, we need you to give some spark to the DOS marketing effort. DOS 5 is going to be a retail product, not just a new-computer upgrade.

It's going to boost Windows performance. DOS and Windows are going to remake the desktop computing business. Here's your chance to make history.

Chase was a bit surprised at Silverberg's quiet salesmanship. Silverberg did not have the rapid-fire, body-slam approach of a lot of Microsoft executives. He did not try to sweet-talk Chase with a lot of hype and inflated promises. Chase kind of liked that. Chase himself was not the slick MBA type, even though he had a master's from the Kellogg School of Management at Northwestern University. Chase liked to identify with the common guy, the end user. If you did that, the marketing pretty much took care of itself.

Still, Chase was a hard sell. Silverberg even began to have doubts whether he was the right guy for the job. Silverberg wanted to make sure whoever stepped into the job also stepped up to it. Any marketing chief for DOS 5 was going to have to have a sincere commitment, a real passion for the job. Yet the more he talked with Chase, the better Silverberg knew he was the perfect fit. Chase had strong values, a good sense of humor, and a forthright, honest, straight manner that meshed well with Silverberg's own truth-in-advertising approach. In November Chase finally said yes. When it came time to move to Building 5, Chase discovered his new office was going to be directly across the hall from Silverberg's. Hoo boy, he thought. We'll find out pretty quick whether this is going to work or not.

As it turned out, it worked in spades. A lot of Microsoft business gets conducted in hallways, during breaks or downtime, or just hanging out, almost like in a college dormitory. Silverberg and Chase could not help but spend quality hallway time together. Over the ensuing months, as the DOS 5 team worked toward its June 11, 1991, launch, the two got to know each other. Silverberg saw in Chase a hard worker who took criticism gracefully, used it to grow, and was always looking to broaden his ability. Chase deemed Silverberg a rare combination of business acumen, technical depth, good instincts, and common sense. Don't let the subterranean profile fool you, Chase learned. The guy was really, really smart, opportunistic, and relentless.

As time passed, the Two Brads became a fixture at product launches, marketing events, and in-house corporate functions. Theirs was a natural chemistry. Silverberg the nuts-and-bolts guy, the wizard behind the curtain, the guy who hated the spotlight. Chase the natural ham, the glad-hander, the guy who loved to sell the vision. Chase always felt a little guilty about being the public figure—he got the credit that Silverberg rightly deserved.

Silverberg's take was just the opposite. He liked to spread the credit around, and he absolutely hated being the focus of attention.

As much as he was involved in the events leading up to it, Chase missed the Pearl Harbor day address. He had scheduled vacation time for early December and, given the sacrifices his wife and two kids had been forced to make through the Windows 95 launch, was not about to change things at the last minute. He would not have learned anything, he later acknowledged, but it would have been fun being there, seeing people respond to the "new" Microsoft. When he got back from his vacation, though, he was surprised to find what an impact the event had had. Even his neighbors were asking about it.

Once back from vacation, Chase had little time for reentry. The company he knew when he left and the company he returned to were two different entities. There was a real buzz in the air. Another Microsoft product cycle was gearing up. A reorganization was brewing, a new division to tackle the Internet. John Ludwig's Memphis upgrade of Windows was moving ahead. Ben Slivka's Internet Explorer team was about to release 2.0 and was cranking on 3.0. There was a barnburner of a deal on his plate: America Online, the old Microsoft nemesis, was making noises about wanting to be on the Windows 95 desktop. As it would turn out, the next twenty-one months would be as intense a time as anyone had seen at Microsoft. And at the wheel, driving the mother ship to warp speed, would be the Two Brads.

Born in 1960 on the same day as, but a year later than, Nathan Myhrvold, Chase grew up in San Francisco a diehard 49ers fan. His first exposure to computers came as an undergrad at Berkeley in the late 1970s, when his father built a Heathkit CP/M machine and installed VisiCalc and WordStar. It ran only on floppy diskettes and had just 56 kilobytes of RAM. So small, it's hard to conceive today, Chase says. Nonetheless, he was struck by the potential of the box. "I just sort of decided computers would have a big impact on society, and got involved," Chase said.

Even at the tender age of nineteen Chase figured it was too late to become a programmer. He would have to take another avenue. After graduation Chase went to work for the office-supply distributor Boise Cascade for three years and learned about distribution channels, sales, and marketing. Then it was back to school—Kellogg. Chase graduated in June 1987 with several job offers. Microsoft's salary offer was the worst of the bunch, but a day of interviewing and talking with Microsofties persuaded Chase that people were not at the company for the money. "Everywhere I looked in the company, I saw people with lots of drive, energy, and enthusiasm," he said. "It was actually pretty contagious."

Chase started work in July in the applications group. His first assignment was Microsoft Works for the Macintosh. Working with Macfanatics was a lot of fun. Works users were mostly small businesses and user-group types. Mac users had a lot of loyalty to Apple and passion for product, Chase found. Under Maples's guidance, by 1989 Chase was working on Microsoft Office, first for the Macintosh, then for both the Mac and Windows. Office was a big hit on the Mac side and destined for similar success in Windows. But by the time Windows debuted Chase, who had spent considerable time on the online documentation for Office on CD-ROM, had joined Silverberg's team.

Chase worked hard on the DOS 5 rollout, but his real baptism by fire came with the gala DOS 6 rollout in front of a 1,000-person-strong user-group gathering in San Francisco's Moscone Center. One of the upgrade's highly touted features was DoubleSpace, a data-compression utility that in effect doubled the amount of storage capacity on hard disks. Slivka's team had built compression into DOS 6, but Stac Electronics and other competitors were raising questions about how robust the system was. Slivka devised a demo where, onstage at the rollout, Chase would accidentally unplug the computer while it was compressing the hard drive. Typically such an occurrence would wreak all manner of havoc on a hard disk, doing everything from damaging individual files to rendering it completely unusable. But Gates would reboot the computer to show that, with DOS 6 and DoubleSpace, all was well. When it came time for the shutdown trick, Gates went off script a tad. "What happens if my kid turns off the machine and then turns it back on?" he asked innocently enough. The rollout was March 31, 1993, just after Gates and bride-to-be Melinda French, a Microsoft product manager, had disclosed their engagement in company e-mail. After Gates's comment at the rollout, there was a long pause. Then Chase, with an impish grin, said, "But, Bill, you don't have a kid!" The audience went berserk while Gates tried to fight back a smile.

The interchange set the tone for future Chase-led rollouts, where informality and a human touch ruled. In characterizing a product's appeal, Chase always kept the end user's situation in mind. He would sit down with the upgrade day after day and get to know it backward and forward, all the while pretending he was Joe or Jill Consumer. What about this feature? What made it cool? That's what made Leno such a great choice for the Windows 95 rollout, Chase thought. The guy was someone everyone could relate to. He knew nothing about computers—even the mouse was a mystery—someone actually had to mouse for Leno. But he could tell what was cool about computers and why someone would want to have Windows 95. Forget about technical specifications and feature sets and channel positioning and all the marketing mumbo jumbo. Tell me what matters about the product to consumers, Chase would say.

By the beginning of 1996, what mattered to consumers was the Internet. Returning from vacation in late December, Chase was pitched headlong into Microsoft's quest for Internet respectability. Already parts of the Pearl Harbor day strategy were falling into place. On the publishing front, Microsoft was moving to purchase Vermeer Technologies Inc. The plan was to build Vermeer's website-building technology, Front Page, into Office. Vermeer, founded in April 1994 in Cambridge, Massachusetts, had caught the vigilant eye of Steven Sinofsky around the time Windows 95 launched. Sinofsky downloaded Front Page off the Web, figuring it to be yet another html editor, and started playing around with it. Wow, he thought, these guys "get" building apps. They're not just gearheads slapping code on a page, this is like an Office application. Sinofsky ran it by Gates, who thought Front Page was pretty cool, especially for a version 1.0 product. Sinofsky also showed it to Chris Peters, who headed up the Office group, and they strategized about adding the Vermeer technology. At a subsequent Internet checkpoint meeting put together by the systems group, Sinofsky demonstrated Front Page. "And it blew everybody away because it was such a cool product, and they'd really gotten it," he said. The response convinced Sinofsky and Peters to pursue a relationship with Vermeer.

One day in November 1995, Peters made a cold call of sorts to Vermeer just to check out the thirty-five-person company. The same day, ironically, another suitor was scheduled to call Vermeer in person—Marc Andreessen. Peters chatted for a while, hinting that Microsoft might be interested in an acquisition. When Andreessen turned up, he was impressed enough to make a pitch to Vermeer's principals, Randy Forgaard, a former Lotus programmer who was the technical side of the collaboration, and Charles Ferguson, coauthor of a 1993 book about IBM called *Computer Wars* and the idea man behind Front Page. Look, Andreessen said, if you guys are interested in being acquired, let us know. "At the end of the day, our heads were spinning," Forgaard recalled. He sensed Microsoft was more committed than Netscape, which already had announced a Front Page–like product strategy with Navigator Gold and LiveWire. Ferguson and Forgaard had dinner in Seattle with Peters and Sinofsky. It was "such a meeting of the minds," Sinofsky recalled, that a deal progressed rapidly. Forgaard felt hesitation only when, in introductory meetings with the Office team, he encountered concern that Front Page and its html foundation would cannibalize Microsoft formats. "They had a few people in the meeting who were kind of Old School Microsoft Office types, who were saying things like the Internet is kind of inconsequential, we want Word to be the default file format on the Internet and this html stuff is terrible." Once Pearl Harbor day happened, however, vestiges of html loathing disappeared. "It was Whoa! Microsoft really gets it!" Forgaard related.

By January 16, 1996, Microsoft announced the purchase of Vermeer in a stock deal valued at $130 million. Front Page was an instant hit. When Microsoft issued version 1.1 in May, it sold 150,000 copies over the next four months. When Front Page 97 was released in late fall, it quickly took the installed base to seven figures.

Microsoft's America Online deal moved less precipitously. When he first heard about it, Chase was not sure what to make of the notion. Since the frosty meeting between AOL kingpin Steve Case and Gates in the spring of 1993, relations between the two companies had ranged from standoffish to incendiary. The following year AOL snatched BookLink from Microsoft's clutches. After the announcement of Microsoft Network at Fall Comdex, 1994, Case was constantly on the warpath, dissing Microsoft at every turn. By the summer of 1995 he was raising antitrust concerns over Microsoft, encouraging the Justice Department to act. Case complained that MSN, by having its own icon on the Windows 95 desktop, was competing unfairly. No other online company could match the distribution might of Windows 95. Partly as a result of his and other Internet providers' complaints, the Justice Department in late spring requested information from Microsoft regarding MSN and Windows 95 sales contracts. Rumblings of the department's investigation continued through the summer. At a meeting with Intel on July 11, 1995, Gates announced that "this antitrust thing will blow over." The statement was in response to a question directly concerning the Microsoft Network investigation, he said later: "The question from the Intel person was a very specific question . . . will Windows 95 ship on time? Will this antitrust thing delay the shipment of Windows 95?" Three and a half years later, the statement, quoted in handwritten meeting notes titled "Gates Unplugged," by Intel executive Steven McGeady, was cast as evidence that Gates was thumbing his nose at the government investigation. Yet Gates's prediction turned out to be accurate: In August 1995 the department announced it would not block

Windows 95 from shipping because of its inquiry. Then the antitrust room went dark. By November 10, 1995, Gates told Reuters he would be surprised "if they were still looking into it." The Justice Deparment declined to comment, but speculation was that with AOL still firmly entrenched at the top of the online services heap, there was little reason to pursue an investigation. With nine times as many subscribers as MSN, AOL qualified more as the monopolist.

McGeady, who wore his enmity toward Microsoft on his sleeve, also was responsible for misattributing one of the Justice Department trial's most inflammatory statements to Microsoft's least inflammatory executive, the understated Paul Maritz. In early 1996, McGeady told John Markoff of the *New York Times* that Maritz had threatened in a meeting with Intel to "cut off their [Netscape's] air supply" by giving away for free equivalent products to those sold by Netscape. Neither McGeady's handwritten notes taken at the meeting nor follow-up memos from the Intel excutives describing the session mentioned the phrase, however. In addition, Jim Barksdale testified that he had first heard the expression from Oracle CEO Larry Ellison, who was referring to Oracle's strategic initiative against its database competitors. The phrase also turned out to be, in general, a popular one around Silicon Valley. In his testimony for the Justice Department suit, Maritz stated, "I never said, in the presence of Intel personnel or otherwise, that Microsoft would 'cut off Netscape's air supply,' or words to that effect."

AOL's air supply circa late 1995 had never looked better. The rumor mill was churning with talk that AOL was negotiating a big deal with Netscape. In the wake of Gates's Pearl Harbor day announcement, Chase figured, it was only natural to assume that the biggest competitor to MSN and the staunchest rival to Internet Explorer would try to combine forces. MSN had bounded out of the gate like a greyhound. In its first three months, it gained more than 525,000 subscribers—a run rate that would halve the company's earlier announced expectation of needing a year to get to 1 million users. As fast as MSN was growing, however, AOL was ramping up even faster. By the end of 1995, its subscriber total stood at 4.5 million—nearly 4 million more than where it had started the year. Chase did not know exactly what the Netscape talks with AOL involved, but he surmised that Netscape's popular website was a leverage point. Everyone using Navigator, and at the time there were an estimated 17 million to 20 million, automatically got shunted to the Netscape home page when they logged on. They could change the home page default setting to another site, but most—an estimated 60 to 70 percent—did not. "It was a huge advantage for them," he said.

Microsoft's site was coming along but had virtually no sex appeal compared to Netscape's. After the Windows launch it had changed from the "Death Star" to "Collage," a rectangular graphic with live text links in a simple list. Collage may have been a conscious play off Mosaic, the original graphical browser, but it is unlikely that anyone on the IE team knew about an NCSA scientific data program called Collage that Mosaic authors Marc Andreessen and Eric Bina had worked on. The Microsoft site included click-on icons for products, for support, for "visit Microsoft," and for the cool link of the day. Oh, and not to be forgotten, MSN. As a matter of policy, all online roads had to lead through the Microsoft Network. The microsoft.com home page was fine for providing nuts-and-bolts product support and getting people launched to other Microsoft things, but it was in no way a destination site on the Web. Despite the Web's growing impact and popularity, there was still no financial incentive for Microsoft to do otherwise. If the Web still meant free, the natural outgrowth was to use it to channel users other places that either cost money or would mean money to Microsoft.

However much it was intended to benefit MSN, the home page's approach—neither fish nor fowl—did not particularly appeal to Russ Siegelman. In his mind, http://www.microsoft.com and http://www.msn.com should be one and the same. When you went to Microsoft's home page, you should be on Microsoft Network's home page. Ultimately this would not only benefit MSN by drawing more paying customers onto the online service, it would help Microsoft build a sense of community around the company. "I thought the most interesting thing would be to create a Windows club on the Net," he said. "They could make it a real virtual community and add a lot of value to Windows and to Microsoft. It was the whole idea of aggregation. You bring all the eyeballs through one point on the Web and make it the starting point to other things."

Siegelman made little progress with the notion of aggregation, however. Instead, the hot metaphor for the Web was *disaggregation* or, as Myhrvold and others called it, disintermediation. A November 27, 1995, memo from Myhrvold entitled "No More Middlemen" laid out the thesis that the Web, because it created a direct dialog between seller and buyer, would cut out the costs, overhead, and inefficiences of the middleman. Gates (and coauthor Myhrvold) had made a similar point in *The Road Ahead* by coining the term "friction-free capitalism."

The theory made perfect logical sense in every theoretical way. Why would sellers bother with the distribution chain if they could reach customers directly? Why would buyers want to pay higher costs associated with marketing and distribution? Newspapers would be the first to succumb, Myhrvold predicted. People would get their news from the Web rather than waiting for a potentially soggy lump of fishwrap to be delivered, if they were lucky, at their doorstep rather than somewhere on the sidewalk or their lawn. Siegelman thought disintermediation was poppycock, but he got nowhere arguing the opposing point of view. "Aggregation was a dirty word in the industry at large, but certainly it was a dirty word with Bill. I will say I did have some pretty heated arguments with Bill about this."

Gates would tell Siegelman, Wait a minute, are you trying to tell me aggregating content will make money? His favorite example was the local newspaper, the *Seattle Times*. I know the guys at the *Seattle Times*, he told Siegelman, and they're going to put up their own website and market to their own customers. And Siegelman would say, Yes, they'll serve a core constituency, but they'll never get critical mass. The people who get critical mass in numbers of eyeballs will be able to build businesses on the Web. Siegelman was becoming increasingly frustrated. "If I was off being not well heard, or being misunderstood, it was on these business model questions more than anything," he said. "I fought bitterly, just bitterly, that Windows 95 should not have a separate entry point. I fought bitterly—and I lost. Bill let all the various groups and interests in Microsoft fractionate Microsoft traffic. It was a huge mistake." Part of Siegelman's frustration stemmed from political infighting. The IE team, particularly Silverberg and Slivka, still did not trust Siegelman's judgment. But the IE team also wanted Windows 95 to be a mantelpiece for Web users. If MSN were the only way to access the Web, where was the perceived added value of Internet Explorer? "There was this notion of whoever controls the page creates the value and allocates the value," Siegelman said. "Multiple times Bill would say, MSN owns the first page when they click on MSN. And when Internet Explorer comes up, they [the Windows team] own that." In October 1998, Microsoft recast msn.com as a portal and announced $60 million worth of new business based on its attractiveness. Portals—aggregated sites that people used as jumping-off points—became all the rage. Russ Siegelman, however, was not around to enjoy the moral victory.

By April 1996, with the AOL deal having left his prize project a weak cousin and with MSN refocusing on TV-like content—a site for teens, a site for women, a games site, a quiz show site, and on down the line—

Siegelman was ready to cut bait. Original content was not his cup of tea. He liked technology, and the technology side of the Web was firmly in Silverberg's domain. "I said, Look, I'll stay in the company but I'm not going to do this any more. It was a hard decision because this was my baby. Like giving up your child for adoption." Once again, Siegelman went to Gates with the message he was ready for another challenge. In Gates's eyes, MSN remained challenge enough. Siegelman soon realized there was nothing left for him at Microsoft. One day a friend from Harvard Business School days, Doug McKenzie, called and invited Siegelman down to visit his Silicon Valley venture capital firm, Kleiner Perkins—otherwise known as the venture firm of John Doerr, the Silicon Valley money man who had backed Netscape and numerous Java start-ups. Siegelman found he "really liked" the KPCB gang's philosophy and signed on. A few months afterward Aboba left to work on NT networking. By fall MSN was on a new and ultimately misguided mission to enhance its service with TV-like special effects and niche interest groups. On November 15, TCI withdrew its $125 million investment. As an online service MSN continued to fall further behind AOL. After finding new life as a "portal," however, the Microsoft site began drawing familiar talent—Slivka, Reardon, Ludwig. Could they work the same magic with Microsoft's online presence as the IE turnaround?

Throughout the fall of 1995, the IE team kept hearing a repeated theme: Software vendors needed to build browsing into their Windows applications. "They told us, I want the html piece, I want the protocol piece, or I want the scripting engine," Slivka said. "It was something Netscape would not do for them." By December Slivka's team was breaking the browser into modules, or components, which could be used by Windows applications vendors to make their programs Internet-smart. "We basically took Humpty Dumpty apart, componentized him, and put him back together again," said Slivka. In one of those sleepless pizza-and-cola jags programmers are famous for, an Internet Explorer whiz kid with the euphonious name of Chee Chew "basically just powered through and did it in a couple of weeks," Slivka said. Performance sucked. The browser was ten times slower than Navigator. But the speed could be bumped up, what counted was the fact that the pieces worked together.

In the second week of January 1996, Gates contacted Steve Case to invite AOL out for a look-see. "Come on out, you're going to like our stuff,"

Gates said. On January 18 an AOL team visited for a preview. Attending the session were Gates, Silverberg, Ludwig, Chase, Slivka, and Chris Jones, an IE programmer. At the time, AOL was wrestling with what to do about its BookLink browser. As browsers became more sophisticated and added features, they became a lot harder to debug and maintain. AOL was discovering that the browser was a lot more work than it had anticipated. It was a point not lost on the Microsoft team, Chase related: "The way we architected IE 3.0, the product was a huge advantage for AOL. Because our product was componentized [and] what they were trying to do is integrate a browser into their technology. Netscape's product was not architected that way." In an e-mail written three days later, David Colburn, a top AOL dealmaker who attended the meeting, agreed with Microsoft's characterization of Netscape "as a company that merely sells free software with severe architectural handicaps (monolithic vs. modular, html-based vs. file-based). They are right." Colburn had already weighed in on Microsoft's side on January 10 in an e-mail to Case, saying dealing with Microsoft "feels like a better one from a P&L standpoint than the Netscape deal" and "likely to get us to a bigger subscriber base in a shorter period of time. . . . Microsoft seems like potentially the better way to go." Colburn's e-mail on the January 18 meeting also portrayed a side of Microsoft not generally acknowledged: "Interesting to note the contradiction between their claim of manifest destiny re: winning the Internet software battle, and their eagerness to bring us into their fold. . . . Microsoft is clearly feeling vulnerable over the next year or two."

Not that AOL was uniformly in Microsoft's camp. In an e-mail that later got top billing in the Justice Department antitrust suit, AOL executive David Cole wrote of the meeting with Microsoft:

> Gates delivered a characteristically blunt query: How much do we need to pay you to screw Netscape? ("This is your lucky day.")

The Justice Department took the statement as being monopolistic and predatory, and it captured numerous headlines in press accounts, some of which mistook the "screw Netscape" reference as a direct quotation from the Microsoft chairman. But Gates heatedly denied the characterization. Asked about it in an interview following the Justice Department assertions, Gates nearly bolted out of his chair, his eyes ablaze with indignation. "That's a lie!" he exclaimed. "I mean, it's just a terrible lie." Gates's PR executive, Mich Mathews, reminded him, "You're on the record." It did little to rein him in. "Someone from AOL wrote that in some meeting notes, okay? It's nothing to do with me, it's not a quote from me, it's nothing I ever said!" Instead, Gates characterized the tenor of the meeting as the ball being in AOL's court: "Understand, AOL instead of having to write their own browser, they had two companies come to them saying, basically, We'll give you a browser for free! . . . So they are in the driver's seat. . . . Because AOL viewed us as a big competitor, we had to be quite a bit better and trying harder to win, win the business. Which we did!"

Moreover, Gates added, no money or payoff was on the table in AOL discussions. Chase, Ludwig, and Slivka, who also attended the meeting, said they did not hear Gates use such terminology while they were present. It should also be noted that the "screw Netscape" reference was not a direct quotation and was offered as Cole's interpretation of Gates's stance. As with the we-will-bury-you allegation during partnering discussions nearly three years earlier, the e-mail could be viewed as another example of AOL hearing something entirely different from what Microsoft was saying.

Whatever blend of AOL paranoia and Microsoft gamesmanship was at play in browser talks, componentization was a huge win for Microsoft. In a January 24, 1996, e-mail, Case acknowledged as much: "From a pure technology standpoint, it does look like Microsoft may win this one." Still, market share was hugely in Netscape's favor. By this juncture, Netscape was riding its highest crest at 85 to 90 percent. Case wanted Windows 95 users to choose AOL over MSN and was willing to go with Internet Explorer to make it happen. But he also wanted Navigator users to feel they had a home in AOL. Case had watched Bill Gates long enough and hard enough to know the gratifications of having your cake and eating it too.

Case liked being the center of attention. Over a two-month wooing, Case was the three-sport athlete all the prom queens wanted to ask to the Internet Tolo. The week after AOL met with Microsoft, the rumor mill exploded with reports AOL was doing a deal with Netscape. AOL shares rose 12 percent and Netscape's, 11 percent, on reports of discussions between the two. Adding fuel to the speculation was CompuServe's intention to license Internet Explorer, announced the previous month in December. Netscape and AOL talked about a close working relationship where the browser maker would give AOL a royalty-free license in return for $10 million worth of advertising and promotion in the ensuing four years. Netscape also would agree to stay out of the commercial online business.

Case described the deal in a December 11, 1995, draft letter that eventually was made public in the Justice Department antitrust trial.

Case saw no reason to close the Netscape deal while Microsoft wooed him. Netscape was acting in no hurry either. When the AOL side seemed anxious to get the deal moving, Netscape's response was: "You'll get what we give you, when we give it to you, if we decide to give it to you." In his January 21 mail Colburn referred to Netscape as "obstinate," a factor that gave AOL "a great deal of room to cut a deal with Microsoft." Colburn saw Microsoft as a trump card to play off Netscape: "The essential Netscape proposition is that they get out of the online services business and we get behind their struggle for survival. Thus, a stable partnership. From time to time Netscape fails to recognize this. A delay in our negotiations may help them to understand."

Following AOL's visit to Redmond, Chase took over negotiating the deal. After some phone conversations, he flew out on January 30, 1996, to AOL headquarters in Vienna, Virginia. Still a little wary, he got a memorable welcome: "I walked into this reception area where a receptionist was working behind the desk, and they had you sign in. She said, Where are you from? I said, I'm Brad Chase from Microsoft. And she looks at me and goes Oooohhhhhh, rolling her eyes. I thought, Oh man!"

The incident encapsulated the mutually respectful wariness of the AOL-Microsoft relationship over the years and gave Chase a hint of the uphill battle he faced. Over the next two days he negotiated a series of issues with AOL, then took the agreement back to Redmond for more scrutiny and follow-up phone calls. The two sides continued to fine-tune the arrangement over the next six weeks.

The reworking of Internet Explorer was leading to a reworking of the company's internal dynamics as well. In January Jonathan Seybold paid a return visit to Microsoft to get updated on the Internet strategy. Compared with his earlier September visit, the company was utterly transformed. "People who had been infighting were now cooperating. There was a sense of unified purpose and forward momentum. Everything was different." Much of the credit could go to Gates, Seybold believed. More than any other CEO or corporate leader, Gates understood the necessity of throwing out the old model. "Bill truly understands that the past is past."

Even when the past is only two and a half months in the hopper. On

February 20, 1996, Microsoft announced it was creating an Internet Platform and Tools Division, to be headed by Brad Silverberg. Internet division? To those recalling Gates's Pearl Harbor day pronouncement just ten weeks earlier, it sounded like the electric company was creating an electricity division. Silverberg, who had argued from the beginning that Internet development needed a separate identity at Microsoft, was not surprised. "I figured he'd come around. It was the right thing. . . . Our group wasn't going to do everything there was to do with the Internet in the whole company. It wasn't like, okay, if this is the Internet, it goes to the IPTD. It was really meant to be the vanguard of core Internet technologies. Kind of be the chief internal missionaries, spokespeople, stakeholders."

Whatever the mission, Silverberg now had more than 2,000 hardcore Internet evangelists working for him. There was something to be said for strength in numbers.

At Gates's annual Executive Retreat for upper management February 22 through 24, the Internet colored every discussion. By March 12, human-resources director Mike Murray was sending out e-mail to 20,000 Microsoft employees around the world with the message, "The Net is the Bet." Microsoft's internal challenge, Murray wrote, was "to discard the status quo and the comforts of a large company, so that we're as hungry and as vigilant as a small Silicon Valley start-up." To help move the process along, Murray was not only authorizing once-elusive Internet access internally to everyone, he was moving Microsoft network services onto a company-wide intranet, or internal Internet connection. "Let's earn our way into the next century," Murray exhorted.

With the Net being the bet, MSN was suddenly out in the cold, and with it Blackbird. Toward the end of 1995, the Blackbird team had been moved out of MSN into Bob Muglia's Development Tools division. Muglia saw potential for some of Blackbird's technologies. But the overall concept of a proprietary publishing protocol died on the vine. At a product review in early 1996 with the Blackbird team, Gates made the observation, "I don't see how this would be appealing to anyone except a teeny teeny group of people with a high-speed connection." He might as well have been issuing a post mortem. To the extent it contributed toward key concepts such as style sheets and two-dimensional layout in Microsoft's browser efforts, Blackbird is fondly remembered. Ultimately it bet on the wrong horse, however.

In March 1996 there arose an extraordinary series of events. More than any other chronological sequence, this was when the lines in the sand were drawn demarcating future competition over the Internet. In the first two weeks of the month, Netscape and Microsoft held back-to-back Internet developers' conferences in San Francisco's Moscone Center. At Netscape's DevCon (Developers Conference), Marc Andreessen announced that, by the end of the quarter, Navigator would, with 25 to 30 million users, surpass Windows 95 and Office installed bases in popularity. Jim Clark, recovering from emergency oral surgery, had on his Microsoft boxing mitts. "I don't have anything against Microsoft except that they're trying to kill us," he groused to the opening-day throng. Still, "I don't think any one company is going to dominate the Internet," he added. John Doerr gave one of his patented psyche jobs, drawing on his favorite metaphors of the time. Some people thought the Internet was overhyped, he said. "I think it's underhyped." The Internet was like a drug. "You rub it on venture capitalists and they get all wild and crazy." And Jim Barksdale, describing a new line of Internet-intranet servers, announced that Netscape was not just a browser company any more. "That's last year's view," he said. The Netscape browser-server jumbo combo was, in functionality, "similar to BackOffice and Lotus Notes." Netscape had shown you could actually make money competing with freeware, Barksdale added — referring indirectly to IE and Mosaic, "most of which was written by our people at the NCSA." Then the kicker. Barksdale had a joke he liked to use to illustrate the power of marketing. What is bottled-water maker Evian spelled backward? N-A-I-V-E. "If Evian can differentiate water, we sure ought to be able to differentiate a browser," Barksdale vowed.

Behind Netscape's strategy was a larger scheme. The Mountain View company was using its browser as a Trojan horse to become a full-fledged Internet-based computing platform aimed at unseating Windows on personal computers. A Netscape browser-server combination using bits of Java here and plug-ins there would be all a Web user would need for day-to-day computing tasks. A Windows-less world was nigh. "The big part of why we're here," Andreessen told the audience, "is to build a platform."

It was proud talk, heady talk. It was pro-Internet but also anti-Microsoft. The crowd of 3,000 was young and hip and wired. Barksdale, asked about reports that Netscape had limited the number of Microsoft attendees, grinned and said, "We told them they could send six of theirs if they would take six of ours" — at the Microsoft Professional Developers Conference (PDC) also at Moscone the following week. DevCon was a testament to Netscape's vaulting ambition of industry leadership. Breakout and birds-of-a-feather sessions went far beyond the company's core products. There were sessions on programming business applications in Java, developing real-time multimedia applications, doing virtual reality applications for the Web. Cool, cool, cool! The overwhelming assumption, based on the vision of the time, was that all these things would be vital to the Internet's, and by extension Netscape's, future. Netscape, as the company in charge of moving the industry forward onto the Web, was taking on everything. DevCon gave profile to a startling string of acquisitions by Netscape through the year, aimed at ensuring it would be on the inside track of the Internet race. On January 31, 1996, it acquired InSoft, maker of network communications and collaboration multimedia, in a stock deal eventually worth $124.6 million. On February 12 it "pooled interests" with Paper Software, which did virtual reality and 3-D software. On March 4 Netscape picked up Netcode, a Java tool maker, in a pooling-of-interests deal. In August it entered a joint venture called Navio to put its browser on TV set-top boxes, in telephones, game players, and other information appliances. For what Barksdale liked to call an itty-bitty Internet company, Netscape was flexing big strategic muscle. Each was acclaimed at the time as the right move. It seemed obvious that a company founded on a product widely perceived to be free needed to broaden, diversify, enhance.

Throughout DevCon rumors rippled that Netscape and AOL were on the verge of signing a deal. Barksdale had no comment but was visibly upset at a *Wall Street Journal* story hinting that Microsoft was trying to bollox up the deal. "All options are still open" was all he would say.

The following Monday—March 11, 1996—it appeared Netscape had trumped Microsoft. America Online announced it had agreed to license Netscape Navigator. Netscape's stock jumped 15 percent with the announcement. Coming on the eve of Microsoft's PDC, the announcement especially seemed to sting the Redmond giant.

Yet the day after, Gates and Case were telephonically united in a conference call announcing a sweeping new deal between the two online superpowers. AOL had decided to make Internet Explorer its default browser, Case announced. No money was exchanging hands, it was quid pro quo all the way. AOL in return would get a choice, but not prime, position on the Windows 95 desktop—in an online services folder. It was a concession: AOL had wanted positioning similar to Microsoft Network, which had its own icon on the Windows desktop. Gates had held firm on that one. The online services folder would have to do. It was a key differentiation that in later accounts of the Justice suit was mistakenly cast as AOL receiving as prominent a position as MSN on the Windows desktop. By Wednesday,

March 13, Case joined Gates onstage at the PDC, extolling the virtues of Internet Explorer.

AOL's stock jumped 14 percent, Microsoft's, 5 percent. Netscape's slid, but only $1—perhaps because Case went out of his way to point out that Netscape Navigator would still be available for AOL users of the Global Network Navigator. GNN was the Web's original news service started by UNIX book publisher and Web pioneer Tim O'Reilly. AOL had purchased the service and was making Netscape its default browser.

At Netscape's Mountain View headquarters, Jim Barksdale was not a happy man. A months-long dance with AOL was ending in estrangement. Netscape had known that AOL was talking to Microsoft, but when they shook hands, Barksdale had thought Netscape had won. "We were worried about the exclusivity of the product and what kind of preferential treatment we were going to get and whether or not they were going to do the same deal with Microsoft. So we asked. And our lawyers were told that night the deal was signed, no, no, they weren't going to do anything like this with Microsoft."

But was it in writing? Not exactly. Netscape's attorneys had pressed for a written guarantee, but negotiations had gone late into the night. As Barksdale put it: "Everybody's dog tired, had been working all weekend, the lawyers had been up for three or four days, and we were led to believe that we didn't have to insert this one last little clause because they weren't going to do this. So we didn't, and that was our mistake." When Case called him while jetting across the country to appear with Gates at the PDC, Barksdale told him, "Gee, I wish you'd told me [earlier]." Case told Barksdale that "they were going to embed Microsoft [Internet Explorer], but they would distribute ours." It was the truth, it just was not the deal Netscape thought it was getting. Componentization had won the day for Microsoft.

Onstage and in a private briefing with a dozen journalists afterward, Case carried on a delicate balancing act, taking care to be non-exclusionary in his comments. Asked why AOL had chosen Microsoft's browser, given his rancorous relationship with the company, Case said flatly, "I'm quite impressed with [their] technology. Microsoft is going to move forward and work together [with developers] and move this industry and move this medium into the mainstream." AOL had decided several months earlier that although it could continue to develop the BookLink browser technology, "it probably made more sense for us to partner as opposed to trying to replicate what other people are doing." Only 11 percent of American households had online service: "So the opportunity is to try to figure out a way to reach the mainstream audience." Ergo, the Windows placement. Yet getting onto the Windows desktop, although important, was no guarantee of success, Case noted. Bundling merely got people to give you a look, and maybe a tryout, he said. It could not "force people to subscribe." Instead it was the content and community, "the overall experience," that got you the eyeballs. "That's really where the rubber meets the road."

Case's March 1996 posture was in stark contrast to AOL accusations made two and a half years later during the Justice Department trial. There Colburn said the company did the deal because Microsoft could offer it something Netscape could not: a place in a folder on the Windows desktop. AOL's dilemma was a dramatic illustration of the Microsoft duality for many companies, which wanted the visibility and market share that Microsoft could offer but resented its control over the PC desktop.

At the PDC, all was sweetness and light between Microsoft and AOL. Gates was ecstatic: "Working with AOL on the browser is a very big deal for us. We really are going to measure the success of a lot of what we're doing here by getting a lot of sites to use these active technologies." This was a key point. Microsoft was using the AOL deal to spread notice of its own new strategy, called Active Platform and based on ActiveX, whose functionality rivaled Java's. Just as Netscape was building a platform out of its browser, Java, and servers, Microsoft was spreading the Windows platform over the Web with ActiveX.

The name ActiveX was the three-headed brainchild of the ubiquitous Thomas Reardon, Chris Jones, and a tall, Tom Poston–lookalike program strategist named Cornelius Willis. The whole thing came together pretty fast, Reardon recalled: "Two weeks before the PDC, ActiveX did not exist. We were sitting around scratching our heads, like we know we've got to get this OLE control in here, and we've got ths whole idea of an architecture. . . . We had kind of introduced active terminology at Pearl Harbor day, and Cornelius comes up with this idea, Well, let's go active everything! Chris and Cornelius literally seven o'clock at night sitting around with a white board and Cornelius was writing different terms down and he comes up with ActiveX. And we're all laughing at him. And three days later he has bumper stickers!"

Although the name was new, ActiveX ran on a well-broken-in engine. It was OLE, object linking and embedding, repositioned for the Web. As J Allard had originally postulated in his "killer app" memo, the Internet opened up countless new ways to use OLE for everything from publishing and whizzy effects to transactions and video. Plus it was a way to match or, Microsoft hoped, exceed what Java had to offer, at least for Windows users. Why not just go with Java itself, especially since Microsoft was announcing at the PDC that the deal with Sun had been finalized? Even as Microsoft sewed up the license, things were turning rocky with Java.

At the PDC, Paul Maritz rolled out ActiveX with great fanfare, heralding a new era merging the "best of the PC, and best of the Web." The intent was not to "kill Netscape," Maritz said, adding in his understated way that nevertheless "We do not intend to remain a distant second in this [browser] market." Was Microsoft, as Barksdale had suggested the week before, leaving itself open to antitrust inquiry by giving away the browser and merging Windows with the Web? "If the Justice Department wants us to stop doing things that we think users find attractive . . . then they'll have to make that case," Maritz replied, unconsciously prophetic. "What we're trying to do is create what we think users want."

If ever there was a time for Justice Department investigators to act against Microsoft, the company clearly was extending an invitation in the spring of 1996. The AOL megadeal and competitive thrusts head-to-head against Netscape were tantamount to Microsoft tests of antitrust boundaries. Yet the department, contacted after the Professional Developers Conference and asked specifically about antitrust action involving the AOL deal, would state only that the investigation of Microsoft was ongoing. At that point there was still no official closure of what was assumed to be an MSN investigation, but no indication either that the investigation was broader than the online services market.

Chase nailed down the AOL deal in a flurry of phone calls and e-mails. So last minute was the deal that there was not even time to make up a press release; a single-sheet media alert lacking company letterhead and time-stamped 6:00 A.M. invited the press to participate in a conference call. The Java deal, announced March 12, was similarly frantic, signed by Baratz and Muglia after a marathon eighteen-hour negotiation binge stretching till 4:45 A.M. In words that later took on piquant irony, Alan Baratz, Sun's JavaSoft president, was quoted in a press release saying that "Microsoft's commitment to Java is both impressive and comprehensive, and this agreement makes them one of the leading Java supporters." Muglia's comment was more pointedly prophetic: "We intend to be the premier supplier of Java-compatible tools to Internet developers."

So much was set to happen at the conference, there was no need for a crowning touch. But one came anyway. Midway through the opening session, a familiar figure in T-shirt and jeans bounded onstage to talk about his company's Web strategy. A familiar figure everywhere except at Microsoft conferences, that is. When Steve Jobs came out, there was an audible gasp in the audience. The former archrival of Microsoft? Onstage here? Jobs, shorn of the long silky beard that had made him look like an extra from *Jesus Christ Superstar*, immediately picked up on the reaction.

"Well, this is really weird, isn't it?" he said with one of his winning grins. You know, it was funny, he went on. In recent weeks he had been looking to partner with a browser company to spread his WebObjects technology at NeXT. And what had been happening was really ironic. Netscape had been treating him the way he would have expected Microsoft to treat him, and Microsoft had been treating him the way he would have expected Netscape to treat him. The comment, reflecting a common sentiment in Silicon Valley at the time, drew laughter and applause from the developers but rattled the cages at Netscape and haunted the company for months afterward. The previous fall Netscape had initiated a developers program. But it was vastly undermanned, especially for a company turning its products into a platform.

Watching Jobs's masterful performance, the Two Brads, Reardon, Jones, and the rest of the browser gang were delirious with triumph. In twelve weeks from Pearl Harbor day to the Moscone PDC, Microsoft had won over two archrivals—the two Steves, Case and Jobs—and brought longtime rival Sun Microsystems and Java into the Windows fold. Who would have thought? Yet that was the whole point to J Allard: "It just set the whole tone for like, throw all your expectations out the window. Or Windows. Marketing expectations. Technical expectations. We're going to show you a Microsoft you had no idea existed. A Microsoft on the Internet."

Allard almost missed the whole shebang. In the weeks leading up to the conference, he had been working killer hours with the rest of his team to get Internet Information Server rolled out in time to have high impact. On February 1, 1996, at 3:47 P.M., it was time to rock 'n' roll. In an e-mail to everyone from Gates and Allchin on down, slugged "high" under "importance," Allard went giddy over his team's accomplishments:

I'm happy to announce that Gibraltar build 157 has released to manufacturing as the 1.0 version of Internet Information Server. The investment that we've made in the architecture, performance and reliability of this product represents a great platform for the next generation of Internet applications. The early success that we've had in running sites like www.microsoft.com, www.superbowl.com, www.msn.com, and www.nba.com are a sign of things to come.

For Allard, IIS was the culmination of the dream set in motion that long-ago day in 1991 when Steve Ballmer asked him to make the pain go away with TCP/IP. It was the manifestation in raw shipping code of his "killer app" memo, there for the world to behold, use, and enjoy. Four-plus years of pedal-to-the-metal product development, and finally Allard could sit back and begin enjoying the fruits. IIS would be a surefire hit at the PDC, Allard figured. As for him, it was time for a break. He had never taken a vacation. When his family set up a skiing trip in Utah, Allard figured it was time. The second week of March, he would be hitting the slopes, decompressing, taking a whole nine days off in a row. A week before he was scheduled to take off, Allard pulled out a brochure for the PDC from his interoffice mail. There was a picture of Bill and Maritz and Allchin and Allard and . . . wait a minute! Allard?! "I'm like what the fuck is my picture doing in there! And I'm a keynote speaker! And I'm like what the hell's this all about, it's like Microsoft Internet strategy, blah blah blah and it's like come listen as J Allard describes blah blah blah and it has something that says how important I am so that people will register for the conference. And I'm just blown away by the thing."

Allard stormed into the office of Cameron Ferroni, heading up Win32 for the NT team. "Tell me who I need to talk to to fix this!" he demanded. Well, Ferroni said, Paul asked me who would be good and I recommended you. "Tell him I can't do it, I've had this thing planned for nine months, I'm owed vacation forever!" As normally excitable as Allard was, he could be downright histrionic when exercised. Ferroni passed the word along at the next executive meeting for the conference: Oh, by the way, he said, J can't do the talk. There was silence. Maritz asked why. "Uh, well . . . " and Ferroni gave him the whole rundown. Maritz, in the way only Maritz can, clasped his hands together, looked straight ahead at the wall across from the table, and said calmly, "I would really prefer if J did that talk."

Allard went down, gave the keynote, and was glad he did. He ended up onstage with Jobs, and the two went out for coffee afterward and spent an hour talking. And clicked immediately. Allard's first computer had been an Apple II. Jobs was a boyhood hero. And Allard's Web server work paralleled Jobs's approach. Jobs's WebObjects was the foundation for e-commerce, or business and transaction, services on the Web, with content tied to databases and custom applications. Allard had the same high concept with Active Server Pages on IIS. Hey, he thought to himself, I'm not that far off base after all! On that high note, he left for the airport to go skiing with his family.

Also watching the Steve Jobs Microsoft Hour with intense interest was Brad Silverberg. Apple's old boss still had the touch, Silverberg marveled. More than once he gazed out at the crammed auditorium, thinking: The universe is shifting once again. Three months earlier every face in that room would have said Microsoft did not yet get the Net. Today they were marveling at how fast the supertanker had turned around.

To Slivka, the PDC marked Microsoft's critical turning point in the war for the Web. The newly componentized IE was nowhere near ready even for serious testing. Although he had slapped it into a developers' kit and called it an alpha version, he hoped no one would take it seriously. Still, the PDC was where Microsoft delivered on its promises. It showed Active Platform, showed how to take html and put it into a Visual Basic application, showed how DocObjects made it a snap to display Office documents in the browser, showed the Microsoft Java Virtual Machine for the first time. The daily-nightly grind was paying off, Slivka decided: "It felt like, you know, we're there. We're in the game now. We're ahead of Netscape on some things. From that point on it was a matter of just grinding it out. A lot of hard work, getting the beta out in May and then shipping in August. We were running pretty hard for quite a long time."

In a basement hallway after the Gates-Case appearance, Silverberg talked excitedly, like a junior product manager, about the benefits of componentization. Have you heard of PointCast? he asked. Sure, he was told. You could not work in a news organization and not know about PointCast. Well, Silverberg said, PointCast would derive huge benefit from componentization. Netscape had promised them a plug-in, Silverberg said, but PointCast was really not meant to be a plug-in. It was a separate application. A screensaver, but a broadcast agent as well. If the PointCast folks could just use off-the-shelf components for their Webified application, it would let them concentrate on the real value of what they did—the content. Point-Cast broadcast updated news, stock quotes, sports scores, whatever you wanted, across your PC screen. It was like TV on a PC. It was all the rage on the cool, cool Web.

Why should PointCast want to write its own browser? Silverberg asked rhetorically. It's not the business they want to be in. Oh, and by the way, he added, his face aglow with competitive zeal, we never restrict. Our enrollment is completely open. Anyone can come to our conferences. Barksdale, he's pretty slick. He's, oh, shucks, I'm an ole country boy. You gotta watch him. I'm not slick, Silverberg continued, never tried to be. It has its shortcomings sometimes. But with me, what you see is what you get. No one absorbing Microsoft's new Web strategy, no one watching Case and Jobs and Java embrace and extend, no one witnessing the strategic partnering and technological acceleration of the Microsoft PDC that spring could leave Moscone Center thinking otherwise.

Chapter 16

¨GOD BLESS GATES!¨

T he March developers' conferences demonstrated more clearly than any other time the confrontational inevitability of the businesses of Microsoft, Netscape, and Sun Microsystems. Everywhere Bill Gates turned, he saw competition—for Microsoft, for Windows, for the Internet. "The Internet opportunity and the competition have us as charged up as we've ever been," he wrote on April 10, in a memo titled "The Internet PC." Gates was intent on reinforcing Maritz's "Best of the PC and best of the Web" motto and identifying Netscape's strategy "to make Windows and the Apple Macintosh operating system all but irrelevant by building the browser into a full-featured operating system with information browsing." Microsoft, Gates advised, had to beat Netscape to the punch with Windows. The first step: an add-on to make any Windows folder a Web page, complete with descriptive text and graphics, links to files and folders, a feature that ultimately was fully expressed in Nashville, the code name for Internet Explorer 4.0.

What really was bugging Gates, though, was the refuse-to-die "Network Computer," the diskless $500 machine that was still being held up as the Windows-beater. At the PDC, Gates had mocked the NC as "a term that's not well-defined. Whenever you have zero volume, it's hard to define a term." What about the NC would make it preferable to a PC? Gates asked. No screen? No disk drive? No keyboard or graphics or sound? If you want a quality computing experience, Gates suggested, "There's nothing in a PC that you get to leave out." What really nettled him was the inconsistency of the NC strategy. The whole point was seemingly to replace Windows with the browser. Yet if you went with NCs, you lost browser richness. Much of what the browser did, including updating, required PC capabilities, especially if you were looking for sound and video. Besides, the big NC draw, its $500 price point, was sure to lose its distinction as PC volumes increased. "In the not-too-distant future you'll almost certainly see capable PCs priced well below $1,000," Gates wrote. Not-too-distant translated, in actual terms, to about a year and a half. "I'm betting on the PC, as I always have," he concluded. "I'm betting on Windows, too."

Where Bill bet, Ballmer raised. By May 9, 1996, Ballmer was answering queries about Netscape versus Microsoft at roundtable briefings by folding his hands flat on the table in front of him, focusing his great furrowed brow, and chanting in a quiet (for him) but unmistakable tone: "Netscape is making noises about becoming an operating systems company. That is bad bad bad bad bad . . . " Shaking his large pumpkinesque head slowly back and forth, his mouth grim and tight. Along the stairwell of Building 15 at Microsoft was displayed a contemporary sculpture of an upside-down chair with arms and legs sticking out at unnatural angles. A handwritten sign taped to it said "Netscape chair"—an assessment Ballmer undoubtedly would have seconded, assuming he was not its author in the first place. Netscape's products were untested. "All they are is one big, broad, rolling beta test!" he exclaimed. Netscape's whole business model was suspect, he asserted, slapping his big basketball-callused hands together. "You charge sometimes and give it away sometimes, [and] you confuse the channel!" Ballmer's point echoed a Gates reservation about Netscape's approach to "free": "It distorted the distribution channels. When people say to Michael Dell, 'Why don't you offer the Netscape browser?' Well, they didn't give it away [to him]! Anyone who called up and said, 'Okay, I want to distribute it,' Netscape forced them to actually charge the price." It was true. Dell Computers would install Netscape on new computers if requested. But it passed along the fee it owed Netscape to the purchaser.

On May 19, in a long e-mail titled "Some Thoughts on Netscape," Gates credited Netscape with a number of "clever" technological and marketing accomplishments. He had spent his Think Week playing with a number of

Netscape products, Gates wrote. "This reinforced the impression that I think all of us share that Netscape is quite an impressive competitor." Gates included a table comparing Netscape products with Microsoft equivalents—in several cases questioning whether there *was* a Microsoft equivalent, particularly in the server arena. Gates admonished the IIS gang that they had to get cracking on matching and exceeding the capabilities of Netscape's Enterprise Server and Proxy Server. Within a year, Gates predicted, Microsoft would be on par or ahead. "It's less clear to me how we compare to other Netscape [server] products," he added. J Allard made Gates a prophet. The occasion, duly noted in a typically Allard-effusive e-mail, took place on April 3, 1997, when the Netcraft Web survey reported "we have successfully passed Netscape . . . at long last." Allard & gang had beat the Gates prediction by six weeks.

On the client side, in a section titled "Browser War," Gates noted Netscape "realized they have a problem" with lack of componentization. Microsoft had been winning too big and too often on that front for it to escape notice in Mountain View. Gates's browser observations included a startling proposal: "I am still a very big fan of us putting the source code of the key parts of IE out on the Web (without commercial reproduction rights) so that universities who want to 'extend' browsers use ours for their experimentation." Somewhere J Allard was smiling. A year and a half later, Netscape would embrace the open-systems principle by posting Navigator source code on the Web in its entirety, for the Internet community to embellish and enhance.

To gain parity, Gates reminded his executives that "there are lots of ways to spend money." You could pay people directly to use the browser, Gates said, but "this is too blunt an instrument." A more subtle method was to give them "Internet money," the equivalent of coupons or reimbursements, in order to "bootstrap" subscriptions to the Web tied to IE. Third, "you can have contests they win for using the browser." Fourth, "you can spend money to advertise the browser so that content providers are giving you visibility." Fifth, "you can pay content providers to do unique things to exploit your browser." Sixth, "spend money on distribution including massive airdrops." Boom, boom, boom: All six proved that Gates the technologist and CEO was just as cunning a marketer when he chose to be.

Netscape was not the only source of Microsoft concern. At the end of May, Sun announced Java Beans—a technology that enabled developers to write Java applications capable of crossing networks and running on any type of computer. When Silverberg and Muglia found out about the Java

Beans announcement at Sun's JavaOne Conference, their jaws dropped. First, Sun had told them nothing of the technology. Second, Java Beans sounded suspiciously like Microsoft's plans for its Common Object Model. As Silverberg recounted it:

> The week or so before, Microsoft developers went to Sun and discussed in good faith Microsoft's not-yet-disclosed ActiveX plans and how we had a nice architecture for component communication that solved a lot of holes in Java and further was language-independent. The Sun engineers were very impressed with what they heard. But then a week later, Sun announced Java Beans, which basically was a Java-only version of what Microsoft disclosed to them. The initial announcement was completely lacking in any technical details; it was clear that they just invented it in the week since Microsoft disclosed to them. . . . The Java Beans announcement was a sneak attack.

Muglia was equally perplexed. The episode sent him a signal that Sun was acting in less than good faith.

At the time, little was made public of Java's brewing clash. Instead, mainstream media were starting to pick up on the emerging clash between the two browser companies. With Microsoft and Netscape both hammering on versions 3.0 of their browsers, and both expecting to be out sometime in the summer, a thunderclap of cool products meeting heated competition was imminent. In the March 25, 1996, issue of *Newsweek*, a Steven Levy story on the competition put a new phrase into the public consciousness. "Blood in the Browser War," the headline read.

The rumbles from Redmond were having little demonstrable impact on Barksdale and his self-described itty-bitty Internet company. The wily Mississippian had consistently put the best face possible on Microsoft's rivalry. "God bless Gates!" he had exclaimed on a trip to Seattle February 12, 1996. "What he does is in effect legitimize this market." Where Gates liked nautical metaphors to describe the Internet's impact on Microsoft—sea change, tidal wave—Barksdale, perhaps in light of his surname, preferred dog analogies: It's going to be a dogfight. It's not the size of the dog in the fight but the size of the fight in the dog. Microsoft has a bigger bulldog to feed. If you can't run with the big dogs, stay on the porch. Peter Currie, Netscape's CFO, kept a whole collection of Barksdale's epigrams, which those around him called Barksdaleisms.

Barksdale had a kind of canine combativeness in his genes. He was a descendant of the first cousin of Brigadier General William Barksdale, a Mississippi congressman and Civil War leader of the Fighting Mississippians. The general was renowned as one of the Rebel forces' most fearless, aggressive leaders. Stories of General Barksdale's kindness and courage pepper numerous historic accounts of the war. Ultimately, what shone through about the general was his love of combat. Historian Shelby Foote, in *The Civil War: A Narrative*, quotes one of Barksdale's soldiers saying the general had "a thirst for battle glory." In *The Killer Angels*, his Pulitzer Prize–winning fictionalization of the Civil War, Michael Shaara movingly described Barksdale's final, fatal charge into the teeth of Union regiments at Gettysburg: "Barksdale was going straight for the guns, running, screaming, far out in front, alone, as if in a race with all the world, hair streaming like a white torch. Longstreet rode behind him, his hat off, waving, screaming, Go! Go you Mississippi! Go!"

In a private interview at a Seattle hotel, Barksdale saw room for both companies, saying: There's this belief, most prevalent here in Seattle, that the only way for Microsoft to win is to put us out of business. But that would be a shame. That would be a crying shame to say that a company like mine that comes up with a good product—for Microsoft to say, Oh gee, we'll now put it in the operating system, thank you very much. Nobody would ever develop another piece of software.

Q. It's happened a lot of times.
A. It doesn't happen every time. They give away Money, it's free, Intuit's doing fine. They [Intuit] have a better product.
Q. What about Adobe's fonts?
A. It's existed okay. I will grant you, there haven't been a whole lot of these stories. I don't want anybody saying we're against Microsoft, we don't appreciate what they've done. They created companies like ours. If they didn't have that operating system with their set of plug-ins and their set of platforms, our business wouldn't be here.

The comments, coming seven months after Microsoft's allegedly anticompetitive threats against Netscape, were in stark contrast to Barksdale's later testimony at the Justice Department antitrust trial, where he said: "I have never been in a meeting in my thirty-three-year business career in which a competitor had so blatantly implied that we should either stop competing with it or the competitor would kill us."

Barksdale liked to rally his own troops with another God quote, from

Voltaire: "Dieu n'est pas pour les gros bataillons, mais pour ceux qui tirent le mieux." God is not on the side of the big battalions, but for those that can shoot straight. As long as Netscape focused on product development, the company would do fine, Barksdale said. Netscape had built-in mail. Microsoft did not. Netscape had table frames. Microsoft had tables, but not frames. "They're about six months behind," he said. In Internet time, six months equaled three and a half years.

But Microsoft had had its own version of Internet time since the very beginning, when Gates and Allen and Harvard sidekick Monte Davidoff worked round the clock, sleeping at their terminals, to get BASIC done for the MITS Altair. Microsoft hours, it was called. It meant sixty-, seventy-eighty-, even on rare occasions ninety-hour work weeks where eating and sleeping were highly integrated into programming and production. Keith Moore had worked Microsoft hours putting together the first NT ftp server for Allard. Chee Chew had worked Microsoft hours ripping apart Internet Explorer to do componentization. By the time Silicon Valley began talking about Internet time, Slivka had the entire Internet Explorer 3.0 team working Microsoft hours. Responsible for getting code whipped into shape for AOL's, and others', use, Slivka's team felt like it was working inside a clothes dryer, spinning and spinning hotter and hotter. Reprogramming the browser in components was like building the Eiffel Tower over again from scratch. All-nighters became the rule. One morning around 12:30 A.M. Slivka and two other IE programmers, Chris Jones and John Cordell, walked out from Building 5 to the basketball court for a quick break. Slivka recalls one of them saying "Hmmm, what's wrong with this picture? We should all be home in bed with our wives." Instead they shot a couple of rounds of HORSE, then went back to work. His efforts on behalf of Internet Explorer earned Slivka a new designation from Lisa, who began referring to him as "my mythical husband."

Slivka continued to hire team members right and left. A key pickup was Chris Wilson, a Web whiz who could say something no one else at Microsoft, and few outside of Netscape, could say. Wilson had worked on the original Mosaic browser at the NCSA with Andreessen, Bina, and the crowd and had teamed with Jon Mittelhauser on the original Windows version of Mosaic. He had been hired away from the NCSA by Spry chief David Pool just before the Clark-Andreessen recruiting trip to Champaign. "I knew Marc had been talking to Jim Clark and I knew they were planning on starting a company and they were planning to do set-top boxes," Wilson said later. "I had absolutely no interest in doing that." Shortly afterward he got a call from Andreessen asking indirectly about joining up with the new venture. Clark thought there was a chance Wilson could wriggle out of his Spry contract if he wanted and asked Andreessen if he should have a lawyer look into it. Andreessen told him no, it was probably not going to be real important. Wilson was pretty much settled on staying in Seattle.

Wilson brought considerable Mosaic savvy to the Spry operation. The same qualities made him an apt candidate for the IE team. Aided by Wilson's former Spry colleague Peterson, Slivka and Reardon recruited Wilson over. Wilson went to work on cascading style sheets, a technology that enabled richly formatted text to resemble a special-effects graphic. Different colored backgrounds, text superimposed over images and photos. For all their whizbang effects, however, style sheets transmitted far faster than graphics with text—a boon at a time when modem speeds were still at 14.4 kbps and lots of new users were connecting over regular phone lines. Creative artists starved to do magazine-y things on the Web saw cascading style sheets as liberation, like being let out of Designer Jail. At its first Web designers rollout on July 15, 1996, Microsoft blew away 22,000 website developers at fifty sold-out North American theaters during a day-long, satellite-linked tutorial. In the frenetic advance of the Web, one new feature, one added tool, could swing entire operations over to a new technology. Cascading style sheets held the promise of that kind of impact. Significantly, Navigator did not support them. For the first time, there were rumbles that Microsoft was passing Netscape in browser implementation. "Cutting edge" had entered the Microsoft lexicon.

Silverberg was eating it up. IE development was like having a constant tailwind riding his bike. Everyone was pushing together, with hardly any management or direction. No pep talks, no motivational meetings, no org charts or timelines. The IE effort had even broken the Golden Rule of project development: the spec sheet. "We didn't have huge specs," Silverberg recalled. "People in other groups were horrified that we didn't have detailed specs. But we didn't need them." It was a matter of like minds unified into one intellectual force. The whole team had the Internet coursing through their veins. They just got it. They just did it.

Adding to the Microsoft turnaround talk was a long cover story by Kathy Rebello in the July 15, 1996, issue of *Business Week*. "The Untold Story of How the Internet Forced Bill Gates to Reverse Course," the subhead read. The story, replete with colorful anecdotes and a time line disclosing the roles of Allard, Sinofsky, Slivka, Silverberg, and others, was the talk of the industry. Microsoft the clueless not only was getting the Net, it was becoming cool. And irony of ironies, it was Chris Wilson, coauthor of Mosaic for Windows, the man Netscape let slip away, who had helped lead the surge.

Down in Mountain View, Microsoft's momentum was having an impact. On July 18, 1996, Netscape's chief of software development, Richard Schell, sent a detailed memo to Maritz outlining a long litany of complaints dating back to the spring of 1995. Schell complained of poor Windows 95 technical support, of not getting the phone dialer APIs till October, well after Windows 95 shipped in August. Netscape had not gotten adequate information about Internet shortcuts, Schell stated. The Windows NT 3.51 Service Pack 3.0 had not been delivered promptly by Microsoft. AcceptEx APIs had been delayed.

Schell had picked on the wrong guy—Maritz, perhaps the most detail-oriented individual at Microsoft. By August 15, in an e-mail carrying the telling time stamp of 5:44 A.M., Maritz had responded with a painstaking four-page, point-by-point rebuttal. It was Maritz with a twist—restrained and understated, only in this case seething with pent-up outrage. Despite the indignation implied by the hour of posting, Maritz resorted to no stronger a term than "incorrect" in characterizing Schell's litany of accusations. Microsoft had supplied the phone dialer APIs in preliminary form in July and August 1995, not October. Microsoft's Windows 95 developers had given direct technical support on the phone-book adapter and TCP/IP in July and August, and Maritz had e-mail to prove it—from Netscape programmers expressing their gratitude. As for Internet shortcuts, "your statement that we failed to provide Internet Shortcut documentation is just plain wrong," he asserted. Mail from Marc Andreessen himself had thanked Microsoft for providing Netscape with a prototype .dll in the spring of 1995. Netscape had dropped the ball by not providing feedback at that time. As for Windows NT 3.51, Microsoft had sent the service pack to manufacturing December 1, 1995, and within four days had gotten a unit to Andreessen via overnight delivery. "J Allard of Microsoft telephoned Andreessen personally to advise him that there were updates to Windows sockets that Netscape might want to utilize." Likewise, the AcceptEx API had been delivered at the same time to Netscape.

Overall, Maritz complained, it was ironic that Netscape was accusing Microsoft of the practices that many software vendors, including Microsoft, found Netscape engaging in. "Netscape is not living up to its many public pronouncements that it would provide support to enable products from other vendors to interoperate with Netscape products," he asserted. It was one thing for Netscape to pursue a strategy it considered in the best inter-ests of its company and customers, but "Netscape appears to be announc-ing one strategy and pursuing another that is diametrically opposite." Maritz cited Netscape's website, which blocked non-Netscape browsers in certain areas, as a prime example. JavaScript was another example: Netscape had implemented the language and evangelized it without sub-mitting it to the Internet Engineering Task Force or the World Wide Web Consortium (W3C). Netscape also was withholding documentation and tools for Navigator plug-ins, which vendors like Microsoft needed to make their applications Navigator-compatible. Furthermore, Maritz said, Netscape was doing extensions to html, the lingua franca of the Web, with-out publishing them or submitting them to the W3C for approval.

The handwriting that Maritz saw on the wall was that Netscape, because its market share hovered between 70 and 80 percent of all browsers, was in the process of creating an environment where users had to use Navigator to get the "best stuff" on the Web. Extending html unilaterally would lead to a situation where parts of Netscape's and other websites would be unview-able, or go black, without Navigator. "By contrast, Microsoft has adopted the following policy: Every significant enhancement to html that we pro-pose will be submitted to W3C before being implemented in Internet Ex-plorer," Maritz pledged. "Submitted," rather than "approved," was a key qualifier. Maritz left the door open for Microsoft to move forward on en-hancements while the consortium considered whether to bless them. But the submission process promised that Microsoft's embellishments would be open and above board.

In closing, Maritz noted that Netscape wanted to license Microsoft's Windows 95 dial-up scripting engine while at the same time it had refused to allow Microsoft to license its Commercial Applications Server. "I would be pleased to talk to you about that. I would also like to discuss Netscape's refusal to allow more than a small handful of Microsoft developers to attend Netscape developer conferences (we put no limitation on Netscape atten-dance at our conferences)."

There it was again. The issue simply was never going to go away. Netscape never responded to Maritz's letter.

To Silverberg, the Schell e-mail smacked of CYA—cover your ass. Per-haps some suits, some Silicon Valley lawyers, trying to trump up antitrust charges had gotten to him. Perhaps Schell's bosses had wakened to the fact that Microsoft was surpassing Netscape in the features arena and wanted to know why. There seemed little other explanation for why Schell would wait as long as a year and a half after the fact to raise serious allegations. This was all water well under the bridge. What was going on?

The Redmonders' intuition about lawyers getting involved proved correct. On August 12, 1996—not coincidentally the day Internet Explorer 3.0 was released on the Web—Microsoft nemesis and Netscape attorney Gary Reback fired off an eight-page letter to assistant attorney general Joel Klein listing a litany of consent-decree accusations. Included were a host of charges that later turned up in the Justice Department lawsuit: exclusionary contracts with computer makers to keep Netscape's browser off of newly shipped computers, and various inducements, such as software and hardware incentives, to Internet service providers that would make Internet Explorer their "preferred" browser and steer customers away from using Netscape Navigator.

To Silverberg, Slivka, Chase, Cole, and the rest of the Internet Explorer team, the Justice Department rumblings were, in a way, mere confirmation that Microsoft had not only caught up with, but surpassed, Netscape's product line. The way they saw it, Netscape was running out of innovation and new ideas and was turning to the government in an effort to anchor the Microsoft sprint. The Justice Department stuff was a diversionary tactic. How could Microsoft, with something like 15 percent market share, be anti-competitive? Netscape is the elephant, Silverberg liked to say. We're the mouse. "The fact is we're ahead [on features] and Netscape knows it, so it wants to change the topic of discussion away from IE 3 versus Navigator 3."

On that front, Microsoft was doing decidedly well. Although the competition was tight, Microsoft wound up winning the large majority of head-to-head comparisons, including CNET, *Computer Reseller News, USA Today, Boston Globe, Seidman's Online Insider*. Nine out of ten major reviews went in Microsoft's favor. The tenth was a big one—*PC Magazine*—but Silverberg liked to point out that Netscape won only because Navigator had better cross-platform implementation. And even on that point Microsoft was not exactly slouching. IE on the Mac ran faster in half the memory Navigator required and supported things like plug-ins, frames, and animated GIFs. And Navigator did not have Java support for Windows 3.1, despite everyone's assumption it did. Still, Navigator had UNIX and a better reputation for cross-platform support, factors that merited the *PC Magazine* nod.

IE 3.0 held a barrelful of new features. It was faster—significantly so. Its look was crisper, more three-dimensional. Mousing over a toolbar icon put a square around it and changed its appearance from gray to colored, so you knew when it was clickable. Icons themselves were bigger, better designed. Users could create Internet shortcuts simply by dragging a hyperlink to their desktop. A dialog box kept users informed as to how long a download would take. Among experienced users, a big plus for IE 3.0 was the customizable ToolBar. CoolBar, the team called it. It enabled users to create quick links, buttons for common commands and URLs, and generally configure the look of the browser to suit their own style. When it was first conceived, CoolBar seemed like a straightforward enhancement. But the coding turned out to take longer than expected, and the process introduced new bugs to the upgrade. In June, two months before IE 3.0 shipped, things were still a little unfinished for Silverberg's tastes. He began pressuring Slivka et al. to dump CoolBar and focus on the ship date. "They floundered for what seemed like an eternity. Up till the end, the designs were not that good and it didn't feel very good. They couldn't get the feel right. I got frustrated by it for sure. . . . I hated to tie up those good developers for sooooo long!"

Slivka listened patiently to Silverberg's concerns, then told him: Don't worry. We'll get it done. Silverberg also was lobbying for dumping cascading style sheets and PICS, the parental-screening standard being adopted to filter pornographic material on the Web. Slivka stood firm. "I explain that those are not critical path. He [Brad] continues to harp on these features over the next few weeks, but in the end lets us leave them in. CoolBar gets a lot of critical praise."

In the end, Silverberg admitted that Slivka was right: "The CoolBar team finally did get it right. I'm so glad they did, because it turned out great and created a buzz that helped IE 3 a lot."

One feature set that Silverberg insisted IE 3.0 had to include was accessibility for handicapped and disabled people. IE 3.0 was the first browser to build in accessibility features. For many of the disabled, mouse movement was difficult if not impossible. IE 3.0 offered keyboard navigation of a Web page. By pressing the TAB or SHIFT plus TAB buttons, users could hop from icons, buttons, and links. Pressing ENTER would open a link. SHIFT+F10 would display a context menu for a link, CONTROL+N would generate a new window . . . in all, there were more than a dozen keyboard options. And sight-impaired users could enlarge the fonts easily with IE's font toolbar button. For Silverberg, the IE 3.0 accessibility push was partly to make amends for past shortcomings: "During the development of Windows 95, we were not as aware of the importance of the accessibility community's needs as I wished. In retrospect we should have done better.

After the release, members of the disability community talked to me in more detail about their needs, and educated me. . . . The disability community was initially quite hostile to Microsoft—understandably, since it was much easier for them in the DOS world."

On most other features, Internet Explorer had excelled. IE had built-in stuff like streaming audio and video, MPEG video playback, ActiveX. In an e-mail shortly after IE 3.0's release, Silverberg defended the browser's progress:

> The bottom line is that I really believe IE 3.0 is the product more focused on the needs of the average end-user. . . . We have come a long way in one year and as a matter of fact we were full force ahead on IE development as early as 1995, whipping out 2.0 by the end of the year. We delivered three versions since the launch of Windows 95, while delivering great Mac and Windows 3.1 clients as well. Our commitment to cross platform is real and the pace won't stop there. Basically, we want users to get past the hype and just try our product and decide for themselves. That will be the true test in our eyes.

The crowning touch was Walt Mossberg's glowing review in the *Wall Street Journal*. Despite a couple of places where Netscape Navigator won—including cross-platform capability and the ability to attach Web pages to e-mail—IE got the genial curmudgeon's nod as the better browser. IE was "easier to use and has a cleaner, more flexible user interface," Mossberg intoned. "Internet Explorer seems to have been designed with more attention to the needs of average, nontechnical users. On top of that, it's free if you download it from the Web, while Navigator costs $49." Mossberg, the consistently No. 1–rated tech journalist by *Marketing Computers* magazine, wielded unmatchable clout. When Silverberg read the review, his heart pounded with triumph. To the ultimate product guy, none of the noise about Internet time and market vision and Java mattered. What mattered was the thing people could hold in their hands and install on their computers. And in that arena, Microsoft was back on top.

Silverberg regarded the IE 3.0 effort as a magic moment in Microsoft history. "Look at what was accomplished, and how quickly!" he enthused. "It was like we captured lightning in a bottle." From that time forward, whenever the IE 3.0 team members would get together, there would be "a knowing smile, an everlasting bond," Silverberg said. Like they had walked on the moon together.

Componentization in the browser had given Microsoft an edge, Netscape marketing chief Mike Homer acknowledged. "What's happened is that because they have a fairly component-oriented software . . . they were able to put a lot of those components together and get IE 3.0 on Win 95 out the door quickly. On the other platforms we're six months ahead of them. And since we're doing product iterations in six months, we're a generation ahead of them. We're not slowing down, we're speeding up. . . . On the server side, our product family is far, far ahead of Microsoft."

Barksdale was equally bullish. "A lot of times companies like Microsoft, their strength can be co-opted. You can use it to your advantage. There are other ways to coexist, to be a good partner with them in many accounts, co-habitate, live with them, and use their products very well to augment our products." As for antitrust talk, Barksdale emphasized that Netscape had hired outside counsel—Gary Reback of Wilson Sonsini—to investigate the issues. Would Netscape consider a civil suit against Microsoft? "I personally don't think it's a big win for us to pursue it in a public forum," Barksdale asserted. Placed in the context of the Justice Department suit eighteen months later, the words seemed eerily contradictory.

For Reback, it was a second crack at Microsoft. In a brief dated January 10, 1995, Reback challenged the July 1994 consent decree between the Justice Department and Microsoft on grounds the department "simply proposes to shut the barn door now that the horse has already gone." In a footnote, Reback noted the memorandum was being submitted to Federal District Judge Stanley Sporkin "on behalf of certain clients that prefer to retain their confidentiality." Although the clients were never identified, Reback's firm—Wilson Sonsini—had represented Netscape in legal matters since its founding as Electric Media in April 1994. Reback's inch-thick brief helped persuade Judge Sporkin to reject the consent decree. Sporkin's ruling, however, later was overturned by the District of Columbia Court of Appeals after some pointed questioning of Reback in a hearing on April 24, 1995. "Suppose you represented somebody who wanted to blackmail Microsoft and didn't have any interest in the antitrust laws whatsoever in terms of economic competition?" Reback was asked. When he hesitated, the chief judge declared, "By definition, once you say from an anonymous source . . . if we weigh that, it should always be valued at zero or less." Reback started to rebut, but the judge cut him off with: "Always."

As defiant a front as Barksdale & Crew were putting on, signs were appearing that the Netscape clipper ship was listing. From a May 1996 high of $75, Netscape shares had fallen to around $35 by the end of August as investor confidence eroded. Marc, Bark, and Clark had sold substantial chunks of stock while the price was falling—2.48 million shares by Clark alone. Too much can be made of insider selling, whose timing and, in some cases, amounts are governed by company regulations. But *Webweek* quoted CDA/Investnet president Robert Gabele as saying that insiders probably felt the stock "highs were awfully lofty." In its SEC financial statements, Netscape also had upped the Microsoft risk factor from the IPO's boiler-plate a year earlier. Now the problem was not just withholding of technology and bundling IE with Windows 95, Microsoft also was leveraging "its dominant position in desktop software to secure preferential distribution and bundling contracts with third parties such as ISPs [Internet service providers], online service providers [AOL, CompuServe] and VARs [value-added resellers]," Netscape's 1996 annual report stated. Nowhere was the fact mentioned, however, that Netscape had filed complaints with the Department of Justice and submitted e-mail and other documentation to its investigation.

Whether the defection in ISP accounts was caused by Microsoft incentives, as Reback charged and the annual report reiterated, or by improved Microsoft technology was open to debate. On July 31, 1996, Microsoft issued an upgrade of Windows 95 called OSR2—for OEM Service Release 2. Included were a number of minor bug fixes, but the big win for OSR2 was integration with ISPs, including AOL, CompuServe, and AT&T. Just a week before the release, Microsoft had scored a huge deal with AT&T, reaching an agreement with the telecom giant to distribute IE 3.0 with AT&T's WorldNet Service beginning in the fall of 1996. WorldNet Service would be included on Windows 95 computers from that time forward, and AT&T would offer IE 3.0 on its CDs and floppy diskettes distributed to Internet customers. The deal was a blow to Barksdale, the guy who had marshaled the AT&T purchase of McCaw Cellular and been wooed to be CEO of AT&T when Bob Allen announced his intention to step down. If anyone should have had an inside track to signing up AT&T's default browser, Barksdale would have been the candidate. But Microsoft had its own card to play on the AT&T side. Sitting across the table from Brad Chase during negotiations was none other than Microsoft's former e-mail/BackOffice patriarch, Tom Evslin.

Evslin had been a busy guy since leaving Microsoft eighteen months earlier. First on his agenda at AT&T had been dismantling the phone giant's investments in proprietary data services, including Ziff-Davis Interchange and AT&T Network Services and "a lot of other stuff that never saw the light of day." The next step was to throw all of AT&T's eggs into the Internet basket. By August 1995 Evslin and AT&T communications executive John Petrillo were announcing the WorldNet Internet access service from AT&T. "We've always taken great pride in the fact that at AT&T we refocused four months earlier than Microsoft," Evslin later recalled, referring to Gates's Pearl Harbor day address as the point where Microsoft began its turnaround. In actuality, Microsoft refocused much earlier, and it took AT&T till the following March of 1996 to begin offering WorldNet dial-up. Evslin is also quick to acknowledge that "Microsoft did a much better job of their refocusing."

The WorldNet deal later drew the attention of the Justice Department, which cast deposed testimony from Silverberg in ominous terms. According to the department, Silverberg had told AT&T during negotiations: "You want to be part of the Windows box [desktop], you're going to have to do something special for us. There are very, very few people we allow to be in the Windows box. If you want that preferential treatment from us, which is extraordinary treatment, we're going to want something very extraordinary from you."

According to the Justice complaint, the "something special" was that AT&T could not distribute, advertise, promote, or even mention any other browser besides Microsoft's. Evslin flatly denied that to be the case, saying, "We were not exclusive with Internet Explorer. We continued to give our customers a choice, Navigator or Internet Explorer, and in fact we were still paying Netscape for Navigator and not paying for Internet Explorer. All that was public. So it was more expensive for us if someone chose to have Navigator instead of IE, but we did feel our customers should have a choice and that's the deal we made." Evslin, however, had not been deposed or interviewed by the Justice Deparment.

Silverberg's reaction to the department's filing: "It's mindboggling that the government somehow finds something wrong. I think it clearly exposes how unjust their actions have been. AT&T wants something special from us. We're supposed to do it for nothing, just because they're AT&T? I'm not a lawyer . . . but I understand the underlying principle of a contract is mutual exchange of value. You do something for me that I value and I do something for you that you value."

When the AT&T WorldNet service was inaugurated, customer inquiries left the impression both options were open:

Q. Can I use Netscape with your service?

A. Yes.

Q. What's the difference between it and Internet Explorer?

A. IE is better integrated with AT&T's network. Otherwise functionality is the same. IE is probably better supported because our technicians are more familiar with it.

The sine qua non, as Silverberg put it, was that users could always obtain Navigator from any ISP, even if it was by downloading Navigator using Internet Explorer.

The major OSR2 technological attraction for ISPs was a feature called the Internet Explorer Administration Kit, abbreviated IEAK. The kit made it easier for ISPs to set up, configure, and provide support for the Microsoft browser. ISPs could customize the browser to "brand" it with their own name or logo: Spry, AT&T, AOL, whatever. And they could provide automatic links to their own home page or website. IEAK also worked well as a tool for corporations to assign levels of security and features to different users. IEAK was not sexy or exciting, but it was the kind of trenchwork Microsoft knew would pay dividends. As Silverberg put it: "Microsoft definitely put a lot of effort into the IEAK and listened carefully to what the ISPs wanted. We saw a real opportunity there, to give them a great customization kit that would make their lives much easier. The tools they got from Netscape were poor [and expensive]; we thought that we could build great partnerships and deliver a superior product and service to ISPs. It paid off."

The browser wars of 1996 and 1997 captivated the industry and dominated the media. But the real campaign for the future of the Web was being waged behind the scenes, on a technological front much less visible to and comprehended by the public. While the focus was on Internet Explorer versus Navigator and Java versus ActiveX, the incipient war within the war was over protocol and formatting standards. With versions 3.0 of both browsers, initial skirmishes were on the verge of turning into a battle royale.

The basic confict had to do with the bread and butter of the Web, html. As modest as its origins were, html was growing up. As Silverberg, Slivka, Ludwig, Reardon, and the other Internet renegades had surmised early on, html would blossom, eventually, into a publishing tool capable of bringing numerous special effects and whizbang layouts to the Web. In versions 3.0, both Microsoft and Navigator supported html 2.0 and some of its leading features, including standard frames and tables and the ability to run video and inline sound on a Web page.

Fair enough. But the storm on the horizon was caused by the two companies' divergence on developing standards in the World Wide Web Consortium and Internet Engineering Task Force. True to Maritz's promise, Microsoft was supporting, as well as helping to drive, future standards, including html 3.2, still under development. IE 3.0 did enhanced frames and tables, enhanced font support, and the "html and style" specification—the glue that bound style sheets to html. Most significantly, Microsoft supported the html layout control and object tag support for html. Netscape supported a tag called the embed tag, which it had developed without the consortium's support. Although Microsoft considered the embed tag proprietary, IE 3.0 supported the tag for compatibility reasons.

For the time being, the browsers were living with each other, albeit living dangerously. As long as IE 3.0 supported both W3C and Netscape-developed standards, Web users could view pages via both broswers. As long as both browsers worked, the Web's universal viewing capability remained intact. But it would not be long before compatibility began to disintegrate. Maritz already had sounded the alarm in his long August letter to Schell: "We find this hard to believe, but it's true: The Netscape Web site deliberately searches out and excludes non-Netscape browsers from significant parts of the site. It also looks for and excludes browsers that use JavaScript-compatible scripting languages, such as JScript in Microsoft's Internet Explorer. . . . Some areas of the Netscape site display a message [to users of Microsoft's Internet Explorer and other browsers] saying, 'Sorry, this demo does not work for your version of Navigator.'"

It was part of a disturbing historical pattern, Maritz complained. In the fall of 1995, Netscape had prevented Internet Explorer users from entering the Netscape general store on the Web. "Searching for and locking out non-Netscape browsers is not a very 'open' thing to do, under any definition," Maritz complained. The practice contradicted Netscape's numerous platform statements by Andreessen and other executives, posted on its website, pledging support for open standards on the Web, Maritz added.

In "Netscape Pulls a Fast One," columnist Raphael Needleman at *CNET* later blew the whistle on Netscape's open-standards practice. On September 22, 1997, Needleman charged that "For all its protestations that it runs an 'open standards' company, Netscape is using the supposedly defunct Layer tag again, this time on its *home page* [emphasis Needleman's]."

The column was a bit of a mea culpa for Needleman, who earlier in the year had accused Microsoft of playing fast and loose in its criticism of Netscape on standards issues. "Well, Microsoft, I really hate to say this, but I was wrong, and you were right," Needleman wrote.

Things on the standards front would get worse before they got better, however. Beginning early in 1996, Adam Bosworth, a Microsoft systems programmer with a quicksilver ingenuity, began work on a supercharged html he called dynamic html. Code-named Trident, Bosworth's project was aimed at giving html things users might expect only from ActiveX or Java—interactivity, animated icons, flashing buttons, and other special effects. It was another one of those cool tools that won the favor of developers searching to give their sites that extra pop to differentiate them from all the clutter on the Web. Although ActiveX was intended to supply the things dynamic html did, Bosworth saw that ActiveX by itself posed enough drawbacks to steer developers off using it. Although Netscape had pledged support for ActiveX, Navigator was not yet compatible with it. ActiveX also ran only on Windows, not on the Mac or UNIX. And although it was intended as a Web technology, ActiveX was viewed as a *Microsoft* technology—proprietary, closed, controlled by one very big company. Then there was the security problem. Web hackers had a field day with ActiveX bugs. Programmer Fred McLain, who lived within spitting distance of Microsoft, cooked up a demo to illustrate how a malicious hacker could remotely tunnel into a Web user's computer over the Internet and not only lift private information from the user's hard disk but change files and crash the system altogether. McLain impishly called the demo "Internet Exploder," and illustrated it with a mushroom-cloud photo of a hydrogen bomb detonating. For his trouble, McLain found his demo's digital signature—the passkey that identified him as a responsible Web user—canceled by VeriSign, the company that registered sites for clearance with ActiveX. Technically, McLain was in violation of the VeriSign pledge not to use ActiveX for malicious purposes. Under the VeriSign system, in fact, he could be traced and possibly prosecuted. McLain considered the loss of privileges a small price to pay to illustrate ActiveX's weaknesses. In any case, the damage had been done. Despite a number of strategies aimed at clearing its name and ensuring user safety, ActiveX never shook the security stigma.

Bosworth's genius was to take a standard Web technology that people already trusted and give it the pizzazz Web developers so eagerly sought via Java and ActiveX. As much resistance as there was to Java, which was slow and never really met its promise of easy cross-platform compatibility, and

ActiveX, the Web community welcomed dynamic html with open arms. The second half of Microsoft's savviness with dhtml, as it soon was abbreviated to, was how closely it worked with the World Wide Web Consortium's standards-approval process. Closely coordinating the dhtml development process with the W3C had two huge impacts in favor of Microsoft: It reinforced the company's long-standing declaration that it supported open standards, and it encouraged Netscape to adopt the Microsoft-W3C approach rather than continuing down a path of developing its own html extensions.

Dhtml had another of those classic checkered Microsoft histories. Its core origins lay with a circa 1994 technology called Forms Cubed, which was aimed at providing Web-like interactivity on Blackbird and MSN. Forms Cubed was yet another lightning rod for controversy between the online services gang and Internet renegades at Microsoft. Leading the way against the whole Forms Cubed ideology was Thomas Reardon. "My job in the whole wide world was to agitate, to say, Look, we've done all this massive investment in OLE and OLE controls . . . the idea that html would just be a control set of Blackbird was upside down. In fact, I thought the browser would be the overall experience. We would have controls in the browser," he stated.

Aligning with Reardon was Slivka, who saw html growing and growing while Blackbird painted itself into a corner. In the opposite camp was Bosworth, the guiding force behind Forms Cubed. Reardon spent much of 1995 arguing the html case. He started by researching cascading style sheets and supporting Chris Wilson's proposal to include them in IE 3.0. The all-out success of style sheets with the developer community helped persuade Bosworth that the future of Forms Cubed was html, as Reardon recalled it: "Cascading style sheets brought html a lot closer to Forms Cubed in terms of visual richness. Through that process we went from yelling at and arguing with Adam's team in a sort of over-my-dead-body kind of way to finally collaborating with them. That led to the creation of the Trident project."

Being the company liaison with the World Wide Web Consortium, Reardon could carry the dynamic html message to its standards committees. Bosworth kept the home fires burning. Although the outside world had little indication of it, the core of dhtml actually shipped with IE 3.0 in August. Called the html layout control, it was not quite ready for prime time because the W3C had not had enough time to bless it with final approval. "Nobody used it because, we learned, Web publishers only use the thing that's out there on everybody's desktop, not the things that are only in small proportion," John Ludwig recalled. "We really went to work at getting that all molded back into the html control." By October 1996 Trident was far enough along to start doing broad demos. At Microsoft's Site Builders Conference on October 28, 1996, it got a shaky introduction in a glitchy demo but was nonetheless well received.

The conference marked another huge step forward in Microsoft's Web strategy, with test versions of Front Page and Internet Studio and some pumped-up talks by J Allard and his fellow server Webheads. "Internet Information Server is hot!!!" was the title of Allard's talk, with his usual unprepossessing air. Allard loved numbers, and the numbers were big: Over 120,000 copies of IIS 1.0 had been downloaded in a year, IIS had gone out with each copy of NT 4.0, of which 150,000 units had been sold. More than 45,000 servers ran IIS on the Net, and more than 60 OEMs were bundling IIS with their server machines. Allard was also pumped about the introduction of Active Server Pages. ASPs were yet another boost to interconnectivity of content on the Web. They represented information coming to your fingertips, as author Michael Corning put it in the introduction to *Working with Active Server Pages*. They united the jazz of ActiveX and DCOM and IIS with the power of database access. By December 10, 1996, at 1:39 P.M., the word from Steve Brandli, project lead, was out on the mojo wire, in all caps: "WE ARE DONE!!!" Active Server Pages were due to go live that evening.

The Site Builders Conference was just as memorable for Microsoft's answer to the Network Computer. As unveiled by Paul Maritz, the best-of-the-Web, best-of-the-PC guy, the new configuration was dubbed the NetPC. A gryphonlike creature, half Net, half PC, the NetPC was a buzzword slinger's manna from heaven. It lowered the costs of administering PCs in a large enterprise, increasing return on investment. Zero-administration Windows, Maritz called it, or ZAW. The phrase was an oblique dig at Sun's Scott McNealy, who had been kvetching about the Windows "desktop hairball" and promising "zero administration" costs under Java for most of the year. Zero administration meant the PC configured itself with updated software automatically. No guy with a screwdriver and pony tail going around the office sticking a diskette into each machine to add the latest software patch. ZAW also meant users could log on to different machines in the office. And it meant that the computer was centrally controlled, so it could be shut down or booted up remotely. The NetPC also was aimed at reducing cost of ownership, another term of convenience popular among the organizational bean counters. To answer the Gatesian riddle of what would be thrown out of a regular PC to make a Network Computer, Maritz concluded: Not much. NetPCs lacked expansion slots for things like whizbang sound or video cards, game ports, and so on. NetPCs also lacked floppy diskette drives for careless users to introduce virus-plagued software into the network. And they lacked lots of power: The base configuration called for a 133mHz Pentium processor and just 16MB of memory. But NetPCs, unlike Network Computers, did have a hard drive and did have at least 16MB of memory. They were not meant to be a callback to the days of dumb terminals.

Maritz put as good a face as he could on the concept of the NetPC. Microsoft was trying, after all, to address concerns expressed to it by beleaguered information managers whose CEOs wanted to know why the company had to keep buying a new PC every other year for each employee, especially when computers kept managing to make things expensive and time-consuming. But there was never much enthusiasm for the NetPC at Microsoft. Microsoft was talking the talk of the Network Computer but not walking the walk. Eventually the NetPC simply dribbled into nothing-ness—along with the Network Computer. By mid-1997, $500 was close to the purchase price of a fully equipped PC, leaving the once-attractive price point of NCs a moot consideration.

The initial skepticism over Network Computers expressed by Gates and his field general Maritz back in the tumultuous fall of 1995 had been borne out by market factors. No need for NCs or dumb terminals or JavaStations or Internet appliances or whatever. By 1998 PC shipments were expected to reach 100 million a year, fully five times the 20 million that shipped the year of Gates's Information At Your Fingertips address. The Internet boom simply meant that many more PCs—wildly many more PCs—would be sold.

Chapter 17

JAVANOIA

On May 21, 1997, Jim Barksdale's personal assistant, Joel Rothstein, tried to sneak into a private Microsoft press briefing in San Francisco by posing as a news reporter. The briefing had to do with Microsoft's plans for "push" technology in its upcoming release of Internet Explorer 4.0. Push was so hot that some voices, notably *WIRED* magazine in a breathless cover story, were predicting the end of the browser altogether. Rothstein's cover was blown by Colleen Lacter, a sharp-eyed observer for Microsoft's PR firm, Waggener-Edstrom. Under pointed questioning, he acknowledged he was from Netscape. Rothstein was asked to leave and, red-faced, complied.

The company that despite repeated entreaties had expressly limited Microsoft's presence at putatively "open" developer events had been caught engaging in an act of corporate espionage. As the browser wars raged and the descendant of a Civil War hero faced increasing pressure to respond, it seemed only natural that wartime surveillance tactics should be invoked. Netscape's battle plan depended on outrunning Microsoft. On keeping its six-month lead. To stay on track, Netscape needed to monitor Microsoft's technological progress in any way feasible.

Spying was certainly nothing new in the no-holds-barred competitive landscape of the PC industry. At major trade shows like Comdex and Internet World, companies hired knowledgeable industry consultants to stroll the floors, question exhibitors, write up show diaries, and otherwise report back on what their competitors were doing. Brad Silverberg admittedly liked to prowl the aisles at trade shows with his ID concealed. Online forums were populated with "ringers"—company executives or hired guns who would argue a corporate line or attack a competitor's product without necessarily identifying their affiliations.

In the summer of 1996, an e-mail exchange at Microsoft revealed its intense curiosity about Netscape. This was the height of Netscape's sales success with browsers. Revenue from Navigator in the third quarter was to reach the company's highest total ever, nearly $60 million. That sounded like real money to Gates & Co. An executive meeting focusing on Netscape was planned for August 19. In preparation, company executives were asked to learn all they could about the worthy warrior to the south. "I don't want a lot of guesses about Netscape generated by people who may know less than I do," Gates directed in an e-mail to several lieutenants, including the Two Brads. Let's get head counts and head count plans, Gates directed. Future growth plans. "People are expecting Netscape to make a lot of money. How does that pencil out?" Sales data, broken down geographically. Development practices, recent speeches, "anything about the relationship between Netscape and Sun and Oracle." Why didn't Netscape outbid Microsoft on Front Page and eShop? Gates wondered. "Why haven't they attacked us on these distribution deals more—if AT&T was important enough for them to announce, why didn't they offer AT&T compelling reasons to work with them?" How was Netscape going to respond to ActiveX?

The questions and scrutiny continued well after the August executive session. A week later Ballmer asked sales staff to "coordinate a drill-down on Netscape's browser revenues to understand where they make money." Where was all that money coming from? Computer makers? Internet service providers? Retail sales? Online sales? Breaking down Netscape's revenue stream soon looped in a long and winding e-mail thread of executives and managers. On December 1 Gates mailed executive Amar Nehru, copying Ballmer, Maritz, and the Two Brads: "What kind of data do we have about how much software companies pay Netscape?" Gates was particularly curious about deals with Microsoft archrivals Corel, Lotus, and Intuit. He acknowledged being surprised at how much money Netscape gained from Internet service providers. "Someone should be more concrete about what they [Netscape] get [nonbarter] from the home page. I think it's quite low," Gates stated. It was a continuing, but nonetheless still early, signal of the value Gates saw potentially in Internet "portal" business. Signing off from his e-mail, Gates added: "I don't think this analysis needed to be sent to so many people," drawing an apology from Ballmer:

> I asked amar to send it broadly I may have gone oevrboard we should have been more precise that home page means ads of all kinds sorry The isv revenue we did not dig into it will have to lower one of our other estimates if sizable we will brain-storm how to get a grab.

Whether he got a grab or not, Ballmer was confident enough to boast to *Forbes* magazine writer Jeffrey Young in January, "I've had my whole group of guys—finance, marketing, product development—here around this table. And we pore over [Netscape's] 10-K and financial statements. We know exactly where they make their money." Locker room trash talk? Barksdale thought so: "Oh, he's the biggest bag of wind," he said later when asked about the Ballmer boast. "I wish he'd tell me!" Barksdale joked, before adding soberly, "I thought that was an arrogant statement. I would also say it indicates their predatory nature."

Predatory or not, Microsoft's information-gathering had been done without adopting a false ID. Rothstein's pose was an indication of how high the stakes over "push," the focal point of the browser war circa 1997, had become.

Barksdale himself had fired the opening salvo on November 20, 1996, in a sneak attack at Fall Comdex. For his first and to date only keynote address at the august trade event, Barksdale demonstrated a next-generation component of Navigator, code-named Constellation. What Constellation did was to turn the Windows 95 desktop into a Web page, complete with ticker tape news updates, stock quotes, and internal corporate bulletins. Constellation pushed information to individual users' PC screens without their having to call up various sites or surf for the information. The fact that Constellation also "pushed" the Windows interface aside for a Web-like look was lost on no one. The wily Mississippian appreciated a clever pun as well as anyone. Outwardly he professed at the show that it "would be foolishness" for Netscape to try to "kill Windows." Camouflaging Windows, however, he was willing to try.

Barksdale also enjoyed zinging Microsoft at every chance. Strolling around the stage, loosening the crowd up with a few Barksdaleisms, the courtly Southerner could not resist a poke at his worthy competitors to the North. After calling Martina Lauchengco onstage to assist in a demonstration of a key Constellation feature, Barksdale asked her: "Martina, let me ask you something before we start. Where did you used to work?" When Lauchengco, who had worked on Word and Office, responded, "I used to work at Microsoft," the audience tittered. Later, when Barksdale was assisted in another segment by Alex Edelstein, Barksdale asked him the same thing. Edelstein's response: "Well, Jim, I used to work at Microsoft." More laughter and applause. The interplay made it seem as if Microsoft was losing a swarm of talent to Netscape; in reality, each company had hired the statistically negligible total of half a dozen of the other's exes. Constellation was seen as yet another of Netscape's forays into building an alternative Web platform to Windows. Say good-bye to the Windows desktop. The new PC paradigm was, in Barksdale's term, the Webtop.

When Will Poole saw Barksdale's Comdex demonstration on videotape a day later, the Microsoft strategic business development executive watched it closely, very closely. Poole had been warned by PointCast, the red-hot king of "push," that Netscape "wanted to do a demo of some of our stuff." Poole's response: It was fine with Microsoft "as long as it did not affect our situation" with PointCast. The "situation" was a big, big strategic partnership, a head-turner of a deal that would give PointCast debutante status on the planned push content bar for IE 4.0.

A sandy-haired, easygoing Rhode Island native, the thirty-five-year-old Poole had been recruited by Brad Chase for just such a role. Poole had strong Silicon Valley connections. A Brown University graduate, he had worked at Sun Microsystems in Boston before migrating to the peninsula, where he in 1991 cofounded San Mateo–based eShop, an Internet commerce company that had developed one of the first Web malls, eShop Plaza. Microsoft liked eShop's technology enough to buy the company on June 11, 1996. Microsoft needed eShop's code for its e-commerce server, Merchant Server, which Gates rolled out with considerable fanfare at the Microsoft Site Builder Conference in October 1996.

Poole's mission was to figure out potential strategic deals for Microsoft involving emerging technologies, a tall order given Silicon Valley's enmity toward what its denizens routinely referred to as the Evil Empire. Even after making the move to the Northwest, though, Poole retained the air of a valley guy. His pitch: Valley attitudes toward Redmond were out of date— particularly the conviction that Microsoft never made any money for third-party companies. The reality is, we do, Poole would point out. "And we can enhance the technology of third-party companies."

Case in point . . . PointCast. In mid-August 1996 Poole was at a venture-capital briefing when he ran into Jon Feiber, a PointCast board member whom Poole knew from his valley days. They got to talking. As Feiber described PointCast's game plan, it occurred to Poole that its push strategy would mesh nicely with Microsoft's. PointCast was less interested in the technology side of push than the content side. It wanted to expand its role as an aggregator—a company whose product brings variegated content together in interesting and compelling ways. The best-known aggregators are TV networks, and PointCast knew there could be huge bucks in the Web version of TV. So did Microsoft, which wanted to build push technology into its Active Desktop blending Windows with the Web. "Jon was characterizing PointCast as a media company," Poole said. "And I said, That's great, because we're a platform company. There could be a partnership opportunity here."

So began weeks of talks that Poole later described as progressive disclosure. PointCast's technology did wonderful and unique things with the popular but uninspiring programming language C++. PointCast could do moving text, flashing emblems, and other whizzy stuff. Even if the technology per se wasn't the bread and butter of PointCast's future business model, it was cool, and the company wanted to hang on to much of it—or at least receive top value for it. As for Microsoft, Poole wanted to make sure PointCast created more synergy than conflict with its own multipronged Internet strategy. As it turned out, the PointCast deal was a classic Microsoft gambit—one that had the industry talking for weeks.

For Microsoft to partner effectively, Poole said, he had to convince the company to go "out of our way" to show its technology strategy. "There were numerous technical briefings with PointCast," Poole said. Microsoft briefed PointCast on Normandy, its suite of Internet servers expected to combine a host of content and community services for businesses and corporations building Web and intranet presences. Microsoft also gave early views of its ActiveX strategy for Windows and websites, including the next generation of its browser, Internet Explorer 4.0. In the testosterone-laced valley parlance, this is called opening the kimono or, only slightly less offensively, lifting your skirts. In a safer metaphor, Microsoft went the extra mile to convince PointCast of its strategy.

As far as Microsoft's own push strategy was concerned, the Internet Explorer team wanted to do its own flavor; there was a possibility that the PointCast technology would conflict or compete. Microsoft wanted to partner with other content providers beyond PointCast; a deal with such a high-profile player might alienate or disaffect potential partners. And what about Microsoft Network's plans for TV-like content on the Web? Would a PointCast deal in effect cannibalize one of Microsoft's own? It was a risky game: Was PointCast a technology company, which it claimed to be less and less of, or a content company, which it clearly was promoting itself as?

Those were the issues on the table when word of the discussions reached the desk, or at least computer monitor, of Redmond's No. 1 dealmaker.

When Poole queried Gates, "Bill was pretty clear that we are going to work with content providers and we are going to partner on platforms." You *can* have it both ways, Gates had suggested: "Platform partnerships and content deals would stand on their own merits." In a way it was the ultimate Darwinian act: Your own children got no favored status in the survival of the digital fittest. In the New Web Order, Gates would go on to say in a speech to a hostile Newspaper Association of America gathering on April 29, 1997, sometimes you partnered and other times you competed with the same people. You just had to be smart about knowing when to do which.

Several aspects of Microsoft's strategy appealed to PointCast chief Chris Hassett. First off was componentization. PointCast needed something to replace its internal browser. Hassett himself had written the browser to provide Web surfing functionality in PointCast, and even though it was getting old in Internet years it could still do 80 percent of what it needed to do. But PointCast was not interested in keeping it updated with newer versions of html, the hypertext markup language that provided the Web's lingua franca for linking, and other browser enhancements. Although PointCast could have built in Netscape's Navigator browser, Netscape strategy called for keeping its brand name out in front of users. Moreover, Netscape could not offer integration with Windows at the operating system level the way Microsoft could.

The more Microsoft and PointCast talked, the better the deal sounded to Hassett. They even came up with a solution to the MSN problem: Make Microsoft Network a prime channel on the PointCast Network. It would bring MSN eyeballs—which Microsoft expected to number 4 million pair by the end of the year—to PointCast while reducing any potential rationale for PointCast viewers to defect to MSN. Win-win, Hassett thought. He compared PointCast's role to that of a TV network: "As ABC or CBS or NBC is to the airwaves, we are to the Internet." The networks don't produce the content, such as a Seinfeld series, but they do pull together the best stuff they can, find sponsors, and get it to the appropriate demographic. Poole ultimately put the Microsoft factor in perspective: "One of Chris Hassett's mantras is we've got to get more people on the Internet. Not the bleeding-edge surfers, people who just want to use stuff. And this partnership could provide a big boost in that direction."

By the first week of December 1996 it was all over but the lawyering. The deal entered the phase Poole later dubbed the 6:00 A.M.-to-midnight shift. It started on an early December Thursday morning and ended with a holiday party the following Saturday night. Conference calls all day long Thursday and Friday. They might have gone all night, Poole averred, except for the fact that a key attorney lived on Bainbridge Island and had to take the last ferry from Seattle home. After three days of marathon teleconferencing, a bleary Hassett signed the agreement in a corner of the room at the PointCast holiday party.

The following week the earth shook at Internet World, the big Mecklermedia trade show in New York City's Javits Center. Just three weeks after Barksdale touted PointCast technology for the Windows-killer Constellation, Microsoft landed PointCast as the poster child for its forthcoming Channel Bar in IE 4.0. "This is a big day for not just Microsoft and Point-Cast but the entire Internet community," said Chase, who with Hassett led a press conference on Wednesday, December 11. The announcement not only marked a giant coup for Microsoft but raised questions about Netscape's whole push strategy. Was this an exclusive deal? Or was Point-Cast free to be a channel on Netscape's Constellation as well? It was hard to tell: Chase seemed to lean toward the exclusivity side, while Hassett seemed to be resisting it. No clear response emerged, giving the impression that maybe there was some built-in flexibility. And both sides were decidedly mum on whether any money had changed hands in the deal.

For Chase, Poole & Crew, there was an aspect of justice served to Microsoft's PointCast coup. The notion of an active desktop—Barksdale's Webtop—in Windows was originally a Microsoft concept. At his Pearl Harbor day address a year earlier, Gates had shown an early demo of an html desktop—a Web page on the Windows 95 desktop. At the following March 1996 Professional Developers Conference, Active Desktop had made its grand debut. But Thomas Reardon warned in an e-mail to the IE team that Netscape might try to "push" Windows off the PC desktop. Netscape had purchased Paper Software and with it a slender and soft-spoken whiz kid named Mike McCue. McCue's inventiveness found its expression in

Constellation, which seemed to be plowing new turf and got mass exposure earlier with Barksdale's Comdex address. But Microsoft considered the "Webtop" its own innovation.

Microsoft would have been earlier to the gate but for a troublesome technical limitation. The IE team discovered as it worked to implement the vision behind the Pearl Harbor day demo that Windows could not display its desktop icons on top of a Web desktop. What came to the rescue, said Joe Belfiore of the IE team, was Trident. "It was a technical limitation before Trident that if you wanted to have some content on the desktop, you would lose your desktop icons. You could not overlap the icons on top of your html content. Once we got Trident we were able to fix that." Microsoft's approach also was more conservative than Constellation, Belfiore explained. "We wanted to do more usability tests, and talk to customers more, before we did a wholesale html desktop implementation." Things were moving so fast on Internet time that enterprises were starting to complain that neither they nor their employees had much chance of keeping up.

While Microsoft was pushing back against Netscape, Sun Microsystems was trying to push aside Microsoft. Center stage, once again, was Java. The previous August, while Microsoft was drilling down on Netscape's financing, Java had gotten a $100 million shot in the arm from ten high-profile tech companies investing in a Java Fund managed by John Doerr's venture-capital firm, Kleiner Perkins. Among the backers were Netscape, IBM, Compaq, Oracle, TCI, Cisco Systems, and Sun. With the Java honey pot flowing, start-ups were sprouting like mushrooms in Silicon Valley garages.

At the same Fall Internet World where Microsoft announced the Point-Cast coup, Java was all that display booths, overhead banners, and keynote speakers could talk about. Sun rolled out a "100 percent pure" Java initiative aligning the industry's top names together in an effort to agree on Java standards. Notably missing from the list was Microsoft. Shades of the Java Beans bushwhack! The Two Brads were incredulous. Silverberg had awakened that Monday morning to read in the *Wall Street Journal* that Microsoft had refused to join the 100 percent pure consortium. Just the night before Chase had learned that anything like a "pure" initiative existed. "We've been blindsided," Chase complained. Combative JavaSoft president Alan Baratz, a former director of strategic development for IBM who liked wearing jeans and pointy-toed snakeskin boots, said Microsoft had been told about the consortium the previous week and had asked to think things over. The ensuing silence was taken as a no. Silverberg said Microsoft was "not invited till Monday afternoon—after JavaSoft [Sun] had already told the press we had been invited and declined. Anything JavaSoft says differently is not true. It is sad to see such posturing from them." Silverberg said Microsoft was still thinking it over: "We are looking forward to details of this program to see how we can participate. We ship more Java-compatible products than any [other] licensee. We love Java."

It was not 100 percent pure love, however. There was a good deal of paranoia mixed in as well. In an e-mail September 30, Gates had sounded the Java alarm in response to a long memo from Bosworth warning that Java posed a better alternative to programmers than Microsoft's equivalent technologies, particularly COM, Microsoft's Common Object Model initiative. Java was not just a language, Bosworth emphasized. It was an entire programming architecture—one that had certifiable advantages over Windows. Gates's response: "This scares the hell out of me." What can we do to make Windows the best place for Java applications to run—to make them "unique enough to preserve our market position?" Gates asked. "Understanding this is so important that it deserves top priority." Gates's comment later was cast as concern over Java the programming language. In reality, he explained in an interview, it was Java's runtime engine—the thing that enabled Java applications to run on Windows computers. If Java applications ran as well or better on Windows computers than equivalent Windows applications, then Microsoft was in big trouble: "If you're not taking advantage of Windows [when you run Java], then Windows becomes a commodity." Generic, devalued, and irrelevant. "It's ambiguous," Gates emphasized, "because the term Java formally means just the language. But the thing that's often most relevant is the runtime."

What ultimately threatened Microsoft about Java, however, was its control being in the hands of a sworn archenemy, Sun. "Who decides what is impure or pure?" Silverberg demanded rhetorically. "What is the purity test? What happens to people or products that are impure?" To Silverberg the JavaSoft initiative sounded like some medieval pogrom aimed at ethnic cleansing of objectionable heathens. When Microsoft had proposed turning Java over to an open standards committee akin to the W3C or IETF, a JavaSoft executive told the company, Don't lecture us about standards committees. We know all about them and want no part of them for Java. Refusing to "open" Java continued as Sun policy despite pressure from critics like Web pundit Jesse Berst, who chided the company repeatedly for its hypocrisy on the topic. Microsoft never did join the 100 percent pure campaign, which fizzled the way industrywide initiatives are wont to do.

Microsoft did, however, mount a campaign to shake Java free from Sun's clutches. The 100 percent pure campaign signaled not only a Sun offensive against Microsoft but a potential industrywide jihad as well. It was eating away at a man with a plan—and with some time on his hands. With the completion of IE 3.0, Ben Slivka found his lust for technological challenge in need of a new outlet. Java seemed to him the biggest threat to Microsoft extant, and he wanted to address it. Almost daily he saw his company getting beat up on Java by Sun and the other constituents of what Ballmer called NOISE—Netscape, Oracle, IBM, Sun, and Everyone else. Everyone else being those who bought into the anti-Microsoft Silicon Valley campaign, that is. By spring of 1997, Slivka was mobilizing a strategic defensive. Once again the product guy had too many thoughts swirling inside his head to contain. On April 14, a Sunday night, at the hoary hour of 3:09 A.M., Slivka sent Bill Gates a note: "I'm working with Paulma [Maritz] to set up a 2–3 hour review for you on our Java efforts (I hope before your May think week)." Based on a previous meeting with Gates, Slivka wanted to cover several points, among them: "How do we wrest control of Java away from Sun?"

It was one of six key themes to Slivka's strategy outlined in the e-mail, but the only one that got played up later in the Sun and Justice Department lawsuits against Microsoft. The reference was cast as predatory, a signal once again of how Microsoft wanted to rule the world. To Slivka, the query was straightforwardly pragmatic. Sun had control and wanted to use it to kill Windows and make Microsoft irrelevant. Slivka did not care if Microsoft controlled Java. As he later pointed out he had not said, "How do we gain control over Java?" He did, however, want to prevent Sun from controlling Java.

Microsoft's we-love-Java approach was good PR but had done little to shake Sun's grasp. The previous fall, Slivka had cautioned Charles Fitzgerald, a gonzo marketing lead for Java with a flair for combative phrase, "we have to be careful about being negative about Java, precisely since there is so much religion about it—for the same reason that Scott McNealy is probably doing Java (and Sun) a disservice by being so extremely, rabidly anti-Microsoft." The ideal was simply to say "Java is great for XYZ, and you can do even better when you couple it with Microsoft technology."

The campaign was not sticking, however. The quotable McNealy, repeatedly referring to Microsoft as the Death Star, was zinging the Redmond giant weekly at Java conferences and industry meetings. Berst was having none of the Microsoft love pledge. As hypocritical as he saw McNealy's

"openness" about Java (while Sun and not an industry standards group controlled the technology), Berst also detected a Microsoft campaign to "kid-
nap Java." By December 1996 and the announcement of Sun's 100 percent
pure campaign, the question of what to do about Java was plaguing Microsoft's leading Windows minds. In a midnight message dated December
18, John Ludwig warned Silverberg, Bob Muglia, David Cole, Slivka, and
Chase that "we all know that we have lost the attention of the leading edge
of the ISV [software developer] industry." Java, he added, "is the next big
industry-transforming idea." Ludwig mapped out a campaign to become
"the lead purveyor of Java," including using Microsoft's sophisticated distribution channels, and comarketing dollars. Microsoft also needed, Ludwig
asserted, to come up with a "next big idea." The last "needs to be one that
is perceived as an order of magnitude improvement in programming productivity." Easier said than done, but Ludwig had taken the first step by
saying it.

Slivka thought he had the answer: dhtml—"a very big deal," he wrote in
response the same day. Active server pages were another Microsoft win,
Slivka added: "But even if I'm 100 percent correct," he noted, "is anyone in
the industry ready to hear either of these messages right now, while the Java
tom-tom beats on?" Slivka added to Ludwig's list by proposing a $100 mil-
lion Windows venture capital fund (archnemesis of Java Fund?), technological bake-offs between Microsoft's Visual Basic and Java, and a ramping
up on natural-language processing for Windows. The last, which enabled
computers to interpret normal everyday speech into computer commands,
would make Windows vastly more appealing than Java, Slivka was certain.
By New Year's Eve, Microsoft Office chief Jon DeVaan, not particularly in
a partying mood, chided his fellow strategists that they were falling squarely
into Sun's traps with happy-Java talk. "My opinion is, Java does not have to
be the next big industry wave," DeVaan intoned. "Unfortunately, we are
handing the mantle of industry leadership over to Java with no fight whatsoever." DeVaan's rejoinder: 32-bit Windows, with its raft of powerful applications, including Office, could just as easily eat Java alive.

The hydra-headed strategy was evoking colorful analogies and roiling
competitive juices but not making Microsoft much headway in the marketplace. In January Slivka drew up a presentation entitled "Microsoft API
Strategy: Java Is Our Destiny." As Slivka saw it the challenge was to maintain the Windows market share and still "surf the Java wave." Java "is a wonderful opportunity to modernize and enhance Windows," he concluded,
taking issue with any notion that the embrace-extend approach would com-

moditize the Microsoft cash cow. Twenty-first-century Windows, Slivka pledged, "will be a result of our faith in Java's architectural benefits and more great execution."

Two weeks later, on February 7, Slivka hosted a Microsoft Java summit at a Silicon Valley hotel with Microsoft partners to discuss improving Java. Attending were Borland, Powersoft, Metrowerks, Symantec, and even a Sun representative, Java's éminence grise, programmer James Gosling. Slivka's follow-up e-mail noted that little progress had been made. But he identified issues that later got intense lawyer scrutiny, including a pledge by Microsoft to "not do the cowboy thing." In other words, Microsoft would not try to subvert Java with its own enhancements. "Neither I nor any of the other Microsoft attendees made any pledges not to enhance Java," Slivka later asserted.

Faith in Java? Not do the cowboy thing? Meeting in Silicon Valley with archrivals to talk about improving kill-Windows software? To Bill Gates, it smacked too much of sleeping with the enemy. By March, Slivka made his pitch to Gates, whereupon, as a Sun attorney later put it, the Microsoft chairman handed Slivka his head on a platter. Slivka took issue with the characterization: "Bill got pissed, yes! But I still have my head, thank you very much!" Gates expressed livid concern that Windows was being co-opted by Java infatuation. "Why don't you just give up your options and join the Peace Corps?" Gates was reportedly to have said by David Bank in the *Wall Street Journal.* As Slivka afterward confessed in e-mail, "It is disappointing that Bill chooses to flame like that without giving me a chance to educate him." Gates "is convinced my group is trying to kill Windows, and I clearly haven't said the right things to show him otherwise."

Gates said later he was not impugning Slivka's allegiance to Windows, but rather thought that Windows was being sold short in the Java strategy. Slivka wanted to promote Microsoft's Java programming functionality—class libraries—to developers. The libraries competed with Sun's Java libraries and were even considered superior in most camps, especially for programming Windows applications. The theory was that Microsoft's tools would aid the Windows cause, even if they were being used for Java. But Gates saw things otherwise. Embrace and extend did not always work: "He [Slivka] wanted to promote our Java runtime piece. . . . So then I was saying, that undermines the Windows asset." Gates saw the strategy as "creating essentially a competitor to Windows. In terms of funding our R&D to do new things and support and all that, you can't be creating a free product that replaces Windows!" To Gates, here was where Slivka's "communistic" inclinations had really come into play. Slivka's guys "were kind of panicked" over Java, Gates believed. "My primary thing was to make Windows better and allow Java developers to get at Windows." The strategy, called JDirect, "is the most straightforward way of allowing the Java guy, if he wants to, no coercion there at all, to use the richness down inside of Windows itself." Ludwig seconded: "Hey, if you want to program in Java, you like its benefits, but you want your program to run great on Windows, where 99 percent of your customers are, then JDirect is the thing." JDirect shipped with Internet Explorer in the fall of 1997.

While Slivka and Gates wrestled over Java standards, the Two Brads "pushed" out standards for Web browsing. At Spring Internet World in March 1997 in Los Angeles, they rolled out a new technology called Channel Definition Format, or cdf for short. Cdf was based on an underlying standard called xml, for extensible markup language. Xml had two big things going in its favor. First, it was a proposed World Wide Web Consortium standard, meaning it was likely to be open and universally supported. Second, "push" archrival Netscape had endorsed it. That did not mean that Netscape, whose push technology had its own, different underpinnings, supported cdf. At a hastily assembled press gathering at Internet World, Andreessen trounced the concept, saying "We don't understand why it is necessary. We think it will die on the vine."

Like dhtml, cdf was an extension of a standard that Microsoft was willing to take its time with and work for approval of from the World Wide Web Consortium. It also signaled Microsoft's increasing leadership in the standards arena, an area where Netscape, by dint of its huge market share, initially had dominated. Reardon & Crew's long hours with the W3C standards committees were paying off. Although Microsoft still was widely suspected of trying to engineer standards, Netscape was more often cited as the maverick.

What did wither on the vine was "push," an Internet technology whose hypesters forgot to check with user demand. Beta tests with large enterprise customers had revealed that the notion of replacing Windows with a Web page did not sit well with information system administrators or end users. Workers, even Web-savvy ones, wanted an old familiar shoe to slip into when they sat down in the morning to get their work done. Whatever drawbacks Windows had, it was comfortable, familiar, and effective. Netscape first, and then Microsoft itself, came to the same conclusion. By the time its version 4.0 of Internet Explorer was released, on September 30, 1997, Microsoft's push technology was relegated to a Channel Bar on the right side of the Windows screen. The bar included high-profile push partners like Disney and PointCast. But users did not have to invoke it, and Microsoft provided a simple procedure for getting rid of it and its associated Active Desktop altogether. In less than nine months, push went from the hottest concept around, the innovation that was finally going to make the PC become like a TV, to the slag heap of technological overkill.

No matter. Microsoft was well on the way to completing its Internet quest. On June 28, 1997, Brad Silverberg began a monthlong solo bicycle trip from Arlington, Washington, about forty-five miles north of Seattle, to Banff, in the Canadian Rocky Mountains. It was something he had been promising himself to do for years but, under the gun with MS-DOS, Windows, and Internet development through much of the 1990s, had scarcely had time to even think about. With IE 4.0 all but out the door, Silverberg finally gave himself a break. Not the kind of baking-on-the-beach, vegging-out vacation the typical business executive might take. No, Silverberg still loved a challenge, whether in work or play. A 1,500-mile, self-supported bike ride up some of the tallest passes of North America was just the kind of thing to help him unwind.

As it turned out, the trip came to an abrupt end. Silverberg was in his fourteenth day out, at Fernie, British Columbia, when he made a routine call home. The voice mail shocked him. "If this is you, Brad," his wife, Jean, said on the message, "I went to Germany to pick up Danny." Silverberg had to call a friend to find out that Danny, his eleven-year-old son, had been stricken with appendicitis during a trip to Europe. Silverberg cut his trip short, flew home, and caught the next flight overseas to be with his son. By August 20, with Danny fully recovered, Silverberg was back on his bike in Calgary. He spent the next ten days completing his itinerary, averaging fifty-eight miles and nearly 3,000 vertical feet of climbing per day. For Silverberg, it was important to always finish what he started.

Four weeks after his bike trip ended, Silverberg saw the original Microsoft vision for the Internet manifested with the rollout of Internet Explorer 4.0. There Windows and the Web came together in a marriage of feature and functionality. It had been nearly four years since Silverberg first wrote, in response to Ballmer's "great front end" e-mail, "I see a big opportunity here. Chicago as the gateway to the information highway." Nearly four years since he had sat at the Shumway Mansion and argued in favor of Internet protocols and against a commercial online system. Nearly four years since he had gotten a quasi-skunkworks browser project started within the Chicago programming effort. For Silverberg, nothing could ever diminish the heroism he saw in Microsoft's Internet metamorphosis: "We believed in open standards and the power of Windows and what they could do together to transform the way people used information. We had to fight and fight hard. The online contingent had Bill's ear better than we did. But we believed in ourselves and we hung in there and we pushed hard and kept pushing. And in the end, all the work was worth it. We knew the Internet belonged in Windows. And we were right."

The September 30, 1997, rollout at San Francisco's Fort Mason had a climactic air of celebration and triumph, with not a little relief mixed in. Many of Microsoft's browser old-timers were on hand. In his keynote, Gates stuck his neck out a bit, predicting that by the time IE version 5.0 was released, Microsoft would have majority market share. By the following fall it happened, although the figure had to include America Online's browser share. Gates rattled off a litany of Microsoft wins, including twenty major corporations representing 300,000 desktops, fifty-plus PC makers representing 40 million units sold the previous year, fourteen major ISPs and 100 content providers. Silverberg later put the rollout in perspective: "With IE 4.0 we felt we had won. The reviews by then were overwhelmingly in Microsoft's favor. Market share was rising steadily. Netscape was talking about how the browser was no longer important to them. It was almost curious how they abandoned the browser. They simply stopped improving it. It was almost like they gave up on the very thing that had brought them so much success."

Enlivening the rollout was a huge, 14-foot-high, three-dimensional "e" in the shape of the distinctive IE "e" logo, which at the time appeared in the upper right-hand corner of the browser. Gee, it would be a shame to just throw the thing away, the IE gang thought. Thomas Reardon, Hadi Partovi, Joe Peterson, Joe Belfiore, Chris Jones, and Yusuf Mehdi had an inspiration. They found a flatbed towtruck driver and spent a good two hours sweet-talking him into hauling the "e" down the peninsula to Netscape headquarters. The guy said no way, he'd be seen. They came up with a backroads route. Still, he balked. Reardon and Peterson dug into their pockets and came up with $300. There's another chunk just like that one upon delivery, they said.

Partovi and Peterson rode with the driver while the others repaired to a bar in the marina district. Some time later a call came to Reardon from "Agent E." Security was patrolling the Netscape parking lot. The IE gang was going to make another pass and bail if the cops were still there. Ten minutes later the call came, "The package has been delivered . . . over and out." Reardon, sharing drinks with the Two Brads and a couple dozen other Microsofties, went wild. The group started challenging each other to a lemon-drop drinking contest. Reardon had no idea how deceptively potent those little citrus shots could be.

The following morning Netscape workers were greeted by the sign leaned up against a tree with a note attached that said: "It's just not fair. Good people shouldn't have to feel bad. Best wishers, the IE team." Mike Homer turned the prank into a publicity stunt. By midmorning a group of Netscape engineers had brought out a big Styrofoam model of Mozilla, Netscape's mascot lizard, to stomp on the "e." Homer drew up a sign trumpeting browser share figures—according to Netscape's calculations: Netscape 72, Microsoft 18. Netscape's adroit handling of the incident was a surprise to the Microsoft contingent. Microsoft's PR agency had argued strenuously against the prank on grounds that it could backfire. But all turned out well, Silverberg later noted: "The noteworthy part is that it is the singular instance I can recall in the entire history of Netscape post-Spyglass where they have done *anything* with good humor toward Microsoft."

Any levity in the browser wars was soon dispelled, however. On October 7, 1997, Sun Microsystems sued Microsoft in northern California Federal District Court for breach of contract regarding its Java license. On October 16 assistant attorney general Joel Klein and his staff summoned Microsoft attorney Bill Neukom and his team to Washington, D.C., for a two-hour discussion of antitrust issues. The discussion was amicable and covered a range of issues, but the Microsoft contingent had a feeling something was up. Klein's line of questioning had largely to do with integration of Internet Explorer 4.0 with Windows. Four days later, on October 20, Klein and attorney general Janet Reno filed a complaint in federal court that Microsoft was in violation of its consent decree. The complaint later died after a ruling by the Circuit Court of Appeals, but by May 1998 Klein had expanded the case into a broader Sherman Act antitrust action against Microsoft. The battle that Microsoft had won in the marketplace was shifting to the vastly untechnological terrain of law and justice.

By then, the lighthouse for Microsoft's Internet development would be gone. In December 1997, Silverberg returned from his sabbatical ready to lead IE to the next level. Instead, he found IE leadership being moved under Jim Allchin in an executive reorganization. On December 22, in a meeting with Allchin, Maritz, and Gates, Silverberg got the news that "pieces of IE" would move under Allchin's direction. The move had vaguely to do with Allchin's conviction that making browsing a separate product available on other platforms—the Macintosh and UNIX—undermined Windows' appeal. Silverberg had argued just the opposite: IE on other computers made Windows all the stronger by offering compatibility with its leading market features. On December 23, Allchin sent e-mail to leading Windows managers about the change. Perhaps sensitive to Silverberg's reservations, Allchin equivocated: "I do not know how you guys come out on this. If you have opinions, I suggest you send them to Bill and Paul." As for Silverberg, he deliberated over the holidays, then decided to take an extended leave of absence. The move left the tightly knit IE team suddenly feeling unraveled. When John Ludwig got the news on January 12, he was visibly distraught. "I don't want to talk about it," he said in a choked voice at the close of an interview. "It's just, today is a bad day." Although he kept in touch with Microsoft and, at Gates's invitation, attended executive retreats and planning sessions, Silverberg stayed on leave. By February 1999, there were rumors he was considering returning in a massive reorganization at Microsoft.

It was not to be. In early March Silverberg took a weeklong snowboarding trip to the interior of British Columbia. Before leaving, he made the decision not to return, but told no one. He wanted to try it on for size. The trip went well. The snow was fantastic, the mountains breathtaking. Silverberg waited for remorse or uncertainty to kick in. Neither ever did. Instead, he felt great: "My gut said it was the right decision. I like my free time. . . . It reminded me how much I enjoy my current life and am not ready to give it up." Silverberg remained in touch on a consulting basis with the company that had been his life for nearly a decade. Most of his contact initially was with Ballmer, who was putting together a sweeping reorganization of Microsoft aimed at accelerating the company's Internet leadership and getting the oft-delayed Windows 2000 out the door. Ballmer had structured the reorganization along consumer lines, with Maritz heading a division focused on developers, Allchin marshaling Windows 2000, and Muglia overseeing applications. An online/consumer division targeted at Silverberg would be split between Brad Chase and Jon DeVaan, a longtime Office executive. But the reorganization's biggest impact was to close the curtain officially on the Brad Silverberg era at Microsoft.

CRISIS!

In May 1998, seven managers from the Internet Explorer and Internet Information Server teams entered as a team in The Game. The annual competition had been put together by Joe Belfiore years earlier, before Belfiore became involved himself in Microsoft's Internet efforts, as an outgrowth of a Stanford University game Belfiore had founded called BARF—The Bay Area Race Fantastique. The Game was a sort of brainy version of Extreme Sports, except that instead of scaling mountains and fording rivers, competitors had to figure out a series of fifteen scavenger-huntlike clues. The competition is heavily Microsoft-based but also features civilian teams. For the 1998 edition, they were asked to travel to Los Angeles for a long weekend. Reardon, J Allard, David Treadwell, Joe Peterson, Chris Jones, James Gwertzman, and Hadi Partovi made the trip. All were Game virgins. They were allowed one vehicle. Otherwise the only instructions were to show up and be prepared for anything. The Reardon-Allard team brought CD-ROMs, a satellite telephone for logging wirelessly onto the Internet, scuba gear, a global positioning system setup, walkie-talkies, and a nineteenth-century Boy Scout handbook, which actually turned out to be of use.

The Internet team had no idea how it would do. One clue left them climbing through sewers in Newport Beach, only to find an envelope with the number 17. After half an hour of head-scratching, someone got the idea to call the local police and ask what 17 might refer to. The clerk suggested lifeguard stations, which were numbered 1 through 30. The team found a flag buried in the sand, with another clue that had Peterson swimming in scuba gear 100 yards offshore for the next clue. From there they went to a family fun center, where they had to crawl through a maze for the next clue.

For one clue, a bunch of live bugs crawled out of the envelope. Inside was an engineering diagram that, when translated, offered a series of 1s and 0s. The Boy Scout manual held nineteenth-century Morse code, which it turns out is different from twentieth-century code. The 1s and 0s spelled out UCR, for University of California at Riverside. The campus, it turned out, had an entomology museum—that's right, a museum of bugs.

The breakthrough clue for the Internet team turned out to be an envelope with ten plastic baggies, each containing an unidentified substance. The clue was posted in the middle of the desert, far outside of L.A., with no stores for assistance. The first envelope held cinnamon, a no-brainer. After that, the clues got decidedly harder. One team resorted to knocking on a farmhouse door at 8:00 A.M. on a Sunday morning for help. The Internet team had Chris Jones. In a matter of moments, Jones raced through the baggies, getting things like cream of tartar first crack. Matching the first initial of the spices with the telephone keypad gave a phone number with the next clue.

The Internet team blew away the competition.

"You know what you win?" Reardon asked rhetorically later. "Nothing. We went to a fast-food stand by the Griffith Observatory and got hot dogs. I had a tofu dog. The whole thing does demonstrate the ridiculous competitiveness of our industry."

Around the same time as The Game, Ben Slivka drew up a case study of the browser wars. Under "Wins for IE," Slivka listed the telling technological advantages IE carried to the marketplace. Componentization. ActiveX controls (insofar as they worked better than Netscape's plug-ins). CoolBar. Outlook Express, the mail client. NetMeeting. NetShow. Comic Chat. Personal Web Server. And localization to twenty-two languages. And under World Wide Web Consortium standards that Microsoft supported early and often: cascading style sheets, PICS (the standard for filtering pornographic or other unwanted material from websites), the object tag, and dynamic html.

Microsoft implemented the fastest, slickest, least-buggy Java virtual machine and provided the best Java tools. In the Java Superbowl on April 3, 1997, a Microsoft team of junior programmers beat four other entrants, including a team from Sun, by a wide margin. The victory was less than well received; instead of announcing Microsoft as the winner, sponsors merely read the scores and ended the event abruptly. Granted Microsoft's work on Java was in the cause of Windows, but Microsoft did not claim altruism as a corporate obligation. Slivka's final take on Java: It was just a "third-rate clone of Windows. You couldn't do anything in Java that you couldn't also do for Windows, and the Java version was slower and typically had fewer features." The Internet, not Java, was the real deal, Slivka maintained.

Microsoft surpassed Netscape in the Web server arena, and then some. By November 1997 the IIS team was ready to roll out 4.0. Allard made it an occasion not easily forgotten. About 2:00 P.M. on wrap day, six team members and Allard left to play poker. The game wound up at 4:00 A.M. "Several bottles of Scotch and numerous cabs were involved," Allard reported later. After testing and product support signed off a few days later, Allard ordered margarita sno-cones in the lobby, a "refreshments" party that even got stoic Paul Maritz to leave his office. Then it was off to Seattle's Broadway Grill, a gathering ground for the city's more progressive lifestyles, where the group had drinks with a $5,000-a-night dominatrix who happened by. Then it was off to the International District and three hours of Japanese karaoke, enlivened by middle-age Asian divorcées table-dancing to Chic's "Le Freak." All this was capped off at an after-hours dance club. Again, many cabs. A week later, at the official ship party on December 3, Allard and the "heavy lifters" rented out Planet Hollywood for the evening. Allard was DJ, Treadwell ran the video, and the event reached near seismographic proportions before migrating to a karaoke bar. Incriminating photos and cab rides home closed out the festivities.

NT Server had come from behind. Microsoft surpassed Novell and UNIX in new network server sales in 1997 with 36 percent of overall sales, compared to NetWare at 26.4 percent and UNIX at 20.7 percent. In 1998 NT was the only network operating system to show year-to-year growth, other than freebie Linux, which held less than 10 percent of the market. By the end of 1999 market-trend analyst firm International Data Corporation forecast that NT would pass UNIX in installed base—the number of computers running it. Sometime in the year 2000, IDC predicted, NT would pass NetWare as well.

The true endorsement of Allard's vision came one day in 1998 when he was driving along Broadway on Capitol Hill in Seattle. He passed a clothing store that had been a fixture on the avenue for nine years, had started out with a little cart in the retail mall and just went great guns, growing 35 percent annually. Then all of a sudden it shut down. Doors locked. Windows empty. All 3,500 square feet. All that remained was a huge thirty-foot banner stretched across the storefront, for all passersby to see. BIG SALE! it read. STORE CLOSING! MOVING TO THE WORLD WIDE WEB! Allard used it as a guidepost: "The sign was up two or three months. And when recruits would come to Microsoft I'd drive them by that place, and that was my interview. I hop in the car and drive them across the bridge. And I tell them, you want to change the world? It's possible. I don't know what Web server he's using. I don't know if he has a Netscape mailbot on his website. It doesn't matter. We got to help change things."

Yes, there were fiascos. Slivka's study found IE strategy wanting when it came to push channels, virtual reality, ActiveX Controls (insofar as ActiveX failed to solve the security problem), and secure payment protocols in general. Microsoft Network missed the boat initially with awkward Internet support, then comically tried to imitate TV with embarrassingly bad video content. The Java implementation, despite its technical excellence, divided developers and lost PR points. A too-self-assured, can't-you-see-I'm-right approach dealing with the industry at large sparked the most sweeping antitrust lawsuit since the the the Ma Bell breakup. If anything, Microsoft was victimized by its own success, was guilty of thinking it was always right because it usually was.

Microsoft also had the fortune of errant competition in some cases. As publishing legend Jonathan Seybold put it, Microsoft more often than not benefited as much from competitors' mistakes and wrongheadedness as from its own right moves. Netscape had driven down similar dead ends as Microsoft on the browser front—3-D, virtual reality, streaming audio and sound, and groupware. All were diversions and distractions that kept the fast-moving company from protecting its huge advantage in the browser arena. Analyst Stephen Auditore of Zona Research in Silicon Valley, an inveterate duffer, liked to say that Microsoft had infinite mulligans. It was rich and powerful and obsessed enough to absorb any number of errant moves without losing the overall match. Netscape had no such thing as infinite mulligans. Each mistake cost the company. Netscape's designated Pied Piper and technovisionary Marc Andreessen later told *Business Week*'s Steve Hamm that during the crucial version 3.0 period he felt "sidelined" and undirected. Despite product quality problems and deadline slippages,

Andreessen was so unmotivated at one point he rarely got to the office before noon. As for Eric Bina, the programming dynamo who wrote much of the original Mosaic before joining the early Netscapers, he wound up spending a huge amount of time on a top-priority project to create a next-generation browser from Java. Blending Navigator features with Java functionality, the project was code-named Javagator. By early 1998 it had been scrapped. Andreessen even went so far as to say Java on the client (browser) side was dead. In a remarkable admission reported by Wylie Wong in *Computer Reseller News*, Andreessen credited not his own company but Microsoft with "doing the work" to make the Java runtime faster and better. Gates's initial take on Java, uttered in full fury in the fall of 1995, thus proved oracular. Rebuking Java Man George Gilder in a private meeting, Gates had declared: "Somebody who thinks that because of a browser that anybody can clone, because of a language that is magic, they can overthrow the world—that person can't even think two chess moves ahead. You're not even in the game I'm playing."

The game Gates and his driven band of Internet idealists were playing was called Passion. Mission. Magnificent Obsession. Whereas the Java and Network Computer and browser-as-platform boosters were committed to the bringing down Windows with the Web, the Microsoft monomaniacs were intent on building up Windows with the Web. It was negative energy versus positive flow. "Their agenda is anti-PC," Gates told Stewart Alsop's Agenda conference of industry leaders in October 1997. "Ours is pro-PC." Where the Microsoft minions kept to the straight and narrow, making the PC and Windows great, they succeeded beyond anyone's wildest imagination.

That was the good news. When he scanned the PC landscape for an equivalent piece of bad news, Gates did not have to squint. In the spring of 1999, eight years after his "Think Week" memo outlined Microsoft's challenges for the 1990s with Novell and networking, IBM and operating systems, the FTC and antitrust, distributed computing and Information At Your Fingertips, the Microsoft chairman took another look at the computer landscape and saw even more assaults on his fortress. AOL had purchased Netscape and aligned with archrival Sun in a partnership that could create the long-sought new Internet platform of computing. An "open-source software" movement had sprung up, dedicated to giving away for free the types of systems and applications Microsoft depended on for the majority of its revenues. Leading the bandwagon was Netscape, which in early 1998 had decided to post the source code for Navigator on the Web. Linux, a freely dispensed operating system, was getting critical raves and gaining market share. What would be Maritz's and Allchin's answer to the Linux revolution? Apache, still the leading Web server, was still being given away for free. How was Allard's IIS effort ever going to make a dent in Apache's domination? There was Novell, whose NetWare 5.0 had turned the "embrace and extend" tables back on Microsoft, building in compatibility with NT. Novell was on the comeback trail. NetWare even had improved directories. Jim Allchin's NT project, renamed Windows 2000, would have Active Directories, which was going to blow everyone away. But it kept facing delay after delay after delay. There was Corel, slaving away to build Linux applications like WordPerfect Office. What was Sinofsky's Office 2000 team doing to head off Corel's gathering momentum? Jini, another brainstorm from Bill Joy, was taking aim on becoming the Windows of the Internet by offering a way to connect and communicate with any device anywhere in the world. What was Myhrvold's Advanced Research group doing to bottle Jini? There was Netscape, whose latest Navigator had, in the opinion of no less than Walt Mossberg in the *Wall Street Journal*, moved ahead of IE, at least temporarily. What was the IE 5.0 team doing to recapture Mossberg's affections? And another Windows clone effort, called Wine for Windows emulator, was under way at Corel. Shades of Sun and Novell, the former with Wabi, the latter with at least two efforts over the years that Gates knew about to build Windows clones. Gates took a figurative look in the mirror and asked himself, What am I doing to make sure Windows stays better than any other single piece or collection of pieces of software out there?

Microsoft was being sued in Washington, D.C., by the Justice Department and the attorneys general of nineteen states, sued in Connecticut by Bristol Technology, sued in Utah by Caldera, sued in California by Sun Microsystems. In an interview during the thick of the Justice Department case, Gates summed up his and his company's entire philosophy of existence: "I mean, the biggest paradox of this DOJ thing of all is you're taking an episode that proves more than anything what a competitive business we're in, and how we could lose it all, and you're taking that episode and trying to say that we're a monopolist. Well, read the e-mail! We're talking about life and death in every piece of e-mail. The tension there, the okay, okay, that has to be free, okay, okay, we need to do this, can't you see it? Go look at any other company. They don't have this kind of thing going on."

Microsoft had just come off another record quarter, posting a 75 percent profit gain. Its stock was at an all-time high, $167 a share. The company's cofounder, his Microsoft holdings alone worth $83 billion, was the world's richest individual. Microsoft was the world's top-valued company on Wall Street. Polls showed continued public faith that the company had benefited consumers and the economy. Yet everywhere he looked, Bill Gates saw crisis after crisis after crisis.

How the Web Was Won draws on more than 500 hours of interview time over the past three years, more than 1,000 e-mail messages from court files and other sources, an equivalent amount of e-mail correspondence between the author and sources, and research from my writing as well as that of other staff members of the Seattle Times throughout the past decade. I also am indebted to colleague Stephen Manes for the use of interviews and research material gathered for our book, Gates—How Microsoft's Mogul Reinvented an Industry and Made Himself the Richest Man in America.

In cases where other authors and journalists contributed definitive ideas and information relevant to my narrative, they are credited in the body of the text. I apologize for any I may have missed or inadvertently overlooked. Much good work unfortunately becomes anonymous with time, absorbed into the information soup of today's global network.

Full annotations, a bibliography, and other supporting research may be found at the book's website, www.webwon.com.

Generously making time for in-person interviews were, from **Microsoft**: Bernard Aboba, J Allard, Jim Allchin, Steve Ballmer, Anthony Bay, Joe

Belfiore, Brad Chase, David Cole, Charles Fitzgerald, Bill Gates, Dave Heiner, John Ludwig, Yusuf Mehdi, Bob Muglia, Bill Neukom, Tod Nielsen, Peter Pathe, Will Poole, Jeff Raikes, Thomas Reardon, Dan Rosen, Alec Saunders, Brad Silverberg, Steven Sinofsky, Ben Slivka, Rich Tong, David Treadwell, Brian Valentine, Cornelius Willis, Chris Wilson. From **Netscape**: Marc Andreessen, Jim Barksdale, Jim Clark, Andrea Cook, Peter Currie, Alex Edelstein, Martin Haeberli, Eric Hahn, Hugh Hempel, Chris Holten, Mike Homer, Chris Houck, Roberta Katz, Daniel Klaussen, Bob Lisbonne, Kandis Malefyt, Mike McCue, Jon Mittelhauser, Tom Paquin, Todd Rulon-Miller, David Rothschild, Greg Sands, Rick Schell, Rosanne Siino, Aleks Totic. From **Sun Microsystems**: Alan Baratz, Bill Joy, Scott McNealy, Eric Schmidt. Other interviewees in person included: Paul Allen, John Perry Barlow, Tim Berners-Lee, Jesse Berst, Doug Colbeth, Michael Dertouzos, John Doerr, Esther Dyson, Mike Folk, Ping Fu, George Gilder, Rob Glaser, Andy Grove, Martin Hall, Chris Hassett, Chris Hopen, Mark Jarvis, Evan Kaplan, Tim Krauskopf, Mike Kwatinetz, Ed Lazowska, John Markoff, Trish Millines, Patrick Naughton, Dick Nolan, Kim Polese, David Pool, Bob Ratliffe, Danny Rimer, Clay Ryder, Russ Siegelman, Larry Smarr, Dwayne Walker, Ann Winblad.

Those who granted telephone interviews included, for **Microsoft**: Steve Brown, Collins Hemingway, Keith Moore, Cameron Myhrvold, Jonathan Roberts, Henry Sanders, John Shewchuk; and for **Netscape**: Martina Lauchengco, John Paul, and Joel Rothstein. Others who contributed by phone included Jay Amato, Phil Barrett, Dave Coursey, Tom Evslin, Randy Forgaard, Joseph Hardin, Naveen Jain, Drew Major, Walt Mossberg, Daniel Oran, Eli Patashnik, Bob Quinn, Gary Reback, Marcia Rotunda, Jonathan Seybold, Rick Sherlund, Enid Slivka, Mike Tyrrell, Andy van Dam, David Weld, and Dave Winer.

So many people generously shared their time that it would take a volume of equal proportion simply to thank them all adequately. I must start with my colleagues at the *Seattle Times*, including Managing Editor Alex MacLeod, Assistant Managing Editor Dave Boardman, and Personal Technology Editor Mark Watanabe for their encouragement and support throughout the two-year project. Vince Kueter of the *Times* library provided valuable research assistance. I also relied on the award-winning reporting of staff members, including Michele Matassa Flores, Jay Greene, James Grimaldi, Greg Heberlein, and others.

Prying into the affairs of a private corporation, especially one under federal investigation, is a sensitive process at best. Microsoft made available most of the individuals I requested time with and assisted in factual research as well. Public-relations liaison from Waggener-Edstrom performed tireless interference on my behalf. Most heroic were the efforts of Karla Wachter, who pestered numerous busy executives into taking time for interviews and e-mail exchanges. Also vital in their assistance were Mich Mathews, on behalf of Bill Gates, and Marianne Allison, Pam Edstrom,

John Pinette, Claudia Husemann, and others. Colleen Lacter provided vital early assistance. At this writing she was undergoing treatment for lymphoma, a form of cancer from which we all wish her a speedy recovery.

I conducted several hundred hours of interviews and also communicated by e-mail with hundreds of sources. Thanks particularly to J Allard, Steven Sinofsky, Ben Slivka, and Brad Silverberg for going the extra mile and not once showing impatience at my repeated getbacks and requests for more information. Without their assistance the book could not have captured the flavor or detail of Microsoft's turnaround on the Internet. In the thick of depositions and public scrutiny, Bill Gates generously granted two extensive interviews. Also going out of their way on my behalf were Steve Ballmer, Brad Chase, David Cole, Jim Allchin, Thomas Reardon, John Ludwig, Bob Muglia, Peter Pathe, Dan Rosen, Mike Murray, Natalie Yount, Russ Siegelman, Bernard Aboba, and Anthony Bay.

Microsoft was not the only company to provide generous access. Netscape, with Suzanne Anthony, Donna Sokolsky, and Chris Holten acting on my behalf, provided considerable time with founders Jim Clark and Marc Andreessen, as well as with CEO Jim Barksdale and numerous other executives. Sun Microsystems, through Susann Vagadori, Susan Stanbaugh, and Lisa Poulson, arranged time with Bill Joy, Scott McNealy, Alan Baratz, Eric Schmidt, and others. Novell's Drew Major provided invaluable background with liaison Blake Stowell. Patrick Naughton of Starwave, Kim Polese of Marimba, Chris Hassett of PointCast, Tim O'Reilly of O'Reilly & Associates, and numerous other industry executives were extremely helpful in backgrounding me. John Doerr of Kleiner-Perkins also gave valuable insight into the way Silicon Valley works. Finally, Paul Allen, at the arrangement of Susan Pierson, shed light on his "wired world" and the early Microsoft networking vision.

Several colleagues and sources, including individuals at Microsoft, Netscape, Novell, and America Online, reviewed parts or all of the manuscript for accuracy and readability. I nevertheless am solely responsible for any errors. Because this book has an associated website at *www. webwon.com*, I anticipate being able to rectify any inaccuracies brought to my attention.

I must also thank Jonathan Seybold, Dave Winer, Mark Anderson, Steve Rubel, Mike Kwatinetz, and Jesse Berst for their penetrating insights into Microsoft and our technological times.

None of the above could have happened without the steadfast support of my agent, Joel Fishman, and my editor at Broadway Books, Charles Conrad. No thanks are adequate for their help in conceptualizing the book and shaping the manuscript. Also assisting at Broadway were Ted Sammons, Becky Cole, Rebecca Holland, and David Drake. Thanks to Matthew Martin for expert vetting and to Debra Manette for superb copyediting.

Finally, I must thank my wife, Cecile, whose recollections of her own efforts on *The Circle of Simplicity* enabled her to tolerate yet another project. A two-author household is a marital minefield. Happily, we survived another walkthrough.

DUE DATE

27.50